Lecture Notes in Computer Science

Commenced Publication in 1973
Founding and Former Series Editors:
Gerhard Goos, Juris Hartmanis, and Jan van Leeuwen

Springer
Berlin
Heidelberg
New York
Hong Kong
London
Milan
Paris
Tokyo

Jutta Eckstein   Hubert Baumeister (Eds.)

Extreme Programming and Agile Processes in Software Engineering

5th International Conference, XP 2004
Garmisch-Partenkirchen, Germany, June 6-10, 2004
Proceedings

Springer

Volume Editors

Jutta Eckstein
Independent Consultant
Thierschstr. 20, 80538 Munich, Germany
E-mail: jutta@jeckstein.com

Hubert Baumeister
Ludwig-Maximilians-Universität München, Institut für Informatik
Oettingenstr. 67, 80538, Munich, Germany
E-mail: baumeist@informatik.uni-muenchen.de

Library of Congress Control Number: 2004106717

CR Subject Classification (1998): D.2, D.1, D.3, K.6.3, K.6, K.4.3, F.3

ISSN 0302-9743
ISBN 3-540-22137-9 Springer-Verlag Berlin Heidelberg New York

Springer-Verlag is a part of Springer Science+Business Media

springeronline.com

© Springer-Verlag Berlin Heidelberg 2004

Typesetting: Camera-ready by author, data conversion by PTP-Berlin, Protago-TeX-Production GmbH
Printed on acid-free paper   SPIN: 11011590   06/3142   5 4 3 2 1 0

Preface

Software development is being revolutionized. The heavy-weight processes of the 1980s and 1990s are being replaced by light-weight, so called agile processes. Agile processes move the focus of software development back to what really matters: running software. This is only made possible by accepting that software development is a creative job done by, with, and for individual human beings. For this reason, agile software development encourages interaction, communication, and fun.

This was the focus of the Fifth International Conference on Extreme Programming and Agile Processes in Software Engineering which took place between June 6 and June 10, 2004 at the conference center in Garmisch-Partenkirchen at the foot of the Bavarian Alps near Munich, Germany. In this way the conference provided a unique forum for industry and academic professionals to discuss their needs and ideas for incorporating Extreme Programming and Agile Methodologies into their professional life under consideration of the human factor. We celebrated this year's conference by reflecting on what we had achieved in the last half decade and we also focused on the challenges we will face in the near future.

The focus of the whole conference was on learning and interaction. We brought practitioners together in different sessions to discuss their experiences in solving software problems. XP 2004 facilitated the swapping of ideas in a number of ways, including featured talks by professionals on the cutting edge of extreme programming and agile processes, technical presentations, activity sessions, panels, posters, code camps, workshops, tutorials, and other opportunities to exchange and elaborate on new findings. XP 2004 also featured a PhD symposium for PhD students and a trainer and educator track for everybody with a vested interest in training and education.

This volume is divided into several topical sections. First you will find full papers, then the abstracts of the invited talks, followed by the abstracts of the posters and demonstrations. Then you will find the papers of the trainers' and educators' track, right before the abstracts of the PhD symposium papers. Next, all accepted workshops are presented, followed by the panels and the activities to conclude the book.

The papers went through a rigorous reviewing process. Each paper was reviewed by at least three program committee members and was discussed carefully among the program committee members. Of 69 papers submitted, only 23 were accepted as full papers. These papers were grouped into six categories, focusing on the following themes:

- Acceptance Testing: These papers focus on different ways of dealing with the problem of creating acceptance tests. Most of them suggest a framework that supports the customer as well as the developer to ensure the functionality of the system.

– Scalability Issues: This section collects all the papers dealing with agile development in a larger setting. Some of them consider the aspect of dispersed development, others the issues that arise when outsourcing parts of the development, and others discuss the problems and solutions of diverse agile practices, such as continuous integration, in a large team.
– New Insights: These papers present various new ideas in the field of agile development. Some suggest the use of agile development in a different field such as open source development and others explore new techniques such as agile specification driven development.
– Refactoring: This section contains papers discussing problems and solutions within the practice of refactoring. Large refactorings is one topic, whereas refactoring in a legacy system is another one.
– Social Aspects: All papers focusing on social aspects are collected in this section. The characteristics of XP teams and different roles in agile teams are one focus, employee satisfaction is another.
– Practitioner Reports: Several authors report on their experiences with agile development. You will find papers about the influence of user participation in agile development, the loss and gain with adapting the agile process during development, as well as agile project controlling.

Next you will find the abstracts of the invited talks, right before we present the posters and demonstrations. Posters and demonstrations are ideal for presenting preliminary research results, experience reports, late-breaking developments, or for giving an introduction to interesting, innovative work.

Then you will find the papers and posters of the trainers' and educators' track. This track was aimed at industry and academic professionals who are interested in teaching and learning extreme programming and agile processes. Professionals from academia and industry were invited to discuss their needs and ideas for integrating extreme programming and agile processes into training plans and courses.

The next section presents the abstracts of the PhD symposium papers. In the symposium, students presented and discussed their research objectives, methods, and (preliminary) results.

After this, all accepted workshops are presented. The XP 2004 workshop program provided a forum for groups of participants to exchange opinions and to enhance community knowledge about research topics and real-life applications of agile processes. The workshops also provided the opportunity for representatives of the technical community to coordinate efforts and to establish collective plans of action.

In the last section you will find the descriptions of the activities and the panels. Panels and activity-sessions were lively, participatory, educational, and entertaining. They offered an interactive opportunity to share perspectives, debate opinions, and communicate best-practices.

These proceedings contain conference versions of the papers, posters, demonstrations, and panel position statements as well as the papers of the trainer and educator track and the abstracts of the PhD symposium. Besides a collection of ideas and experiences, they represent an aspect of collective learning and understanding within a community of people who came together in Garmisch-Partenkirchen for five days in June 2004.

We would like to thank everybody who contributed to XP 2004; the authors, the workshop and activity leaders, the tutorial speakers, the panelists, those who served on the various committees, our sponsors, those who offered their experience of running previous XP conferences, the staff of the conference center in Garmisch-Partenkirchen and, last but not least, the participants.

April 2004   Jutta Eckstein
                                                              Hubert Baumeister

Organization

XP 2004 is organized by Software und Support Verlag in cooperation with the Institut für Informatik of the Ludwig-Maximilians-Unversität München.

Executive Committee

General Chair:	Martin Fowler (ThoughtWorks Inc., USA)
Program Chair:	Jutta Eckstein (Germany)
Academic Chair:	Hubert Baumeister (LMU Munich, Germany)
Tutorial Chair:	Rachel Davies (UK)
Workshop Chair:	Vera Peeters (Belgium)
Panels and Activities:	Steven Fraser and Joshua Kerievsky (USA)
Poster Chair:	Rachel Reinitz (UK)
Educators Track Chairs:	Helen Sharp and Mike Holcombe (UK)
PhD Symposium Chairs:	Barbara Russo (Italy)
Chair of Social Activities:	Nicolai Josuttis (Germany)

Program Committee

Ann Anderson (USA)
Barbara Russo (Italy)
Bernhard Rumpe (Germany)
Charles Poole (USA)
Daniel Karlström (Sweden)
David Hussman (USA)
Diana Larsen (USA)
Dierk König (Switzerland)
Don Wells (USA)
Erich Gamma (Switzerland)
Frank Westphal (Germany)
Giancarlo Succi (Italy)
Helen Sharp (UK)
Hubert Baumeister (Germany)
Jim Highsmith (USA)
Joe Bergin (USA)
John Favaro (Italy)
José H. Canós Cerdá (Spain)
Joseph Pelrine (Switzerland)
Joshua Kerievsky (USA)
Laurie Williams (USA)
Linda Rising (USA)

Marco Abis (Italy)
Martin Fowler (USA)
Martin Lippert (Germany)
Mary Lynn Manns (USA)
Mary Poppendieck (USA)
Michael Hill (USA)
Michele Marchesi (Italy)
Mike Holcombe (UK)
Nicolai Josuttis (Germany)
Paul Grünbacher (Austria)
Rachel Davis (UK)
Rachel Reinitz (USA)
Rick Mugridge (New Zealand)
Ron Jeffries (USA)
Scott W. Ambler (USA)
Sian Hopes (UK)
Steve Freeman (UK)
Steven Fraser (USA)
Till Schümmer (Germany)
Tim Mackinnon (UK)
Vera Peeters (Belgium)
Ward Cunningham (USA)

Table of Contents

Refactoring

Social Issues

Practitioner Reports

Invited Talks

Posters

Demonstrations

Trainers and Educators Track

Ph.D. Symposium

Workshops

Panels and Activities

Author Index

The Video Store Revisited Yet Again: Adventures in GUI Acceptance Testing

Johan Andersson and Geoff Bache

Carmen Systems AB, Odinsgatan 9, SE-41103 Göteborg, Sweden
geoff.bache@carmensystems.com

Abstract. Acceptance testing for graphical user interfaces has long been recognised as a hard problem. At the same time, a full suite of acceptance tests written by the Onsite Customer has been a key principle of XP since it began [1]. It seems, however, that practice has lagged behind theory, with many practitioners still reporting weak or no acceptance testing. At XP2003, we presented our successes with text-based acceptance testing of a batch program[2]. In the past year we have extended this approach to apply to a user interface. We have developed an approach based on simulation of user actions via a record/replay layer between the application and the GUI library, generating a high-level script that functions as a use-case scenario, and using our text-based approach for verification of correctness. We believe this is an approach to GUI acceptance testing which is both customer- and developer-friendly.

1 XP Acceptance Testing

We should be clear what we regard as the primary aims of acceptance tests. These are the standards by which we judge acceptance tests and approaches to acceptance testing:

- The tests should model the actions of a user as closely as possible.
- Writing the tests should be quick, painless and require as few programming skills as possible,
- Running the tests should be as smoothe as possible - press a button and watch them go green/red.
- Maintaining the tests should not be too laborious.
- Tests should be as stable under changes as possible. In particular they should be independent of things like font, user interface layout and internal design.
- Tests should document the features of the system in as readable a way as possible.

Let's also be clear at what we are not aiming for. While the following are worthy aims, they are mainly the responsibility of other practices, for example Unit Testing or the various replacements for it that we described in last year's paper [2].

- The tests should not aim to improve or document the design.
- The tests should concentrate on indicating the presence of errors, not primarily help in fixing them.

J. Eckstein and H. Baumeister (Eds.): XP 2004, LNCS 3092, pp. 1–10, 2004.

2 Introduction

Our open source acceptance testing tool, TextTest [3], has traditionally been a console application that we have used to test UNIX batch tools. Recently, however, we wrote a GUI for it, and wanted to be able to test this GUI using a variation of the same approach. We have come up with an approach to do this that we found to be highly effective. For the sake of this paper, however, we thought that we would use what we have learned to revisit the classic Video Store problem, as this is likely to be more familiar to readers and avoids the meta-situation of programs testing themselves! The Video Store has been used to illustrate a few aspects of XP already, from refactoring to unit testing.[4]

TextTest is written in Python, and its GUI uses the PyGTK library[5]. The examples are therefore taken from this environment.

3 The Theory: Principles of Our Approach

3.1 Separating Simulation from Verification

Acceptance testing of GUIs has traditionally been regarded as one activity. Perhaps due to our background with applications that do not have an interactive aspect, we have come to regard it as two, largely independent activities: simulating the interactive actions of a user in some persistent way (e.g. a test script) and verifying that the behaviour is correct when performing these actions. For future reference we refer to these as *simulation* and *verification*.

This simplifies matters somewhat because it removes the need for a tool that does both, decoupling the activities. Each tool can then concentrate on being good at one thing only. Armed with a pre-existing verification tool, TextTest[3], (discussed later) which has proved successful in the world of batch applications, the main challenge of testing a GUI is to find an effective approach to simulation.

3.2 An Agile Record/Replay Approach

Record/Replay approaches have a strong theoretical appeal to us. To be able to create tests as a user simply by clicking around the application under test seems to be the easiest imaginable interface. Many tests can be created quickly, it is totally clear to the person creating them what they represent, no (potentially error-prone) code needs to be written per test and the only qualification for writing them is understanding the system under test, which is needed anyway.

Record/Replay tools are nothing new. A wide range of them exist, of which QCReplay[6] is the one we have most experience of. In recent years, a bewildering array of open source varieties for Java have appeared as well[7]. They are generally based on intercepting mouse clicks and keyboard input, recording them in a script, and asserting behaviour by taking screen dumps ("photographing" the screen)

They are not renowned for their popularity in the Agile community, however. They tend to produce long, low-level scripts which are extremely tied to the environment at the time when they were recorded.[8] For example:

1. Taking screen dumps is fragile under changes of font settings or window manager.
2. Moving the mouse across a GUI generates lots of focus-in events, focus-out events, mouse-over events etc. The application is only connected to (*'listening for'*) a fraction of these, so they fill up the script with junk.
3. Even relevant events are recorded in very low level terms, with commands like click(124, 21). Change the GUI layout and all bets are off: everything must be re-recorded.

In short, they do not embrace change. They are fun for a while but usually a maintenance headache in the long run.

For this reason, they have been abandoned by many in favour of data-driven approaches, that sacrifice some of the advantages listed initially for the ultimately greater gain of maintainibility in a changing world. We, however, have tried to rehabilitate record/replay in a more agile and maintainable form. In our view this requires a radical change to the way it works.

3.3 Test Scripts as Use-Case Scenarios

We believe that the fundamental difference between acceptance tests and unit tests is that acceptance tests have a customer focus and unit tests have a developer focus. A GUI acceptance test therefore has a lot in common with a Use-Case scenario. It should be a description of an interaction sequence between the user (actor) and the system under test from the point of view of the user. It should not describe what happens internally in the system, instead, as a Use-Case scenario, it should aim to give a user-readable statement of what happens during the actor/system interaction in the high-level language of the domain.

Such a test has two major advantages over the kind of test generated by traditional record/replay approaches. It is easy to read and functions well as documentation of system behaviour. More importantly, it is much more independent of the mechanism by which the use-case has been implemented.

We therefore want the test script that we will record and replay to be a high-level natural language file describing what the user does in the terminology of the domain. This fits well with the chosen verification approach, of comparing high-level natural language files produced by the system.

How can this be done? It is clear that it is not possible to write such a record/replay tool that sits on top of the application, starting, stopping it and recording its events at the system level. We need a layer between the application and the GUI library which can be told something about the terminology of the domain and the intent of the application rather than its mechanics.

4 Applying the Theory: Simulation with PyUseCase

We have developed an open source record/replay layer for PyGTK, "PyUseCase"[9], extending it as we have needed to, in the process of testing

TextTest in the past year. While this scripting engine will only be useful to other PyGTK developers, the approach is possible with any GUI library.

To summarise, it differs from other record/replay tools in the following respects:

1. It does not generate scripts in any particular 'language'. What comes out is a high-level use-case description in the terminology of the domain.
2. The relationship between it and the application is reversed. Instead of sitting on top of the application and starting and stopping it, it sits between the application and the GUI library.
3. It is assertion-free, i.e. it is a pure simulation tool. Another tool (e.g. TextTest) is needed for verification.

4.1   Creating a Domain-Language Script

(Note that PyGTK's terminology of 'connecting to signals' may be understood better as 'listening for events' for readers used to other GUI libraries)

Our ideal is to be as close as possible to the terms in the user's domain, and not use the terms of the GUI layout or the mechanics of how it is used. For example, when the user of VideoStore clicks the 'add movie' button, we want the script to simply say

```
add movie
```
rather than
```
click('add movie') or
click(124, 21)
```
This has obvious advantages. It's about as stable under changes as is possible : it survives as long as the user can in some way add a pre-selected movie at that point. It is not dependent on the user interface layout, the choice of widgets for the purpose of adding movies or the internal system design. It also leaves the reader in little doubt as to what happens at this point.

How does it work? We need our developers to connect the GUI widget signals to script commands at the same time they connect them to the methods that will be called when the user performs some action. This tells the script engine how to record the emission of that signal into a use-case description, and how to convert it back again.

For example, PyGTK programmers might implement the 'add movie' button like this:

```
button.connect('clicked', addMovie)
```
where addMovie is the method that actually performs the change, and button is the widget. To use PyUseCase, they would instead write

```
scriptEngine.connect('add movie', button, 'clicked', addMovie)
```
Instead of connecting the addMovie method directly to the signal emitted when the button is clicked, they connect it indirectly via the script engine, giving the user action a name at the same time. This is not much of an extra burden for the programmers. They just need to give names to everything the user can do via the GUI by adding extra arguments to their 'connect' statements.

This is basically the only API to PyUseCase. The syntax varies a bit for different widgets, and for more complex widgets like list views you need to tell it how to parse the arguments for selecting rows, etc. You also need your application to know about record and replay mode, so it can forward these things to PyUseCase.

Note that we only tell the script engine about signals we are connected to anyway. This means that any signals we aren't connected to won't be recorded by the script, whatever the user does with his mouse.

5   Verification with TextTest

TextTest and its usage were discussed in some detail in last year's paper[2]. The basic idea is the same, though it has gained many more features and users since then, including a GUI.

Essentially, the developers ensure that the system writes a plain-text 'behaviour file' describing what it is doing. This file will contain all information considered useful to the customer: internal state, parsing and response to user actions, text that has appeared on the screen. Verification is achieved by the customer saving this file (and any other text-convertible generated files considered relevant) at the point he is happy both with what he is able to do with the system and how the system responds to his actions. Note that this is not a 'system diagnostic' file and should be free of statements that only have meaning to developers. Developer-statements should be written to a different file, which can also be generated and saved, but whose contents will not be viewed by the customer. By convention the 'behaviour file' is simply written to standard output.

A test-run then consists of replaying what the customer did and checking the system's text output for any differences from when the customer approved it. Differences will show up as test failure, though they may be saved and turned into the new correct behaviour if the customer approves the change. In conjunction with a simulation tool, this can be used on a GUI just as easily as on a batch application.

This has several advantages over requiring the customer to select assertions to make per test. In essence, many more verifications can be made, at a level of detail largely determined by the developers, who have a better overview of this. The customer has one less thing to worry about, and cannot "forget" to make some vital assertion. He can concentrate on using the system in an appropriate way and looking out for correct responses from it.

The tests consist only of automatically generated plain text. This removes the need to write any code per test. Your tests then depend on your program's behaviour file, but not on its internal design. This means refactoring will not disturb the acceptance tests, and you will not end up needing to maintain a lot of test code once you have a lot of tests. Bugs in your test code will not be hiding bugs in your real code.

Also, a customer without development skills can interact with the behaviour file, even if he isn't writing it. It is written in natural language and describes in words what is happening. He can spot if the important number he saw on the screen didn't appear in the behaviour file, for example. If the verification is implemented as a load of Java test code, he can only hope it does what he intended when writing the test.

6   Customer-Developer Interaction

We have developed a test-first approach to using these tools. This requires close interaction between the customer and the implementing developers. The process looks something like this. (See the appendix for examples of it in action!)

1. The customer does the simulation to record the test. He does as much as he is able of what he wants to be able to do, generating a use-case script and a behaviour file that records system responses.
2. The customer can force-fail the test by editing the use-case script (giving the system some 'command' it does not yet understand). This tells the developers to add some user capability.
3. The customer can also force-fail the test by editing the behaviour file, if the system responded incorrectly or incompletely. This tells the developers to change the behaviour.
4. The developers take this test and implement the functionality, taking care to make the system output descriptions of important new system actions to the behaviour file.
5. The customer repeats the simulation with the new improved system (if needed). When he is happy, the new test is added to the suite of acceptance tests.

In this way development can be considered to be 'driven' by acceptance tests, in that tests describing work to be done are provided by the customer before that work is begun by developers. However, we have found this process most practical for small incremental user stories, which are hopefully the daily stuff of XP projects. Where the user wants completely new screens or totally different behaviour, it's more practical to describe this in words to developers and only try to create acceptance tests when some attempt has been made to provide the functionality. This is also likely to be the case in the very early stages of a project when there is not so much around to write tests on yet. It is still possible to use the approach for larger steps: but it requires a bit more of the test writer and is more prone to tests needing to be re-written when the functionality is present.

With this process in place, we have also experienced less of a need for unit tests. See our XP2003 paper[2] for details.

7   Other Benefits of the Record/Replay Layer

The fact that our record/replay tool sits between the application and the GUI library means it is a part of the application, rather than an optional extra for the testers. This opens up some interesting possibilities for using it for other things than directly recording and replaying tests.

7.1 Refactoring the Tests

Everything possible has been done to keep the scripts short, high-level, and change-resilient, staving off the evil day when they get too hard to manage easily by pure record/replay. But applications get big and complex, and maybe that day will come anyway. As we don't have a language with syntax, we cannot take the approach of refactoring out common code by hand. We need some other way of updating a large number of tests when their use-case scripts prove to be insufficiently resilient.

Fortunately, we have the possibility to run in record and replay mode simultaneously. This enables us to automatically update a great deal of tests very quickly by telling the script engine to keep the old names for 'replay' only, while introducing the new ones for 'record'. This will work well where use-case actions disappear or change description. It works less well when new use-case actions need to be introduced to a lot of pre-existing tests, or when one conceptual 'use-case action' starts to require several clicks. This requires another approach, which we have called "GUI Shortcuts".

7.2 GUI Shortcuts: Towards a Dynamic User Interface

The record/replay layer is available at any time to any user of the system. This raises the possibility that individual users can personally tweak the user interface and eliminate repetitive actions by making use of the record/replay capabilities.

Most people have at one time or another ended up using a GUI in a repetitive way. They generally do not need all of its capabilities, and may have to make 5 or so clicks just to reach the screen they usually work with. Or for example, who hasn't at some time or other been frustrated by constant pop-up dialogues that demand "Are you sure you want to do this?" or something similar. This can be minimised by good user interface design, but fundamentally applications have to be configurable for their power users, and this can make them unwieldy for their novice users.

The user can simply record a "shortcut" for his repetitive actions. He goes into record mode at the appropriate point, records his usual five clicks (or OKs all his annoying pop-ups), and then gives the script he has recorded a name. A new button appears at the bottom of his screen, which he can click whenever he wishes to repeat what he did. This will save him time and repetitive work.

In the case of maintaining scripts when a user action starts to require more than one click, you can rely on the fact that shortcut names are recorded in scripts if they are available. Therefore, you would record a shortcut for the single click in the old system, run in record and replay mode simultaneously as described previously to insert the shortcut into all tests, and then simply re-record the shortcut (by hand) in the new system.

8 Conclusion

We feel that true Acceptance testing of GUIs can best be achieved by trying to make record/replay approaches more 'agile'. This in turn is best achieved by an approach that separates simulating user actions from verifying system behaviour and uses co-operating, but separate tools for these things.

Simulation of user actions will be most change-resilient if it records use-case descriptions that are independent of the mechanics of the GUI, and this can only really be achieved by a record/replay layer between the application and GUI library, rather than one that sits on top of the application. PyUseCase is such a tool that works for PyGTK applications.

Verifying system behaviour is best done by a tool that compares automatically generated plain text. Organised plain text is easy to update and maintain and is independent of the system's internal design. TextTest is such a tool that will work for a program written in any language.

9   Appendix: Examples from the VideoStore

9.1   Step by Step: Fixing a Bug in VideoStore

Let's suppose that the system allows the user to add two movies with the same name. This isn't good, so we as customer want to create a test for it. Here's what we would do.

1. Open TextTest's test creation functionality for the VideoStore application.
2. Enter 'DuplicateMovieBug' as test name, describe problem in description field. Create test.
3. Press 'Record Use-Case' button. TextTest will then start VideoStore in record mode, which forwards this mode to PyUseCase. We use the GUI to enter a movie 'Star Wars', add it twice, and then quit.
4. The test now contains a use-case script generated by PyUseCase. It looks like this:
   ```
   set new movie name to Star Wars
   add movie
   add movie
   quit
   ```
5. We now have the chance to edit this script, but it describes what we did and reproduced the bug, so we don't need to.
6. Press 'Run Test' button. TextTest now starts VideoStore in replay mode (using our generated script), and collects VideoStore's behaviour file. It looks like this:
   ```
   'set new movie name to' event created with arguments 'Star Wars'
   'add movie' event created
   Adding new movie 'Star Wars'. There are now 1 movies.
   'add movie' event created
   Adding new movie 'Star Wars'. There are now 2 movies.
   'quit' event created
   ```
   The 'event created' lines are created by PyUseCase when it successfully replays a script event. The 'Adding new movie' lines are simple output statements from VideoStore describing what it is doing.

7. We can now edit this as well. System behaviour was wrong, so we do so, replacing the second 'Adding new movie' line with a suitable error message.
8. Now we're done. The test is handed over to the developers, who can run it and will be given failure on the line we edited. They can then fix the problem, and get VideoStore to send the error message to both the behaviour file and the screen.

9.2   Step by Step: Adding New Functionality to VideoStore

Let's suppose that we want to be able to sort the list of movies alphabetically. This functionality doesn't yet exist.

1. Open TextTest's test creation functionality for the VideoStore application.
2. Enter 'SortMovies' as test name, describe functionality in description field.
3. Press 'Record Use-Case' button as before. TextTest will then start Video-Store in record mode. We enter two movies 'Star Wars' and 'Die Hard'.
4. These are in the wrong order, so we want to sort them. But we can't do that yet. We quit.
5. TextTest then shows us the script it has generated. It looks like this:
```
set new movie name to Star Wars
add movie
set new movie name to Die Hard
add movie
quit
```
6. We now have the chance to edit this script. We wanted to do something we couldn't, so we add a line sort movies before the quit command.
7. Press 'Run Test'. TextTest now starts VideoStore in replay mode, using our script and collects the behaviour file. It looks like this:
```
'enter new movie name' event created with arguments 'Star Wars'
'add movie' event created
Adding new movie 'Star Wars'. There are now 1 movies.
'add movie' event created
Adding new movie 'Die Hard'. There are now 2 movies.
ERROR - 'sort movies' event not understood.
'quit' event created
```
8. We can now edit this as well. System behaviour was wrong, so we edit the file, replacing the 'ERROR' line with 'I'd like to press a sort button here. It should sort the movie list into alphabetical order' (or whatever, just to make a difference appear on this line when the test is run)
9. Now we're done. The test is handed over to the developers, who can run it once again and will be given failure on the line we edited. They can then add the sort button, and probably a little print-out to the behaviour file saying what order our beloved movies are in. When they swap order suitably, the developers return the test to the customer.
10. The customer can now review what happens. If he is happy that the system behaves correctly, and that both user and system actions are correctly recorded in their respective files, he saves the new behaviour and checks it in to the acceptance test suite. If not, the process iterates.

References

1. Beck, K.: Extreme Programming Explained. Addison-Wesley, 1999.
2. Andersson, J., Bache, G. and Sutton, P.: "XP with Acceptance-Test Driven Development: A Rewrite Project for a Resource Optimization System" in Proceedings of the 4th International Conference on Extreme Programming and Agile Processes in Software Engineering (XP2003). Italy, 2003.
3. TextTest is open source and can be downloaded from http://sourceforge.net/projects/texttest
4. An entire chapter on writing a Video Store GUI with unit tests is present in Astels, D.: "Test-Driven Development: A Practical Guide" Prentice Hall, 2003 A discussion of refactoring with the same problem can be found in van Deursen, A. and Moonen, L.: "The Video Store Revisited - Thoughts on Refactoring and Testing" in Proceedings of the 3rd International Conference on Extreme Programming and Flexible Processes in Software Engineering (XP2002). Italy, 2002.
5. PyGTK is available from http://www.daa.com.au/ james/pygtk/. It comes as standard with Red Hat Linux versions 8.0 and onwards.
6. http://www.centerline.com/productline/qcreplay/qcreplay.html
7. At least 6 record/replay tools for Java can be found at http://www.junit.org/news/extension/gui/index.htm
8. The tool 'Android' gives a beautiful example of the kind of low-level script you get from recording a test that does $1 + 2 = 3$ in xcalc. http://www.wildopensource.com/larry-projects/article1.html
9. PyUseCase isn't formally released at time of writing, though it hopefully will be by the time of XP2004. It is in any case bundled with TextTest as TextTest itself uses it for its own testing.

Test Driving Custom $\mathcal{F}it$ Fixtures

Rick Mugridge

University of Auckland, New Zealand
r.mugridge@auckland.ac.nz

Abstract. $\mathcal{F}it$ is an automated testing framework, developed by Ward Cunningham, that is a great way to develop automated customer tests. Custom *fixtures* can allow us to express some tests in a more convenient, expressive and direct form for customers (and ourselves). The open-ended and generic nature of the $\mathcal{F}it$ framework enables new custom fixtures to be easily incorporated. We show how to test drive the development of such custom fixtures using `FixtureFixture`.

Keywords: Customer testing, tdd, $\mathcal{F}it$.

1 Introduction

$\mathcal{F}it$ uses HTML tables to express data-driven tests. Each test table specifies a $\mathcal{F}it$ fixture, which defines how the tests in the table are to be interpreted [1]. Three standard fixtures are provided with $\mathcal{F}it$. `ColumnFixture` tables are for testing business rules involving calculations. `ActionFixture` tables are for testing sequences of actions that change the state of the system under test. `RowFixture` tables are for testing that collections in the system under test contain the elements that are expected.

New types of fixtures can allow us to express some tests in a more convenient, expressive and direct form for customers (and ourselves). For example, the Socket Acceptance Testing framework (SAT) uses a custom fixture that has been used to test a chat server [2]. A test may involve several clients interacting with a server, where the actions of each client is represented in its own column of a SAT table. This makes it easier to see the impact of the actions of the clients on the state of the server over time, going down the table.

Clearly, a test driven approach to the development of complex custom fixtures is desireable. What sort of tests are needed for such fixtures?

When we write tests for applications using $\mathcal{F}it$, the tests in a table pass when there are no unexpected values and no exceptions are thrown. However, when we test or define a new type of fixture, we also need to specify what is to happen when tests don't pass. We can do this in terms of the *markings* (colours and extra information) that we expect in the table report, as provided by $\mathcal{F}it$.

We introduce `FixtureFixture`, a fixture for testing and test-developing new types of fixtures for $\mathcal{F}it$. A `FixtureFixture` table embeds another table within it in order to test or define it. `FixtureFixture` was developed test-first, using

J. Eckstein and H. Baumeister (Eds.): XP 2004, LNCS 3092, pp. 11–19, 2004.
© Springer-Verlag Berlin Heidelberg 2004

itself. It has been used to define the standard $\mathcal{F}it$ fixtures and six generic custom fixtures.

We begin by looking at examples of $\mathcal{F}it$ tables, based on ColumnFixture and RowFixture, and the reports that result from running them in Section 2. In the next Section, we show FixtureFixture tables that test (or define) some aspects of these standard fixtures. We then show in Section 4 how FixtureFixture itself was developed test-first using FixtureFixture tables. We consider some design issues in Section 5 before concluding.

2   Markings in Table Reports

After running test tables, $\mathcal{F}it$ provides feedback by producing an HTML report. For example, consider the $\mathcal{F}it$ report in Fig. 1 for a ColumnFixture table. All but the first two rows of the table are independent calculation tests, where the *plus()* value is expected to be the sum of *a* and *b*. The first two tests in the table pass and are marked green. The third test fails and is marked red, along with the *actual* value.

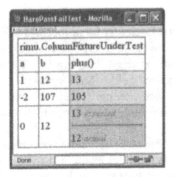

Fig. 1. Report of ColumnFixture table with last row wrong

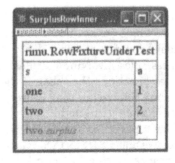

Fig. 2. Report of RowFixture table with an unexpected third row

A RowFixture table checks that the elements of a collection from the system under test are as expected. A report for such a table marks row cells that have unexpected values and rows that are "missing". Any "surplus" rows, that were unexpected, are added to the reported table. For the example shown in Fig. 2, the first two rows were expected but a third was also actually present.

3   Testing with FixtureFixture

To automatically test an existing or custom fixture, we need to specify what *markings* (colourings and added text and rows) we expect from tests in a table that uses our new fixture. The obvious way to do this is to use $\mathcal{F}it$ itself.

A `FixtureFixture` table (the *outer* table) encloses another $\mathcal{F}it$ table (the *inner* table). All but the first row and first column of the whole table make up the inner table. For example, the table shown in Fig. 1 is embedded inside the table reported in Fig. 3. The first (outer) column specifies the *markings* that we expect in the resulting $\mathcal{F}it$ report for each of the cells of the corresponding inner row.

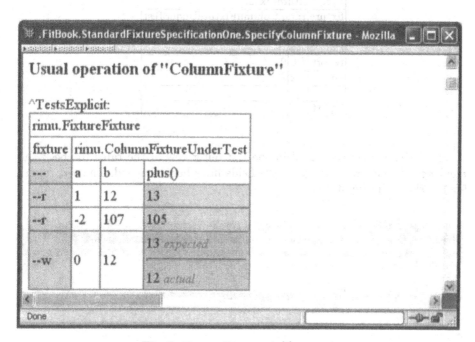

Fig. 3. `FixtureFixture` table report

The first inner row (ie, the first row of the inner table) in Fig. 3 specifies the name of the fixture. The second inner row includes the names of the fields and methods (for the `ColumnFixture`). We expect these three cells to be left *unmarked* ("-") in the report. The first outer column specifies the expected *markings* as "---", with a "-" for each of the three cells (trailing "-" are unnecessary).

For the third inner row, the last cell is expected to be *right* ("r") and to be coloured green. As the other cells in that row remain unmarked, the expected *markings* is "-- r". For the fifth inner row, the last cell is expected to be *wrong* ("w") and to be coloured red. Hence the expected *markings* is "--w".

A blank cell in a `ColumnFixture` table is filled, in the report, by the current value of the column's field or method. We need to be able to test this *marking*. We use a *report* row in the `FixtureFixture` table, which checks the values of the previous row. For example, in the third inner row of 1, the cells are empty, so their values should be added in the report. The *report* in the fourth inner row checks that the two cells in the previous (empty) inner row of the report each have the value "0", the initial values of *a* and *b*.

Table 1. Empty Cells in the Report

rimu.FixtureFixture			
fixture	rimu.ColumnFixtureUnderTest		
	a	b	plus()
report	0	0	0
--r	1	2	3
report	1	2	3

Similarly, a *report* is used in the last outer row of the table to check the *markings* of that inner row after the fields have been changed. The $\mathcal{F}it$ report for 1 is shown in Fig. 4.

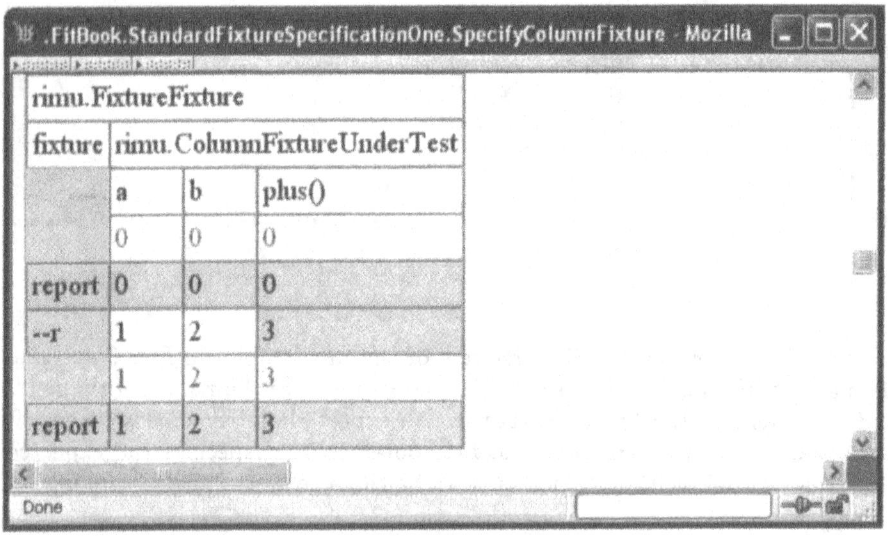

Fig. 4. Report of Table 1

Finally, we need to specify that we expect extra rows to be inserted into a reported table. For example, 2 shows a FixtureFixture test for the report of the table shown in Fig. 2. The markings of the outer cell of the last row of 2 start with "I". This means that an inner row is expected to be inserted here, with the given markings ("w") and the given text ("two surplus" and "1").

Table 2. Report extra row

rimu.FixtureFixture		
fixture	rimu.RowFixtureUnderTest	
	s	a
rr	one	1
rr	two	2
Iw	two surplus	1

4 Developing `FixtureFixture` Itself

These ideas were used to develop `FixtureFixture` itself, using an inner table with a fixture with known behaviour. The fixture class used is transparent as possible; class `FixtureUnderTest` has actions that correspond directly with the *markings* that it makes in a reported table[1].

We began with an inner table with fixture `FixtureUnderTest`, as shown in 3. The single cell of the inner table contains the action "r", which means that the cell itself will be marked as *right* (green) by `FixtureUnderTest`. This corresponds to the expected *marking* of "r" in the first column.

Table 3. Right table for `FixtureFixture`

rimu.FixtureFixture	
fixture	rimu.FixtureUnderTest
r	r

This fixture class was then extended to handle the other cell *markings*, for *wrong* ("w"), *exception* ("e"), *ignored* ("i") and *unmarked* ("-"). A table with all the *markings*, in various combinations, is shown in 4. We also test that trailing "-" are not needed.

The code for fixture `FixtureUnderTest` is very simple and direct. Each action encodes the *markings* to be carried out. For example, "rw" codes for the first cell to have *marking right* (green) and the second *wrong* (red). The fixture code is kept as simple as possible, so it's quite clear what it does. Given that its role is rather like a test (in some sense tests and code mirror each other), we avoid introducing any generality.

4.1 Testing Added Text in Reports

We can now define the handling of extra text in reports, with two tables. In the fourth row of 5 we use the action *reports* of FixtureUnderTest to add the text "reported" to the fourth cell of that row.

---

[1] See [3] for further details.

Table 4. Colouring table for FixtureFixture

rimu.FixtureFixture									
fixture	rimu.FixtureUnderTest								
r	r								
w-	w								
i	i								
e-	e								
-	-								
rw	rw	wrong							
ri	ri	ignore							
iw--	iw	w							
iw	iw	w							
rwrwiwiee-	rwrwiwiee-	w	r	w	i	w	i	e	e

Table 5. Reports

rimu.FixtureFixture				
fixture	rimu.FixtureFixture			
	fixture	rimu.FixtureUnderTest		
r		reports		
w-rw	report		reported	no

We doubly nest FixtureFixture to allow us to test the results of the inner FixtureFixture. The last row of this table checks that *report* reports correctly. The "reported" cell matches but the "no" cell doesn't. As not all the cells match, the *report* cell and the last cell are both expected to be wrong, as shown in the report in Fig. 5.

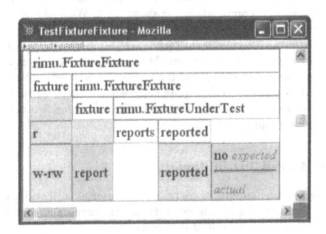

Fig. 5. Report of Table 5

In the fourth row of 6, we test that a cell is marked *wrong* with an inserted message. This is carried out with the action *wMsg* of FixtureUnderTest. The fifth row then uses *report* to test the *markings*. We also test that the report fails when the message doesn't match, as in the last row.

Table 6. Reports from *wrong*

rimu.FixtureFixture		
fixture	rimu.FixtureFixture	
	fixture	rimu.FixtureUnderTest
rw	w	wMsg
rr	report	wMsg expectedMessage actual
rw	w	wMsg
ww	report	Message

4.2 Testing Inserted Rows in Reports

FixtureFixture can test that the contents of rows have been inserted in a reported table. For example, consider the tests in 7. The action *insertTwoRows* inserts two new rows into the report of the inner table after that row; each row consists of a *right* cell containing the text "one" and a *wrong* cell containing the text "two". The fourth and fifth row of the overall table in 7 specify that rows will be added in those positions, with the given markings and text.

Table 7. Row insertions

rimu.FixtureFixture		
fixture	rimu.FixtureUnderTest	
	insertTwoRows	
lrw	one	two
lrw	one	two

Other tests were developed to ensure that an error is given by FixtureFixture when rows are unexpectedly inserted in the report by the inner fixture, when the inserted rows contain text that don't match the actual inserted rows, and when an expected row insertion doesn't occur.

4.3 Testing That Problems Are Handled

We also need to test that FixtureFixture correctly handles awkward cases, such as when a fixture doesn't exist or it is not specified. For example, 8 tests that a *wrong* results when the unknown class UnknownClass is specified as a fixture in the inner FixtureFixture table.

Table 8. Unknown fixture class

rimu.FixtureFixture		
fixture	rimu.FixtureFixture	
-w	fixture	UnknownClass
report		UnknownClass : Unknown Class

5   Design and Other Approaches Considered

Several issues were considered in the design of `FixtureFixture`:

- We need to be able to easily read the tables. We don't want them cluttered with unnecessary detail.
- We expect each outer test to be *right*, and to count in `fit.Summary`. Counts from inner tables need to be ignored so that we can just check the summary and/or the $\mathcal{F}it$ runner output to see that the (outer) tests have all passed.
- FixtureFixture needs to be sufficient to test most aspects of the standard fixtures. We don't want to have to specify the reported value of every cell, as many are not of interest — we always have to make tradeoffs when we write tests.
- We're not interested in matching the fine details of the HTML in cells.
- We want to work within $\mathcal{F}it$ as it is currently defined (release 2003-9-15).

Several other approaches were considered for `FixtureFixture`:

- A table could be followed by another, special one that defines the fixture tests instead of using embedding[2]. But we don't want to count *right*, *wrong*, etc of the table under test in our overall count, as that means we'd have to manually check the results. And it may not be so easy to see the correspondence between the two tables. On the other hand, this approach avoids mixing the two levels together.
- Each row of the table under test could be followed by a testing row with expected *markings*. But it's messy to mix colorings and cell values which have changed (although two rows could've been used).
- Instead of having a single cell to encode the expected *markings* for the inner row, we could've used the same number of cells as in the inner row. But this would've led to bulky tables. And it's difficult to handle tables with varying numbers of rows. $\mathcal{F}it$ doesn't currently allow nested tables, so nesting wasn't an option.

6   Summary

The $\mathcal{F}it$ framework is very powerful and open-ended, allowing for a wide range of fixtures to be used in testing. Custom fixtures can be developed to enable tests to be expressed in a more convenient, expressive and direct form.

---

[2] This is the approach used with *fat*, which has somewhat different aims [1]

$\mathcal{F}it$ tests can be applied well to testing fixtures themselves, by embedding a table inside a FixtureFixture table. FixtureFixture tests that cells of the inner table have the correct *markings*. The *marking* codes are cryptic, but it doesn't take long to get used to them. FixtureFixture can also test, with *report*, that a cell has an appropriate value in the generated report and that appropriate rows have been added.

FixtureFixture has been used to test/define several of the standard fixtures, as well as to develop and to test FixtureFixture itself [3]. We don't expect to use FixtureFixture to test everything about a fixture. For example, we are unable to directly check that the right exception has been thrown. However, this is dependent on the programming language being used.

FixtureFixture has proved to be very useful in understanding the behavior of the existing, standard fixtures of $\mathcal{F}it$ as well as in developing six new generic custom fixtures.

Acknowledgements. Special thanks to Ward Cunningham for making $\mathcal{F}it$ publically available, for pointing out problems for FixtureFixture with inserted rows in reported tables, and for feedback on an earlier version of this paper.

References

1. For an introduction to $\mathcal{F}it$, see http://fit.c2.com.
2. Rick Mugridge and Ewan Tempero, "Retrofitting an Acceptance Test Framework for Clarity", *Agile Development Conference*, Salt Lake City, June 2003, pp92-98.
3. A longer version of this paper, the $\mathcal{F}it$ test tables (for FixtureFixture and the standard fixtures), and the fixture code are all available at:
www.cs.auckland.ac.nz/~{}rick/fit/FixtureFixture/.

Putting a Motor on the Canoo WebTest Acceptance Testing Framework

Jennitta Andrea

jennitta@agilecanada.com

Abstract. User acceptance testing is finally getting the attention and tool support it deserves. It is imperative that acceptance tests follow the best practices and embody the critical success factors that have been established over the years for automated unit testing. However, it is often challenging for acceptance tests to be repeatable, readable, and maintainable due to the nature of the tests and the tools currently available for automation. The key contributions this paper makes to the agile community are: first, it provides concrete examples of applying test automation patterns to user acceptance testing, and secondly it provides a description of various extensions to the WebTest acceptance testing framework that facilitate developing automated acceptance tests according to these established best practices.

Keywords: Automated testing, Canoo WebTest, framework extension, test automation patterns, testing strategy, user acceptance testing

1 Introduction

Years of test first development using automated unit testing tools and frameworks, like Junit [1], have resulted in a collection of best practices that enable key critical success factors, namely: automated tests that are *repeatable*, *readable*, and *maintainable* [2]. Automated tests create the safety net that enables a team to confidently evolve a system incrementally, and to be assured that it is production-ready. A team must be able to efficiently develop tests that they trust, specifically, tests that are free from side effects, and that perform predictably every time they are executed. Because the tests encode system requirements, it is important that the tests are more readable than the system code itself. When there is as much test code as system code, the tests must be maintainable, so as to continually keep their benefits higher than their costs.

It is imperative that both acceptance tests and unit tests follow best practices and embody these critical success factors. It is often more challenging for acceptance tests to accomplish this because of the nature of the tests and the tools available for automation. Acceptance tests embody real business workflow scenarios, thus all input and validation occurs as a result of interaction with the user interface, and execution through all of the layers of the application.

J. Eckstein and H. Baumeister (Eds.): XP 2004, LNCS 3092, pp. 20–28, 2004.
© Springer-Verlag Berlin Heidelberg 2004

This paper describes a series of customizations made to the Canoo WebTest [4] acceptance-testing framework that were implemented during the course of an XP/Scrum project to develop automated acceptance tests that are repeatable, readable, and maintainable.

2 Acceptance Testing Strategy

Automated software testing is not simply about tools and techniques for automating tests. In fact, the choice of tool should be one of the last decisions made when developing a testing strategy because the tool should enable the overall strategy, rather than drive it. While this paper is ultimately about a tool, we are obliged to start with the strategy. Software projects must balance many different, often competing, concerns when developing a testing strategy. The testing strategy as a whole considers the significance of each type of testing, including: unit, acceptance, usability, performance, security, etc. Decisions made about the one type of testing are likely to have an impact on the choices made about another type. For example, a system with an extensive unit test suite will tend to focus the content of acceptance tests on workflow concerns rather than on detailed business rule validation.

The team builds their acceptance testing strategy by considering questions like the following: What is the budget for user acceptance testing? Is the purpose of the test to specify requirements, to assess quality, or both? Who is responsible for writing the test specification? Who executes the tests and assesses failure? How are the tests executed? How often? How are the automated tests kept in sync with the test specifications? What parts of the system does the automated test touch? What techniques should be used? What tools should be used? The answers to one question are often inter-dependent on other ones. Some answers may contradict each other, making the formation of the strategy all the more challenging.

The experience described in this paper is based on a particular project with an acceptance testing strategy driven by budgetary concerns. Specification, automation, and execution of the acceptance tests were allotted an average of twenty hours per week of a single developer's time. The remainder of the strategy, including tool selection, had to facilitate automating as many tests as possible in a short timeframe. Given the size and complexity of the system, this budget was not sufficient to automate acceptance tests for the entire system, so the developer and customer collaborated to define the smallest possible set of representative tests for the highest priority areas of the system. The customer did not have time to automate the tests themselves, but reviewed the automated tests in order to sign off on them. While automating acceptance tests was considered late in the project, the system was built unit test-first, ensuring acceptable test coverage of small-grained business rules. Thus the acceptance tests were required to focus on overall workflow scenarios, using the user interface in ways that a real user would. After a limited exploration of various techniques and tools, including HttpUnit [6], FIT[5], and a custom framework to generate test code from an excel spreadsheet [10], the Canoo WebTest framework was the tool selected for this project.

3 Canoo WebTest

Canoo WebTest is a layer on top of HttpUnit, where the tests are specified using descriptive XML targets (like clickbutton, verifyitle, etc), and executed via Ant [7]. The key characteristics of WebTest that made it a good fit for this project, are: a scripted approach to testing against the user interface (as opposed to a record-playback approach [8]); a succinct, high level specification language; readable and detailed output reports; and the interpreted execution, which made test development very fluid. The output reports were probably the most important characteristic for this project; not only do they provide visual clues as to the success/failure of each individual step, they also include captured screen shots. This facilitates a slow motion replay of the test, which is used by the customer to verify the correctness of the test, and can be used to debug the test when necessary.

The development team immediately recognized issues related to weak tool support for XML development and cross-technology refactoring, especially when contrasted to the powerful capabilities they exploited when developing Java with Idea [9]. In addition, the noisy XML syntax within the specifications was deemed to hinder readability. This latter concern was not a showstopper because the customer is able to review the output reports instead of the XML test specification.

4   Customizing Canoo WebTest

The examples in this section are fragments from a real acceptance test for a system that is used by hospitals to archive inactive patient records (called volumes). A patient is identified by a chart number, and may have one or more volumes. A volume is essentially a file folder that contains treatment details for a patient. If a patient has not received treatment for five or more years, their volume is considered to be inactive. Before boxes of inactive volumes are physically sent to an off-site storage location, a user enters the data associated with each volume into the Volume Archiving System (VAS). The acceptance test takes the volume and box through their normal life cycle (volume created, added to box, box moved off site, volume removed from box). It also demonstrates the following business rules: (a) creating a new volume will create the associated chart if it doesn't exist, (b) a box may contain duplicate volume numbers, (c) chart numbers are not unique across sites.

This section displays fragments of a single acceptance test, not necessarily in the order they would appear in a complete test. The entire acceptance test, which is too large to include in this paper, can be found at [11]. The WebTest extensions described here have been submitted to [4].

Critical Success Factor 1: Repeatability

The rhythm of test-first development is: write a test, watch it fail, and then make it pass by developing the missing system capability or fixing the incorrect behavior [3]. Once the test is complete, it should pass repeatedly, whether it executes by itself or within a test suite. When a completed test fails, we need to quickly and accurately pinpoint the cause: did the test uncover a bug in the system, or is the test faulty? We strive to eliminate time spent debugging tests, especially the nasty situations when side effects of one test cause a different test to fail (the interacting test smell [2]). Best practices for achieving repeatability focus on making tests independent. Ideally, a test should operate on its own unique data set, and should clean up after itself (the clean slate approach [2]).

The most obvious shortcoming of the WebTest framework is the inability to manage the test fixture data directly from within the test. By default, one must use mechanisms external to the test to setup the precondition data and remove it when the test has finished. It is generally possible to setup independent test data for a number of tests in advance, however, this approach creates the mystery guest test smell [2], and reduces the readability of the test.

Our solution was to develop various new framework components in Java that enable creating precondition data directly within the test and cleaning it up when the test ends[1]. Example 1 shows the use of the two new Ant tasks: **preconditions** and **cleanup**, which act as bookends to the body of a test. Other custom domain specific Ant tasks are contained within these wrappers, and are responsible for creating or deleting a specific type of domain object. To keep the test readable and succinct, the test specification includes only the attributes of the domain objects that are necessary for understanding the tests. All other attributes are generated 'anonymously' within the Java implementation of the custom creation/cleanup Ant task.

---

[1] For those familiar with the WebTest framework, the following is a high level summary of the changes made. Text in **bold** font are new classes/methods we introduced; text in *italic* font are existing framework classes/methods. **PreconditionWrapper** extends *StepContainer*, and contains a sequence of steps of type **PreconditionStep** (an extension to *TestStepSequence*). The project specific subclass of **PreconditionStep** overrides the method **doCommonPreSetup** to perform all of the necessary one-time data base initialization tasks. It then executes each specific fixture setup step, which creates and populates one or more domain objects, and registers them as being ready for persistence. The final task is to override **doCommonPostSetup** which causes the objects to be stored using a specific persistence mechanism. Following this same pattern, we added **TearDownWrapper** to the framework, which contains a sequence of steps of type **TearDownStep**. Modifications were made to the WebTest framework in order to accommodate these new classes. *TestStepSequence* recognizes the two new wrappers and process them appropriately. *TestSpecificationTask* keeps track of the teardown steps. A finally clause was added to the *Engine's doExecute* method to ensure the teardown steps are executed after a test failure. The final piece is to write custom fixture setup and cleanup steps for the business objects needed by the test. These steps create business objects, populate them and register them for persistence.

```
1.  <preconditions>
2.      <site name="site1"/>
3.      <site name="site2"/>
4.      <volume name="v1c1s1" chart="chart1" site="site1" box="box1"/>
5.  </preconditions>
.......
6.  <cleanup>
7.        <deleteSite name="site1"/>
8.        <deleteSite name="site2"/>
9.        <deleteVolume name="v1c1s1"/>
10. </cleanup>
```

Example 1. Preconditions and Cleanup

Critical Success Factor 2: Readability

It is crucial that all tests are readable, as they are the definitive reference for the system requirements. It is *even more* imperative for acceptance tests to be readable, because the customer is responsible for signing off on them and must fully understand them. A number of best practices help improve readability, namely: write the test declaratively (focus on *what* not *how*); write the test succinctly (include only the details that are pertinent to understanding the test); and make the test unambiguous (ideally, two different people with a similar understanding of the business domain should understand the test in the same way).

WebTest's steps (e.g. clickbutton, verifytext, etc) and output reporting facilitate developing readable tests, especially compared to writing raw HttpUnit and only having the red/green bar for feedback. In practice, we found that because user acceptance tests capture multi-step workflow, they tend to be fairly long. Even when reviewing the WebTest output report, the reader quickly becomes lost in a forest of low-level tactical details related to using the user interface. They must consciously re-construct the intent of the sequence of steps in order to understand the big picture. A series of simple adjustments to the framework and the report formatter improved this situation greatly.

A new attribute, **description**, was added to the *testSpec* target (see Example 2). This free-form text attribute is intended to capture an overall summary of the test and is displayed at the beginning of the test output.

Another new step container, called **group**, is used to assemble related steps together under a higher-level description (see Example 3). The primary purpose of this container is to enable the steps to be visually grouped together in the output report, giving the reader the big picture; steps 13-20 must be performed in order to create a new volume in VAS.

11. <testSpec name="basic volume and box lifecycle" **description**="This test takes the volume and box through their normal life cycle (volume created, added to box, box moved off site, volume removed from box). It also demonstrates the following business rules: (a) creating a new volume will create the associated chart if it doesn't exist, (b) a box may contain duplicate volume numbers, (c) chart numbers are not unique across sites."/>

Example 2. Description attribute

```
12.  <group stepid="create a volume">
13.      <clickbutton label="${mainMenu.button.addVolume}"/>
14.      <verifytitle text="${addVolume.title}*" regex="true"/>
15.      <setinputfield name="${addVolume.field.boxNum}" value="box1"/>
16.      <setinputfield name="${addVolume.field.chartNum}" value="chart1"/>
17.      <setinputfield name="${addVolume.field.volNum}" value="v1c1s2"/>
18.      <setinputfield name="${addVolume.field.date}" value="2003-11-13"/>
19.      <clickbutton name="${addVolume.button.save}"/>
20.      <verifytitle text="${addVolume.title}* regex="true"/>
21.  </group>
```

Example 3. Group step

We also added a simple custom step to the framework that corresponds to the fail() assertion from junit, called **forceTestFailure.** This facilitates an active to-do list style of writing tests that ensures the system will remind us when a test is incomplete rather than comments in code or notes on scraps of paper.

Critical Success Factor 3: Maintainability

Test first development yields as much (or more) test code than system code, thus we have to be as concerned (or more) with the maintenance costs of test code as compared to system code. Refactoring is a common practice on agile projects, because the system continually evolves over time as new features are developed. Acceptance tests are modified to reflect changes to business rules and screen details. Maintenance costs can be reduced if the acceptance tests don't break when UI elements merely change position on the screen. While development tools greatly assist the maintenance effort through powerful refactoring features, developers remain responsible for making design decisions that enable system and test code to be modified efficiently. This section contains a series of refactorings that were performed on the test specification fragment shown in Example 3.

A user goal level use case [12], e.g. to create a patient volume, is achieved through a number of detailed interactions with the user interface (entering text into fields, clicking buttons, etc). The acceptance test suite contains multiple instances of the same user goal level use case, so a strategy for code reuse must be devised. The simplest possible thing to try initially was to use XML componentization within the test specification. The WebTest framework was extended with a new step, **storeVariable,** as a simple way to pass parameters to an XML component. Example 4 is the result of refactoring the original test specification fragment (Example 3) to reference a common XML component.

```
22.  <group stepid="create a volume">
23.      <storeVariable name="${param.boxNum}" value="box1"/>
24.      <storeVariable name="${param.chartNum}" value="chart1"/>
25.      <storeVariable name="${param.volNum}" value="v1c1s2"/>
26.      <storeVariable name="${param.date}" value="2003-11-13"/>
27.      &createVolume;
28.  </group>
```

Example 4. Test spec with custom XML component reference

The body the original test specification fragment was moved into the createVolume XML component (see Example 5), with specific values replaced by references to the stored 'parameters'.

```
29.  <clickbutton label="${mainMenu.button.addVolume}"/>
30.  <verifytitle text="${addVolume.title}*" regex="true"/>
31.  <setinputfield name="${addVolume.field.boxNum}"
         value="#{param.boxNum}"/>
32.  <setinputfield name="${addVolume.field.chartNum}"
         value="#{param.chartNum}"/>
33.  <setinputfield name="${addVolume.field.volNum}"
         value="#{param.volNum}"/>
34.   <setinputfield name="${addVolume.field.date}"
         value="#{param.date}"/>
35.  <clickbutton name="${addVolume.button.save}"/>
36.  <verifytitle text="${addVolume.title}* regex="true"/>
```

Example 5. The custom XML component

While this was a simple and workable solution, it falls short of being maintainable. The same tools cannot be used to refactor XML acceptance testing components and Java unit tests and system code. The second approach was a natural progression towards this end, namely turn the XML components into custom action steps (i.e., Ant targets), written in java. Example 6 is the result of refactoring the previous test specification fragment (Example 4) to reference a custom action step that embodies the desired behavior. The **storeVariable** attribute is no longer necessary, as the parameters are passed to the Java implementation via the specified attributes (e.g., boxNumber).

```
37.  <createVolume boxNumber="box1" chartNumber="chart1"
             volumeNumber="v1c1s2" archiveDate="2003-11-13"/>
```

Example 6. Test spec with custom action reference

The createVolume XML component (see Example 5), is replaced with a custom Java class (see Example 7), that encodes each detailed step as method calls that are implemented in the **CustomActionStep** super class.

```
38.   public class CreateVolumeActionStep extends CustomActionStep {
39.       private String archiveDate, boxNumber, chartNumber, volumeNumber;
40.       private static final String STEP_ID = "create volume";
41.   public void doExecute(Context context) {
42.       verifyParameters();
43.       super.doExecute(context);
44.       clickbutton(context, Properties.mainMenu.button.addVolume);
45.       verifyTitle(context, Properties.addVolume.title);
46.       setinputfield(context,Properties.addVolume.field.boxNum, getBoxNum ());
47.       setinputfield(context,Properties.addVolume.field.chartNum, getChartNum());
48.       setinputfield(context, Properties.addVolume.field.volNum, getVolumeNum());
49.       setinputfield(context, Properties.addVolume.field.date, getArchiveDate());
50.       clickbutton(context, Properties.addVolume.button.save);
51.       verifyTitle(context, Properties.addVolume.title);}
```

Example 7. Specific custom action step

The **CustomActionStep** superclass provides Java access to each of the WebTest steps (see Example 8 for the implementation of the verifyTitle step). Each method integrates with the WebTest reporting infrastructure, so that the output reports look the same as they did previously.

```
52.   public abstract class CustomActionStep extends GroupWrapper {
53.       public void verifyTitle(Context context, String title) {
54.           VerifyElementText step = new VerifyElementText();
55.           getStepSequence().getSteps().add(step);
56.           step.setStepType("verify title starts with");
57.           step.setType(ELEMENT_TYPE_TITLE);
58.           step.setText(title);
59.           step.setRegex(true);

60.           try {
61.               step.notifyStarted(context);
62.               step.doExecute(context);
63.               step.notifyCompleted(context);
64.           } catch (Exception e) {
65.               throw new StepFailedException(e.getMessage(), step); } }}
```

Example 8. Generic support for custom action steps

5 Conclusions

The key drivers from this particular project's acceptance testing strategy that guided the tool selection decision were: the customer must be able to read the test specification in order to sign off on it, the acceptance tests must capture significant system workflow scenarios and must use the user interface as the primary touch point, and the tests must be developed as quickly as possible.

After a short and limited tool evaluation period, the Canoo WebTest framework was deemed the best choice for satisfying these key drivers. Was it the only choice? No, the list of acceptance testing tools and frameworks is impressive, covering the full spectrum of techniques. Was it a good choice? Yes, the framework is solid and feature rich. While it was missing some key capabilities to meet our standards for developing repeatable, readable, and maintainable acceptance tests, the framework proved to be easily extended. Was it worth the extra effort? Yes, the introduction of framework support for custom precondition, action, and cleanup steps enabled the team to develop a domain specific testing language. The elements from this testing language formed the building blocks for quickly developing user acceptance tests.

Acknowledgements. It's been my privilege for many years to work with and be mentored by Gerard Meszaros and Shaun Smith on test automation best practices. The work customizing Canoo WebTest was made possible with the cooperation, insights, and participation of: Linda Duhn, Allen Ho, Tom Kuntz, Amy Law, Eric Liu, Chris Klementis, Brad Marlborough, Jim McDonald, Robert Purdy, Lynne Ralston, Dave Shellenberg, Brent Sprecher, and Ross Taylor.

References

1. Junit, http://www.junit.org/index.htm.
2. Meszaros, Gerard and Shaun Smith "Test Automation Manifesto", XP Agile Universe Conference, 2003.
3. Beck, Kent, *Extreme Programming Explained,* Addison Wesley, 2001.
4. WebTest, http://webtest.canoo.com/webtest/manual/WebTestHome.html
5. FIT, http://fit.c2.com
6. HttpUnit, http://httpunit.sourceforge.net
7. Ant, http://ant.apache.org
8. Meszaros, Gerard, et al al "Agile Regression Testing Using Record & Playback", XP Agile Universe Conference, 2003.
9. Idea, http://www.jetbrains.com/idea/
10. Andrea, Jennitta, "Generative Acceptance Testing for Difficult-to-Test Situations", XP2004 Conference, 2004
11. http://agilecanada.com/wiki/Wiki.jsp?page=JennittaAndrea
12. Cockburn, Alistair, *Writing Effective Use Cases*, Addison Wesley, 1997.

Generative Acceptance Testing for Difficult-to-Test Software

Jennitta Andrea

jennitta@agilecanada.com

Abstract. While there are many excellent acceptance testing tools and frameworks available today, this paper presents an alternative approach, involving generating code from tests specified in a declarative tabular format within Excel spreadsheets. While this is a general approach, it is most applicable to difficult-to-test situations. Two such situations are presented: one involving complex fixture setup, and another involving complex application workflow concerns.

Keywords: Automated testing, code generation, domain specific testing language, test automation patterns, testing strategy, user acceptance testing, XML, XSL

1 Introduction: Acceptance Testing Difficulties

As a result of the agile movement, teams now pay more attention to their testing practices, and seek out the advantages of automated testing. Acceptance tests[1] are performed to ensure a system has suitably implemented the user's requirements. The primary objective of an acceptance test is to ensure the core business rules are implemented correctly in the context of the overall application workflow.

Automated acceptance tests are used in a wide range of situations, motivated by a variety of different goals. The purpose commonly mentioned in testing literature is to support custom software development in a test-first manner; the acceptance tests describe the essence of what is to be developed, and objectively signal when it is complete [1]. Application integrators use acceptance tests to specify, manage, and verify outsourced or commercial software components [2]. Acceptance tests are being created after-the-fact for existing legacy systems to support both ongoing maintenance and application renewal [3].

Due to the nature of acceptance tests, a number of difficulties may be experienced when automating them that may not be experienced when automating unit tests for the same system. *Direct customer involvement* is crucial to the acceptance testing process. It also raises the bar for the usability of automated testing frameworks to

---

[1] Also known as customer tests, functional tests, system tests, etc.

J. Eckstein and H. Baumeister (Eds.): XP 2004, LNCS 3092, pp. 29–37, 2004.

ensure the customers can read and potentially write the automated test themselves. There are additional implications for test management, including: maintaining synchronization between the customer test specifications and the automated tests, and maintaining the tests as the user interface and/or workflow evolve over time. *Poor performance* of an automated acceptance test suite is often an issue because the tests typically operate on the user interface, and involve all of the application layers and other integrated components. Stubbing out a problematic component is a common solution to performance problems, but unless the application was originally designed for testability, selective stubbing is often impossible. *Test data management* is another area rife with difficulties. Acceptance tests are automated to accelerate and standardize regression testing. The key to achieving reliable and repeatable regression tests is the use of unique test-specific data rather than real production data [4]. If the application has not been designed for testability, it is often difficult to create the test data, or to control the execution environment in order to create a specific event.

This paper examines how a particular project overcame these types of difficulties, and developed an innovative acceptance testing strategy: generating the code to automate acceptance tests that are specified in a declarative tabular format. For the project this was not just the simplest thing that could possibly work, it was the *only* thing that could possibly work.

2   Motivation: Invention through Necessity

We did not set out to create an alternative approach to automating acceptance tests. Our expectation was that an existing framework (e.g.: FIT [5] HttpUnit [6] jWebUnit [7] WebTest [8] to name just a few) would be used to automate our tests. As it turned out, none of these highly capable frameworks was up for the combination of challenges we faced on project Alpha[2].

The first hurdle was the large number of acceptance tests that had to be written in a very short period of time. For a variety of reasons, acceptance testing was considered late in the game; in addition, the critical system features being tested did not have adequate unit test coverage. To compensate for this, and to increase the users confidence in this part of the system, the acceptance test suite was larger than normal to include coverage of the business rules as well as the overall workflow. We started with ~100 tests, and expected this number to increase as subsequent releases introduced new features. The strategy for managing the integrity of such a large suite of acceptance tests was to ensure the test specification created by the business expert was directly executable. We could not afford the time or potential for error associated with translating a user specification into an automated test. A number of frameworks being considered were dropped from the list because coding the tests directly in Java was out of the question.

---

[2] Not the real name of the project.

The core challenges were architecturally rooted, thus much more problematic. Alpha was part of a family of applications, which together supported a large corporate business process. A number of the other related applications supplied portions of the precondition data referenced in Alpha's acceptance tests. Due to incomplete application integration, and technological and architectural differences between the applications, creating the precondition data required by the tests was complex and convoluted, a common side effect when testability is not a key architectural consideration. No single framework could work the magic required to dynamically set up the precondition data; we definitely needed to think outside of the box.

3 Overview: Code Generation Approach

An outline of the code generation approach is shown in Fig. 1. The customer defines their acceptance tests in a tabular format within *Excel spreadsheets* using a formal domain specific testing language. An *XML* representation of the test is created as a result of running a custom macro within the spreadsheet. Members of the development team use *XSL* to transform the XML test specification into an executable *test*, which encodes the detailed steps required to interact with the *system under test*, using the syntax and mechanisms required by the target *testing framework*. An important result of this is that the *front end* can drive many different *back ends*. The XML generated from the spreadsheet can be manipulated by any number of XSL specifications to create automated tests based on any of the available frameworks (e.g., Junit, HttpUnit, jWebUnit,WebTest).

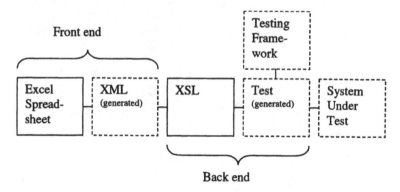

Fig. 1. Code Generation Components

Inspired by FIT, our goal was to provide the customer with a declarative, clean, and powerful testing language for defining acceptance tests. The customer already frequently used Excel spreadsheets to specify calculated outcomes, so we decided to use them to document the entire acceptance test. The customer had numerous tests to write in a short amount of time; human error was minimized wherever possible by taking advantage of Excel's cell cross reference and calculation features.

Fig. 2 provides an example acceptance test for a system that is used by hospitals to archive inactive patient records (called volumes). A patient is identified by a chart number, and may have one or more volumes. A volume is essentially a file folder that contains treatment details for a patient. If a patient has not received treatment for five or more years, their volume is considered to be inactive. Before boxes of inactive volumes are physically sent to an off-site storage location, a user enters the data associated with each volume into the Volume Archiving System (VAS).

This is one of the simplest acceptance tests for VAS, which demonstrates the following business rules: (a) adding a new volume will create the associated chart and/or box if they don't pre-exist, and (b) volumes for the same chart may be archived in different boxes.

1	Test Scenario	1		
2	Feature Name	Add Volume		
3	Description	Dynamically create boxes as necessary when volumes are added to the system. Volumes for the same chart may be archived in different boxes.		
4	Preconditions			
5		Volume		
6		Volume#	Chart#	Box#
7		1	1	1
8	Processing			
9		AddVolume		
10		Volume#	Chart#	Box#
11		2	1	2
12	Expected Results			
13		Volume		
14		Volume#	Chart#	Box#
15	unchanged	1	1	1
16	created	2	1	2
17				
18		Box		
19		Box#		
20	created	2		

Fig. 2. Example Excel Spreadsheet Test Specification

This specification is declarative in that it focuses on *what*, not *how*; it gives no hint of the gory details associated with actually executing the test. It is clean because only the essential concepts are described; we have the assurance that everything else that needs to be taken care of will be. It is powerful because the various table and column headings form a domain specific testing language that is familiar to the customer.

The body of the test (lines 4-20) is divided into three sections:
- **Preconditions** identify the data that is expected to be in the system prior to running the test. The table heading (line 5) defines a business object, and the column headings (line 6) reference attributes of the object. Each row represents a separate object (line 7). Many different business objects can be specified in the preconditions section, following the same pattern shown in the example.
- **Processing** refers to workflow, or user goal level use cases [9](line 9), supported by the system. Each column heading (line 10) represents user input that is required at some point within the workflow. Workflow is processed sequentially in the order specified in this section.
- **Expected Results** are described in the last section in terms of the changes made to the business objects. The appropriate verbs (e.g., created, updated, deleted) are placed in column 1.

The XML corresponding to the spreadsheet is shown in Fig. 3. A custom macro within the spreadsheet understands several simple rules about placement and the use of color within a test specification: fields describing the test start in cell (1, 1) and end at the first yellow line; major sub-sections of the test are found in lines highlighted in yellow; domain classes and their attributes are found in lines highlighted in grey; domain objects exist in the uncolored rows. The XML is semantically equivalent to the excel spreadsheet, but in a different (and noisy) format. The macro generically handles test specifications from any business domain, supporting any number of domain classes and associated attributes.

```
1 <test TestScenario="1" FeatureName="Add Volume" Description="Dynamic..." >
2 <Preconditions><classes>
3        <class name="Volume">
4              <object Volume#="1" Chart#="1" Box#="1"/>
5        </class> </classes></Preconditions>
6 <Processing><classes>
7        <class name="AddVolume">
8              <object Volume#="2" Chart#="1" Box#="2"/>
9        </class> </classes></Processing>
10<ExpectedResults><classes>
11       <class name="Volume">
12             <object verb="created" Volume#="2" Chart#="1" Box#="2"/>
13             <object verb="unchanged" Volume#="1" Chart#="1" Box#="1"/>
14       </class>
15       <class name="Box">
16             <object verb="created" Box#="2"/>
17       </class></classes></ExpectedResults></test>
```

Fig. 3. Example Generated XML

While this is one of the simplest acceptance tests for VAS, the actual steps required to carry out the test (either manually or automated) are significantly more complicated. Automated tests contain the details of the application workflow and proper test data management, and are typically divided into four sections:

- **Fixture Setup** (lines 4-7): Create a unique volume object with the specified attributes (note, the business logic will also cause the chart and box to be created). All remaining required attributes are generated as unique, 'anonymous' values [4]. Persist this object in the database.
- **Exercise System Under Test** (lines 9-11): Ensure the objects that will be created by the test (lines 15 and 20) do not exist prior to running the test. Navigate through the screens to accomplish the user goal of adding a volume to a box. The values listed on line 11 are used as inputs as appropriate within this workflow. For this application, this simple workflow involves logging in, and navigating through 3 different screens.
- **Results validation** (lines 12-17): Navigate through the application to ensure that: the objects that should have been created actually exist, the objects that should have been deleted no longer exist, and the objects that should have been updated have the new values. Each of these validations involves multi-screen navigation starting from the main screen.
- **Fixture teardown** (lines 4-7, 12-17): Remove any objects created in the preconditions (line 7). Remove any objects created as a result of exercising the System Under Test (line 15, 20).

4   Project Alpha: Difficult Fixture Setup

As described in Section 2, the motivation for this code generation approach was to find a solution to the complicated test fixture setup problem experienced by project Alpha. Test data creation was a multi-step process performed partially using: Alpha's user interface, another application's user interface, Alpha's java API, and a series of carefully hand-written SQL scripts aimed directly at several databases (a simplified outline is shown in Fig. 4). Multiple XSL code generators were developed to take information from the XML specification and transform it into a specific step in the data loading process. The standard acceptance-testing tool for the project was QA Run [10]. The testing team developed a customized script-based interface to supplement QA Run's standard record-playback interface.

This is a case where the *front end* and the *back end* of the tests are radically different. Because the data creation process was so complex and time consuming, the code generated to handle the fixture setup stage pre-loaded all of the data for an entire test suite while still insuring that each test operated on it's own unique data set (private fixture data [4]). The key critical success factor for pre-loading private fixture data is to follow a naming convention that ensures each test references only its own data. The test scenario and feature name from the header part of the test specification (lines

1-2 of the spreadsheet; line 1 of the XML) were encoded into the test data during the code-generation process.

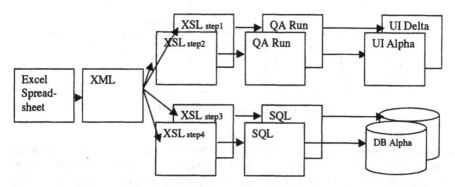

Fig. 4. Multiple Targets for Fixture Setup

This turned out to be a remarkably elegant and efficient solution that resolved both the technical challenges and the usability requirements. The business experts were able to quickly develop acceptance tests, given the declarative, and domain-oriented specification language. This approach addressed all of the problems and constraints related to loading the test data, and did so in an error-free and consist manner. Ultimately, less time was spent automating the large number of acceptance tests using the code generation approach, as compared to having to hand-code each test from a customer specification.

5   Project Bravo: Complex System Workflow

The results from project Alpha were so encouraging, that a second project was immediately sought out to verify the general applicability of the approach. Project Bravo[3] also considered acceptance testing late in the game, but was very different from project Alpha in a number of ways. First, a disciplined (unit) test-first process was followed during application development. As a result, the system was very testable; none of the fixture setup difficulties experienced by Alpha were experienced on this project. Because the intricacies of the business rules were well covered by the unit tests, far fewer acceptance tests were needed as compared to Alpha. The team had been using HttpUnit to unit-test the user interface, so this was the target tool for the second code-generation case study (see Fig. 5).

While Bravo did not share the difficulties of Alpha, there were different project characteristics that made this approach compelling as an option. Bravo is very rich in features, supporting many detailed business workflows. Because the declarative nature of the spreadsheets focuses on the business intent (what), not the detailed steps

---

[3] Not the real name of the project.

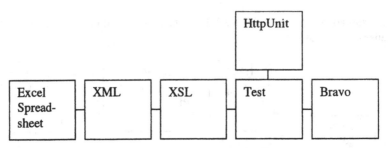

Fig. 5. Code Generation for project Bravo

within the workflow (how), the test specifications will remain quite stable while the actual system evolves over time. In addition, the highly collaborative and fluid design approach taken by the team results in user interface and workflow details that are not solidified until relatively late in the sprint. Thus the *front end* of the tests can be defined early on, and the *back end* of the tests can be developed later once the details have been worked out. Furthermore, as the system evolves over time, test maintenance will typically be localized in a small number of XSL components; once the code for the acceptance tests are re-generated they are all brought up to date.

While this approach worked well the second time, it wasn't necessarily the best strategy for Bravo. The customer was not responsible for actually writing the tests, so it was not as crucial to have a user-friendly specification. As a result, the XSL code generation layer was deemed to be extra overhead, requiring specialized skills and tools that the team had not needed thus far. Because the number of acceptance tests automated on Bravo was quite low (in the order of ten to twenty), hand-coding the tests in a more direct fashion was acceptable. The team ultimately decided to use an extensively customized WebTest framework [11] for hand-coding the acceptance tests.

6   Conclusions

While there are many excellent acceptance testing tools and frameworks available today, this paper presents an alternative approach, involving generating test code from acceptance tests specified in excel spreadsheets. This approach has been tried on two substantially different projects, providing insights about its applicability. Although this is a general-purpose approach, it is not a silver bullet. In particular, the project must weigh the extra cost of developing the code-generation layer against the resulting benefits. In particular, if there are a manageable number of tests, and an existing acceptance testing framework can be used directly, then the code-generation approach would likely introduce unnecessary overhead. Thus, the most basic criterion for applicability is that the situation is too difficult to test using an existing framework directly. One or more of the following project characteristics further increase the appropriateness of this approach:

- The customer writes the acceptance tests themselves and needs a simple, domain specific testing language to express the concepts clearly.
- Acceptance tests act as requirements and are focused on capturing strategic concepts (e.g., overall business rules and relationships) rather than tactical details (e.g., application steps to enact the workflow). Decoupling the specification from the automation makes this separation of concerns possible.
- A large number of tests must be automated in a short amount of time. The tests contain calculations and interrelationships between the data that a spreadsheet supports well.
- The user interface evolves over time, and test maintenance is a concern.

Does the automated acceptance testing world need yet another approach? For a difficult-to-test project like Alpha, the code generation approach worked exceptionally well, in a situation where nothing else could have possibly worked.

Acknowledgements. It's been my privilege for many years to work with and be mentored by Gerard Meszaros and Shaun Smith on test automation best practices. The work described in this paper would not have been possible without the courage, insights, and contributions of members of the *Alpha* project team: Bryan Ambrogiano, Kevin Holroyd, and Bud Newman. The work was significantly improved by the insights and contributions of the *Bravo* project team: Amy Law, Robert Purdy, Lynne Ralston, and Ross Taylor.

References

1. Beck, Kent, *Extreme Programming Explained,* Addison Wesley, 2001.
2. Andrea, Jennitta, "An Agile Request For Proposal (RFP) Process", ADC, 2003
3. Meszaros, Gerard, et al "Agile Regression Testing Using Record & Playback", XP Agile Universe, 2003
4. Meszaros, Gerard and Shaun Smith, "Test Automation Manifesto", XP Agile Universe, 2003
5. FIT, http://fit.c2.com
6. HttpUnit, http://httpunit.sourceforge.net
7. jWebUnit, http://jwebunit.sourceforge.net/
8. WebTest, http://webtest.canoo.com/webtest/manual/WebTestHome.html
9. Cockburn, Alistair, *Writing Effective Use Cases*, Addison Wesley, 1997.
10. QA Run, http://www.compuware.com/products/qacenter/qarun.htm
11. Andrea, Jennitta, "Putting a Motor on Canoo WebTest Acceptance Testing Framework", XP2004 Conference, 2004.

Moomba[1] – A Collaborative Environment for Supporting Distributed Extreme Programming in Global Software Development

Michael Reeves and Jihan Zhu

Information Environments Program
School of Information Technology and Electrical Engineering
The University of Queensland
Brisbane 4073, Queensland, Australia
m.reeves@uq.edu.au, jihan@itee.uq.edu.au

Abstract. Global Software Development (GSD) is an emerging distributive software engineering practice, in which a higher communication overhead due to temporal and geographical separation among developers is traded with gains in reduced development cost, improved flexibility and mobility for developers, increased access to skilled resource-pools and convenience of customer involvements. However, due to its distributive nature, GSD faces many fresh challenges in aspects relating to project coordination, awareness, collaborative coding and effective communication. New software engineering methodologies and processes are required to address these issues. Research has shown that, with adequate support tools, Distributed Extreme Programming (DXP) - a distributive variant of an agile methodology – Extreme Programming (XP) can be both efficient and beneficial to GDS projects. In this paper, we present the design and realization of a collaborative environment, called "Moomba", which assists a distributed team in both instantiation and execution of a DXP process in GSD projects.

Keywords: eXtreme Programming, CSCW, groupware, distributed teams, awareness, coordination

1   Introduction

Global Software Development [1] stems from the Software Industry's desire for globalisation of business to derive increased market-share and from its' desire to gain a competitive edge through outsourcing, subcontracting and forming strategic partnerships. Rapid advances in computer networks, telecommunication and internet technologies have made it possible for developers from different geographical locations and technical specialities to form virtual teams in a distributed setting. This allows teams to jointly develop the same artefact of software in a collaborative way. However, GSD represents a radical shift from the way software is engineered traditionally in a collocated team setting. Many challenges arise due to GSD's

---

[1] Moomba is an Australian aboriginal word meaning: "let us get together and have fun" which captures well the synergistic spirit that our collaborative environment endeavours to create.

J. Eckstein and H. Baumeister (Eds.): XP 2004, LNCS 3092, pp. 38–50, 2004.

distributive nature, where developers are dispersed at different development sites across many countries and time zones. Four aspects of software engineering process are most impacted by the distribution of team members, these include - project coordination, awareness, collaborative coding and effective communication.

A software development process is needed in a GSD project to coordinate the activities of the project and govern the project's lifecycle. The question is then which software process best lends itself to GSD. In recent years, Extreme Programming (XP) has proven to be a popular methodology for its' relatively 'lightweight' approach which encompasses many valuable user-centric design principles and usability values. The XP methodology relies predominately on the development team working in close proximity, ideally within the same workspace to facilitate tight communication. To allow XP to be utilized within distributed environments, it is necessary to introduce communication and awareness support that is closely comparable to collocated XP practices. Several efforts have been made to apply XP methodologies to a distributed setting, notably in TUKAN and MILOS [2, 3].

A collaborative environment is essentially any virtual workspace specifically designed to support communication and awareness to afford a strong sense of coherency within a group. It should integrate with existing systems used by the organization, such as document repositories coupled with versioning and configuration control tools (such as CVS), databases, videoconference facilities and e-mail systems. This can provide improved communication through use of notifications, document sharing and an increased understanding of the software process. This will allow for greater collaboration among team members by unifying people with diverse skills into a more cohesive unit. The goal of the Moomba collaborative environment aims at creating an online virtual community by encouraging cooperative teamwork. Moomba implements a three-tier awareness model based on the model inspired by Rodden [4]. This model describes the interactions of users with a shared workspace in terms of a spatial metaphor.

The rest of the paper is organized as follows. Moomba's three-tier awareness model for support collaborations in DXP software process is defined and discussed in section 2. A realization of the three-tier awareness model use as part of our collaborative development environment is described in section 3. Related work is reviewed in section 4, followed by conclusions and future work in section 5.

2   Moomba's Awareness Model

"Workspace awareness is the up-to-the minute knowledge a person requires about another group member's interaction with a shared workspace to collaborate effectively" as defined by Greenberg et al.[5]. People can use this awareness information to help coordinate their work based on an understanding of the activities of others. To determine how Moomba supports awareness it is helpful to determine how different types of awareness can be categorized. According to Greenberg [5], there are several categories of awareness that must be used to provide effective collaboration.

Table 1. Four types of group awareness.

Type of Awareness	Description
Informal	Basic knowledge about the presence of users sharing a workplace.
Group-structured	Knowledge people's roles and responsibilities, their position on an issue, their status and group processes.
Social	Information people maintain about others in a social or conversational context.
Workspace	Knowledge a person requires about another group member's interactions in a shared workspace.

It is essential that the awareness system captures enough information about the interactions of the users within the workspace, and provides awareness support through the appropriate notification of events. Careful consideration should be made to the value or importance each awareness sub-type brings to the system to ensure an effective and compact awareness model.

2.1   Rodden's Spatial Awareness Model

Several models have been developed to deliver awareness information without flooding the user with irrelevant information. A well-known model presented by Rodden describes the interactions of users with a shared workspace in terms of a spatial metaphor. Within the spatial model, artifacts are arranged in a three dimensional space. As users interact with various artifacts, other users may see where their team members are positioned. The important concepts used by this model are *focus* and *nimbus* as described in [6].

- *Nimbus* describes the location (s) where a user is located in the workspace.
- *Focus* describes the location(s) at which the user may be looking.

TUKAN's Awareness Model

TUKAN, developed by Schümmer and Schümmer [2], uses this specialized spatial model with focus and nimbus. The focus includes all objects that are of interest to the user, while the Nimbus includes all positions in space where the object might influence other objects. TUKAN automatically arranges the artifacts within the artifact space according to the following relationships:

- **Structural** relationships like inheritance
- **Usage** relationships such as calling class method
- **Version** relationship between artifacts with the same version

Based on these relationships a semantic distance function can be used to find the range between two artifacts. A color-coding scheme is used to visualize the distance to the nearest team member in the nimbus. Thus this information can be used to indicate the presence of users working on related artifacts, which may encourage pair programming. The same distance can be used to measure possible configuration conflicts. Potential conflicts between artifacts are represented using a weather metaphor in TUKAN.

2.2 Moomba's Three-Tier Awareness Model

The Moomba three-tier awareness model extends TUKAN's awareness model to support a greater level of awareness. This particularly includes workspace knowledge and group-structure awareness needed to support DXP. The collaborative space model used by TUKAN provides detailed awareness information in relation to the project artifacts. However, we believe that TUKAN's awareness model is somewhat passive when supporting pair-programming, as the awareness model is fundamentally based on the proximity between two programmers' foci. It is our belief that a greater level of support for workspace knowledge and group-structure awareness holds the key to creating a sense of community among the development team.

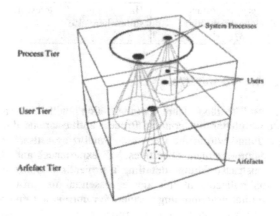

Fig. 1. Illustrates Moomba's three-tier awareness model

Moomba's three-tire collaboration model can be visualized within cubic space as illustrated in Fig.1. The cubic space has three planes, each corresponding to a tier of awareness within the collaborative environment. The top tier represents system entities that provide social and group-structure awareness. The middle tier captures awareness information regarding interactions and collaboration performed by users, while the bottom tier focuses on software artifact interactions. The projection cones in Fig. 1 represent the interactions and relationships between each tier in the awareness model.

The model is essentially a means to capture awareness information of interest to team members. At each tier of awareness, there are many types of the associated events that need to notify different team members. However, not all events are relevant to each team member. Different types of events must be handled differently by the collaborative mechanisms that support awareness. We have adopted an event classification system defined by Schlichter et al [6] to categorize these events. In general, the events are classified into four awareness modes as describe in the Table 2.

Synchronous awareness is concerned with events that are currently occurring in the collaborative environment. This is in contrast to asynchronous awareness, where events have occurred in the past. Coupled and uncoupled awareness is used to categorize events according to the user's focus in the workspace. Participants collaborating on the same artifact and are aware of each other is considered coupled awareness. While uncoupled awareness is information that is interesting, but not related to the user's current focus of work.

Table 2. A scheme for classifying awareness events.

	Synchronous	**Asynchronous**
Coupled	What is currently happening in the actual scope of the work?	What has changed in the actual scope of the work since last access?
Uncoupled	Things of importance, which occur currently anywhere else?	Has anything of interest happened recently somewhere else?

2.3   The Process Tier of Awareness

The process tier is used to place team members along with their interactions with project artifacts into a collaborative context. Process entities are used to form relations among user entities found within the user tier. Analyzing a user's responsibilities, roles, ambitions, self-improvement objectives, XP experiences and skill sets allows process entities to construct relations detailing a project's organizational and social structure. Information collected at this tier is essential for providing users with knowledge about potential programming partners for current and future collaboration on the project. Events associated with the process tier include events related to potential collaborators and requests for interactions. An example of events for the process tier is illustrated in the Table 3 (not comprehensively listed).

It is important to realize that the events listed in Table 3 do not represent what is captured by the process entities. What the process entities capture basically consists of information regarding relations between user entities and the user entity's relationship with the artifact-tier.

2.4   The User Tier of Awareness

The User tier is essentially a simplified version of TUKAN's collaborative space. All software artifacts evaluated to be of interest or relevant to the user are added to their focus. Whereas TUKAN arranged artifacts within the artifact space by analyzing the semantic structure of each class, Moomba uses an artifact's collaborators, as defined by the Class, Responsibility and Collaboration (CRC) cards.

Table 3. A classification of events in the process tier.

	Synchronous	Asynchronous
Coupled	• A potential collaborator has become online / offline • An expert in current work interest has become on-line / offline • A task which matches a programmer's skill sets is available	• Changes in potential collaborator's schedule and plans. • Requests for pair programming / task negations left by collaborators.
Uncoupled	• A pair-programming request has arisen in an area of my learning interest • On-line technical seminar has started • On-line status of the rest of team	• New member has joined the team since last access • Staff departure

Awareness information similar to TUKAN is captured at this tier. Moomba provides information regarding the presence of users as they interact with software artifacts. Knowing that a user is working on the same or related artifacts can resolve potential configuration conflicts. When a potential conflict is detected programmers can work together to resolve the problem. Thus continuous integration can be achieved while coding. In addition to resolving conflicts, knowing that another user is sharing the same artifact or an artifact closely related can encourage users to work collaboratively. Examples of events belonging to the user tier are listed in the Table 4:

Table 4. Examples of events belong to the user tier.

	Synchronous	Asynchronous
Coupled	• Potential conflicts • Sharing the same artifact	• Version changes to this artifact since last access. • Configuration changes to this artifact
Uncoupled	• Any changes to collaborating artifacts (as defined in CRC)	• Version changes occurred on not closely related artifacts

2.5   The Artifact Tier of Awareness

The artifact tier is concerned with capturing events generated when a user modifies a shared artifact. It is more specificly interested in events limited to the scope of an artifact. This is how the user level is able to determine potential conflicts and the presence of potential collaborators. However, the artifact tier is of particular importance when users are engaged in a pair programming sessions. Examples of events in the artifact tier are listed in Table 5.

Table 5. Examples of events belong to the artifact tier.

	Synchronous	Asynchronous
Coupled	• Actions performed by oneself • Actions performed by collaborator	• History of changes the current shared artifact
Uncoupled	• Actions performed on other instances of the shared artifact	• History of all changes to other instances of the share artifact

Moomba's collaborative editing system is based on the relaxed WYSIWIS (what you see is what I see) model. This corresponds to the ability of participants to each work in seperate sections of the document. The model is nesscessary to allow the document's participants the freedom to browse its contents, while not disrupting their pair's position. For example, while pair programming one user may check the implementation of method, while their parnter continues to code. Moomba allows two or more users to remotely collaborate on a shared artifact simultaneously. The shared artifact is not limited to the project's source files, so it covers the possibility to create or modify user stories or tasks collaboratively.

3   A Realization of Moomba's Collaborative Environment

Moomba's collaborative environment consists of a set of tools which integrate these support mechanisms to facilitate the instantiation and execution of a DXP process. We begin by describing the overall architecture of Moomba. Each of tools will be discussed in the next section. Examples are then used to illustrate how Moomba's tools can be applied for supporting a DXP process.

3.1   Overall Architecture

The overall architecture for Moomba is illustrated in Fig.2. Moomba consists of three main tools: HyperStackXP – a web portal for project coordination and tracking; a collaborative server – for coordinating manipulation and management of shared artefacts; and MCIDE - a collaborative programming environment for pair-programming in Moomba. In addition, both the web portal and the collaborative server are integrated with CVS code/document repositories and a user database.

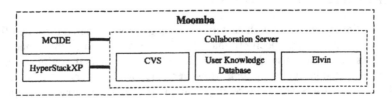

Fig. 2. An illustration of Moomba's collaborative environment architecture.

3.2   Web Portal – HyperStack XP

Moomba offers a flexible, web-based project management web portal - HyperstackXP to help streamline the project management and planning. Its goal is to support both coupled and uncoupled asynchronous event notifications. It is essential to keep users informed of any project changes through indirect communication. Each user's web interface is customized to receive notifications or updates based on the user's responsibilities within a project. HyperstackXP contains a rich set of functionalities, although not all features will be described in this paper. A selected few screen shots demonstrating the functionalities of HyperstackXP are included in Fig.3. The web portal integrates process execution with a user database to simplify project management, minimize overhead, and notify requirement changes. It incorporates key XP practices such as release planning, iterating planning and tracking, and story and task management.

Tracking Project Overall Status. Hyperstack provides overviews on the current status of a project by release and iteration. This allows developers the quickly assess the project's status. User stories and task requirements are organized into releases and iterations. In a distributed environment where members frequently change it important that the system has a good support structure to help new users become familiar with the project.

Supporting Planning Game. Release Planning lists all the stories that have not been completed or planned for an iteration. This allows users to group selected stories to be added to the current or a future iteration. The Iteration display can be used to show users their tasks and assignments. In most XP projects, task assignment is generally decided by allowing users to signup for a particular task as soon as it becomes available. The drawback with this approach is it may be difficult for all users to be present each time a new task is added. This is especially true with large distributed projects, where the development team is typically dispersed across many time zones. Moomba handles this dilemma by maintaining a user's presence within the system when the user is offline. The system has the responsibility within the system to 'act' on the user's behalf. For example, Moomba detects that a new task has been added to system, which requires extra functionality to the applications sound API. Using information from the user knowledge base and analysing user involved with related artefacts, the system can notify potential users that a task may be of interest.

Pair-Programming Partner Finder. The Finder is essentially an advanced search through the user database with the goal being to find a programming partner. The Finder defines the search criteria based on the requirements or attributes a user may be interested in. This can then be used to search each user's profile for pair compatibility. For example, a user may choose to use the Finder to collaborate with another user at a particular skill level, coding interest or programming role. This feature is also helpful for pairing new users to more advanced and experienced users to balance and develop the XP team.

User Profile Management System. The user profile management system is a collection of information relating to each user's: Programming interests, ambitions, project goals, XP experience, programming experience, availability, project schedule, time zone, performance rating given by peers, and completed user stories and tasks. The user database can help bring together users for pair programming by using Moomba's Pair-Programming Finder. The user database is created when a new user joins the development team and some fields are dynamically updated each time a user has completed a task. For example, after each successful task completion, the user's performance is rated by peers; the user's XP experience and programming experience also increase. The manager updates their skills set when a user has successfully completed a task that requires new skills or has completed a training course.

3.3   Moomba's Collaborative IDE (MCIDE)

Moomba's collaborative editor supports all the functionality usually found in today's leading development environment. This includes syntax highlighting, code completion, find/replace, indentation and a symbol finder. Moomba allows two or more users to remotely collaborate on a shared artifact simultaneously. The shared artifact is not limited to the project's source files, but can allow users to create and modify user stories or tasks collaboratively. The editing is completely unconstrained and users can insert and delete characters at any location.

The most important feature for supporting text-based collaboration involves making all participants aware of each other's changes to a document. Taking this into account, it is paramount that the input generated by each user be distributed to all participants, so that consistency among participants is maintained. To further add awareness, a participant's contribution to the document can be visualized using a different background colour to emphasize what they have typed. It is important that the collaboration be based on the relaxed WYSIWIS model. The main advantage being participants have the freedom to scroll to any location within the document without affecting what other participants are doing. However, this freedom can lead to reduced awareness. Thus there is the requirement to provide appropriate widgets to allow participants to be aware of each other activities. Moomba features several widgets to counter the lack of reduced awareness. These widgets are shown in Fig 4.

The functionality of Moomba can also support collaborative debugging of programs. Each collaboration session allows participants to collaboratively control program execution, while receiving essential debugging information. Participants have access to information regarding the call sequence of each thread and its variables. The editor also allows participants to follow the execution of a program within the source code. Currently, only the textual output of an executing program can be shared. For programs, such as applets, only the host will be able to see the output sent to the screen. Moomba also allows users to execute groups of JUnit tests. The results of the tests are distributed to all participants within session. Users can move to the failed test by clicking of the error message listed in the Testing output window.

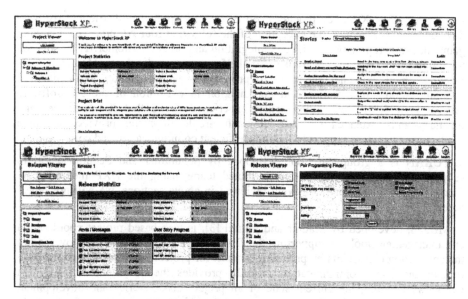

Fig. 3. Screen shots demonstrate (clockwise: project overall progress statistics, user-stories sorted into iterations, pair-programming partner finder, and the status for a release.

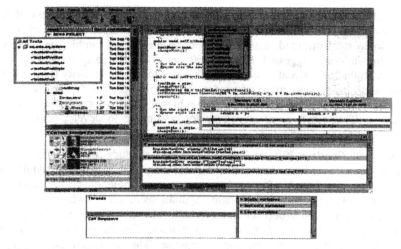

Fig. 4. Moomba's collaborative features allow participants to editor, build, test and debug a project collaboratively.

4   Related Works

The term DXP was first used by Kircher et al [7] when they investigated the possibility of extending the agile methodology XP to distributed software engineering settings by relaxing the team's collocation constraint. Their empirical study showed that almost all of XP's key practices can be directly applied in distributed software development. This is with the exception of the following four XP practices: planning game, pair-programming, continuous integration and on-site customer. Their solution to collocation constraint is to use off-shelf groupware (such as Microsoft Net-meeting, email and chat channels) to provide awareness support to facilitate to communication, collaboration and coordination in execution of the XP software process in a distributed setting. Their experience shows that XP principles and practices can be extended into distributed software developments, provided that there is adequate awareness support to facilitate efficient communication and collaboration.

TUKAN is a groupware tool developed by Schümmer and Schümmer [2] to support software development in distributed teams using the DXP methodology. Since TUKAN has been extensively reviewed in above sections, we will not repeat here.

MILOS, developed by Maurer and Martel [3], is web-based project coordination and management tool for supporting the DXP software process. MILOS overcomes the collocation constraints by providing support for project coordination, information routing and team communication. MILOS provides the development team with overviews detailing the current state of all project tasks, stories and development plans. The system easily allows for accessing the information generated from a task. This information can be viewed within a standard Web browser. The support for pair-programming is done by Microsoft Net-meeting.

Baheti et al [8] conducted an empirical investigation to the effectiveness of pair-programming in distributed teams. This was achieved by comparing the performance level between a distributed team and a collocated team within an academic environment. It was suggested that the efficiency of the dispersed teams was comparable to that of collocated teams, with respect to the productivity (lines of code per hour) and quality (test subjects' grades) of the code produced. The results also showed that the distributed pairs showed a higher level of communication and collaboration. This result gives incentives for continuing to develop and improve collaborative tools for distributed pair-programming.

Damian and Eberlein [9] conducted an empirical study of the efficiency of groupware tools such as Microsoft's Net-Meeting for supporting requirement negotiation in a distributed software development environment. The results suggest that the group performance in requirement negotiations in a face-to-face setting is no better than in distributed group setting; and collocated negotiators actually manage conflicts less well than the distributed negotiators. This is because face-to-face negotiations are usually more emotionally intense. The results appear to confirm experiences reported in Kircher's DXP work that used groupware communication tools such as Microsoft Net-Meeting might not hinder the decision-making ability of a distributed team.

Starbase CodeWright™ 7.0 [10] is a commercial programming environment. CodeWright's most attractive and relevant feature is known as CodeMeeting that serves the function of a shared editor that allows pair-programming over a distributed environment. Pairs see the same source code simultaneously and can take turns writing, editing and commenting the source. CodeWright also features a text chat feature that drastically speeds up development time, as an external messaging system is not necessary. The awareness support provided by CodeWright is comparable to the third level as defined in our awareness model.

RECIPE™ (REal-time Collaborative Interactive Programming Environment) [11] is a prototype for an internet-based real-time collaborative programming environment. Its goal is to allow physically dispersed programmers to collaboratively design, code, test, debug, and document the same software source code. The awareness features supported in RECIPE are comparable to the third level as defined in our awareness model.

5   Conclusion and Future Work

Workspace knowledge and group-structure awareness in distributed teams is crucial for facilitating strong collaboration required by distributed teams to practise XP in GSD projects. While TUKAN's awareness model provides detailed awareness information in relation to project artifacts, Moomba's three-tier awareness model extends TUKAN's awareness model to support a greater level of awareness. This particularly includes workspace knowledge and group-structure awareness which are vital for seamless collaborations at project coordination and management level. Moomba's collaboration environment supports our awareness model by using two collaboration tools: a web portal – HyperstackXP and a collaborative editor - MCIDE.

In future work, intelligent agent systems will be investigated to automatically support some of the functionalities in the process tier. For example, match-making agents will replace the current the finder for searching potential pair-programming partners. A reputation agent will automatically rank a developer's performance. The direct communication in the current system uses Microsoft Net-meeting to provide video and audio. In the future work, the video and audio conferencing facility will be fully integrated to the collaborative editor. The usability of Moomba's collaborative environment is currently under evaluation at a commercial company. Features and functionalities in both HyperstackXP Web portal and MCIDE collaborative editor will be refined according to the usability study report. The final product of Moomba will be release as open-source software.

References

1. Damian, D., Workshop on Global Software Development. 2002, Web Conference Proceedings on "Global Software Development" available at http://www.cis.ohio-state.edu/~nsridhar/ICSE02/GSD/PDF/summary.pdf.
2. Schümmer, T. and J. Schümmer. Support for Distributed Teams in eXtreme Programming. in Proceedings of Second International Conference on eXtreme Programming and Agile Processes in Software Engineering (XP2001)",. 2001. Cagliari, Sardinia, Italy: Addison Wesley, pp. 355-377.
3. Maurer, F. Support Distributed Extreme Programming. in Proceedings of Extreme Programming and Agile Methods - XP/Agile Universe 2002, Lecture Notes in Computer Science. 2002. Chicago, IL, USA: Springer-Verlag Heidelberg, pp. 13 - 22.

4. Rodden, T. Population the Application: A Model of Awareness for Cooperative Applications. in Proceedings of International Conference on Computer Supported Cooperative Work. 1996, pp. 87-96.
5. Greenberg, S., C. Gutwin, and A. Cockburn, Using distortion-oriented displays to support workspace awareness. 1996, Dept of Comp. Science, Univ. of Calgary, Canada.
6. Schlichter, J., M. Koch, and M. Bürger. Workspace Awareness for Distributed Teams. in Proceedings of International conference on Coordination Technology for Collaborative Applications - Organizations, Processes, and Agents, Lecture Notes in Computer Science. 1998. Singapore: Springer Verlag, Berlin, pp. 199-218.
7. Kircher, M., et al. Distributed eXtreme Programming. in Proceedings of Second International Conference on eXtreme Programming and Agile Processes in Software Engineering (XP2001)",. 2001. Cagliari, Sardinia, Italy: Addison Wesley, pp. pages 66-71.
8. Baheti, P., et al., Exploring pair programming in distributed object-oriented team projects. 2002, In Web Proceedings of 17th Annual ACM SIGPLAN Conference on Object-Oriented Programming, Systems, Languages, and Applications - Educator's Symposium 2002, available at:
    http://collaboration.csc.ncsu.edu/laurie/Papers/EdSymDistPPFinalSubmission.pdf.
9. Damian, D. and A. Eberlein, Groupware Support for Requirements Negotiation in Distributed Software Development. 2001, Web Conference Proceedings on "Global Software Development" available at
    http://sern.ucalgary.ca/~maurer/icse2001ws/submissions/Damian.pdf.
10. Borland, Starbase CodeWright, http://www.codewright.com/.
11. Shen, H. and C. Sun. RECIPE: A Web-based Environment for Supporting Real-time Collaborative Programming. in Proceedings of IASTED International Conference on Networks, Parallel and Distributed Processing, and Applications (NPDPA 2002). 2002. Tsukuba, Japan, pp.

When XP Met Outsourcing

Angela Martin[1], Robert Biddle[2], and James Noble[1]

[1] Faculty of Information Technology, Victoria University of Wellington
Wellington, New Zealand
{angela, kjx}@mcs.vuw.ac.nz
[2] Human-Oriented Technology Laboratory, Carleton University
Ottawa, Canada
robert_biddle@carleton.ca

Abstract. Outsourcing is common for software development, and is the context for many projects using agile development processes. This paper presents two case studies concentrating on the customer role in projects using outsourcing and extreme programming (XP). The studies follow an interpretive approach based on in-depth interviews, and suggest some tensions between some contractual arrangements in outsourcing, and the XP process. In particular, one suggests XP worked well in the context of their particular outsourcing arrangements, and the other study suggests difficulty in aligning XP with a different set of outsourcing arrangements.

1 Introduction

Outsourced software development has become commonplace in today's business environment [3, 5]. The outsourcing environments of today are complex, involving multiple organisations for different services: management, development, infrastructure and integration, to name but a few. Agile development, as it moves into the mainstream of software development, will come face-to-face with the realities of these complex outsourcing environments. Outsourcing arrangements typically result in the XP customer residing in a separate organisation to the development team. Our research [6, 7], which focuses on the XP customer role, quickly brought to the fore that outsourcing is an issue facing the XP customer.

In this paper we present two case studies that highlight the practical realities faced in using XP with complex outsourcing arrangements. In the next section we outline some of the related work in this area, followed by our research method. The fourth and fifth sections outline the two cases, while the final section presents our conclusions.

2 Related Work

Members of the agile community have begun to raise some of the issues potentially associated with outsourcing arrangements and agile development.

J. Eckstein and H. Baumeister (Eds.): XP 2004, LNCS 3092, pp. 51–59, 2004.
© Springer-Verlag Berlin Heidelberg 2004

Ambler [1] argues that outsourcing is riskier than it initially appears and organisations should seriously consider an alternative to outsourcing; that of running a small internal agile development team. Ambler's main argument is that the agile alternative may gain many of the intended cost savings without some of the inherent risks of outsourcing. So while Ambler does raise the question of whether the organisation really should be outsourcing, he does not provide detailed advice to the practitioner on how to effectively work in an outsourced environment.

Poppendieck & Poppendieck [9] take a different tack. Recognising that there is a perceived barrier to agile development in an outsourcing situation, they have explored the potential implications of different contracting models. The contracting models they have reviewed and analysed include fixed-price, time-and-materials, multi-stage, target-cost, target-schedule and shared-benefit contracts. They conclude that contracts that allow optional scope are more likely to create effective software development environments. Since the publication of their book [9], the Poppendiecks have run a series of workshops [10] at international conferences that are aimed at further evolving our understanding in this area.

3 Research Method

Information Systems Development (ISD) methodology researchers [2, 8] have expressed a growing concern that existing ISD methods do not meet the needs of today's business and software development environments. Studies [8, 7] in this area have begun to explore practices in natural settings in order to begin to address these issues. Given this trend, we have used interpretative in-depth case studies to explore our research questions within their natural setting, software development projects. We used semi-structured in-depth one-on-one interviews to collect the data for this paper. Two outsourced projects are explored, in the first we interviewed 5 project participants and in the second we interviewed 3 project participants. The interviewees, in both cases, have covered the spectrum of core XP roles including the customer, programmer, coach and tester. In the second case, the participants moved between roles over the life of the project. All interviews were taped and later transcribed in detail. The interviewees were asked to validate both the transcriptions of the interview and the interpreted findings. We use a number of quotes from the interviews to illustrate our findings in this paper; names have been avoided or invented to preserve anonymity.

4 Project Endeavour

This section tells the story of Project Endeavour, an outsourced XP project involving:
- KiwiCorp, a large New Zealand company, is the customer organisation
- DevCorp, a large consultancy, is the development vendor and
- BureauCorp, a large software services company, is the infrastructure vendor

The data that forms this section was collected in a series of interviews with both KiwiCorp and DevCorp project participants, near the completion of the project [6, 7].

4.1 Case Description

Project Endeavour is seen as a success by both KiwiCorp and DevCorp, and part of that success was attributed to the use of an agile development method. Project Endeavour had been attempted by KiwiCorp previously, but each previous attempt was unsuccessful. In fact, the KiwiCorp customer representative notes that when her manager was handed this project to 'sort-out':

> *"We felt we could probably only do it if we used [DevCorp] ... because we had such a lot of confidence in them based on previous experience ... [later in the interview] ... we knew what they were capable of, ... they could actually deliver what they said they could ... a key value of working with [DevCorp is that] it was a joint effort" – Customer, KiwiCorp*

The project was approximately 15 months long, and at its peak the project team had 11 full-time experienced team members. Initially the project was a traditional waterfall project and was divided into three phases, planning (deciding what to build), development (building the application) and implementation (user acceptance testing, training and roll out). The planning phase focused on gathering requirements using standard workshop techniques and involved a series of user workshops that were attended by the business users. At the end of the planning phase it was decided to use XP for the development phase. The requirements gathered during the planning phase were used as a basis for the XP user stories. The implementation phase was retained as this approach meshed with the existing practices of KiwiCorp and BureauCorp.

The relationships amongst these three companies, outside of the specific project, are complex and also worth noting. The items of particular interest are:

- KiwiCorp and BureauCorp have a business alliance, they work together to deliver outsourced services. Each company also delivers services outside of the alliance.
- BureauCorp is the outsourced vendor for all KiwiCorp's internal infrastructure.
- BureauCorp and DevCorp both have software development service lines and compete against each other in this area.

Please see the technical report of this research [6] for further information concerning Project Endeavour.

4.2 Participant Reflection and Discussion

During the course of the interviews, the participants reflected on their experiences with XP and outsourcing. These reflections are outlined and discussed in this section.

Time and Materials Contract. The project manager from DevCorp reflected on some of the benefits they encountered working on a time and materials contract, rather than working on a fixed price arrangement:

> *"We were very fortunate that we were working on [a] time and materials contract with [KiwiCorp], if we were working on a fixed price per itera-*

tion ... I would have had to be a lot harder on the client... I would have to have been a lot more strict about things like getting change signed off and if circumstances came along [e.g. infrastructure difficulties caused by BureauCorp] and we lost a day ... I'd have to go back to the client and say well actually you've lost a day ... therefore you need to subtract that functionality [from this iteration] ... I was sort of able to let that ride with the client ... It didn't become blindingly obvious to me until I was [discussing the issue with a manager responsible for a fixed price XP project] ... if at the end of the iteration if we had not finished all of the stories on the wall we would just put them into the next iteration, but [on the fixed price project] they've still got to finish them without getting any more money" – Project Manager, DevCorp

So a fixed price contract arrangement would result in a changed working relationship between the two companies. In a fixed price arrangement, the vendor needs to add an overhead to the process to ensure the sorts of issues noted above, would be at the client's expense and not the vendors. However, the project manager also noted some of the limitations of the time and materials approach encountered on this project:

"We didn't establish criteria for [the customer to complete acceptance testing] this is one of the differences between us [time and materials contract] and a fixed price contract ... if we were working on a fixed price basis we would have had to put some criteria around a sign-off .. .we've not had to do that but what it does mean is that you don't get a very quick turnaround" – Project Manager, DevCorp

The obvious impact of not having agreed delivery dates for acceptance testing was that (a) the defect stream was unpredictable making it difficult to manage the development team's workload and (b) the feedback from the customer was not immediate and hence errors in the development team's understanding remained for a longer time. Perhaps the not so obvious issues are (a) the customer may not realise that their actions caused this chain of events that directly impacts the cost of the project and (b) the customer may not realise that DevCorp team members could interpret the customer's tardiness as a lack of commitment from KiwiCorp, potentially impacting their own commitment to the project. Although it would be possible to negotiate and agree delivery dates in this area the lack of a contractual agreement can make it difficult to enforce these dates. Additionally, it is difficult for a services organisation such as DevCorp to 'chastise' KiwiCorp regarding this behaviour without endangering future work streams from KiwiCorp.

Multiple Organisations. This project not only had three organisations, but three organisations approaching the project with very different processes:

"We were happy to step out of XP and work within the processes that [BureauCorp] dictated for any kind of change or to migrate any software or to actually have any software installed so we've almost had to take the whole infrastructure thing and stick it out of XP" – Project Manager, DevCorp

All of the interviewees agreed that the effect of multiple organisations involved in the project, using a mixture of agile and non-agile processes, affected the timeline of the project, as summed up by this quote:

> "I was fully [committed to] the project but I was ... all of these technical integration issues were just taking up about half the time [and later in the interview regarding the project delay] the big delay has been in the technical integration. You know, just getting the application to work on the software in the various environments" – Customer, KiwiCorp

The term "technical integration issue" was used to refer to all of the issues encountered between DevCorp and BureauCorp. The impact of the inter-organisational issue was that the customer had significantly less time to spend on the requirements and testing tasks. While the customer understood that this impacted the quality of the delivered software, the flow-on delay caused by the quality issues appeared to be eclipsed by the obvious technical integration issues encountered.

The project manager recognised that the relationship between the three organisations was not a simple one and noted:

> "[KiwiCorp] at the end of the day is also a client of [BureauCorp] ... because of the nature of the relationship they have, [KiwiCorp] haven't got any weight to push around, they signed up for these processes and they have to follow them so there is frustration on both sides of the camp' – Project Manager, DevCorp

He also reflected on how to improve the situation between the three organisations next time:

> "We need to actually work together to build something that actually doesn't hinder the project process ... this is my first time working with three parties ... and I think sitting down and sorting [the] rules of engagement out at the start would be something ... I would ...in hindsight, like to have done – Project Manager, DevCorp

Summary. This story focussed on some of the differences between a fixed price and a time and materials outsourcing contract arrangement on agile development projects, concluding that there are benefits and limitations to both arrangements. It also highlighted the types of issues encountered when multiple organisations are involved in the project, which appears to be an increasingly common trend. We need to ensure that agile contracts and approaches are able to work in these complex outsourcing environments.

5 Project Pinta

This section tells the story of Project Pinta, an outsourced XP project involving:
- RCCorp, a large organisation based in Europe, is the customer organisation
- ManageCorp, an international management consulting, technology services and outsourcing company, is the outsourced vendor for all of RCCorp's IT functions and plays the role of proxy customer

- FalconCorp, a large international software product company based in the United States of America, is the development vendor.

The data that forms this section was collected in a series of interviews with Falcon-Corp project participants.

5.1 Case Description

Project Pinta has not been seen as a success by FalconCorp, and part of the concerns with the project have been the use of an agile development method. The project has taken longer than the original schedule, currently more than three times the original estimate, and has yet to be accepted by the RCCorp. The project can be divided into two stages, Stage I covers the originally estimated period and Stage II covers the remaining time. Stage I started out as a typical "death march" project:

> *"Everyone that was on it said it was doomed for failure [but] we were*
> *going to make it work anyway" – Customer Proxy, FalconCorp.*

The team had less than six months to cover almost 30 functional areas, so management quickly scaled the project up to more than 60 people across several XP labs.

Project Pinta is not a typical custom build project, as the intent of this project is to develop a product that will both meet the needs of RCCorp and become a product within FalconCorp's product suite. The labs were structured so that each lab had a customer representative, two of the labs had product managers from FalconCorp and two of the labs had business analysts from the European office of ManageCorp. The ManageCorp analysts had been involved in writing the initial high level requirements that had been accepted by RCCorp. No representatives from RCCorp were on the project.

The team quickly established a pace with weekly iterations. At the end of each week the team produced working software that implemented the prioritised stories. It quickly became obvious that all of the functionality would not be completed by the required deadline, despite everyone's best efforts. However, FalconCorp had committed to deliver the functionality by this deadline. The unintended outcomes of how this unwelcome knowledge was handled are outlined below.

In typical software development projects, *scope creep* must be managed by the outsourced vendor, particularly in an *aggressive* fixed price project such as this one. FalconCorp managed the scope by not exploring exceptions or evolving the requirements:

> *"We had the client on site but we didn't make use of them in [the] way*
> *that we should [as] we didn't want to raise any questions that would lead*
> *to gaps in the requirements that we would ultimately be responsible for ...*
> *and so we built [to the specification] without asking questions ... [our*
> *aim was to build a product that] we could check off and say ... we made*
> *our deadline, we deserve our payment" – Customer Proxy, FalconCorp*

In fact, the level of mistrust and organisational self-protection rose to such a level on this project, that the ManageCorp analysts were removed from the labs:

> *"There [were] roadblocks that were on both sides [that stopped] real*
> *communication. We had the client over here and I remember the first*

week that I was here they were talking about kicking one of the [Man-ageCorp] people out of the labs because they were a spy ...they were going back and reporting what was going on in the labs... You'd think that was part of what they were for but, you know, they thought they were giving a bad impression back to the client ... and so they actually kicked them out of the labs at one point." – Customer Proxy, FalconCorp

The result of this environment occurred at the end of Stage I when members of the team presented the software to RCCorp in Europe:

"It was kind of a sales pitch because they [RCCorp] didn't really test it. We [demonstrated how it worked with] some scenarios instead of letting them just hammer anything, because if you hammered on anything, you [would] have big huge gaping holes" – Customer Proxy, FalconCorp

The demonstration to RCCorp went well, so well that FalconCorp laid off over two thirds of the original staff, as they were now entering *"bug-fixing"* mode. During the first two months of Stage II, new project management was appointed in FalconCorp. These new managers quickly assessed that the project required significantly more work than *"bug-fixing"*. The final decision was to treat Stage I as a throw-away pro-totype and re-write the entire product. The contract was renegotiated and FalconCorp expect to complete the project in mid 2004.

5.2 Participant Reflection and Discussion

During the course of the interviews, the participants reflected on their experiences with XP and outsourcing. These reflections are outlined and discussed in this section.

Scope Definition. A non-negotiable area for FalconCorp as part of the contract rene-gotiation was an up-front requirements gathering and documentation stage. As an indication of the size of the gaps discussed, one of the documents expanded the initial requirements document from a 30 page document to a 250 page document.

Schwaber [11] writes that agile development, in that case Scrum, is not a silver bullet for fixed price contracts. In fixed-price contracts an upfront requirements gath-ering phase is required to accurately estimate scope. It is interesting that FalconCorp did not believe Stage I gave them sufficient knowledge and that an additional signifi-cant up-front requirements activity was commissioned. During the interviews poten-tial reasons were uncovered, including (a) significant product knowledge was lost when the majority of the staff from Stage I were laid off and this was compounded with XP documentation practices and (b) there was a perceived failure of XP by man-agement and so waterfall processes were seen as 'safer' in a contracting arrangement.

Development Process. Stage II of this project has yet to complete but the interview participants' are clear that the project is now much closer to a typical waterfall proc-ess than an XP process. One participant reflected on this change:

" XP [if you go straight from the book] is useless from my perspective ... if you have a fixed scope, a fixed date, well ... how well is that spec going to play in that space – not very, because it relies on the ability to manage that and to change that and impact that over time as realities come out.

Whereas with a contractual arrangement, you can't, you have very little wiggle room to be able to shift that and manage that and change that, and so XP finds itself significantly hampered and you have to start shifting it more towards Waterfall over time, because you just had to deal with the realities of the fact that you must get certain things out in certain timeframes." –Development Coach, FalconCorp

It appears XP will end up taking the blame for the problems encountered within this project in FalconCorp. And while it seems from both of these cases that there are issues with using XP on fixed price contracts without an upfront requirements gathering and documentation phase, perhaps there is more to this case.

Kern, Willcocks and Heck [4] outline a typical outsourcing issue called the *Winner's Curse* that may play a significant role in this case. The Winner's Curse occurs where the winning organisation or person has over-estimated the value of the object being bided on, typically due to inaccurate assumptions made during the bidding process. Inaccurate assumptions in IT outsourcing can range from the Client Organisation's political climate causing long turn-around times through to functional scope complexity, such as the one-line functional bullet item in the original specification that becomes a complex sub-system over the course of the project. The end-result: the organisation or person makes a loss or at least no profit on the transaction. The Winner's Curse is a prevalent issue in IT outsourcing.

In IT Outsourcing the 'Winning' organisation will then typically concentrate on cost-cutting strategies, such as placing inexperienced staff on the project or focussing on the letter of the contract scope not the spirit, to reduce their loss. The end result for both parties is a loss situation, as the resulting software is unlikely to meet the client's needs. Project Pinta exhibits all of the signs of the Winner's Curse.

Summary. This story focussed on some of the typical issues faced by companies in an outsourcing environment. One of the key issues highlighted is the need for an upfront scope definition phase for fixed price contracts, irrespective of the development process. The second issue discussed was the Winner's Curse; that of being the successful bidder for a contract that will result in a loss, or very little profit, for the winning vendor. The Winner's Curse is a prevalent issue in IT outsourcing, irrespective of the contract type or development process, and significantly impacts the project environment. Developers who find themselves with the Winner's Curse should consider carefully what they want from an agile process.

6   Conclusions

We are studying the customer role in agile development, and in this paper we presented two interpretive case studies where XP was used in projects involving outsourcing. The studies are based on in-depth interviews with project participants. In both cases we saw a strong awareness of the interactions between outsourcing arrangements and the XP process. Additionally, we noted that the issues facing outsourced XP projects include general agile issues, outsourcing issues as well as multi-organisational issues.

In the first study, we learned that the agility fostered by continual contact between developers and customer worked well with the contractual arrangements based on time and materials charging. In the second study, we found a more fixed contractual basis for the project, and heard about experience that suggests this clashed with the XP process. In both cases, we saw that the involvement of multiple organisations required accommodation of the different cultures of the organisations, and presented challenges in interpreting the XP customer role.

All these findings show us that for XP to embrace change, an organisational and contractual context is needed that allows change to be embraced without penalty.

References

1   Ambler, S. Outsourcing Examined. Software Development Journal, April 2003.
2   Fitzgerald, B. Systems development methodologies: the problem of tenses. Information technology and people, 13 (3). pp. 174 - 185.
3   Kern, T. The Gestalt of an Information Technology Outsourcing Relationship: An Exploratory Analysis. Proceedings of the Eighteenth International Conference on Information Systems, Atlanta, Georgia, United States, pp: 37 – 58, 1997.
4   Kern, Thomas, Leslie P. Willcocks, Eric van Heck, The "Winner's Curse" in IT Outsourcing, California Management Review 44, no. 2, p. 47-69, Winter 2002.
5   Klepper, R & Jones, W. Outsourcing Information Technology, Systems, & Services. Prentice Hall PTR, 1997.
6   Martin, A. A case study: exploring the role of customers on eXtreme programming projects, CS-TR-03-1, School of Computing and Mathematical Sciences, Victoria University of Wellington, Wellington, 2002.
7   Martin, A., Noble, J., and Biddle, R. Proceedings of the Fourth International Conference on eXtreme Programming and Agile Processes in Software Engineering, Giancarlo Succi (Ed.), Being Jane Malkovich: a Look into the World of an XP Customer. Lecture Notes in Computer Science 2675, Springer-Verlag. 2003.
8   Nandhakumar, J. & Avison, D. The fiction of methodological development: a field study of information systems development. Information Technology & People, 12(2). pp. 176-191.
9   Poppendieck, M & Poppendieck, T. Lean Software Development: An Agile Toolkit. Addison-Wesley, 2003
10 Poppendieck, M. Poppendieck, T (Eds). Proceedings of the Oopsla Workshop on Agile Contracts, Anaheim, California, USA, 2003. http://poppendieck.com/.
11 Schwaber, K. Fixed Price, Fixed Date Contracts at Engage. In Poppendieck, M., Poppendieck, T. (Eds.), Proceedings of the Oopsla Workshop on Agile Contracts, Anaheim, California, USA, 2003. http://poppendieck.com/.

Distributed Product Development Using Extreme Programming

Charles J. Poole

8001 Braddock Road, Springfield, VA 27150
cpoole@suscom-maine.net

Abstract. This paper uses the experience of developing a shrink wrapped software product to examine issues related to distributed software development using agile methodologies. The work is based on the author's time at IONA Technologies as a senior manager delivering their Web Services Integration Platform (WSIP) product suite. It is focused on the issues of distributed development using Extreme Programming (XP) by describing the development effort: its organization, practices, and processes and evaluating, using both qualitative and quantitative measures, the success of four of the practices adopted by the team (distributed stand-ups, cultural exchanges, common source code, and shared vision). Regardless of the ultimate success or failure of the product and development effort, the lessons taken from the experience are valuable and have reinforced many of the observations and experiences reported by others [1,2].

Keywords. Extreme Programming, Agile Methods, Software Development, Project Management, Distributed Development

1 Introduction

Let's get this straight right from the beginning. There would probably be very little argument to the statement that software development works best when the development team is co-located. Extreme Programming [3]and its reliance on on-site customers, stand-up meetings, pairing, etc (or for that matter any of the other Agile Methodologies) is best implemented when the teams are co-located. So why set up distributed development environments? Well, as most are aware circumstances are not always perfect in the field of software development. Acquisitions, off-shoring, telecommuting, the desire to utilize the best available development staff, and open source are but a few examples of reasons why distributed development exist and will continue to exist in the foreseeable future. This paper is not an attempt to promote distributed development rather an attempt to ensure that when you adopt a distributed development environment, for whatever reason, that you have the tools to be successful. In this case those tools are a set of recommendations based on the experiences of the author in a highly distributed development environment in which XP represented the adopted approach to developing a software product.

J. Eckstein and H. Baumeister (Eds.): XP 2004, LNCS 3092, pp. 60–67, 2004.

1.1 Development Organization

Early in 2001 IONA Technologies acquired a company in Santa Clara, California that had developed a suite of Business to Business (B2B) applications, adaptors, and tools. During the first part of 2001 and through 2002 IONA focused not only on integrating the new B2B product suite and associated technologies into a new product strategy and road map but also on bringing the acquired engineering team under its Extreme Product Development[1] engineering umbrella. This meant bringing together efforts from development sites in California, Massachusetts, Virginia, and Dublin, Ireland to produce two new product suites. The first was the Application Server Platform (ASP) and the second was the Web Services Integration Platform (WSIP). The development effort spanned eight time zones and two countries and at times involved over 130 engineers.

1.2 The Product Suite

It is useful in the context of the rest of the paper to gain some understanding of the WSIP product and the role that each of the teams played in implementing the new product suite. The core element of WSIP was developed in Santa Clara. It consisted of a B2B server and associated gateway and system management tools, a set of business process modeling/orchestration and monitoring tools that in addition to supporting standards based business process development also supported the creation and integration of web services into those process flows, and finally a set of business protocol adaptors. The Santa Clara team was also responsible for integration, packaging, system testing, load and performance testing, and manufacture of master CDs. The Reston team was responsible for the enterprise integration component and associated integration adaptors. The Waltham team delivered a web services stack as well as a set of tools to create, expose, and manage web services. This was bundled in a component called XMLBus. Lastly, the Dublin team provided the J2EE application server from IONA's ASP product on top of which the WSIP product could be deployed.

Each of the teams from the various locations had previously produced separate products which now came under the WSIP or ASP heading. Each would need to be integrated into the new product strategy. In some cases integration was nothing more than a wrapper around the existing product in others it was a tightly coupled integration based on various Application Programmer Interfaces (APIs) exposed by the software components and in a few instances brand new applications and application functionality was required to satisfy Product Management requirements.

1.3 The Focus

One of the difficulties in writing this paper was that there is so much to tell about the experiences of the author while with IONA. Transforming such a large organization to using agile methods presented many problems and issues and there is the tendency

---

[1] Extreme Product Development was the umbrella term given to the set of practices and processes developed internally by the IONA engineering and product management and product marketing teams. Its foundation was the XP practices used by the engineering teams.

to want to tell it all at once, something not necessarily appropriate in this instance. So, instead of looking at the broader issues this paper will only examine the development of the WSIP product and the four key practices used as part of the distributed XP effort. It will also focus less on the issues around the development and programmatic execution of the new product strategy and more on the issues related to creating an agile development environment in such a distributed product development team. It is useful to note that the teams in Reston, Dublin, and Waltham were in the process of or had already adopted XP as their development model prior to the acquisition with the Dublin team and its full XP implementation at the forefront.

2 Extreme Team Building – Key Practices

This paper is really all about team building and the critical element of communications in a distributed environment. That is what these four practices represent. Joshua Kerievsky in Industrial XP (IXP) [4] has encapsulated some of this in IXPs project community and project chartering practices. Kent Beck focuses considerable attention to communications and team building in XP. One of the core XP values is communications reflecting a need for broad, regular, open, and honest communications not just between developers but also between the customer (real or proxy) and the development team. XP strategies also include elements that foster team building. The XP facilities strategy suggests an open space arrangement that encourages almost constant communication and situational awareness and the regular planning, visible story cards, and stand-ups create yet more opportunity for communicated a shared understanding of the work and product vision.

However, none of these specifically addresses the issues of distributed development efforts. When IONA's development plan was first laid out, the various implementation teams identified, and the initial stories were created by Product Management, what was left was a disparate group of engineers located all over the globe who needed to work together in an agile way to create a product. When one is looking at a collocated team the natural first step is to pull everyone into the same room and have a kick-off meeting, to recognize face to face for the first time who you're going to be working with. You can't do that as readily or easily when half your team is somewhere else. How do you bring the developers together to work as a team on the new program, to get them to buy-in to a vision as a team? With XP you have iteration planning meetings, daily stand-ups (scrum meeting with Scrum [5]. You plan team activities to improve morale, and create team areas to improve team cohesion and awareness. What do you do if the team isn't even on the same continent? How do you maintain a sense of team with a focus on a common goal and clear and up-to-date understanding of the development effort and their role in it not just in the beginning of the project but through out the entire life cycle of project? So some experimenting was in order. The results are the set of practices or practice extensions identified below.

2.1 Cultural Exchange

One of the things that was discovered very early on was the need to create a common understanding not only of the project and its associated artifacts but also of how members of the team from different parts of the country or world, worked, thought, communicated, and in general dealt with the various issues and problems that arose from the development effort. A Cultural exchange is simple in practice and potentially expensive in the short term but provides benefits that far out way any perceived short-comings. The idea is to exchange one or two developers between remote sites for a few weeks or if possible a few months. The desire is to create a stronger sense of community between the various team members as well as to improve communications by locating someone who knows the remote team intimately and can help people make the right pairings – to talk to the right person.

In putting together the WSIP product it was discovered that the developers in California were having problems getting the WSIP application suite to deploy quickly on the IONA application server and were not using it to do component and system level testing. Instead of being proactive and trying to address the issues with the Dublin developers they switched to another application server and went on their merry way. It's a big problem when your application or product isn't being tested on your own application server. So, we found an engineer in Dublin who was willing to relocate to California for six months and on a regular basis we started sending engineers from California to Dublin for a couple of weeks at a time. It worked. The Dublin engineer got to know the California engineers and likewise the California engineers the Dublin engineers. Each began to understand how the other worked and how to effectively communicate needs and to work with the other team. The Dublin engineer taught the California team how to get stories into the Dublin planning game. The California team was able to demonstrate face to face what the WSIP application suite did and the Dublin team started showing how it could better use the J2EE architecture. Ultimately both WSIP and the J2EE application server were improved to the ultimate benefit of the customer. It didn't happen over night but within a month or two the sorts of problems between the Dublin and California developers no longer became an issue. Similar cultural exchanges occurred between all four of the development sites.

Although not a part of the WSIP project, the practice of a cultural exchange was also used in an off-shoring effort run by IONA. A team of Indian engineers who were to take over the maintenance and enhancement of IONA's old generation CORBA middleware products came to Dublin in 1999 to learn the product. They worked in Dublin setting up a duplicate environment in preparation for the movie to India. The intent was to eventually maintain a regular exchange of engineers and management once the code was moved. This effort highlighted the differences between engineers from truly different cultures. Issues such as understanding and dealing with differences in how authority is perceived between co-workers or between employee and employer or simply interpreting differences in body language all of which was aided by promoting a cultural exchange.

One of the other big benefits to the exchanges can be a breakdown in what might be called the castle complex - teams establishing technical or visionary domains that they are reluctant to share or to collaborate constructively on. This too can be helped with cultural exchanges as was demonstrated between the developers in California and Virginia who through regular exchanges were able to develop a common understanding of each other's domain and to work on creating a viable shared vision and architecture for the WSIP B2B and Enterprise Integration adapters. Unfortunately, in other instances cultural exchanges did not seem to work towards resolving the conflict as there was a significant disagreement between various arms of product management, marketing, and the senior technical leaders over the product direction at the visionary or strategic level and the allocation of resources to those various visions was a constant battle.

2.2 Stand-Ups and Wikis

One of the elements of several agile methodologies (both Scrum and XP incorporate a short daily meeting) is the practice of a daily stand-up. The main focus of such meetings is as a tool for eliminating blockers and to a lesser degree gives each member of the development team the opportunity to hear what others in the team are working on. For distributed teams this practice can be quite difficult to follow given the time difference and the size of the team involved and is a reflection of the loss of communications bandwidth when using distributed development. The following stand-up practices were adopted by various elements of the WSIP development team to help improve this sort of regular communication:

- It was found that a daily conference call during the product delivery iteration was critical to quickly identifying who needed to get together after the meeting to do a little long distance pairing to resolve pending issues or eliminate blockers.
- Stand-ups tended to happen on a daily basis with the co-located team members. And across sites for some components for which there was a smaller number (less than 15) of developers. Daily stand ups involving the whole team were not seen as productive and were never attempted.
- To ensure good communications between the various sites, twice weekly stand ups between remote site team and technical leads and managers were substituted for the daily stand up. Having a conference call a couple of times a week seemed to work out best during the normal development iterations.

Wiki pages were used a lot by IONA. Although not used as effectively as they might have been (no common standards and issues with regular updating) the Wiki pages added the ability to present a distributed story board that everyone in the organization could use to see what each development team was doing. Not all teams used this but where it was used effectively the situational awareness of the developers seemed to be a step above other teams although never as good as using cards posted on a wall or cork board. Any electronic white board, messaging, system, or even defect tracking system (e.g. Bugzilla[1]) could be used just as effectively.

2.3 Shared Vision

How does one work on something if they don't know what it is and how it satisfies the customer's needs, or the business goals and priorities of the company? Here is an instance of abject failure on the part of the WSIP team. As mentioned in the introduction, much of this failure is probably attributable to the lack of a common shared vision by the senior technical leaders, the product management, and the product marketing elements of the team. Their inability to promote the vision they did have in a way that the developers could understand it, buy-in to it, and throw their support behind it also played a part. The result was a group of people moving behind each others backs to try and push personal as well as site specific objectives with executive management. It was not a team effort and for all intents and purposes created a degree of tension that in some instances no amount of extreme anything could over come.

It is critical in developing a shrink wrapped product that those elements of the organization acting in the role of the customer or customer proxy are prepared to create the stories and set the priorities in a consistent and clear fashion based on a common and agreed vision. If there is dissent or differences of opinion you only have a few options: you can work towards compromise between the dissenting voices, you can let them fight it out by letting the two visions compete (takes more resources in a resource limited environment), or you can simply ask the dissenting voices to toe the line or leave (sometimes forcing some to leave to better establish a team with a solid shared vision is more desirable then holding on to a dissatisfied group of people). Over time IONA did a bit of all of the above as part of its efforts reestablish a consistent vision between the customer proxy and the development team as well as between the various development teams.

It is very important to get a handle on that vision and market it to the development team using a simple clear vocabulary. Involve the team in working with the customer or customer proxy to create the vision. The importance of this is indicated by its inclusion in IXP as part of creating a project charter. In a distributed environment it becomes even more critical as it is that much harder to gain that shared vision due to cultural, ideological, and technical differences that seem to be so easily misunderstood and misrepresented and are amplified by the remoteness of a team.

2.4 Common Source

Although mentioned last this is one of the first things that a distributed development team should get right. It includes not only the idea that everyone regardless of location has access to a common source base but that they have access to a common set of automation tools and processes. If you can't build your entire product down to the packaging from a common source base and use a common set of automated testing and production tools then you are going to have a much harder time getting anything out the door. This is true of any development effort but is even more so when considering integration across multiple remote sites. Some of the more important elements of this practice applied to distributed development include:

- Use of a multi-site source control system. Anything will do although some are better than others. Not having it makes code synchronization almost impossible
- The source control system is used to support an automated nightly build and integration capability that includes automated integration and system testing and automatic build and test report generation.
- Access to a common build environment. A developer at any site should be able to easily build and run all of the tests for the purposes of continuous integration testing against their view of the source.

Over time all of the WSIP development sites were able to integrate with IONA's common source control system. Additionally, many man months of effort went into developing automated build and test systems that could be run nightly and kicked off with a single command by any developer. Nightly reporting of integration and system testing results on over a dozen operating system and application server combinations created an environment in which on a daily basis one was aware of the problems in the code. As indicated in the table below this effort was rewarded with significant improvements in the ability of the team to deliver an integrated tested product.

Table 1. Improvements Due to Common Source Access and Automation

Metric	Before adoption	After adoption
Time for complete build and test	2 days – 18 people	6 hrs - automated
Average time from code freeze to shipment	12 weeks – 70 people	2 weeks – 10 people
Time to get successful soak test	6 months – 2-5 people	2 weeks – two people

It is recognized that the above metrics don't necessarily provide a good quantitative measure of the correlation between common shared access and automation and the improvements that are presented. However, it is noteworthy that the only operational changes that occurred in the teams working on building and system testing of the B2B product was the adoption of the practices and processes described above. That is to say, they did nothing but work on the automation of all build, test, and integration systems with in IONA's common source code repository. Hence the inference that these practices and process led to the improvements seems correct.

3 Conclusions

It is useful to note that the creation, management, and in hindsight failure, of the new product strategy had a significant impact on the ability of the engineering team to effectively adopt XP. This fact has been presented as one of many contributing elements and is ultimately the focus perhaps for another treatment looking at the development of product strategies and program management with agile methods in a multi-product company. Ultimately the WSIP product suite failed to claim much in the way of market. It was eventually replaced by other products and strategies. However, the successes and failures that the WSIP engineering team experienced as a part of the distributed development effort taught some significant lessons. First, IONA no longer focuses on large widely distributed teams. Whether by economic necessity or product strategy the engineering group has realigned itself with product business units that are for the most part co-located or have dependencies between only two development sites. The teams in California and Reston no longer exist and efforts run through those development offices have been eliminated or moved to one of the other development teams in Massachusetts or Ireland. Second, the business units themselves have been used to improve on the vision around each product IONA sells. Although the business unit does not eliminate the potential for dissent it does increase the probability of buy-in from the whole team by providing a clearer focus on who the customer is and what their priorities are by elliminating some of the infighting between competing elements in product managment and marketing.

The lessons of extreme distributed development boiled down in the authors eye's to one thing – Communications. Each of the key practices or processes focused on different modes of communication to bring understanding across a breadth of development issues and concerns. Whether it was to better understand the members of the team in another location and the culture (development or otherwise) they exist in or have created, or to having a common view of the source code and daily build and test processes, or to know what blockers people are experiencing that you can help elleviate, or establishing and sharing a common vision in the context of the companies product strategy and vision (and ultimately reflect the needs of the customer) it all was about communications. Utimately distributed development with XP is possible if the lessons of how to effectively communicate are heeded and addressed. It is as though we are turning the nob up on communications and perhaps in some ways is even more extreme (e.g. cutural exchanges) than XP originally laid out.

Author. Charles Poole worked with IONA Technologies for four years from 1999 through 2002. He is currently employed by Computational Physics, Inc. as the Senior Systems Analyst and Architect for a U.S. Department of Defense distributed simulation system. He has continued his focus on promoting Agile Methods through his efforts to integrate Extreme Programming under an Earned Value Management framework

References

1. Martin Fowler's web site, http://www.martinfowler.com/articles/agileOffshore.html
2. Matt Simons, *Internationally Agile*, Mar 15, 2002, http://www.informit.com
3. Kent Beck, *Extreme Programming Explained, Embrace Change*, Addison Wesley, 2000
4. Industrial XP web site, http://www.industrialxp.org/
5. Scrum web site, http://www.controlchaos.com
6. Bugzilla home page, http://www.bugzilla.org

Scaling Continuous Integration

R. Owen Rogers

ThoughtWorks, Inc.
Peek House, 20 Eastcheap
London, United Kingdom
orogers@thoughtworks.com
http://www.thoughtworks.com

Abstract. Of all the Extreme Programming practices, continuous integration is one of the least controversial – the benefits of an integrated, streamlined build process is something that software developers immediately recognise. However, as a project scales up in size and complexity, continuous integration can become increasingly hard to practice successfully. By focussing on the problems associated with a growing project, this paper describes a variety of strategies for successfully scaling continuous integration.

1 Continuous Integration

The practice of continuous integration represents a fundamental shift in the process of building software. It takes integration, commonly an infrequent and painful exercise, and makes it a simple, core part of a developer's daily activities. Integrating continuously makes integration a part of the natural rhythm of coding, an integral part of the test-code-refactor cycle. Continuous integration is about progressing steadily forward by taking small steps.

1.1 Integrating Continuously

Integration should happen continuously, and continuously is more often than you might think. The frequency of integration will vary from project to project, from developer to developer, and from modification to modification. However, as a goal and a good rule of thumb, developers should integrate their changes once every few hours and at least once per day.

Learning how to integrate so frequently requires practice and discipline. Fundamentally, an integration can occur at any point when the code compiles and all the unit tests are passing. The challenge is learning how to write software so that you never stray too far from this point. If you are testing at the right level of granularity and are refactoring regularly, then you should never be more than a few minutes away from this point. This means that you are almost always in a position where you can launch a new integration.

Deciding when to integrate is all about controlling risk. When making modifications in a high traffic area of the code base or when conducting broad refactorings like class renaming or package reorganisation, there is an elevated risk

J. Eckstein and H. Baumeister (Eds.): XP 2004, LNCS 3092, pp. 68–76, 2004.

of impacting other developers or of having merge conflicts when committing. The longer that developers go without integrating, the greater the likelihood of conflicts and the larger the effort required to resolve those conflicts. As the effort of integration increases exponentially in proportion to the time between integrations[2], best practices dictate that when making high-risk changes a developer should start from a clean workspace, focus only on required modifications, proceed with the smallest logical steps, and then commit at the earliest opportunity.

A successful integration is a measure of progress. It provides feedback that the new code runs correctly in the integration environment and successfully interoperates with the rest of the code base. Code sitting unintegrated in a developer's workspace simply does not exist. It is not part of the code base, it cannot be accessed by other developers or tested by the customer. Only when it has been successfully integrated is the benefit of the new code realised.

1.2 Continuous Integration Tools

In order to integrate as frequently as possible, the integration process must be easy to launch. If the integration process requires multiple manual steps then it is easy to forget steps or make mistakes. Ideally, the integration should be initiated by invoking a single, simple command. Build tools such as **make**, **Ant**, or **NAnt** are excellent candidates for scripting the integration process to achieve this.

Automated integration servers, such as **CruiseControl** (Java), **CruiseControl.NET**(C#) or **DamageControl** (Ruby), automate the integration process by monitoring the team's source control repository directly. Every time a developer commits a new set of modifications, the server will automatically launch an integration build to validate the changes. When the build is complete, the server notifies the developer whether the changes that they committed integrated successfully or not. Effectively, integration becomes as easy as checking in code. Using an automated integration server not only makes integration easy, it also guarantees that an integration build will happen. There is no danger of developers forgetting to validate their changes after checking in.

1.3 Practicing Continuous Integration

Tools play an essential role in practicing continuous integration. Having the right set of tools is what changes integration from a painful and time-consuming task into an integral part of the development process. However, with the power that they bring, it is easy to focus on the tools and lose sight of the fact that *continuous integration is a practice – it is about what people do, not about what tools they use.*

As a project starts to scale, it is easy to be deceived into thinking that the team is practicing continuous integration just because all of the tools are set up and running. If developers do not have the discipline to integrate their changes on a regular basis or to maintain the integration environment in good working order then they are not practicing continuous integration. Full stop. Having all the right tools does not make any difference. Tools are great facilitators, but they are only as effective as the discipline of the people involved. Ultimately, continuous integration is about people and the way that they interact to build software.

2 Scaling Continuous Integration

As the success of continuous integration depends on the discipline of the team, it is important to foster an environment where it is easy for the team to be disciplined. However, as a project scales up in terms of the size of its code base or in terms of the size of the team, there are several factors that undermine the discipline of team members, making continuous integration increasingly hard to practice. Understanding these obstacles and their symptoms is instrumental in devising strategies to overcome them.

2.1 More Code

As the size of the code base starts to grow, it takes an increasingly long time to run an integration build. While compilation time does grow with the size of the code base, for most XP projects, the primary factor influencing the build time is the increasing number of tests. If not properly managed, the build time can increase exponentially in proportion to the number of tests executed.

The growing build time means that it takes longer for developers to receive feedback on the results of their integration. It is not uncommon for integration builds to rapidly reach 30 minutes to an hour as a product of the expanding code base. Waiting for the integration to finish before proceeding can amount to a considerable stretch of unproductive time. A natural reaction is to reduce the frequency of commits so as to minimise this unproductive time. However, committing less frequently means that more changes are included in each integration, which, in turn, increases the likelihood of merge conflicts and, if integration problems do occur, increases the difficulty of fixing those problems. Reducing the frequency of commits undermines the benefits of continuous integration.

The growing build time also decreases the window in which a developer can integrate their changes. It is bad karma to leave work after checking in a build-breaking change. Doing so means that your teammates are stuck either fixing your bad code, rolling back your changes, or working around your problems. To avoid this frustrating and embarrassing situation, the easiest thing to do is to commit early enough in the day so that if integration problems do arise, they can be tackled before leaving. However, if you are not ready to commit your changes before this cut-off point then you need to wait until the next day to do the commit. In the meantime, the inclination is to start something new. Doing so, however, only delays and increases the difficulty of the next integration.

The common result is that as the code base grows developers commit less frequently and the practice of continuous integration starts to break down.

2.2 More People

Adding more developers to a project team has two major impacts on the integration process. First, it increases the rate of code production; this only exacerbates the problems of a rapidly growing code base as discussed in the previous section. Second, it means that more people are dependent on a working build. Any developer committing code that breaks compilation or causes some tests to fail has the potential to affect a lot more people.

On a small team, the probability of another developer needing to commit while the build is broken is relatively small. However, as the team grows in size, the overall frequency of commits increases. If the build is broken, developers not working directly on fixing the problem are not permitted to commit their changes. If they were, it could greatly complicate the problems for the people engaged in fixing the build, only serving to increase the time that the build is broken for. Therefore, they are stuck waiting for the build to be fixed.

Rather than wait for the build to be fixed, there is a temptation, whether out of frustration or from desperation, to ignore the build breakage and check in anyway. It might seem innocent enough to sneak in a quick change while no one is looking. However, as the build is already broken, it is very difficult to verify whether or not the new changes actually work properly (either by doing a local build in the developer's workspace or on the integration server). This makes it easy to use the broken build as an excuse for checking in unverified code, and risk ending up in a *tragedy of the commons* situation where a broken build leads to a free-for-all of frustrated developers dumping in their changes.

If bad code has been committed, every developer that updates their local workspace will be affected. Normally it is good practice for developers to check the integration server before updating their workspace to ensure that they can avoid being affected by a broken build. However, because of the lag caused by the growing build, there is a window during which developers may unwittingly pick up the bad code. Pulling down broken code requires figuring how to rollback the broken code from the local workspace which is a hassle at best and a showstopper at worst. Either way, it is a very frustrating and time-consuming experience.

A broken build, especially a protracted one, is a serious broken window in the development process – it undermines productivity and morale. To deal with this broken window, a common approach is to institute a strict and thorough pre-commit procedure that will make it as hard as possible for developers to break the build. The pre-commit procedure typically amounts to requiring developers to run a full integration build locally on their machine before they are allowed to commit their changes.

While this approach may be successful at reducing the likelihood of committing build-breaking code, it has the side effect of greatly increasing the time required to integrate a set of changes. The increased integration time tends to drastically reduce the frequency with which developers will integrate their code. As the goal of continuous integration is to make integrating changes as quick and easy as possible so that developers will do it all the time, this approach is clearly an anathema.

Fundamentally, it needs to be acceptable to break the build. That's what an integration server is there for – to inform developers that the committed code has integration problems. Introducing a stringent pre-commit procedure and turning each developer's workstation into a *poor man's integration server* is not an effective way to deal with integration, and only wastes productivity and undermines morale.

3   Strategies for Scaling Continuous Integration

As the project grows in size, it is easy to use these obstacles as an excuse for dismissing continuous integration as a practice only useful to small projects. This is not the case. By careful attention to when integration starts to become infrequent and when developers start to suffer integration pain as a result, it is normally possible to tune the process to ensure that continuous integration remains feasible. Here are five strategies for successfully scaling continuous integration:

- Establish a maximum build length
- Create targeted builds
- Write faster unit tests
- Smaller teams with local integration servers
- Modularise the code base

3.1   Establish a Maximum Build Length

Keeping the build quick is easier said than done. First you need to determine how quick is quick enough. This requires deciding what an appropriate maximum build length should be and then coming up with a set of strategies for keeping it below that threshold.

The question of how quick is quick enough is a product of the requisite frequency of integration. The frequency with which developers are willing to integrate their code is proportional to the time and effort that it takes to do so. This is a common pattern of human behaviour[1]. If integration takes 20 minutes, it is unreasonable to expect developers to integrate every hour. This would mean that they spend 30% of the iteration integrating their code. If the goal is to give developers the potential to integrate every hour, it is important for integration to take a small enough proportion of the overall development time so as to be unnoticeable. If the integration process is quick enough, taking say two minutes or less, then it can effectively become a background activity that developers can do whenever they are not typing or getting the code to pass. On many large projects this is a difficult goal to reach, so there will be a trade-off between a longer build and a reduced frequency of integration.

---

[1] The **Planning XP** book makes this observation with relation to planning [3]. The amount of time spent planning needs to be proportional to the length of the iteration. Clearly it makes no sense spending two days planning for a one week iteration.

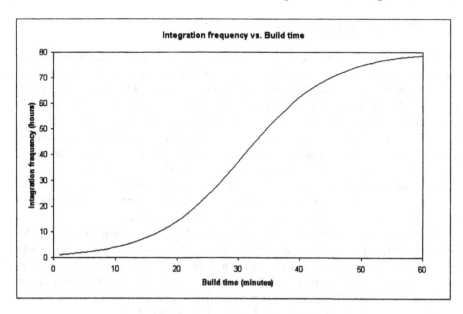

Fig. 1. Integration frequency chart.

Conceptually, the relationship between the frequency of integration and the length of the build is similar to the graph shown in Figure 1. If the build time is below a certain threshold (two or three minutes), then there is no noticeable effort involved in integration and it can be done as frequently as required. As the integration time and effort becomes perceptible, integrations start to become an interruption to the flow of development and will be scheduled accordingly. This drastically reduces their frequency. For integrations of 5 to 10 minutes, it still feasible for developers to integrate several times per day. However, as the build time increases above this threshold, the time and effort involved in integration increase rapidly.

On a recent project that I was on, the integration time was 30 to 40 minutes and developers were integrating their changes once per week on average. The build time rose to almost an hour before being reduced again to more sustainable levels. Developers would typically allocate most of one day to do their integration. Once integrations begin to take this long, there are certain limiting factors that affect the frequency of integration. Factors such as iteration length set an upper limit on integration frequency (developers need to integrate successfully at least once per iteration).

Specific build time thresholds and recommendations will vary from project to project; however, human factors, such as the limits of perceptible time, will remain constant. Keeping these constants in mind will help you to set thresholds and targets that are appropriate for your project.

3.2   Create Targeted Builds

As the build is a central, regularly scheduled task, it is easy to chuck everything into it, including the kitchen sink. It is common to end up with a single integration process that compiles the code, runs the unit tests and the acceptance tests, builds deployment packages for QA and the customer, validates code coverage, and checks coding standards amongst other things. Including all of these tasks in the build is, in general, a good thing because it means that they are running as regularly as possible and the team can benefit from their feedback. However, when included in a single serial integration process, these extra tasks can greatly increase the length of the build. Dividing the build into a set of independent consecutive or concurrent processes is an excellent way to prioritise build tasks and ensure that feedback is given fastest to those that need it most.

When thinking about the contents of the build, it is important to consider the different parties that rely on the integration build and what their requirements are. For developers, it is essential to have a code base that can compile and that passes the unit tests at all times. Creating a separate developer build process that runs only these tasks minimises the build time and thereby increases the potential frequency with which developers will integrate their code.

Feedback on the status of the acceptance tests is also important; however, acceptance tests take substantially longer to run than the unit tests. Deciding whether or not to include acceptance tests is a trade-off between the overhead of integration and the stability of the code base. For most development teams, it is fine to permit acceptance tests to break over the course of the iteration as long as the team ensures that the tests are all passing prior to the end of the iteration.

The other parties that rely on the integration process are typically content with less frequent feedback. QA and the customer often use the build as a means of acquiring a new copy of the system. However, they typically will pick up a new version on an infrequent basis – once per day or on-demand. Setting up an alternate QA/customer build process to package the distributables and run the acceptance tests is a great way of ensuring that these tasks are run regularly, yet do not affect the quick developer build.

3.3   Write Faster Unit Tests

Slow tests are typically the main culprit behind a slow build. Separating unit tests from functional and acceptance tests is key to reducing test execution time. Developers learning XP are typically new to testing and may not have a clear idea of the distinction between these different types of tests. Most developers when they start writing unit tests end up writing a hybrid between unit and functional tests. This is because when testing a particular class, it is easy to end up pulling in and testing the entire web of objects that that class depends on. Without proper testing and design techniques, it is quite common to end up in a situation where practically every unit test hits the database or some external system. The overhead of redundantly testing through multiple layers of the system greatly increases the unit test execution time.

Unit tests, when written at the right level of granularity should run extremely quickly. Thousands of properly decoupled, orthogonal unit tests can execute in a matter of seconds. However, there is an art to learning how to write unit tests like this. Getting to this point requires a lot of practice doing test-driven development and a good understanding of unit testing tools and techniques. Making extensive use of mock objects[4] and dependency injection[1] are essential techniques for testing each class as a discrete and independent unit.

It normally takes some time before getting to the point where every developer can write fast, decoupled unit tests. In the meantime, it is important to repeatedly refactor slow unit tests to keep the build time down. Most automated integration servers report a sorted list of test execution times. As the build time starts to grow, it is good practice to regularly pick the slowest running unit tests and try to refactor them. If refactoring is not possible, move them into a designated functional test area.

3.4   Smaller Teams with Local Integration Servers

It needs to be acceptable to break the build. That is, after all, why you use an integration server. Even negative feedback is good feedback. However, if a large number of people are affected by a build breakage, it is tempting to think that breaking the build is a deadly sin to be avoided at all costs. Stopping developers from breaking the build involves adding overhead to the integration process, which simply ends up decreasing the frequency with which they will commit their changes. Instead, it is important to to allow developers to break the build with relative impunity without adversely impacting their colleagues.

The simplest approach is to organise into small development teams (4-8 developers per team) and to modularise the code base on a per team basis. This modularisation introduces a level of isolation between teams. As each team operates predominately within their own area of the code base, they only need to compile and run the tests for their module. As a result, the build is very quick to run. If a developer commits modifications that cause the build to break only the handful of developers on their team relying on the code in their module will be potentially affected.

Each team can and should set up their own automated integration server. However, there need not be anything special about an integration server; it can be run on any box. If developers practice pair programming then half of the available workstations are sitting idle. There is no reason why a vacant developer box cannot be turned into an integration server.

3.5   Modularise the Code Base

The primary issue with splitting into smaller teams is that it creates the problem of cross-team integration. Teams are effectively delaying full system integration in exchange for a faster, leaner integration process and the productivity benefits associated with it. By delaying the full system integration, teams are potentially building up an integration debt that will be painful to resolve when the integration finally happens.

To mitigate the pain of cross-team integration, it is important to carefully consider the way that modularisation is done. Modularisation should minimise cross-team dependencies. Ideally, teams should be organised along independent vertical slices of functionality – not in accordance with application layers. Modularisation along application layers, albeit the typical, traditional approach to organising software teams is inadvisable because it maximises cross-team dependencies. In a n-tier architecture, any piece of functionality effectively needs to integrate with each of the modules of the other **n** teams. This approach also greatly slows down development as each team depends on all of the other teams to finish their work before any piece of functionality can be judged complete.

Integration with other teams should be done through published interfaces and common value objects. This integration can be accomplished either at binary or source level. Binaries offer the benefit of decreased compilation time (teams do not need to recompile each other's source) and provide a controlled, versioned, releasable unit. However, having the source available helps diagnose and fix integration problems, and helps ensure consistent coding standards across teams.

4   Conclusion

The goal of continuous integration is to maximise developer productivity and minimises integration risk by making integration an easy, natural part of the development cycle. It provides the development team with the invaluable feedback that the code base is continuously in a working, integrated condition. However, continuous integration is considerably harder to practice on projects with large code bases and large teams. The strategies proposed in this paper provide guidelines for successfully scaling continuous integration to deal with these issues. Applying these strategies can help ensure that practicing continuous integration is feasible even for very large projects.

References

1. Fowler, M.: Inversion of Control Containers and the Dependency Injection pattern. *http://martinfowler.com/articles/injection.html*
2. Fowler, M., Foemmel, M.: Continuous Integration. *http://martinfowler.com/articles/continuousIntegration.html* (2001)
3. Beck, K., Fowler, M.: Planning Extreme Programming. Addison-Wesley (2001)
4. Mackinnon, T., Freeman, S., Craig, P.: Endo-Testing: Unit Testing with Mock Objects. Extreme Programming Examined. Addison-Wesley (2001)

Efficient Markets, Efficient Projects, and Predicting the Future

John Favaro

Consulenza Informatica, Via Gamerra 21,
56123 Pisa, Italy
jfavaro@tin.it

Abstract. Economic concepts have provided valuable sources of insight into important concepts underlying agile methodologies. The dynamics of capital markets are understood through the concept of *market efficiency*; an analogy is developed to *project efficiency* for understanding the dynamics of agile projects. The efficient project concept is then used to motivate the preoccupation of agile developers with dealing only with available information at any time and not trying to predict the future. Finally, six lessons of project efficiency are presented.

Keywords: Economics, efficiency, value, market, project.

1   Introduction

> Our highest priority is to satisfy the customer through
> early and continuous delivery of valuable software.
> – The *Agile Manifesto*

One of the ways in which agile methods such as Extreme Programming (XP) have differentiated themselves from other software development methodologies has been their explicit elevation of economic arguments onto an equal (or greater) footing with the more familiar technical arguments. Therefore it is perhaps not surprising that economics and finance have also proven to be a rich source of analogies for explaining the values, principles, and practices of agile methods.

Certainly the most widely disseminated of these has been the analogy of "business options," introduced both in the White Book [1] and in other publications [2], where concepts from option pricing theory are used to support the discussion of flexibility in agile methods. In another recent example [3], the concept of residual income (or Economic Profit), commonly used in financial management to monitor usage of capital resources such as inventory, helped illustrate the notions of "software inventory" and "software in process" currently being promoted in the agile community.

In this paper an analogy is developed between agile project dynamics and the concept of efficient markets from corporate finance.

J. Eckstein and H. Baumeister (Eds.): XP 2004, LNCS 3092, pp. 77–84, 2004.
© Springer-Verlag Berlin Heidelberg 2004

2   Efficient Markets

The ideas leading up to the theory of efficient markets are over a hundred years old. Louis Bachelier, in his doctoral thesis [4] in 1900, put forward the proposition that stock price movements are completely random – an idea considered so preposterous at the time that it was quickly forgotten. (This was unfortunate, because Bachelier not only anticipated the next formulation of this proposition by 53 years, he also anticipated Albert Einstein's work by five years in postulating that stock prices follow Brownian motion. As if that weren't enough, he also managed to contribute several key ideas in the field of option pricing.)

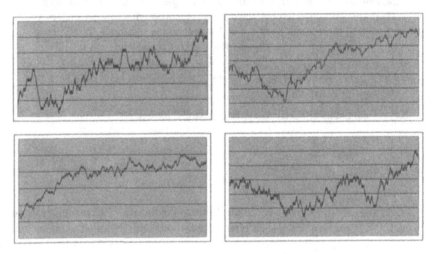

Fig. 1. Which is the real chart of stock prices?

In 1953, Kendall performed an extensive study of patterns in stock market prices, and subsequently reported [5] on the number of patterns he had found: none. To his own amazement, he had been unable to find evidence of *any* regularity or cycles. On the contrary, prices seemed to walk around randomly, as though their direction were being determined by a simple toss of a coin. This report was also greeted by skepticism, even hostility (especially from those making a living from finding patterns in stock prices). But this time the conclusions were harder to ignore: time and again it has proven to be impossible to distinguish between a chart generated entirely by random coin tosses and a chart of real stock prices. Three of the four stock price charts in Fig. 1 were generated for this article from a spreadsheet in which successive up and down movements were determined randomly. Which is the real chart? (The answer is given at the end of this article.)

The reason that the randomness of stock price movements was so hard to accept, of course, is that it seemed to make no sense at all: how can stock price movements be random when stocks are obviously affected in a very concrete way by profits, losses, acquisitions, mergers – in short, by significant events of all kinds? The explanation arrived in the form of the Efficient Market Hypothesis, first proposed formally by Fama in the mid-1960s [6].

In an efficient market, information travels freely among the large number of intelligent, motivated participants (as Malkiel [7] says, "money attracts brains"). As soon as any bit of information becomes available, investors pounce upon it, and its implications are quickly incorporated into the prices of stocks. As a result, the market is always completely "up-to-date" – it reflects all information that is currently available to investors.

Most importantly: not only does an efficient market reflect everything that has happened in the *past*, it also reflects anything that can currently be said about what might happen in the *future*. Legions of investors scrutinize, discuss, and analyze any new information over and over until every useful conclusion from that information has been drawn – *and also acted upon*:

> If today's direction ... does indeed predict tomorrow's step, then you will act on it today rather than tomorrow. Thus, if market participants were confident that the price of any security would double next week ... Why wait? [7]

This is the key insight in understanding the puzzle of random stock price movements. In an efficient market, the incessant activity (motivated by greed and fear) of investors assures that any information that clearly points the way to the future is acted upon without delay. Afterwards, only one type of information remains: *that which does not yet exist*. Its arrival must come as a genuine surprise. But the timing of unexpected new information is *by definition* unpredictable (as Paulos notes [8], it would have been extremely strange to have seen a newspaper headline in 1890 exclaiming "Only 15 years to relativity!"). And therefore, each *new* step by the stock market is taken in response to new information whose timing and impact are necessarily unknown beforehand – a random walk (also called a "drunkard's walk").

Today, more than 50 years after Kendall's report, the degree to which the market is efficient is a matter of lively ongoing debate, but the essential validity of the Efficient Market Hypothesis is widely accepted.

3 Efficient Projects

The Efficient Market Hypothesis turns out to provide a very good conceptual framework for gaining insight into the dynamics of agile projects. Working within this conceptual framework, we now introduce the notion of *efficient projects*.

Before proceeding, it is worth noting that the word "efficient" is used here more in the engineering sense of "completely consuming all input" than in the bureaucratic sense of "well-organized and disciplined" more commonly seen in the software engineering literature today. Another engineering definition of efficiency is "high ratio of output to input": A perfectly efficient market quickly and completely consumes information as it becomes available, converting every bit into investor action. It is this same goal of perfect efficiency that agile projects strive to attain, the rapid and complete absorption of new information and its immediate conversion into implementation.

The concept of *common knowledge* [8] is central to the functioning of efficient markets. Information is disseminated in such a way that all participants are aware of it, and moreover, are aware that others are aware of it. As a result, information is not compartmentalized. Agile projects strive to achieve rapid information dissemination and a state of common knowledge through a variety of techniques including stand-up meetings, pair programming, ruthless refactoring, collective ownership, continual re-estimation of effort and velocity, and the absence of fixed roles that tend to compartmentalize information. Rapid and complete information dissemination is coupled with techniques for rapid conversion into implementation, such as the principle of the Simplest Design That Could Possibly Work.

We can contrast this with traditional projects that might be called *inefficient projects* (in the engineering sense we are using it). At any one time, there is information that is not common knowledge in the project. On the contrary, information is segmented and compartmentalized. This prevalence of "insider information" is partially a result of roles such as, for example, a "Chief Architect," who may act as the sole custodian of much important information. Moreover, information is generally not quickly converted into system functionality. At any one time, there is much information that is not reflected in the current state of the system – much design, much implementation, much testing is still in the future.

4   Predicting the Future

The notion of efficient projects yields insight into the preoccupation of agile practitioners, so puzzling to many, with not trying to predict the future – expressed, for example, in the familiar YAGNI (You Aren't Going to Need It) principle. Many cannot understand why agile projects do not try to deal with the future; paradoxically, this arises from the fact that they deal so completely with the past.

In an efficient project, everything to date – requirements, analysis, design, test, everything implied by the information available – is completely reflected in the *implemented* system. (This objective is also reflected in the so-called Customer Bill of Rights [9], where the customer " ... can cancel at any time and be left with a useful working system reflecting investment to date.").

The less efficient a project, the more the "future is built-in." It is built in by the design that is not yet coded, by tests not yet run, by assumptions and claims made for the future. It is more difficult to change direction because it is predetermined by the very state of the implemented system that does not reflect all currently available information.

In contrast, in an efficient project, as in an efficient market, the future literally *is* unpredictable – because the past and present have been so completely digested. It is ready to react to this unpredictable future (for example, a user decision to introduce a new story). Each new step in an agile project (e.g. an iteration) leads to the rapid absorption and implementation of new information, leaving behind no assumptions about the future, in its own form of a random walk.

5   The Six Lessons of Market and Project Efficiency

In their classic text on corporate finance [10], Brealey and Myers presented six "lessons" that conveyed succinctly the most important implications of market efficiency. It is instructive to revisit these lessons now from the perspective of this discussion. Each lesson is presented and summarized first in its original form for efficient markets, then in an adapted form for efficient projects. Where appropriate, quotes from the original presentation in [10] will be utilized.

Lesson 1: No Memory

Efficient markets have no memory. "[In an efficient market] ... the sequence of past price changes contains no information about future changes." This is the most fundamental message of the Efficient Market Hypothesis: the past does not condition the future – there are no patterns or cycles implied by past movements.

Efficient projects have no memory. An efficient project likewise strives to not build the future into the system. By working only for the present, the project builds in only what is necessary to handle what has happened up to now, so that there are no mechanisms that condition how new information will be handled. For example, in a web project, if the system is built to handle, say, 200 users now, there is nothing in the current implementation (e.g. "hooks") from which to infer that the system might be asked to handle 1000 users in the future. The more efficient the project, the more it will decouple its past from its future, leaving it optimally ready to react to new information.

This is much different from an inefficient project, where the past strongly conditions the future, making it difficult to change course – because so much remains to be done, based upon so many suppositions.

Lesson 2: Trust

Trust market prices. "In an efficient market you can trust prices, for they impound all available information about the value of each security. To [improve on this], you not only need to know more than *anyone* else, but you also need to know more than *everyone* else." Often managers, confident of their superior investing ability, acquire other companies simply because they think those companies are undervalued. But in an efficient market, the phenomenon of *arbitrage* ensures that the values placed on securities (and therefore companies) by investors quickly converge to the correct ones: if the available information indicates that a price is too low, investors quickly take advantage of this and drive the price up; the converse happens when the price is too high. Even when the price is not correct, it is *unbiased*: any error is just as likely to be in one direction as another.

Trust the implemented system. In an efficient project, you can trust the implemented system, because it impounds all available information about what the system should do. In a phenomenon similar to arbitrage, the principles of the simplest possible implementation and refactoring place downward pressure on complexity, while information such as failing tests act to produce upward pressure, resulting in an implementation whose complexity is generally appropriate for the information available. When you try to second-guess the implementation, you are not only saying that you can improve on the consolidated wisdom of the project, but that you have a better idea of where the project is headed next. But since the system impounds all available information, then even if it is not yet completely right, it is still unbiased: there is no reason to think that you have a better idea about what the future holds.

Lesson 3: Read the Entrails

Read the market entrails. Since the prices in an efficient market reflect all available information, it is there that we must go for answers. For example, if the stock price of a company (e.g. Oracle) is sinking in response to the bidding war it is waging to acquire another company (e.g. Peoplesoft), it is the clearest signal available that investors are displeased with this initiative. As another example, reading the entrails of long-term versus short-term interest rates will tell us whether the market thinks that interest rates are set to rise in the future.

Read the system entrails. "Ask the code," as the common saying goes. Since the implementation impounds all available information, it is there that we must go for answers. When there is a question, then look to how the system is actually implemented and performing – an addition to the suite of tests is invariably the best route. If the code smells or, for example, if the system seems to be able to get to 90% of tests passing and can't move beyond, then the system is sending a strong signal that something could be fundamentally wrong with the implementation. In an inefficient project, in contrast, where much important information remains outside the implementation, the system cannot be reliably interrogated for answers.

Lesson 4: There Are No Illusions

There are no financial illusions. "In an efficient market ... investors are unromantically concerned with the firm's cash flows ..." In recent years there have been a number of cases of "creative accounting," where reported earnings were manipulated in order to appear to make them appear higher (think of so-called *pro forma* earnings reported by many tech firms). But the incessant scrutiny of investors has invariably exposed the financial window-dressing and kept the focus on the true cash flows of the firm (with some infamous exceptions during the years of the dotcom mania – and even those were eventually exposed).

There are no functional illusions. In an efficient project, customers are unromantically concerned with the functionality of the system. The unrelenting rhythm of implementation and testing in an efficient project quickly peels off any functional "window dressing" (perhaps in the form of a colorful and flashy GUI) and keeps the focus on whether the customer functionality (e.g. handling a particular set of file formats) is really implemented by the system or not.

Lesson 5: The Do-It Yourself Alternative

"In an efficient market, investors will not pay others for what they can do equally well themselves." The transparency of efficient markets reveals the costs and value of operations undertaken by firms – and consequently a firm must demonstrate to the investor that it can offer something at a cheaper price than he could have done himself. For example, companies that merge or acquire others often try to convince investors that they have added value by "diversifying." But the investor can easily and more cheaply diversify on his own, simply by buying shares in several different companies. There is no reason for him to prefer the generally more costly route offered by a merger.

In an efficient project, customers will not pay others for what they can do equally well themselves. Efficient projects are very transparent: the relentless cycle of estimating and re-estimating stories leads to the customer always knowing the cost and value to him of paying to have a feature implemented within the context of the project, down to a relatively fine grain. He will therefore always have the opportunity of being aware of possibilities to acquire the feature at a cheaper price outside of the project (say, a COTS or open source tool or component that implements that feature perfectly) – or to renounce altogether, when the efficient processes in the project reveal that the cost/value relationship of the feature is not advantageous.

In contrast, in an inefficient project, the implementation is generally not feature-aligned; as a consequence there is generally little or no opportunity to separate out and evaluate features that could be provided in a more cost-effective way outside the project. The customer must simply trust the implementers and hope for the best.

Lesson 6: Seen One, Seen Them All

Seen one stock, seen them all. "Investors don't buy a stock for its unique qualities; they buy it because it offers the prospect of a fair return for its risk." In an efficient market, stocks are perfectly substitutable for each other: investors don't care whether their cash flows are generated by selling cars, computers, or candy.

Seen one implementation, seen them all. In efficient projects, customers don't buy features for the unique characteristics of their implementation; they buy them because they deliver the functionality requested at a fair price, whether it is implemented with objects or with acorns. Agile methods support this view by being relatively technology-neutral: although certain technological categories are recognized to be generally effective (just as certain market sectors are recognized to be generally profitable), agile methods focus on delivery of features at the promised cost and consider the supporting technologies to be essentially substitutable for each other.

6 Conclusions

The notion of efficient markets is central to modern corporate finance: it is the primary mechanism through which the value of capital assets is determined. The notion of efficient projects can help agile project managers understand the mechanisms that lead to the production of software with measurable value. Agile project managers don't try to predict the future, because they strive to have projects that completely impound the past and present. This leaves them free of the baggage of the past and present, and ready to confront an unpredictable future. Of course, neither markets nor projects are ever perfectly efficient all of the time – but the concept provides agile developers a way of understanding what they are trying to achieve.

The upper right-hand chart in Fig. 1 tracks the S&P500 index from 20 November 2002 to 19 November 2003.

References

1. Beck. K., Extreme Programming Explained: Embrace Change, Addison-Wesley, 1999.
2. Erdogmus, H. and J.M. Favaro, "Keep your options open: Extreme Programming and the economics of flexibility," in Extreme Programming Perspectives, M. Marchesi, G. Succi, D. Wells and L. Williams, Editors: Addison-Wesley, 2003.
3. Favaro, J.M., "Value-Based Management and Agile Methods," Proc. Fourth International Conference on Extreme Programming and Agile Processes, Genoa, May 2003.
4. Bachelier, Louis, Théorie de la spéculation, Annales scientifiques de l'Ecole Normale Supérieure, 3° série, 17 :21-86, 1900.
5. Kendall, M.G., "The Analysis of Economic Time Series," Part I. Prices, Journal of the Royal Statistical Society 96 (1953), pp. 11-25.
6. Fama, E. F., "Random Walks in Stock Market Prices," Financial Analysts Journal, September/October 1965.
7. Malkiel, B.G., A Random Walk Down Wall Street, W.W. Norton, 1996.
8. Paulos, J. A., A Mathematician Plays the Stock Market, Basic Books, 2003.
9. Jeffries, R., et al., Extreme Programming Installed, Addison-Wesley, 2001.
10. Brealey, R. and S. Myers, Principles of Corporate Finance, McGraw-Hill, 2000.

Agile Principles and Open Source Software Development: A Theoretical and Empirical Discussion

Stefan Koch

Vienna University of Economics and BA, Department of Information Business,
Augasse 2-6, A-1190, Vienna, Austria
stefan.koch@wu-wien.ac.at

Abstract. In the last years, two movements have been widely discussed in the software development community: Agile and open source development. Both have faced some of the same criticism, and both claim some of the same benefits. This paper poses the question whether open source software development is in accordance with agile software development principles and therefore well within the planning spectrum. To this end, the general principles of both movements are detailed and compared, and some empirical data from open source software development projects is given on any similarities and dissimilarities uncovered.

Keywords. Software Development, Agile, Open Source, Software Metrics, Coordination

1 Introduction

Agile software development has been proposed as a solution to problems resulting from the turbulent business and technology environment faced by organizations engaged in software development [8]. Several methods like Extreme Programming (XP) [1], Scrum, Lean Development or Adaptive Software Development exist that embody the principles of this approach as laid down in the Manifesto for Agile Software Development. While there is some evidence, mostly based on singular projects, of positive practical application of these methods, there is a lively discussion on this topic [2,13]. On the other hand, Boehm in his analysis [3] sees both the agile and more plan-driven approaches as having a responsible center, and argues for a risk analysis of a project's characteristics for determining the right balance of disciplines in each case [4]. All of these contributions have not yet ended the ongoing debate, even if some first empirical results on both use of agile principles and the results in cost, productivity and quality have already been published [15], and seem an important step towards this end. There is one point in the discussion that has as yet been largely omitted: Like agile development, there has been another movement which has received much attention in the last years: Open source software development. Also in this case there is considerable debate about benefits and efficiency [11,5,17]. While any

J. Eckstein and H. Baumeister (Eds.): XP 2004, LNCS 3092, pp. 85–93, 2004.

discussion of agile development contains the words cowboy coding, unplanned and undisciplined hacking or similar terms, from which this movement is seen as different, the term open source is not mentioned. Many of the same arguments brought to bear against agile development are also faced by open source development. So, using the planning spectrum introduced by Barry Boehm, the question is where to place open source development? On the far end with the hackers or more towards XP and agile methods? In order to facilitate this classification, this article seeks to compare both methods, and tries to give some first empirical results on any similarities and dissimilarities. Besides clarifying terms and classifications, open source projects and their wealth of data [10,12] might form additional testbeds for agile development methods, and both movements might learn and benefit from each other.

2   Agile Software Development

Both the business and technology environment continue to change at an increasing pace. In software projects, this leads to more frequent changes during the life cycle. Therefore the main question is how to better handle these changes, not stop them by anticipating and including them in the requirements definition, while still achieving high quality and timeliness. To this end, a group of people created the Manifesto for Agile Software Development that values individuals and interactions over processes and tools, working software over comprehensive documentation, customer collaboration over contract negotiation, responding to change over following a plan, while explicitly acknowledging the value of the latter items. Furthermore there is a set of principles giving more details, stressing the importance of quality in design, especially in simplicity, the honesty of working code, delivered early and continuously, for communication between developers and sponsors, short feedback loops, the importance of motivated and competent individuals interacting face to face and welcoming change even late in the development. There has been a lot of criticism, one of them being that planning, processes and documentation are essential, and agile development is an excuse for hackers to do as they like, coding away without planning or design [13]. Barry Boehm on the other hand sees agile methods as having a responsible center with a fair amount of planning, and as an important advantage of this movement to draw hackers away from pure hacking [3]. Another point of criticism is the reliance on individual competency, craftsmanship, working together in self-organizing teams in intense collaboration including customers [6]. It is argued that the number of developers possessing excellent technical knowledge paired with the necessary social skills is naturally limited. Also the possible size of agile development teams is discussed. While successful projects with up to 250 people are cited [6], others see a limit of 15 to 20 people.

3   Open Source Software Development

Open source (or free) software has generated much interest in the last years, especially following the rise of Linux and several similar projects like GNU project's utilities and libraries, the Perl and Tcl programming languages, and the Apache Web server. Regarding these examples, the notion that software of considerable quality can result from this form of development can not be dismissed. Open source software (using the Open Source Definition) is software under a license that fulfills several criteria, giving the user more rights than most other terms of distribution. These include the free redistribution, the inclusion of the source code, the possibility for modifications and derived works, which must be allowed to be distributed under the same terms as the original software, and some others. One example for a license that fits these criteria is the well-known GNU General Public License (GPL) advocated by the Free Software Foundation, which imposes even stricter regulations. While these definitions pertain to the legal terms of distribution, there is also a distinct form of development associated with open source software. The guiding principle is that by sharing source code, developers cooperate under a model of rigorous peer-review and take advantage of "parallel debugging" that leads to innovation and rapid advancement in developing and evolving software products. The best and most widely used description of this development form is an article by Raymond titled 'The Cathredal and the Bazaar', in which he contrasts the cathredal model of commercial software development with the bazaar model of open source using fetchmail as a case study [14]. In this article, he gives several lessons, which form the guiding principles of this form of software development. These therefore constitute the counterpart of the principles behind the agile manifesto and need to be compared with those and reality in open source projects. The criticism faced by the open source development paradigm has several main arguments, the first being that finding and correcting bugs late in the life cycle during coding incurs very high costs [11], a point also discussed in the context of agile development [16]. In addition, effort by people looking for bugs, but not being able to find or fix them, is hidden by spreading it. The inattendance to analysis, requirements engineering and design causes additional limitations due to architectural problems, hiding of useful code, etc. On the other hand it is argued that due to the high modularity of open source code, which is much more stringently enforced to allow more people to work in parallel, and because the context of an error is not lost due to fast release cycles, the costs for fixing bugs in code are not much higher [5].

4 Comparison and Empirical Data

Using several key areas mostly denoted by the principles of agile development and lessons from Raymond's description of open source software development, both movements are compared. Empirical data is used where appropriate to further emphasize and confirm any similarities and dissimilarities. The data employed is derived from several empirical analyses including Apache and Mozilla [12], GNOME [10] and an analysis of Sourceforge, a repository providing free services like version-control or mailing lists for several thousand hosted open source projects. The main idea for this empirical research was to use existing data on the projects available to the public, especially the version control systems that stores every single check-in of a file by a programmer with additional information like the number of lines-of-code changed, and mailing lists.

4.1   Software Process

Both agile and open source development are no description of a software process as envisioned by this research area. They consist of a set of principles for a software project. While agile in contrast to open source development has several approaches and methods that embody these principles, some of these, e.g. XP, do not have much more detail on the software process, but also restrict themselves to general guidelines. On the other hand, several open source projects have devised elaborate process descriptions, e.g. for release management [9].

4.2   Craftsmanship, Chief Programmers, and Individuals

Agile software development focuses on individual competency and on motivated individuals ('Build projects around motivated individuals.'). This attitude is also described by the term craftsmanship [6], and manifests in pair programming, collective code ownership and mentoring in XP, or chief programmers in FDD. In open source development, Raymond gives a possible explanation for the free effort contributed by using the craftsmanship model, in which the pure artistic satisfaction of designing beautiful software and making it work drives the developers. Empirical data on open source projects show an interesting distribution of the effort invested. While a large number of people participate in the development by giving feedback or testing, a smaller number contributes to the source code, and an even smaller number is responsible for the vast majority of the outcome. In the Apache project, while over 3,000 people submitted problem reports, a core group of 15 programmers out of 400 is responsible for 88% of the lines-of-code [12]. In the GNOME project, which is much more diverse containing several sub-projects, the top 15 of 301 programmers added 48% of the total lines-of-code, while clustering hints at a still smaller 11 person core programmer group. In total, about 1,900 people participated by showing some activity on the mailing lists [10]. Analysis of the Sourceforge repository shows that of more than 12,000 programmers in 8,600 projects, the top 10% are responsible for about 80% of the total source code. Regarding the distribution in single projects, all 65 projects with more than 500k lines-of-code added and at least 5 developers were analyzed. These projects range up to 88 programmers with a mean of 17 persons per project. In the mean, only the top 20.4% of the participating programmers (2.8 people) were necessary to reach 80% of the project's source code. In open source development, each project therefore seems to center around a small number of highly competent and motivated individuals. These individuals, at least some of them, will need to have the social and communication skills necessary to bring larger numbers of people to the project, and hold them there. Open source development can therefore be termed chief programmer teams, as a large number of supporters center around a small inner circle of programmers responsible for most part of actual design and coding.

4.3   Team Size

While successful agile projects of up to 250 people are cited [6], most authors see a size limit at about 15 to 20 persons due to the tightly coordinated teamwork necessary. Both of these ranges are within the bounds of open source projects. As demonstrated above, large projects like Apache or GNOME number a few hundred programmers, but there is empirical evidence for a very small core team in the range of 10 to 20 persons. In smaller open source projects, these numbers decrease accordingly, down to one highly motivated developer with a small team of supporters. The core team seems to have a size of about 5 to 20%, resulting in a group within whom frequent and even personal interactions are easier. While Boehm in his analysis of agile development correctly remarks that 49.9999% of the world's software developers are below average, he concedes that a project does not necessarily require uniformly high-capability people. This seems to exactly mirror the situation in open source projects, where highly capable chief programmers are supported by a larger number of participants.

4.4   Self-Organizing Teams

Agile development stresses the importance of self-organizing teams that are able to rapidly adjust to changing requirements and new challenges ('The best architectures, requirements, and designs emerge from self-organizing teams.', 'At regular intervals, the team reflects on how to become more effective, then tunes and adjusts its behavior accordingly.'). This requires common focus, mutual trust and respect, and intense collaboration. In open source development, a common focus is ensured, as all participants voluntarily join and therefore follow the goals, which might available implicitly in a vision or example like an existing commercial system. In order to efficiently apply the manpower available to the project, self-organization is strictly necessary. As each participant needs only to do what he wants, self-selection will lead to each one doing what he does best and most efficiently. As Raymond writes '...open source hackers organize themselves for maximum productivity by self-selection...'. For the GNOME project it has been shown that the number of participating programmers in each month, at least until the time of operation, closely follows the efficient manpower distribution proposed for commercial software projects [10]. As there is no central management, the community of developers really seems to be able to organize itself accordingly. Of course, coordination is still necessary also in this form of project, and data from the GNOME project shows that the activity on the mailing lists was strongest during the build-up in active programmers, while declining afterwards [10]. This hints at some sort of briefing or introduction necessary for newcomers. If the data of the GNOME project's source-code versioning system is analyzed, in the mean only 1.8 programmers are found to work together on a single file, even larger files are worked on by only a few programmers. This indicates a division of labour on a higher level. In the Apache project [12], data on the problem reports show that this activity is more widely spread than actual programming, the top 15 people only produced 5% of the total reports, and only three of these were also among the core programmers. This again hints at a high degree of division of labour, with the tasks that can more easily be performed in parallel being spread out more than others. In the Sourceforge repository, in the mean 1.2 programmers work an a given file, but as this number might be distorted by the large number of small projects, analysis of the 65 large projects (more than 500k lines-of-code, at least 5 developers) was again undertaken. While the number within this group is slightly higher with 1.5 programmers, it is still rather small and near the GNOME project, further enhancing the findings given above. In addition, when the data from the Sourceforge repository is analyzed using text parsing of the commit log messages by the programmers, distinctive names of design patterns show up at about 10% of the projects. One of the main benefits often associated with patterns is improved communication between developers. In fact, there is a significant positive correlation between the number of participants in a project and the number of different patterns used. This indicates that larger teams seem to have an increased need for the improved communication provided by patterns. As this usage is not prescribed, this can be seen as an additional example of self-organization for maximizing efficiency.

4.5   Team Co-location

Agile development aims at close, personal contact and collaboration within the development team ('The most efficient and effective method of conveying information to and within a development team is face-to-face conversation.'), while open source development is performed by large numbers of developers scattered throughout the world [7]. While the empirical data given above suggests that most work is done by a small inner circle of programmers, which could and also do meet in person sometimes, that the self-organization works remarkably well, and is enhanced especially by the Internet medium, this difference remains. In fact, open source software development sees the Internet with all its tools including mailing lists, source code versioning, e-mail, maybe even video-conferencing, as a means for achieving collaboration that is sufficient ('Provided the development coordinator has a medium as least as good as the Internet, and knows how to lead without coercion, many heads are inevitably better than one.').

4.6   Customer Interactions

In agile development, the continuos interaction and collaboration with the customers is paramount. A short feedback loop is necessary to be able to respond quickly to new information like changes in the requirements. These principles are embodied in practices like customer on site in XP. In fact, agile development sees a development team as spanning organizational boundaries and therefore including customers. The same attitude is at the heart of open source development: Users should join the development community and become co-developers in order to more rapidly improve the software ('Treating your users as co-developers is your least-hassle route to rapid code improvement and effective debugging.', 'Release early, release often. And listen to your customer.', 'The next best thing to having good ideas is recognizing good ideas from your users. Sometimes the latter is better.'). Of course, the necessary precondition for this is the availability of the source code. Even more so than in XP, there is indeed collective code ownership. As has been detailed above, in larger open source projects thousands of people, read users, participate to some degree, not necessarily coding, which only a minority actively does, but in reporting errors, filing change reports or claiming additional functionalities and requirements. In the GNOME project, the nearly 1,900 participants in the mean contributed 10.6 separate postings to the diverse mailing lists. In the FreeBSD project, 82% of the developers indicated that they received some form of feedback on their code, either as a problem report or a bugfix performed on the code [9]. Therefore the open source process is specifically designed to allow customer collaboration, in fact depends on it.

4.7 Early Delivery of Working Code and Feedback

Agile development sees working code as the 'primary measure of progress'. To use this measure in the collaboration with customers, and in order to ensure short feedback cycles, frequent releases of working software are intended ('Deliver working software frequently, from a couple of weeks to a couple of months, with a preference to the shorter timescale.'). These practices increase the motivation for all participants, allow for easier discussion of the current status and therefore increased chances to uncover necessary changes and efficient possibilities for incorporating them ('Our highest priority is to satisfy the customer through early and continuous delivery of valuable software.'). In open source software development, frequent releases are also propagated ('Release early, release often.'). This has several reasons, including that a larger number of users and co-developers should test und debug the code, thus faster finding and correcting any errors ('Given a large enough beta-tester and co-developer base, almost every problem will be characterized quickly and the fix obvious to someone.'). In order to minimize the lost time spent by participants looking for problems which have already been found or even solved, everyone needs to be kept at the current status. This is achieved by releasing new versions even with only a small number of changes. During the early days of Linux, new releases could occur daily. In the FreeBSD project, approximately 200 developers have been granted commit authority, and any change committed by these individuals results in instant creation of a new release [9]. There is an additional effect of releasing open source software often: Keeping developers constantly stimulated and rewarded, as they have new challenges to rise to, and at the same time see the results of their prior work take shape in the form of improved software. This motivational aspect has been mentioned by 81% of the FreeBSD developers [9]. These points correspond remarkably well: Working software is released often to facilitate change, to keep the effort for rework under control, to ease collaboration with the users and customers, and as a primary measure of progress.

4.8 Changing Requirements, Good Design, and Simplicity

Closely connected to frequent releases is the attitude of agile development towards change. As release and feedback cycles are short, changes in the requirements happening anyhow due to the turbulent environment can easily be uncovered, and can more easily be implemented than at the end of the development ('Welcome changing requirements, even late in development. Agile processes harness change for the customer's competitive advantage.'). Incorporating these changes in addition needs an appropriate design ('Continuous attention to technical excellence and good design enhances agility.'). Therefore agile development stresses the importance of having a simple design that allows for easy changes ('Simplicity - the art of maximizing the amount of work not done - is essential.') and refactoring. The same is also inherent in open source development. There is evidence for both the strive for simple designs allowing for change, and also refactoring, if not actually using this term. Raymond describes how he changed to a new development base ('...I'd be throwing away the coding I'd already done in exchange for a better development base...the first thing I did was reorganize and simplify...'). It is also evident in the saying 'Plan to throw one away; you will, anyhow', originally by Fred Brooks, adopted by the open source community. This of course also hints at prototyping and feedback from users. Another embodiment of refactoring can be found in the principles 'Often, the most striking and innovative solutions come from realizing that your concept of the problem was wrong.' and 'Good programmers know what to write. Great programmers know what to rewrite (and reuse).' from Raymond. The strive for a simple design is obvious in the saying 'Perfection (in design) is achieved not when there is nothing more to add, but rather when there is nothing more to take away.' As the data from the Sourceforge repository suggests the usage of design patterns, these could also be used as a target for refactoring later in the life cycle.

5   Conclusion

As both agile and open source development have been hotly debated, claim some of the same benefits, and face some identical criticism, a comparison seems a logical step. Using their main principles, we have discussed whether open source development can be seen as an agile form of development. In several areas, amazing similarities have been found, for example the emphasis on highly skilled individuals or 'craftsmen' at the center of a self-organizing development team, the acceptance and embrace of change by using short feedback loops with frequent releases of working code, and the close integration and collaboration with the customers and users. For these points, empirical indications were found that at least partially confirmed the presence of these agile principles in open source projects. For example, empirical data suggests that an open source project has a relatively small inner circle of highly skilled and productive developers, around which a larger number of participants and users cluster in a highly efficient self-organization. On the other hand, one major difference showed up, the team co-location and personal contact demanded by agile development, which is not seen as a precondition in open source development. In addition, while Boehm and Turner see small product size as agility homeground [4], open source projects have undoubtedly been able to realize quite large products, with similar comments applying for safety criticality, as quality assurance is often cited as a main benefit of open source development. Overall, the question whether the 'hackers' and 'cowboy coders' mentioned by the proponents of agile development and others are indeed the open source software developers of the world may therefore not be so easy to answer as it might seem at first glance. Additional research into the real workings of both agile and open source projects is in order, both to compare them to more plan-driven methods and also among each other.

References

1. Beck, K.: Extreme Programming Explained: Embrace Change. Addison-Wesley, Reading, Mass. (1999)
2. Beck, K., Boehm, B.: Agility through Discipline: A Debate. IEEE Computer **36** (2003) 44–46
3. Boehm, B.: Get Ready for Agile Methods, with Care. IEEE Computer **35** (2002) 64–69
4. Boehm, B., Turner, R.: Using Risk to Balance Agile and Plan-Driven Methods. IEEE Computer **36** (2003) 57–66
5. Bollinger, T., Nelson, R., Self, K.M., Turnbull, S.J.: Open-Source Methods: Peering through the Clutter. IEEE Software **16** (1999) 8–11
6. Cockburn, A., Highsmith, J.: Agile Software Development: The People Factor. IEEE Computer **34** (2001) 131–133
7. Dempsey, B.J., Weiss, D., Jones, P., Greenberg, J.: Who is an Open Source Software Developer? Communications of the ACM **45** (2002) 67–72
8. Highsmith, J., Cockburn, A.: Agile Software Development: The Business of Innovation. IEEE Computer **34** (2001) 120–122
9. Jorgensen, N.: Putting it All in the Trunk: Incremental Software Sevelopment in the FreeBSD Open Source Project. Information Systems Journal **11** (2001) 321–336
10. Koch, S., Schneider, G.: Effort, Cooperation and Coordination in an Open Source Software Project: Gnome. Information Systems Journal **12** (2002) 27–42
11. McConnell, S.: Open-Source Methodology: Ready for Prime Time? IEEE Software **16** (1999) 6–8
12. Mockus, A., Fielding, R.T., Herbsleb, J.D.: Two Case Studies of Open Source Software Development: Apache and Mozilla. ACM Transactions on Software Engineering and Methodology **11** (2002) 309–346
13. Rakitin, S.R.: Manifesto Elicits Cynicism. IEEE Computer **34** (2001) 4
14. Raymond, E.S.: The Cathedral and the Bazaar. O'Reilly, Cambridge, Mass. (1999)
15. Reifer, D.J.: How Good Are Agile Methods? IEEE Software **19** (2002) 16–18
16. Williams, L.: The XP Programmer: The Few-Minutes Programmer. IEEE Software **20** (2003) 16–20
17. Wilson, G.: Is the Open-Source Community Setting a Bad Example? IEEE Software **16** (1999) 23–25

XP Lite Considered Harmful?

Ben Aveling

Faculty of Information Technology, UTS, Australia
bena@triode.net.au

Abstract. It is generally prescribed that XP be adopted in full. However, a review of existing XP adoption case studies suggests that full adoption is exceptional; most companies adopt XP only partially and they adapt XP to fit existing practices and philosophies. Drawing on interviews with industry participants, the paper recommends using XP as a 'tool kit' of techniques and philosophies.

1 Introduction

There is a rapidly growing wealth of case studies of adoption of XP. In the main, good results are claimed. However, early adoptions can be genuinely but atypically successful: „With small projects carried out by highly motivated zealots, success is a lot easier to achieve" (Yourdon 1997, p. 63). Furthermore, most existing studies are post-hoc assessments of their authors' adoption of XP.

What is missing is independent comparative studies. This paper draws on the existing literature and on a series of interviews with practitioners in order to provide a comparative assessment of multiple instances of the adoption and use of XP. In particular, the paper looks at adaptations made in the implementation of XP. Beck and other long-standing proponents of XP believe that partial adoption of XP is undesirable. This study, however, suggests that full adoption of XP is unusual; most organisations adopt XP only partially.

2 Methodology

Existing case studies of the adoption of XP were reviewed and the XP practices followed and omitted were noted, as were comments on the drivers and consequences thereof. Informed by these results, an interview study was undertaken of four companies that had adopted or failed to adopt XP. The author has no commercial relationship with any of the companies reviewed.

J. Eckstein and H. Baumeister (Eds.): XP 2004, LNCS 3092, pp. 94–103, 2004.

3 Literature Review

All case studies reviewed were authored by people reporting their own experiences. As such, the studies' authors were highly involved, financially and emotionally. No case was considered a failure by its author, although many were obviously qualified successes, at best. One must draw on these results with some caution. For example, most projects reported adopting Collective Ownership. This could indicate that Collective Ownership is not difficult to adopt. Alternately, it could indicate that any project incapable of adopting Collective Ownership is doomed to failure.

Table 1 lists practices identifiably used or omitted in each of the case studies reviewed. The results show that it is possible to deviate from the XP practices and still enjoy the benefits of an Agile Methodology. If these cases are typical, it suggests that partial adoption of XP is more common than full adoption of XP.

The most difficult practices to adopt were Metaphor and the 'Customer Practices' of On-Site Customer, Planning Game and Small Releases. The other 'Developer practices' were not generally difficult to adopt. Explanations given for difficulties in adopting practices broadly fell into one of three categories: 1) insufficient discipline; 2) initial temporary failure to understand the practice; or 3) failure to persuade third party stakeholders. The first two categories generally resulted in lower but acceptable productivity. The third category often compromised or prevented various practices, occasionally led to the cancellation of projects and, in one case, led to retrenchments.

Most of the published cases succeeded without an *On-Site Customer*, demonstrating that the practice, while desirable, is not strictly necessary. Several projects used a proxy customer while others used more traditional methods.

Wells and Buckley (2001) report that their attempt to introduce the *Planning Game* resulted in „total disaster". The local culture was that schedules were not driven by estimates but by desired outcome, allowing for an anticipated overrun. Adding this hidden multiplier made accurate estimates appear unrealistically high. The resultant backlash forced the project to revert to conventional scheduling practices. This is consistent with McBreen (2003): „many organisations still seem to think that it is possible to negotiate estimates." Kini and Collins (2003) were more successful but could not fully implement the Planning Game because the customer felt that bug fixes were 'owed' to them and should not be included in the estimating process. Instead, two developers were assigned to fixing bugs with a resulting reduction in effort available for new features. The evidence suggests that customer participation in the Planning Game, while desirable, is not necessary.

There are sufficient examples of successful projects that do not do *Small Releases* to indicate that the practice is not totally necessary. However, omitting Small Releases precludes using the Planning Game to set scope. Further, Small Releases may be an important source of discipline in that the practice dictates release-quality code at all times.

Table 1. Practices identifiably used in each case study

	Johnson (2000)	Wells & Buckley (2001)	Schuh (2001)	Kini & Collings (2003)	Greening (2001)
On-site customer	no	no	no	yes	partial
Planning game	no	no	no	yes	partial
Small releases		yes	no		yes
Metaphor		yes	no		no
Simple design		yes	yes		yes
Testing	yes	yes	yes	yes	partial
Refactoring	yes	yes	yes	yes	yes
Pair programming	no	yes	partial	yes	yes
Collective ownership	yes	yes	yes		yes
Continuous integration	yes	yes	yes		yes
40-hour week		yes	no	yes	yes
Coding standards	yes	yes	no		yes
Whole Team				yes	
Coach		yes		yes	
Stand up meetings			no	yes	
Unqualified Success	yes	no	no	yes	no
	Moore (2001)	Poole & Huisman (2003)	Johnson (2002)	White (2002)	Johansen, Stauffer & Turner (2002)
On-site customer		partial		no	no
Planning game			yes	yes	yes
Small releases	yes			partial	
Metaphor				no	
Simple design		yes		no	yes
Testing	yes	yes		yes	yes
Refactoring	yes	yes		yes	
Pair programming		partial	modified	yes	yes
Collective ownership				no	
Continuous integration			modified	yes	
40-hour week		no		yes	yes
Coding standards	yes	yes		yes	
Whole Team		yes	no	yes	
Coach				yes	
Stand up meetings		yes	modified	yes	yes
Unqualified Success				yes	no

Note: Blank cells are used where it was less than clear if a practice was used or not.

Metaphor appears to be a useful technique, when a project succeeds in finding a suitable metaphor. Most projects succeed without finding a metaphor.

Simple Design was not reported as being difficult to adopt, although several authors reported that it takes time to become adept (eg Lippert et al. 2002, p. 168).

Some level *of Automated Testing* appears necessary to support Refactoring. The evidence suggests that a small degree of laxity in automatic testing is not automatically fatal. For example, Johnson (2000) reports success without Automated Testing but a dramatic increase in progress after its adoption.

The results do not make clear if *Test First* development is or is not essential for Agile Development, but it appears to be significant in producing a Simple Design.

As with Simple Design, *Refactoring* was not difficult to adopt but was difficult to do well: „It took us a long time to learn how to break down a refactoring ... into as small chunks as we wanted" (Lippert et al. 2002, p. 171). Refactoring appears to be essential for developing and maintaining a Simple Design. It appears unlikely that a project could omit refactoring and remain Agile.

Pair Programming was universally regarded by authors as beneficial, although Poole and Huisman found that persuading their engineers of the value of Pair Programming was „one of the hardest things" in XP (2003, p. 229). Johnson (2002) reported successfully using a form of virtual pair programming on a project with developers spread around America. Johnson concluded that the only reason the project succeeded was because virtual contact was heavily supplemented by regular face-to-face meetings. Other projects succeeded without Pair Programming. Pair Programming is clearly not essential but, without Pair Programming, other practices are less rigorously followed, especially those that require high levels of discipline, communication, team alignment or technical knowledge.

It is unclear from the cases examined if *Collective Ownership* could be omitted or not. The main obstacle to Collective Ownership is the minority of programmers with an especially strong desire to avoid scrutiny and/or unwillingness to share in responsibility for the project as a whole.

Continuous Integration demonstrates many benefits and is essential if Refactoring is to be practised. It does not appear to be contentious or difficult to adopt.

40-Hour week, also known as Sustainable Pace, is probably the most contentious practice. It is potentially dangerous, career-wise (Johansen et al, 2002). It also appears to be essential for Agile Development. Without 40-Hour Week, discipline declines, practices are not followed, mistakes are made and shortcuts are taken (Schuh, 2001; Kini and Collins, 2003). Something approximating 40-Hour Week appears to be essential to Extreme Programming. Agile Development appears to require that developers have the time and peace of mind to reflect critically on what they are and should be doing.

Coding Standard has many benefits in its own right. It is important if Pair Programming or Common Ownership is to be practised. It does not appear to be contentious or difficult to adopt. As with Common Ownership, any developer too individualistic and opinionated to accept a common Coding Standard is probably a liability to the team and the project.

It appears that none of the cases studied adopted all 12 of the XP practices. Almost all were happy with almost all of the practices that they were able to attempt. The XP practices appear sound, with the possible exception of Metaphor. However, On-Site Customer appears to be largely unachievable, and Planning Game and Small Releases appear to be an internal exercise for the majority of projects.

Even allowing for bias in reporting, the main obstacles to XP appear to be political, not technical. Wells and Buckley (2001, p. 405) reported that introducing XP practices was successful when and only when the practices could be seen to address a recognised problem. Greening (2001, p. 28) commented that trying to persuade the customer to accept full XP would have prevented any XP practices being adopted.

4 Case Comparison

Interviews were conducted with representatives from four companies that had adopted XP, or attempted to do so. All interviewees were identified through attendance at SyXPAC XP user group functions. Company 3 has engaged the services of Company 4. Otherwise, the companies have no relationship to each other. Interviews were semi-structured, ranged between 1 and 2 hours and were tape recorded and transcribed. The interview guide was based on the literature review discussed above.

4.1 Practices Adopted and Barriers to Adoption

Consistent with the literature review, the companies interviewed did not adopt Metaphor or the Customer Practices (Planning Game, Small Releases and On-site Customer) and did adopt the other 'Developer Practices', excepting Company 1, which all but failed to adopt any practices (see Table 2). Customer involvement was, as the Company 1 interviewee put it, „very difficult to get … It would mean that we would need to change our relationship with them totally." All of the companies interviewed were happy with the results of the practices they had adopted. None of the interviewees expressed interest in reverting to a more Waterfall-based methodology.

Company 2 experimented with *On-Site Customers* but found that giving customers direct access to developers led to uncontrollable scope creep for which it was unable to be renumerated. Using marketing as Proxy Customers proved more successful. While Companies 3 and 4 did not take issue with the demands Whole Team placed on developers, Company 3 reported that their business staff found „being called on constantly [was] difficult and disruptive to their work". In contrast to the more common Proxy Customer, Companies 3 and 4 agreed that the technical lead would act as a 'Proxy Developer', collecting questions from the other developers and meeting for one hour a day with the business staff. While successful, even that was „a big cultural shift for the business to apply that sort of time from their business staff".

No company used *Small Releases* for more than testing. Only final versions were released to the live: „There's a greater organisation and it no longer becomes project issues, it becomes interfaces with other divisions that stops small releases from getting as small as they could be" (Company 4). No company used the *Planning Game* although Companies 3 and 4 implemented a modified version, keeping overall scope fixed while allowing flexibility in the exact implementation of the preset scope.

As a practice, *Metaphor* engenders more curiosity than compliance. In the words of an XP consultant from Company 4, „I don't think it's that people find Metaphor hard. It's they're not quite sure what it means. So that we're not quite sure what they should be doing, yet. And I'm probably one of those people."

Table 2. Practices adopted per company.

	Company 1	Company 2	Company 3	Company 4
Company	Small software house	Small software house	Large corporate	Consultancy
Informant	Developer	Manager	Manager	Developer
On-site Customer	no	no	modified	modified
Planning Game	no	no	modified	modified
Small Releases	no	no	partial	partial
Metaphor	no	no	no	no
Simple Design	no	yes	yes	yes
Testing	no	yes	partial	partial
Refactoring	partial	yes	yes	yes
Pair Programming	no	partial	yes	yes
Collective Ownership	no	partial	yes	yes
Continuous Integration	no	yes	yes	yes
40-Hour Week	no	yes	yes	yes
Coding Standards	partial	yes	yes	yes
Whole Team	yes	yes	yes	yes
Coach	no	yes	yes	yes
Stand Up Meetings	partial	no	yes	yes
Unqualified Success	no	yes	yes	yes

Company 1 banned *Pair Programming* because management did not perceive it as cost efficient: „if I'm only now going to get 4 man hours' work out of what was originally 8 man hours, I can't see the value in that." Company 2 felt Pair Programming was worthwhile only for the initial education of new staff, in part because it made it hard to review the performance of individual developers.

Companies 3 and 4 had a broader view of the benefits of pairing, believing that it increases both productivity and 'survivability'; the ability to survive the loss of individual developers, something that significantly impacted Company 1: „The guy who's leaving tomorrow, he is the only one with any training in the middle-ware".

Adoption of *40-Hour Week*, as with Pair Programming, was sometimes blocked by management perceptions of cost efficiency. However, evidence from Company 1 suggests that excessive schedule pressure may be a false economy: „The code is just Byzantine and brittle. And this is killing us. This is absolutely killing us." A driver for adoption of something approaching 40-Hour Week at Company 2 was staff turnover: „We've never pushed developers to work ridiculous hours because they leave."

4.2 Drivers for Adoption

The engineers interviewed held an extremely positive view of XP. They were no less positive about practices they themselves had not attempted. The managers interviewed entertained basically positive attitudes towards practices they had experienced but were less positive, even dismissive, of practices they had not personally experienced.

Adoption was generally motivated not so much by perceived benefits of XP in general as by perceived shortcomings in the current methodologies. Company 1 said that „what we have been doing ... didn't work last time and isn't working now. XP couldn't be worse", while Company 3 said that „in hearing about the solution we started to understand that it may solve problems that we had. We weren't actively looking for a change in methodology."

4.3 Key Success Factors

The strongest predictor for successful adoption of XP appears to be the competence with which the existing methodology is executed. Factors that drive success with the existing methodology tend to have similar impact on any XP adoption effort. Company 3's culture featured coalition building, executive intervention and generous but tightly managed resourcing. Personal leadership and careful use of rewards had made Company 2 successful. At both companies, the XP adoption effort employed the same tactics – successfully. Conversely, at Company 1, the very factors XP was intended to address crippled the attempt to adopt XP: poor communication, excessive time pressure, a hostile customer, short-termism, a culture of blame and distrust and above all, a refusal to acknowledge the existence of problems: „changing couldn't be worse [but] a bit of pressure came on and it all went out the window".

5 Recommendations

Extreme Programming is the first popular methodology to view software development as an exercise in coding rather than an exercise in management. Kent Beck spends the first 50 pages of his *Extreme Programming Explained* (2000) describing the values and principles of Extreme Programming. Arguably, these are more important than the exact practices: „Kent's most important vision is about ... changing the way people treat each other and are treated in organisations" (Highsmith 2002, p. 52). For Beck, XP is an alternative to the 'Taylorism' he sees as implicit in existing methodologies because Taylorism makes „no business sense [and] no human sense" (Beck 2000, p. 172). Intuitively, XP is humane. The question is, does XP make business sense?

Waterfall structures software development so as to be manageable using traditional procurement and management practices. In particular, it attempts to fix scope up-front. XP determines scope as an ongoing function of the project itself. Unfortunately, this flexibility proscribes funding models that appear incompatible with current business practice. In the words of Company 2: „it's nearly impossible, in any size commercial contract, to not have fixed price, fixed deliverables. It is just not doable. Nobody will ever agree." Even for in-house projects, such as at Company 3, project approval is almost always contingent on a business case demonstrating that benefits sufficiently exceed costs. Full XP denies senior management information they habitually depend upon when assessing the merits of business a case: „Arguably approval processes could be changed to allow anything, if justified but their management can't cope with not knowing what the outcome is going to be for a given spend."

The evidence of this paper is that businesses are insufficiently motivated by Full XP to engage in the required change. It has been suggested that an alternative to Full XP is fully adopting an alternate, less demanding, agile methodology (Cockburn 2002, p. 204). It is sometimes argued that one should adopt an XP practice when it addresses a felt need without challenging any strongly held norm: „We regarded XP as a toolbox from which we could use practices that addressed concrete, recognisable problems" (Lippert et al. 2002).

This author suggests that those wishing to mix-and-match practices begin with an 'XP Lite' consisting of 40-Hour Week, Pair Programming, Single Work Site, Continuous Integration, Simple Design, Test First Programming, Automated Testing, Coach, Proxy Customer, Refactoring, Coding Standard, Stand-Up Meetings, End of Iteration Retrospectives and a degree of Collective Ownership.

Although not enumerated amongst Beck's 12 core practices, Coach, Stand-up Meetings and Retrospectives appear necessary for developers to acquire an understanding of XP and to share local knowledge. I have used the term Single Work Site instead of the more common Whole Team to avoid the inference that the customer's presence, however desirable, is essential. Automated testing and test first programming are often considered to be aspects of a single practice: Testing. My findings suggest they are distinct, Test First being not so much a testing technique as a design technique that produces tests as a side effect.

Evidence from the literature review and the interviews shows that the above practices are not generally politically difficult to implement, perhaps because they are only visible locally. The exceptions are Single Work Site and 40-Hour Week. Single Work Site is not contentious but can be unachievable in companies used to open-plan offices, especially when project teams are not 'long lived'. 40-Hour Week is both contentious and highly visible. Sadly, it is essential, if other practices are to be rigorously followed.

Metaphor may be desirable – there may even be value in an unsuccessful search for metaphor – but Metaphor is, as yet, too poorly understood to be a core practice. The Customer Practices of On-Site Customer, Planning Game and Small External Releases require cooperation from non-developers. The practices are desirable but neither necessary nor easily achievable. Small Internal Releases and Proxy Customer are adequate if not ideal substitutes, even though they do not generate 'customer buy-in'.

6 Conclusion

Organisational cultures enable or prevent adoption of Full XP. Given the variation in organisational cultures, it seems impossible that any single methodological solution could be universally applicable. Experience shows that XP is most often used as a tool kit of practices, all of which offer value, some of which depend on other practices and some of which are politically difficult to adopt. This paper has identified a subset of the XP practices that excludes as many as possible of the difficult-to-adopt practices while still remaining viable. This 'XP Lite' is suggested as a reasonable starting point for many organisations.

References

Beck, Kent (2000), *Extreme Programming Explained*, Reading, Mass.: Addison-Wesley.

Cockburn, Alistair (2002), *Agile Software Development*, Agile Software Development Series, Boston: Addison-Wesley.

Greening, James (2001), „Launching Extreme Programming at a Process Intensive Company", IEEE Software, November/December, pp. 27-33.

Highsmith, Jim (2002), *Agile Software Development Ecosystems*, Agile Software Development Series, Boston: Addison-Wesley.

Johansen, Kay, Stauffer Ron and Turner Dan (2002), „Learning by Doing: Why XP Doesn't Sell", in M. Marchesi et al. (eds), *Extreme Programming Perspectives*, pp. 411-419.

Johnson, Ralph (2000), „Developing the Refactoring Browser", in G. Succi and M. Marchesi (eds), *Extreme Programming Examined*, Boston: Addison-Wesley, p. 323-331.

Johnson, Sue (2002), „Talk Isn't Cheap", in K. Auer and R. Miller, *Extreme Programming Applied*, Boston: Addison-Wesley, pp. 303-4.

Kini, Natraj and Collins, Steve (2003), „Lessons Learned from an XP Project", in Marchesi et al. (eds), *Extreme Programming Perspectives*, Boston: Addison-Wesley, pp. 363-373.

Lippert, Martin, Roock, Stefan and Hening Wolf (2002), *Extreme Programming in Action: Practical Experiences from Real World Projects*, Chichester: John Wiley & Sons.

McBreen, Pete (2003), *Questioning Extreme Programming*, XP Series, Boston: Addison-Wesley.

Moore, Robert (2001), „Evolving to a Lighter Methodology: A Case Study", pdf available online at sel.gsfc.nasa.gov/website/sew/2001/Session2R.Moore.pdf

Poole, Charles and Huisman, Jan (2003), „Extreme Maintenance" in M. Marchesi et al. (eds), *Extreme Programming Perspectives*, Boston: Addison-Wesley, pp. 215-234.

Schuh, Peter (2001), „Recovery, Redemption and Extreme Programming", *IEEE Software*, November/December, pp. 34-41.

Wells, Don and Buckley, Trish (2001), „The VCAPS Project: An Example of Transitioning to XP" in G. Succi and M. Marchesi (eds), *Extreme Programming Examined*, Boston: Addison-Wesley, pp. 399-421.

Yourdon, Edward (1997), *Death March*, Upper Saddle River: Prentice Hall.

White, Richard (2002), „Odyssey", Unpublished Thesis, University of Technology, Sydney.

Agile Specification-Driven Development

Jonathan S. Ostroff[1], David Makalsky[1], and Richard F. Paige[2]

[1] Department of Computer Science, York University, Canada.
{jonathan, dm}@cs.yorku.ca
[2] Department of Computer Science, University of York, UK
paige@cs.york.ac.uk

Abstract. We present an agile approach to Specification-Driven Development, which combines features of Test-Driven Development and the plan-based approach of Design-by-Contract. We argue that both tests and contracts are different types of specifications, and both are useful and complementary for building high quality software. We conclude that it is useful for being able to switch between writing tests and writing contracts, and explain how Specification-Driven Development supports this capability.

1 Introduction

Traditional software development methods stress the elicitation and documentation of a "complete" set of requirements, followed by architectural and high-level design, coding, inspection and testing. This general approach is sometimes described as *plan-driven development*. Agile methods were a reaction to these traditional "documentation driven, heavyweight software development processes" [2], focusing on an iterative design process with rapid feedback in which code appears early [15].

In this paper, we describe an integrated approach, Specification-Driven Development (SDD), which combines the best features of the agile Test-Driven Development (TDD) methodology with the best features of the plan-driven approach of quality-first Design-by-Contract (DbC) [11]. The emphasis in TDD is the production of *executable tests* that act as restricted emergent specifications of collaborative behaviour. DbC emphasises a concept of *contract*, which can be represented using constructs such as preconditions, postconditions, and class invariants for explicitly specifying expected behaviour. At first glance, TDD and DbC conflict, or, as one authority put it:

> If it's a matter of gut feeling, then mine is that the two approaches, test first and Design by Contract, are the absolute extreme opposites with no combination possible or desirable. It's nice once in a while to see a real irreconcilable opposition [13].

We attempt to show that not only are TDD and DbC compatible, but that each can enhance the other. In SDD, both unit tests and contracts are specifications, and there are advantages to using each type of specification in producing reliable systems. TDD is superior for capturing complex emergent behaviour (e.g., trace behaviour) that cannot easily be expressed statically with contracts; DbC is superior for completely specifying

J. Eckstein and H. Baumeister (Eds.): XP 2004, LNCS 3092, pp. 104–112, 2004.

behaviour. The two approaches are compatible: both TDD and DbC are iterative and are based on the view that it is important to produce working code as soon as possible.

We make our arguments in the context of the Eiffel language which has DbC built-in. But, DbC works in other languages such as Java as well [7].

2   Plan-Driven Development

The conventional, systematic plan-driven approach to software development is inherited from systems engineering. Plan-driven development approaches, such as DbC, stress the elicitation and documentation of a complete set of requirements, followed by architectural and high-level design. Code and tests often appear at the tail end of the process. The gap between requirements and code is thus bridged by *specifications*, which describe constraints on behaviour shared between the physical world and the system. Iterations between writing specifications and coding are often encouraged. Incremental approaches to plan-driven development have been adopted, but all still emphasise documentation and traceability between requirements, specification, and code.

Plans can be written in a variety of ways, including structured natural language, UML class and sequence diagrams, and formal methods. There is an associated cost with applying mathematical techniques; in general, it is much more than testing with the benefit of obtaining higher quality [3]. The economic reality is that for most software development, testing and inspections trump formal specifications.

In plan-driven approaches, complete documentation brings with it two main problems. First, there is the problem of keeping the documentation consistent with changes in the design and code. And second, there is the sheer volume of documentation that must be produced. Analysts must document the requirements, designers must create the design specifications, and programmers must document their code. At each stage, additional detail must be added as we do not know who will be reading the documentation; it may therefore be safer to err on the side of caution.

2.1   Design by Contract

DbC is a form of plan-driven development that naturally lends itself to agile development because of the way in which its documentation is expressed. It also has almost all the benefits of mathematical methods – and these are formidable for emphasising software quality first – without the associated cost. Contracts on software are written using preconditions, postconditions and class invariants, providing mathematical specifications. These contracts are written in the assertion language of the programming language itself, and are therefore *executable*; contracts are thus a form of the best kind of documentation, that which executes with the code, and which is always guaranteed to be consistent with the code (otherwise an assertion violation would arise at run-time).

Suppose we need to calculate the square root of a real number to four decimal places. Fig. 1 provides an example illustrating how this might be done using contracts.

There are many benefits to using contracts to document software: contracts are checked every time the code is executed (and violations are immediately flagged); components are self-documenting because the contracts are part the documentation (and

```
class MATH feature
  square_root(x: DOUBLE): DOUBLE is
    require x>=0
    do  -- your algorithm goes here, e.g., Newton's method
    ensure
      (Result*Result - x).abs <= epsilon;
      epsilon = old epsilon
    end
  epsilon: DOUBLE  -- accuracy
invariant
  0 < epsilon and epsilon <= 0.001
end -- MATH
```

Fig. 1. Example of a contract for class *MATH*

inconsistency between code and contracts is impossible). And The benefits of using contracts to document software are as follows: contracts provide design rules for maintaining and modifying the behaviour of components, cf., behavioural subtyping, and a basis for formal verification.

In [11] Meyer describes the "quality-first" DbC design method. Meyer implements quality-first DbC using Eiffel and the BON visual modelling language, both of which support contracts, and for which integrated tool support exists. A brief summary of quality-first DbC in BON/Eiffel follows.

1. Write Eiffel code or produce BON diagrams as soon as possible, because then supporting tools immediately do syntax, type, and consistency checking.
2. Get the current unit of functionality working before starting the next. Deal with abnormal cases, e.g., violated preconditions, right away.
3. Intertwine analysis, design, and implementation.
4. Always have a working system.
5. Get cosmetics and style right.

DbC can be seen as an instance of plan-driven development, but unlike some approaches it does not suffer from the "big design up front" problem, in part because the plans in DbC are validated code. There are two vague steps in the quality-first DbC approach: (a) in step (2) we must get the current unit of functionality working, but how do we progress from informal requirements to a contract or a BON diagram? (b) in step (4) we are told to constantly compile, execute, and test the system but how the testing is to be performed is not explained. These two problems can at least partially be alleviated with the use of TDD techniques.

3   Test-Driven Development

Test Driven Development (TDD) is one of the popular evolving agile methods [1]; it emphasises testing first as a replacement for up-front design. Like all agile methods,

TDD stresses the development of working code over documentation, models and plans. The TDD cycle proceeds as follows: (1) write the test first (without worrying if it does not compile); (2) write enough code to make the test pass; (3) *refactor* the code to eliminate redundancies and other design flaws introduced by making the test pass.

A striking aspects of this approach is the idea that the code that is implemented may not be behaviorally correct: it just has to pass the test. Correctness means passing all the tests. The test is therefore the specification. Another striking aspect is refactoring as a replacement for up-front design (sometimes pejoratively called a "big up front design") [5]. Testing, with tool support, occurs all the time: before and after refactoring, and whenever new functionality is implemented.

Tests are a form of specification, typically (though not exclusively) dealing with normal and expected behaviour. Tests do not provide precise documentation of class interfaces. Thus, they are useful in capturing traces of valid behaviour for scenarios of the system, but may miss the big picture, i.e., the architecture and component views. Thus tests cannot be described as complete requirements. Tests encompass both unit and regression tests, and also what we call *collaborative tests*. These latter tests are related to UML sequence and collaboration diagrams in that they show the messages (method calls) sent between a number of specific objects within a use case. A good example of a collaborative test is shown below, in Fig. 2, for a simple banking system. An account is initialised and withdrawal is made, with the expected result of the account checked for correctness.

```
test_teller_withdrawal_request: BOOLEAN is
  local a: ACCOUNT; t:TELLER_TRANSACTION
  do
    -- initial balance $900 in John's account
    create a.make("John Doe",900)
    check a.balance=900 end
    create t

    -- test scenario
    t.request(a,500)
    t.withdrawal_request
    result := a.balance=400 and t.succeeded
  end
```

Fig. 2. Collaborative test for banking system

The benefits of TDD are many. For one, the cost of verification is spread across the development process. The TDD process also provides low-level information about test failures, on the operation or even statement level, thus making debugging easier. Experience has shown that designs driven by tests tend to exhibit high cohesion and loose coupling, perhaps possibly due to the frequent refactoring and the requirement to keep the design as simple as possible. TDD also allows predictive specification of what code will do, independent of the existence of the code itself. Finally, the tests produced using TDD provide documentation of the design and the design process. The latter, in particular, will be essential for any requisite auditing and review.

The limitations of TDD come in part from the incompleteness of tests: requirements cannot be completely captured by tests in general without enumerating all scenarios. Further, tests cannot deal with phenomena that are in the environment of the system, whereas contracts can express constraints on such constructs.

3.1 Collaborative vs. Contractual Specifications

Test-based unit and collaborative specifications are incomplete, because they consider only specific scenarios. Consider the following unit test, written in Eiffel.

```
test_integers_sorted:BOOLEAN is
    local sa1,sa2: SORTABLE_ARRAY[INTEGER]
    do
        sa1 :=  <<4, 1, 3>>; sa2 := <<1,3,4>>;
        sa1.sort;
        Result := equal(sa1, sa2)
    end
```

in which we create an unsorted array sa1, execute routine sort, and then assert that the array is equal to the expected sorted array sa2. The unit test does three things for us. The test is a precise specification of a unit of functionality (the sort function in the special case of array <<4, 1, 3 >>). The test also drives the design. It induces the public interface of class $SORTABLE\_ARRAY$ with features such as sort. However,

- The unit test specifies that array <<4, 1, 3>> must be sorted. But what about tests for all the other (possibly infinite) arrays of integers?
- The unit test does not test arrays of REAL, or arrays of PERSON (say by age). After all, the class SORTABLE_ARRAY[G] has a generic parameter G.
- It is hard to describe preconditions with unit tests. For example, we might want the sort routine to work only in case there is at least one non-void element in the array. (We could make the sort routine have no precondition, but that would then force us to always program defensively [10, p344].)

By contrast, the contractual specification in Fig. 3 is a precise and detailed specification of the sorted array. The quantifiers can be expressed using Eiffel's agent notation.

The generic parameter G of class SORTABLE_ARRAY is constrained to inherit from COMPARABLE. This allows us to compare any two elements in the array, e.g., the expresion item(i) <= item(i+1) is legal whether the array holds instances of integers or poeple, provided the instances are from classes that inherit from COMPARABLE.

Routine sort is specified via preconditions and postconditions. The preconditions state that there must be at least one non-void element to sort. The unit test did not specify this, nor is it generally easy for unit tests to specify preconditions. The postcondition states that the array must be sorted and is unchanged. This postcondition specifies this property for all possible arrays, holding elements of any type. Again, only an infinite number of unit tests could capture this property.

```
class       SORTABLE_ARRAY [G − > COMPARABLE]  inherit  ARRAY[G]
feature       sort is
          require
              count_positive: count > 0
              elements_not_void: ∀ i | lower ≤ i ≤ upper • item(i) ≠ Void
          do
              ...
          ensure
              sorted: ∀ i | lower ≤ i ≤ upper • item(i) ≤ item(i + 1)
              count_unchanged: count = old count
          end
end
```

Fig. 3. Class SORTABLE_ARRAY

Since contracts and tests are both specifications (the contract being more general), they can both serve to drive development of the code.

Unit tests can be used to automatically check that the code satisfies its specification – just run the tests. Can code be checked against the contracts? One approach would be program verification which provides strong assurance but requires qualitatively more time and effort than testing. The simpler approach is to turn assertion checking on in the programming language. But, unit tests will now be required to execute the code so that contracts can be checked. However, there is a *test amplification* effect, which we discuss in the next section.

While contractual specifications are detailed and complete, they have disadvantages. Consider a class $STACK[G]$ with routines given by $push(x : G)$ and pop. While contracts can fully specify the effects of $push$ and pop individually, they cannot directly describe the last-in-first-out (LIFO) property of stacks which asserts that

$$\forall s : STACK, x : G \bullet pop(push(x, s)) = s$$

By contrast, the LIFO behaviour can easily be captured using test-based collaborative specifications.

4   Specification-Driven Development

Clearly there are benefits to plan-driven development based on DbC, and test-driven development. Choosing between the value offered by the approaches will equally clearly depend on the project at hand. There are surprising commonalities between TDD and DbC, particularly: both contracts and tests are specifications; both TDD and DbC seek to transform requirements to compilable constructs as soon as possible; both TDD and DbC are lightweight verification methods; both methods are incremental; and both emphasise quality first in terms of units of functionality. We claim that it is not necessary to choose between the two approaches *a priori*, and that there are substantial benefits to using TDD and DbC together in a project.

Specification-Driven Development (SDD) provides the ability to use TDD and DbC techniques in the same development. It assumes (a) the availability of a contract-aware programming language (e.g., Eiffel, or Java with a suitable pre-processor), and (b) a suitable testing framework (e.g., JUnit or ETester). The statechart of Fig. 4 describes the approach. It does not dictate where to start – it is the developer's choice whether to start with TDD or DbC based on project context. However, the emphasis is always on transforming customer requirements into compilable and executable code.

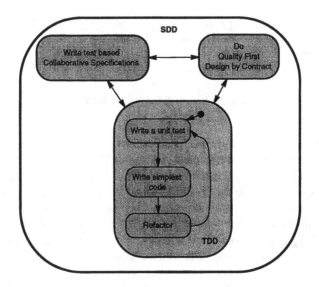

Fig. 4. SDD: Specification-Driven Development

SDD provides more than TDD or DbC individually, as it eliminates some of the limitations with each approach. But SDD is more than the sum of TDD and DbC, as there are synergies between the approaches. In particular, contracts act as *test amplifiers*. When writing a contract, it is easy to make mistakes, or write a contract that is simply too weak and which underconstrains the system. Some of these flaws will be caught by executing the system; but this is not sufficient in general. Writing tests to exercise the contracts (i.e., which validate and invalidate each pre- and postcondition) can help validate the tests, and can also help drive the production of tests.

4.1 Some Observations

SDD can start with writing tests (as illustrated by the left-most state in the statechart), or with writing contracts. However, there are two reasons to prefer writing unit tests before contracts:

Closure: A unit test provides a precise description of a unit of functionality and hence also a clear stopping point – you write just enough clean code to get the test to pass. Contracts do not provide clear stopping points for units of functionality in quite the same way, thus allowing for the possibility of unnecessary design.

Collaborative specification friendly: tests can formalize instances of collaborative specifications more easily than contracts, as illustrated by the last-in-first-out property of stacks.

Contracts, of course, can provide precise documentation of the complete behaviour of code in a way that tests cannot (as illustrated in Fig. 3). Contracts also provide preconditions; tests cannot document or check for preconditions. Finally, contracts can supply a qualitative level of assurance for code beyond that of testing in the case of program verification, and can act as an automatic test amplifier in the case that assertion checking is turned on.

In summary:

1. Contracts are good for fleshing out the design while making underlying assumptions explicit.
2. Contracts spell out the logical assumptions underlying a design more completely and concisely than unit tests.
3. Tests are good for writing collaborative specifications; as such, they are likely to be more appropriate early in the development process when scenarios are being refined to executable constructs. Contracts are good for constraining the design to meet the requirements.

Table 1. SDD synergies – $SDD > max(TDD, DbC)$

TDD lacks:	Quality First DbC has:
Good Design Documentation	✓ Self-Documenting Design (automated using seamless and reversible BON)
Detailed interface specifications of normal and abnormal behaviours	✓ Contracts and contractual specifications
TDD has:	**Quality First DbC lacks:**
✓ Collaborative specifications	Units of functionality for Quality First
✓ Automated Tests (JUnit/ETester)	Systematic regression tools for exercising contracts
Synergies:	
✓ Contracts are test amplifiers	
✓ Contractual and collaborative specifications provide lightweight verification of the design	

5   Conclusions

We have investigated the compatibility and complementarity of TDD and DbC, in producing a new agile approach called Specification-Driven Development. Our conclusion is that TDD and DbC are complementary technologies and can be used synergistically, but also to supplement limitations: contracts make design decisions explicit that may only be implicit in tests; and tests can better capture requirements (such as the LIFO property on stacks) than contracts.

We are providing tool support for the Eiffel language that allows TDD and DbC to be used together. This support comes via the ETester framework, documented elsewhere

[8]. ETester is specifically designed to make it easy to write unit tests and tests involving contracts. Additional work on an Eiffel plug-in for Eclipse will also make use of ETester.

Our work has similarities to that of Feldman [4]; his work focused particularly on the relationship between contracts and refactoring, whereas we have focused on the assistance that contracts provide to the TDD process. Feldman in particular makes the point that using contracts can reduce the amount of tests that need to be written because contracts cover the correctness of methods. We disagree on this point as tests must still be written to exercise the contracts, and to particularly deal with contracts that underspecify behaviour. However, we do agree with Feldman's findings that contracts work synergistically with refactoring.

Table 1 summarises our conclusions.

References

1. Beck, K. *Test-driven Development: by example*, Addison-Wesley, 2003.
2. Beck, K., A. Cockburn, R. Jeffries, and J. Highsmith. Agile Manifesto www.agilemanifesto.org/history.html. 2001.
3. Berry, D.M. Formal methods: the very idea — Some thoughts about why they work when they work. *Science of Computer Programming*, 42(1): p11–27, 2002.
4. Feldman, Y. Extreme Design by Contract. In *Proc. XP 2003*, LNCS, Springer-Verlag, 2003.
5. Fowler, M. and K. Beck. *Refactoring*, Addison-Wesley, 1999.
6. Gamma, E. and K. Beck. JUnit: A cook's tour. Java Report, p27-38, 1999.
7. Leavens, G.T., K.R.M. Leino, E. Poll, C. Ruby, and B. Jacobs. JML: notations and tools supporting detailed design in Java. In *OOPSLA 2000 Companion*, ACM, 2000.
8. Makalsky, D. ETester Unit Testing Framework. Available at www.cs.yorku.ca/eiffel/etester, 2004.
9. Martin, R.C. *Agile software development*, Pearson Education, 2003.
10. Meyer, B. *Object-Oriented Software Construction*. Prentice Hall, 1997.
11. Meyer, B. Practice to Perfect: the Quality-First Model. *IEEE Computer* 30(5), 1997.
12. Meyer, B. Towards practical proofs of class correctness. In *Proc. ZB 2003*, Springer-Verlag, LNCS 2651, p359-387, 2003.
13. Meyer, B. Personal communication, June 2003.
14. Paige, R. and J.S. Ostroff. The Single Model Principle. *Journal of Object Oriented Technology*, 1(5): 2002.
15. Williams, L. and A. Cockburn. Agile Software Development: It's about Feedback. *Computer*, 36(6): p39-43, 2003.

Towards a Proper Integration of Large Refactorings in Agile Software Development

Martin Lippert

University of Hamburg, Software Engineering Group & it-wps GmbH
Vogt-Kölln-Straße 30
22527 Hamburg, Germany
lippert@acm.org

Abstract. Refactoring is a key element of many agile software development methods. While most developers associate small design changes with the term refactoring (as described by Martin Fowler and William F. Opdyke), everyday development practice in medium- to large-sized projects calls for more than fine-grained refactorings. Such projects involve more complex refactorings, running for several hours or days and sometimes consisting of a huge number of steps. This paper discusses the problems posed by large refactorings and presents an approach that allows agile teams to integrate large refactorings into their daily work.

1 Introduction

Refactoring is part of everyday programming practice in agile software development[1]. The use of small-scale refactorings such as *Rename Method* or *Extract Interface* is well understood (see [6], [12]), many of them now being directly supported and automated by an Integrated Development Environment (IDE).

Of greater complexity are refactorings that introduce or remove pattern-like structures into a software system. The Refactoring to Patterns catalogue by Joshua Kerievsky provides an overview and handbook for some of the GoF patterns in [9]. Alur, Crupi and Malks describe J2EE-oriented pattern refactorings in [4]. Initial prototypes for automating these refactorings using specialized tools have appeared within the research community (see [3, 16]).

This paper focuses on refactorings that go beyond these small or pattern-based refactorings. In medium- to large-scale projects, we sometimes have refactorings that cannot be realized by means of a few renames, etc. For example, a refactoring that restructures the central inheritance hierarchy of a non-small system might affect several hundred or several thousand references to these classes. Such a refactoring could easily take several days or weeks, maybe even months to complete.

---

[1] This paper focuses on agile software development. Refactoring may also be part of any other development method.

J. Eckstein and H. Baumeister (Eds.): XP 2004, LNCS 3092, pp. 113–122, 2004.

While the scope and complexity of these refactorings is highly diverse, the term "large refactoring" has different connotations to different people. We therefore define some basic terminology before going on to introduce large refactorings and discuss them in more detail.

1.1 Integration Steps

An important concept in agile software development projects, especially when using Extreme Programming (see [1], [11]), is the idea of continuous integration. This means that changes and improvements to the system are realized in small steps. This paper subsumes all the changes made by one programmer (or pair of programmers) between two integrations under the term *Integration Step*.

Integration steps are not allowed to take more than one day each, the guideline for many agile development methods being to integrate by the end of the day (or throw the code away). Their duration thus ranges from minutes to hours. Each integration step must result in a properly running system and is integrated into the team's common code base.

Consequently, every task, requirement, feature or user story must be realized by proceeding in integration steps. Everything has to be done within this framework.

1.2 Small Refactorings

Many refactorings described in [6] can be realized within a single integration step. Such refactorings are called *Small Refactorings* in this paper. Examples are *Rename Class* (with a proper IDE) or *Extract Method*.

2 Large Refactorings

Some design changes and improvements cannot be realized completely within a single integration step[2]. Kent Beck and Martin Fowler describe this in their chapter on *Big Refactorings* in [6]. To fit these refactorings into the general concept of integration steps, they have to be split into smaller chunks. This is already a common task for user stories within Extreme Programming. The same is necessary for big refactorings to enable them to be handled within an agile development project[3].

It is quite difficult to decide why and when refactoring is big rather than small. Basing this purely on the number of changes to the system seems inappropriate. Mod-

---

[2] The reasons why these larger design changes occur even in the presence of merciless refactorings are not analyzed in detail in this paper.

[3] We do not discuss the possibility of realizing large refactorings in a separate branch of the system because the paper's focus is on integrating large refactorings into everyday development practice.

ern IDEs offer automated refactoring support allowing several hundred places in the code to be changed in a few seconds. While the impact on the team is most significant in a big refactoring, it is becoming more and more apparent that big refactorings are best characterized by the time the team takes to complete them. The term *Large Refactoring* is thus defined to reflect this.

Definition:
Large Refactorings are refactorings that cannot be realized within a single integration step.

This definition of large refactorings includes refactorings that span only two or three days. It might be an exaggeration to call them "large" refactorings. The real focus of this paper is on refactorings that take weeks or months rather than a few days to complete. Nevertheless, many of the problems we have observed with three-month refactorings (see below) also occur with refactorings that span only a few days – only on a much smaller scale. Thus ideas on how to deal with these problems are just as applicable to two- or three-day as they are to three-month refactorings. Of course, the proposed approach becomes more important, the more time the refactoring takes.

2.1 Why Are Large Refactorings More Problematic than Small Ones?

Large refactorings differ from small ones not only in terms of their size or the time they take. Beck and Fowler emphasize in [6], for their big refactorings, that it is of crucial importance that all members of the team are aware of the big refactoring, that they know where it is going and how it affects their daily work. This is important because large refactorings have to be split into a number of steps (as discussed above). Each step of the large refactoring is realized and integrated into the common source-code repository of the system.

Fig. 1. A large refactoring split into small steps. Each R describes a refactoring step. Time runs from left to right.

If integrated into the general development process, this is done parallel to other developers of the team working on the system. The complete integration flow of the team may look like this:

Fig. 2. A complete integration flow. The steps for the large refactoring and the normal development (D) are interlocked.

This situation can cause a number of difficulties, especially if the large refactoring is complicated and runs for several weeks or months. Frequently observed problems are:

- **Interim states of large refactorings:** Interim states of large refactorings become visible to the team. This means that all developers may be confronted with changes made to the common code base as a result of the large refactoring. In this case, the system typically contains code parts that follow the new structure as well as code parts that are not yet adapted to it. By-passes in the code are often used to make this possible. Such situations – dealing with new and old parts of the code's structure – can confuse developers who are not familiar with the details of the refactoring. In addition, it is hard for the developers to keep track of all the by-passes and different code states.

- **Teams get lost:** Sometimes teams get lost in large refactorings. This often happens because the team has to implement a large number of changes over a lengthy period of time. After several weeks of doing the refactoring alongside the daily feature development, and faced with hundreds of changes, a huge number of deprecated methods and different parts of the system following different designs, individual team developers may get confused. Sometimes they even end up forgetting the main goal of the refactoring, resulting in an unfinished refactoring.

- **Unfinished refactorings:** One risk with large refactorings is that they never get finished. Developers simply forget to finish the refactoring completely, perhaps because major parts of the refactoring are finished or other things distract them. This mostly results in code-structure flaws. Parts of the system conform to the new structure, while other parts follow the old one. This situation can even result in a code structure that is, overall, worse than before the refactoring.

- **More complex planning:** A large refactoring is much more difficult to plan and predict than small refactorings. While a team is doing a large refactoring, the rest of the system changes, too. Team members implement new features or do small refactorings at the same time that other team members are working on the large refactoring. Changes to the system can have an impact on future large-refactoring steps.

Another important planning issue with large refactorings is that they need to be integrated somehow into the release and/or iteration planning. This is necessary to reserve development time for the refactoring and to concentrate the work on such bigger design changes.

2.2 Consequences

Faced with the challenge of more complex design changes, many projects opt for one of the following alternatives:

- They avoid more complex changes to the structure and make do with a bad system design.

- They stop normal system development to concentrate exclusively on the large refactoring.

Since both alternatives appear unsuitable in agile software development, this paper analyzes in more detail the issues surrounding large refactorings. The goal is to work out a way of dealing with large refactorings so as to make them manageable in the daily development practice of agile projects.

3 Explicit Refactoring Routes

As described earlier, a large refactoring has to be split into a number of smaller steps. These steps are not chosen randomly. They describe a route from the current to the desired design. This route is called a *Refactoring Route*. Its key features are:

- A refactoring route subsumes a number of steps that lead from the current to the desired design.
- Each step should be realizable within one or more integration steps.

Following the definition of integration step (see Section 1.1), this means that a large refactoring has to be split into a number of steps, where

- each step results in a running system
- each step can be realized in a maximum of one day

This relates directly to the mechanics sections for each refactoring in [6], especially for big refactorings. But such sections are written generically, e.g.: "Decide which job is more important and is to be retained in the current hierarchy and which is to be moved to another hierarchy" from the *Tease Apart Inheritance* refactoring ([6], pp. 362ff). With a concrete large refactoring, the refactoring route could be described in a much more concrete and meaningful way for the team using the concrete class names and concrete concerns of the system.

In Extreme Programming projects, the individual steps for a large refactoring can be written on separate task cards – enhanced by an overall card describing the large refactoring as a whole. But experience with large refactorings has shown that this is often not enough. The above-mentioned problems still remain.

3.1 A Refactoring Plan

This paper proposes enhancing refactoring mechanics and tasks cards for large re-factorings. Key to this is the concept of an explicit refactoring route written in the form of a *Refactoring Plan*.

A refactoring plan consists of a sequence of *Refactoring Steps*. A refactoring step is of the same scope as one or multiple integration steps. An example of a refactoring step is: "Analyze all usages of class A and shift them to usages of class B, where possible". Depending on the size of the project, a refactoring step may have to be split into multiple integration steps or can be done within a single integration step.

The entries of a refactoring plan reflect the concrete system and the route that makes sense for the large refactoring in the concrete situation. The team thus arranges the refactoring steps in the order in which they are to be realized.

To track the progress of the large refactoring, each step of a refactoring plan can be marked as finished, work-in-progress or open. The steps of a refactoring plan can be rearranged, deleted or adapted, if necessary[4].

3.2   Refactoring Plans in Practice

Refactoring plans serve two different purposes. On the one hand, the team can use refactoring plans to discuss, rethink or replan large refactorings. They are thus vital elements in the development process. On the other, they allow developers to keep an eye on the refactoring while developing new features, thus serving as a map and a reminder.

Typically, a refactoring plan for a concrete large refactoring is drawn up by the team while discussing what refactoring needs to be done. The plan is initially sketched out on a sheet of flipchart paper and pinned on the wall to make it visible to the whole team.

When the team is working on the refactoring, they usually pick the next open step from the refactoring plan and mark that step as work-in-progress on the paper. Once they finish the refactoring step, they mark it as finished.

It sometimes happens that the steps in the refactoring plan have to be replaced or rearranged. In this case, the team or pair doing the refactoring discuss the changes. As a result, a changed refactoring plan is communicated to the team in the same way the old refactoring plan was.

3.3   Forms of Refactoring Plans

Refactoring plans can take different forms and be at different stages of expansion. Three possible variants are:
- **The Manual Refactoring Plan:** One way of dealing with explicit refactoring plans is a simple, manual approach, using a handwritten plan on a flipchart or whiteboard visible to all members of the team. This is the simplest form of explicit refactoring plan, and one that has been successfully used by us in a project context.
- **The Electronic Refactoring Plan:** Greater potential for team support is offered by an electronic version of a refactoring plan that is part of the project source base. A simple and suitable tool can help to integrate refactoring plans

---

[4] Examples of refactoring plans can be found at [10].

into the IDE to make them directly and easily visible to all project members (e.g. via specialized views in the Eclipse Java Tooling, see [5]). The electronic version makes it easy to modify the plan and facilitates teamwork across different locations (a handwritten plan being more suitable for a single location). We have also used a wiki page to sketch out and track a refactoring plan. The downside of electronic refactoring plans is that they do not attract the same attention as a big poster-size plan on the wall.

- **Vision – the Connected Refactoring Plan:** In addition, electronic refactoring plans could be connected to the source code to allow navigation from finished refactoring steps to changed parts of the source code and vice versa. This is useful to find information on large refactorings, together with the changes they have introduced into the code. Developers can easily find out whether the large refactoring has affected the code they are going to work on.

- **Vision – the Refactoring Map:** To make it easier for developers to check whether their work is affected by a running large refactoring, the idea of a *Refactoring Map* emerged. A refactoring map displays the complete system in a map-like form. The parts of the system affected by changes due to the refactoring are marked (e.g. in a particular color). The developer can use the map to see at a glance if the large refactoring comes close to the part of the system he is working on.

3.4 Implications of Refactoring Plans

Refactoring plans can change the way developers deal with large refactorings in agile development projects. The anticipated benefits from using refactoring plans include:

- All developers of a team are aware of ongoing large refactorings and can observe the progress.
- Developers can easily see which large refactorings are not yet finished. This prevents the team from forgetting unfinished large refactorings.
- The team can track the progress of a refactoring. This can help to plan the refactoring effort required in current and future iterations.
- The risk of getting lost within a large refactoring is reduced by the refactoring plan. Developers can watch the plan while immersing themselves in the refactoring. They can check whether the current activity really yields a benefit for the overall refactoring or not.
- Developers can recognize changes and by-passes within the code that are introduced as part of a large refactoring (using the electronic version of a refactoring plan).

3.5 Consequences for Project Planning

The discussion of large refactorings reveals that agile development projects need to pay explicit attention to large refactoring tasks. While small refactorings are part of everyday programming practice – and thus not a separate project-planning issue – large refactorings need to be taken into account in the planning process. They must be scheduled somehow during iteration and release planning as they could easily take up a large part of an iteration's development time.

4 Related Work

In [13], Don Roberts and John Brant describe a tool designed to support mass changes to source code automatically. Basically, they took the source-code transformation engine of their Smalltalk Refactoring Browser (see [2]) and used it to automatically modify Smalltalk source code following a user-written script-like list of rules. This rule script is used by the transformation engine to modify the source code.

Unlike us, Roberts and Brant adopt an "all-at-once" approach, in which a large refactoring is basically prototyped using their rule engine. If the complete path through the refactoring is found, they execute the rule-based script for the refactoring in one step. Their approach completely ignores the communication issues of an agile team. The team's developers have to live with situations in which many lines of code change from one day to the next. In addition, the approach of working on a fixed version of the system to do the refactoring (or writing the rewriting rules) involves similar risks to doing the refactoring in a separate branch (merging, major changes to the head version, etc.). Another drawback of their approach is that writing rules on top of parse trees can be quite complicated for developers not used to thinking in terms of parse trees (see [13]).

Nevertheless, using a rewrite engine like the one they propose to realize parts of large refactorings is a conceivable solution. It would be most powerful for refactoring steps with simple transformations but a high number of dependencies on these changes.

Tammo Freese has proposed a way of using *Inline Method* refactoring to facilitate API changes within an application (see [7]). His work demonstrates an elegant way to split API interface changes into smaller steps. This technique could be used to split large refactorings into smaller steps.

In [8], Tammo Freese describes an approach designed to facilitate what he calls global refactorings within agile development teams. The basic goal of his work, with regard to the topic of this paper, is to facilitate automatic refactorings that affect large parts of the system. He proposes a specialized version-management system that is aware of refactorings and is therefore able to merge refactoring results automatically. This approach could be quite useful for developers dealing with large refactorings. While this paper focuses on a different issue, namely how to integrate large refactorings into the daily work of an agile team, individual steps of a large refactoring could be supported by a refactoring-aware version-management system.

The concept of a refactoring plan is derived from the work on process patterns for situated action (see [14], [15]). The authors use process patterns to reify typical work processes in application domains. Their process patterns replace workflow systems with a more flexible way to describe common processes and deal with them individually. Unlike the process patterns, refactoring plans are written for a concrete refactoring only. They cannot be reused for similar refactorings and they do not serve as a template for multiple refactorings.

5 Conclusion

This paper introduces the notion of large refactorings and emphasizes that they are an important issue in today's agile software development methods. The main problems and characteristics of large refactorings are presented and briefly discussed. The paper focuses on the team issues posed when dealing with large refactorings, in contrast to a formal approach designed to somehow automate large refactorings. The focus, then, is on the problems faced by agile teams when dealing with large design changes.

The concept of explicit refactoring plans is presented, which are designed to integrate large refactorings into the daily programming work of an agile software development team. These plans combine the notions of situated process patterns and task planning to create a simple and easy-to-use concept. They aim to help teams manage large refactorings smoothly within an agile development project.

While electronic refactoring plans have yet to be implemented, initial experience with manual refactoring plans has been gained and shows promise. Nevertheless, what the paper presents is more a concept for supporting teams dealing with large refactorings than a proven solution. Further research is needed to verify the suitability of the presented approach in a larger number of projects.

Acknowledgments. My thanks go to Axel Schmolitzky, Holger Breitling and Marko Schulz for their comments on draft versions of this paper, and to the other members of the Software Engineering Group at the University of Hamburg for their comments and discussions on the topic in general. I would also like to thank Stefan Roock for his work and feedback on the topic.

I am particularly indebted to the following participants of the OT 2003 *Workshop on Large Refactorings*: Peter Marks, Erik Groeneveld, Peter Hammond, Alan Francis, Ray Farmer, Pascal Van Cauwenberghe, Peter Schrier, Marc Evers, Willem-Jan van den Ende and Matt Stephenson, as well as to the participants of the OOPSLA 2003 *Workshop on Beyond Greenfield Development*, especially to Kyle Brown for his feedback. My very special thanks go to Brian Barry for his comments and the idea of refactoring maps.

References

1. Beck, K.: *Extreme Programming Explained – Embrace Change*, Addison-Wesley (2001)
2. Brant, J., Roberts, D.: *Smalltalk Refactoring Browser*.
   http://st-www.cs.uiuc.edu/~brant/RefactoringBrowser.

3. Cinnéide, M. Ó.: *Automated Refactoring to Introduce Design Patterns*, Proceedings of the 22nd International Conference on Software Engineering, Limerick, Ireland (2000)

4. Crupi, J., Alur, D., Malks, D.: *Core J2EE Patterns: Best Practices and Design Strategies*, Prentice Hall PTR (2001)

5. Eclipse Project: http://www.eclipse.org

6. Fowler, M.: *Refactoring – Improving the Design of Existing Code*, Addison-Wesley (1999)

7. Freese, T.: *Inline Method Considered Helpful: An Approach to Interface Evolution*, in: Extreme Programming and Agile Processes in Software Engineering, Proceedings of the 4th International Conference XP 2003, Genova, Italy, LNCS 2675, Springer (2003), 271-278

8. Freese, T.: *Software Configuration Management for Test-Driven Development*, in: Extreme Programming and Agile Processes in Software Engineering, Proceedings of the 4th International Conference XP 2003, Genova, Italy, LNCS 2675, Springer (2003), 431-432

9. Kerievsky, J.: *Refactoring to Patterns*, Addison Wesley (2004)

10. Lippert, M.: *Refactoring-Plans – Examples and Experiences*, http://www.martinlippert.com

11. Lippert, M., Roock, S., Wolf, H.: Extreme Programming in Action – Experiences from Real-World Projects, Wiley & Sons (2002)

12. Opdyke, W. F.: *Refactoring Object-Oriented Frameworks*. PhD thesis, University of Illinois at Urbana-Champaign, Dept. of Computer Science (1992) Tech. Report UIUCDCS-R-92-1759.

13. Roberts, D., Brant, J.: *Tools for Making Impossible Changes*, to be published in IEE Proceedings-Software, Dec. (2003)

14. Suchman, L.: *Plans and Situated Actions. The Problem of Human-Machine Communication*. Cambridge University Press (1987)

15. Wulf, M., Gryczan, G., Züllighoven, H.: *Process Patterns - Supporting Cooperative Work in the Tools & Materials Approach*, Information Systems Research Seminar In Scandinavia: IRIS 19; proceedings, Lökeberg, Sweden, 10-13 August, 1996. Bo Dahlbom et al. (eds.). - Gothenburg: Studies in Informatics, Report 8 (1996), pp. 445 – 460

16. Zannier, C., Maurer, F.: *Tool Support for Complex Refactoring to Design Patterns*, in: Extreme Programming and Agile Processes in Software Engineering, Proceedings of the 4th International Conference XP 2003, Genova, Italy (2003), LNCS 2675, Springer (2003), 123-130

An Agile Approach to a Legacy System

Chris Stevenson[1] and Andy Pols[2]

[1] ThoughtWorks Technologies (India) Pvt Ltd.
Diamond District, Airport Road
Bangalore, India
CStevenson@thoughtworks.com
http://www.thoughtworks.com
[2] Pols Consulting,
5 Granary House, Hope Sufferance Wharf,
St Marychurch Street, London SE16 4JX, UK
andy@pols.co.uk
http://www.pols.co.uk

Abstract. We describe how a small, successful, self-selected XP team approached a seemingly intractable problem with panache, flair and immodesty. We rewrote a legacy application by delivering new features, a radically different approach to those previously applied. This proved to be a low cost, low risk proposition with a very high payoff for success. Most importantly it provided users with new functionality quickly that could never have been retrofitted into the legacy system. In the longer term it may give a migration strategy for replacing the legacy system.

1 Background

InkBlot is a large financial legacy application feeding dozens of other applications and supporting up to 100 in-house traders on a daily basis. The system was originally developed in the 1990s and the original team disbanded long ago. There are many external apps that talk directly to the database.

There are no clean external interfaces, which means that we have no idea who is connecting to the system and what they are doing in the system. In fact all external access uses the same well-known username and password.

Business logic is distributed across 1600+ stored procedures, some of which are 3000+ lines of SQL, and exist in multiple versions. Whenever a stored procedure was changed, a new version was added because no-one knew who was using the old version.

There are no primary or foreign keys on the 250+ tables, and triggers are used to maintain data 'integrity'. Code was not under source control and written in a mixture of 4GL, C, SQL and unix shell scripts.

2 Our Evolving Strategy

There had been several previous initiatives to improve the system. The most recent was an attempt to rewrite a key part of the system in a language that we

J. Eckstein and H. Baumeister (Eds.): XP 2004, LNCS 3092, pp. 123–129, 2004.

knew (Java) on the assumption that this would increase understanding of the system and make it more amenable to refactoring.

This strategy did not work.

With hindsight the reasons for this failure are clear: we were attempting to change the legacy application itself, therefore we were likely to break it before we fixed it. Also since we were rewriting what was already legacy code, we were by definition writing legacy code.

For example if (say) 75% of the code is unused or irrelevant (probably a lower bound in this legacy application) then working on that proportion of the code is wasted time. Even worse, since there are bugs in the legacy application that other parts of the system assume or work around, we would need to reproduce the bugs in our new code.

The refactoring effort was started as a spike, and morphed into a multi-month project - it should have been time-boxed to prevent this. Also note that this approach, even if it could have worked, was slow, demoralising and would have provided (again by definition) zero benefit to the business.

The drive for the original rewrite came from development management and developers not business and users. Management drive was to improve reliability of the system. This was incorrectly interpreted as a mandatory requirement to rewrite existing code. At one stage we were told specifically 'no business value work is allowed'.

When the rewrite failed we decided a new strategy was needed.

Therefore our rule of thumb is: Don't reproduce legacy code

Next, we got a good customer proxy[1] who was able to identify the key problem in the use of the system by front office staff. The system was being used as a reporting tool, using stored procedures that would run for up to 5 minutes before producing a result. This frustrated the users who ended up running the reports continually, adding to the load on the system.

When we asked the users what they wanted, they had very clear ideas about what was wrong. Of course none of them mentioned the part of the system we had been working on – to them it was invisible. If we had persisted on the original rewrite we would not have solved their problem. The area of the system we were focussed on was not even the one causing their problem.

Therefore our rule of thumb is: Always ask the users what the problem is

Deciding that our users knew better where they were hurting, our next approach was driven by user requirements. We wrote a greenfield application to extract data from the legacy application database and display it to users in a flexible and timely manner. An already successful team was given the task of

---

[1] Customer proxy: Someone from the development organisation acting as a proxy for the customer, when an onsite customer is not possible.

writing a quick one-week spike to prove that the required data could be extracted in real time. This gained the trust of our customer proxy and gave the team the confidence to continue.

This proved to be very easy and *'How difficult can it be'* became the team's motto.

Our approach was low risk in that we didn't change the legacy application, and so the potential cost of failure was small. However the payoff for success was extremely high. The new system obsoletes legacy application functionality incrementally while delivering regular new features to users.

The new system only extracts the key relevant data from the legacy application, ignoring the irrelevant code and database tables, and makes no changes in the legacy application. This means that the team gains an understanding of the important parts of the legacy system while ignoring those parts that do not matter.In fact we use only 10 of the 250+ tables in the legacy application.

Therefore our rule of thumb is: Refactor a legacy application by delivering new business value

3   How We Built the Team

We started the Greenfield application with a team of two people who had just successfully completed an unrelated project. They were bored and looking for something challenging to sink their teeth into. The legacy application team's credit bank was at zero, so there was no confidence in their ability to deliver using this new strategy. The new team believed in the new strategy and lobbied project management hard to get a chance to try it. The new team was given permission to start work unofficially to validate the approach.

The first story was to prove to our customer proxy that we could extract the data in real time, without impacting the performance of the legacy application. This proved to be easy, and basic functionality was implemented rapidly, leading to much more confidence in the approach. As time went on and our and confidence grew, we raised our heads above the parapet more and more, until we were able finally to demonstrate the app to our users. Up to that point all conversations with the users had been theoretical.

Therefore our rule of thumb is: Incrementally build trust - prove that you can do the hardest part of the system

After the initial spike[2], people around the team were infected by their enthusiasm, and lobbied to join the team. The team grew to 6 and then fought

---

[2] Spike: An experiment to explore a possible solution to an unfamiliar problem. So-called because a spike is "end to end, but very thin", like driving a spike all the way through a log.

hard to keep that size. This self-selection meant that the team had a unique ethos and passion. Since everyone wanted to be there the team was committed to the success, and members took collective responsibility for the success of the project.

Therefore our rule of thumb is: Build a small, self-selected team

Unlike some XP teams that we have seen, we did not allocate cards to specific programmer pairs. Instead the cards were placed on a whiteboard near the team, and we would take them when we had finished another story. Interestingly even the boring cards were picked up early, as the team's pride was at stake.

We initially planned to have one-week iterations, and most of the time that was fine. Occasionally a piece of work would come along that would block other avenues of development. When this happened we planned for a short 'blitz' to complete the work as soon as possible. This meant that some of our iterations turned out to be quite short - some as short as three days. We sometimes finished all of the work planned for an iteration early, and again in this case we would have an early planning meeting. We found that variable iterations worked well and helped us keep the development focused.

Therefore our rule of thumb is: Don't get hung up on process

We would regularly call each other on bad code or small mistakes. When the build broke, we would very quickly call out to the culprit. In fact we did not use automatic integration, because we were integrating ourselves about every 10-15 minutes, and would just shout out if the build had broken.

Team discussions were ego-less but opinionated, and we were all willing to be wrong. Discussions about the system were very robust, but once we had thrashed out a solution, the group would invest in the idea. Ideas were always owned by the group, not individuals.

Single pairs felt very uncomfortable with architectural refactorings that would affect a large proportion of the code base. So we would spend half an hour around a whiteboard to thrash out the details, and then the whole team would work on that refactoring only, until we could commit and move on to something else. Before the first release we refactored the back end architecture completely 4 times in this way, approximately once every couple of weeks. This meant that the architecture stayed flexible and easy to adapt.

Therefore our rule of thumb is: Involve the whole team with larger refactorings so the team can move on as quickly as possible

We built our own culture and rituals as the project progressed. For example every afternoon about 3pm we would disappear to the local coffee shop for a half hour. Discussions there were often (but not necessarily) about code problems, but the primary benefit was that it gave the team a known break point, so that we could maintain a higher pace. Some of our best work happened after these breaks, as the brainstorming and fresh air gave us more energy.

The team socialised together outside work hours as well. When we released we went to a local bar for rounds of Flaming Absinthe - a ritual that we occasionally regretted the next day.

Therefore our rule of thumb is: Effective teams need break points

4 Delivering

There were people who had no confidence in the team's ability to deliver. Others feared that failure would reflect on them, or the solution compromise the existing legacy application. We approached these antibodies in the same way we would approach a customer - teasing out their fears and requirements and building them into our process as carded activities. We anticipated these sorts of problems and brainstormed the expected antibodies and our response to their concerns. All members of the team were aware of politics surrounding the system and able to 'sing from a common hymn sheet'.

One particularly effective strategy was 'don't say no, say later'. We would take the fear on board (literally carding it and putting it on the whiteboard) for a later iteration, by which time we would have proved that it was no longer an issue, or the initial reason for the request had changed or been forgotten. Fears could then be prioritised in the same way as any other piece of work.

Therefore our rule of thumb is: Treat politics as a user requirement

Our initial increments were tested using static data loaded into a test database. We were able to simulate some of functionality of the legacy application. However, we did not appreciate the complexity of the real system's behaviour until we connected our system to the live database.

We could not rely on our unit tests and simulations because these only reproduced what we thought the legacy application did, not what was actually happening. In particular, some external systems that we did not know existed, were directly manipulating crucial tables in ways we were unaware of.

Within minutes of connecting to the live database we noticed inconsistencies and bugs that had been in our code for months. This meant that we had to rethink a large part of the back end of the system. We ran the system with live data for a month before delivery, and built tools to automatically compare the results of our system with those produced by the legacy application. These became our most important integration/user acceptance tests. We did have some of our own 'stress tests' but these were not used for functional testing of the system.

After our first release we no longer left the test system connected to live, and we lost a lot of our reliability. In fact our second release had to be rolled back as bugs were exposed within minutes of going live. Ironically the main piece of functionality of this release had been to allow us to record and play back the events generated by the live system, so that we could improve testing. We had relearned our lesson - and when we connected our test release to the live system again, we managed to do a successful release.

Therefore our rule of thumb is: A System that connects to a legacy system must be tested using live feeds.

Even though we had live data feeds to tease out business rule bugs, we still had gui bugs that eluded our unit tests. With hindsight we would like to find ways of introducing robust and flexible acceptance tests much more early in the process. Gui testing is still an open issue for us. We have been bitten by it on several occasions, but have yet to find an effective solution.

Three months into the project (around Iteration 12) we showed the system to key business users and asked them to try it for a while. The system had been running on live data for a month by this stage. The system was so popular that we had problems removing access to the system - when we released the final version, there were still 20 users running the original, some of whom we had not actually given it to. We had designed the system to automatically deploy new versions, so the upgrade was not painful.

We never told the users that they must use the new system. Nor did we remove access to the old system. We relied on making the system so compelling that there was no reason to use the old. This also meant that we stayed focused on the users real requirements.

Because we had actually been 'live' for a month, the first release was an anti-climax. The Project Manager of another team commented that he could not believe we were releasing that week - none of us were staying late and no one worked weekends. In fact our coffee breaks in the afternoons continued.

Therefore our rule of thumb is: Engage users and they not only won't they turn it off, they will fight some of your battles for you.

After delivery of the first release we suffered from a bout of 'post-delivery depression'. We concentrated on technical infrastructure problems and refactorings without adding any business value. The team became bored and unmotivated, and the team lost its spark.

Once we got back on business value, the team's demeanour lifted and we sparked again, but we had lost a couple of iterations. A dynamic team like this needs problems and challenges to remain motivated.

Therefore our rule of thumb is: Keep giving a good team motivated by giving them new hard problems - don't waste a good team

5   Reflection on the Experiences

The project has now been going for seven months. We gave some users a test version to try after two months. They continued to use this version for two months until we delivered the first official release four months into the project. We are about to deliver the fourth release.

We are still running the new system in parallel with the legacy system. We are currently adding major new functionality that is missing from the legacy application and has been an outstanding feature request for some time.

We are also working to enable the new system to operate independently from the legacy application, so that eventually we can switch off the legacy application.

Our project was initially kicked off as a strategic short-term fix. The organisation was planning a long-term project to replace the legacy system, for delivery in 'a couple of years'. Due to the success of our project, this rewrite has now been put on hold.

The team has been asked by other parts of the business to spike solutions to hard problems. This enhanced the motivation of the team.

Looking back on our experiences, we find that our "rules of thumb" paid off well on this project, and we intend to try them out on future projects to see how well they stand up under different circumstances.

Acknowledgements. The InkBlot team for letting us put our ideas into practice and for making development of the system a pleasure.

Special thanks to Alistair Cockburn for encouragement and advice; to Martin Fowler, Joe Walnes, Gregor Hohpe, Tim Bacon for thoughtful feedback; Ben Authers for de-geeking our prose; and to the London Extreme Tuesday Club (XTC) for their continuous stream of good ideas and discussions.

Cynical Reengineering

Kristoffer Kvam, Daniel Bakkelund, and Rodin Lie

Telenor, CRM, Business Logic,
{kristoffer.kvam,daniel.bakkelund,rodin.lie}@telenor.com

Abstract. This paper presents a solution for saving large systems from increasing entropy. The solution is proven on a large middleware platform giving good results. The method's objective is to rework the system so that reengineering investments pays off. Reaching agile practices is the methods basis. In order to reach the objective the method cynically relies on measurements to find unwanted characteristics of the system. Subjective opinions due to ownership and politics are ignored in the method. An extensive open source tool, the Cosmos Radar, is given to the community to make these measurements. Various symptoms and measurements are identified and approaches to solutions are discussed.

Keywords: Reengineering, Refactoring, Software Metrics, Open Source

1 Introduction

1.1 Challenge

One of the major challenges we face in software development are the old systems. Systems having reached maturity often have a mysterious tendency to produce highly unexpected errors and maintenance is a pain. Taking inspiration from the Second Law of Thermodynamics some call this phenomenon increasing system entropy: In time a system experiences increasing disorder if not explicitly tended to [1]. This disorder adds unnecessary complexity to the problem domain's inherent complexity, something many organisations experience as their systems mature. A great deal of time is being spent fixing bugs and testing the fixes while development of new functionality is costly, risky and likely to introduce regression errors.

Techniques within the Agile initiatives such as automated acceptance testing, test driven development, continuous integration and refactoring all aim at preventing systems to end up as described above [2]. This idea works well with new systems development, but what about all the existing systems?

One alternative is a complete rewrite, but the cost might not pay off the investment. Rewriting a system is a risky and tricky affair, but not something we shall venture into in this paper.

The other alterative is to facilitate agile practices by reengineering the old system. This process is not free of challenges, whereof some of the more obvious ones are:

J. Eckstein and H. Baumeister (Eds.): XP 2004, LNCS 3092, pp. 130–138, 2004.
© Springer-Verlag Berlin Heidelberg 2004

- How to get management acceptance?
- Where to start?
- What to prioritise?
- How to reduce risk?

In addition to this you will most likely have very important organizational challenges, such as the process and culture change needed to establish the agile practices. These are not in the scope of this paper.

The following presents a solution to the challenges mentioned above (save the cultural and process related ones). The solution is based on quantitative measurements to make objective reengineering decisions. As a means of obtaining the measurements a new free open source tool, the Cosmos Radar [6], is introduced.

1.2 Telenor

Telenor is Norway's largest telecommunications company with numerous international interests.

COS is a middleware system designed to give front-end applications a consistent view across multiple back-end systems. There are more than 20 front end applications serving retail outlets, customer support, large corporate customers and internal functions. The back end systems include Sybase and Oracle databases, network connections and mainframes, all of which are logically interconnected through the use of batch jobs, scripts and database stored procedures.

COS has evolved over 5 years into a large system, composed of many subsystems. After a period of sustained development the problems were manifold. The system state corresponded well with the description of increasing entropy as defined above.

The Pareto project was instigated with solving the problems. The results presented here rely heavily on the work done during the project.

2   Objectives

A project proposal that sounds like "saving the system from the entropy spiral" will likely face scepticism from management. The project's business case must show that the increased life of the system defends the investment. After all, a very sensible alternative from a business point of view is to let the system die a silent death and invest in new development or buying a packaged solution. (In some cases that will also be the better solution.) The following issues must be taken into consideration when deciding the reengineering roadmap.

2.1   Reduced Time to Market

Reducing the time from an idea is created to it is put into production is a critical competitive factor for businesses today. Often the willingness to pay for a change is very high but the organizations ability to implement the changes is limited and time consuming. Hence, reducing the time to production of highly prioritised changes is often the most important factor for the business.

2.2 Increased Flexibility to Change

Having a flexible system architecture usually means being able to introduce large changes into the system at low cost and low risk. Flexibility also increases insight into the systems secrets causing general maintenance costs to decrease. Finding system bottlenecks and optimising performance will also be much easier once the systems architecture is flexible.

2.3 Reduced Number of Critical Errors

Developing zero defect software is one of the observed merits of agile practices such as XP [3]. Unfortunately, this is not the track record of the typical mature system one faces. Even small changes can have catastrophic effects on the stability of the system. Since these mature systems often are heavily depended on, downtimes can amount to painful losses for the business. Consequently, a focus on this area is usually appreciated by the organisation.

3   The Cynical Reengineering Method

A reengineering project is likely to have a mandate corresponding to the objectives mentioned above. In the targeted system there are probably several causes to the problems. Below, typical causes are identified and means of measuring them are presented. Once you have identified the most pressing problems, ways of attacking them are needed. We give you details on that. An unfortunate problem with a reengineering project is that you discover so many issues you want to resolve, but must prioritise the problems that give the greatest benefit for the company. The Prioritisation section summarises and gives insights into that issue.

3.1 Metrics

Object oriented metrics [4] can be used to analyse various characteristics of a system. Unfortunately, in a stand-alone form their value is often limited as a means for architectural decision-making. Questions like what values are acceptable for this system, how can they be combined to add more value and what metrics to emphasize usually arises.

To give true insight you need to see the metrics' dynamical nature and the value of combining them to form a more high-level view of the system. You are interested in how the characteristics of your system changes over time. In this way you can easily see which aspects of the system that are trending negatively and consequently where countermeasures are needed - a dynamic view.

Another issue is the particular metric's value in a reengineering project. Our experience is that most of the symptoms you search for cannot be found by the classical metrics. Instead, knowledge of the system must be combined with various measurements to produce valuable reports. A tool like the Cosmos Radar can help you with that.

We worked with many different views of the underlying metrics, but ended up with combining some selected metrics to get at picture of the amount of redundant code, illegal dependencies and code rot.

3.2   Redundant Code

Problem. As time goes, old code tends to be forgotten. When changes are done developers forget to (or are not given any time to) clean up the code. Code may be inaccessible or simply never used. This redundant code decreases the maintainability of the system. Our experience with redundant code is that the readability decreases, build cycles go slower and the impression of the system is more complex than what it inherently is. The last issue is important when considering system flexibility. Time is spent analysing regression effects and testing code that is worthless for the business.

Removal of redundant code is one of the easy wins in a reengineering project. It is among the tasks with the lowest risk that you can do in the code base.

Solution. We use two techniques to find redundant code: static analysis and statistics from the production environment showing the usage of public access points into the system. When you start removing public entry points, new rounds of static code analysis will most likely report large amounts of internal unused code that can be removed, and so goes the cycle: remove, analyse, remove, analyse. As this process goes on, the code base diminishes and becomes more manageable.

Static analysis of the code base can give valuable insights into the inaccessible parts of the code such as private methods, fields and inner classes that are never accessed. In a similar manner, you can also statically find the unused classes in the system.

Access points typically refer to the publicly available component services of the system. The largest part of redundant code in the system can be found by instrumenting all public access points and detecting which are never used in production (no client applications calling the methods). For a mature system not being maintained with dedication to the redundant parts, the system will most likely have a considerable amount of unused code that may be removed.

Being Cynical. Code that is detected as unused through static code analysis may be removed immediately, but some care should be taken to avoid deleting classes that are only accessed through mechanisms such as reflection in Java. When the unused entry points are detected these should be deprecated and allowed to remain in the system for enough time for the clients to report in wrong deprecations (e.g. methods that are used very seldom, but still are important). In this way you will avoid deleting skin-dead code. Still, our experience is that in many cases you need to be ruthless. Clients often report that they have references to the code that you deprecate - references that more often than not originates in client code that also is unused and redundant. Pushing and involving them a little extra on code removal may often create gains for both.

3.3 Illegal Dependencies

Problem. Illegal dependencies are dependencies that cause unnecessary entangling of the parts of your system. It is obvious that since there are some dependencies that are "illegal" there must also be some that are "legal". The definition of which are what arises from a defined "dependency graph".

A dependency graph contains a set of sub-systems (that make up your system) and the legal dependencies between these (making up the edges in the graph). For each sub-system it says what code belongs to it (e.g. which java-packages comprises a specific sub-system). The dependency graph should be a directed acyclic graph.

Sources for defining this structure might be found in architecture documents and by doing interviews with system domain experts. Once the work is done you actually have a declared and measurable definition of the vertical and horizontal layering of the system. Based on such a graph it is easy to see whether for example the integration layer framework makes use of customer functionality (which probably is not desirable).

A particularly unwanted problem area are cyclic dependencies [2]. Cyclic dependencies in a system appear when one module calls another module which again directly or indirectly calls the first module. This is a major pain that results in a plethora of problems that all directly negatively affects the objectives of a reengineering project.

The immediate result of these cyclic dependencies is code entangling. Different subsystems with different responsibility depend on each other. This greatly increases the risk for regression errors, and the burden of development and testing changes become large. Hence, flexibility to change and the number of critical errors suffer.

The second problem with cyclic dependencies is that you have to build and deploy all components for each release. It is not possible to develop, build and deploy a single module, and bug fixes are risky since they need to be patched into the system. In sum, such dependencies hinder incremental builds and deployment into production. The end result of that is slow time to market of prioritised functionality.

Solution. The advantages gained from removing illegal dependencies between subsystems are numerous, but as in many other circumstances in life; with great gain comes high risk. Mature systems are not likely to have automated acceptance tests that you can use for regression testing. Unit tests are probably not used either. Going into details in this area is not the scope of the paper, but having a clear strategy for both of these testing elements are essential before one starts to do massive restructuring of the code base.

Once the testing strategy has been developed and proved to work for the system, one can start removing the illegal dependencies. There are several ways to remove illegal dependencies and these vary greatly with the nature of the system. Still, some are probably typical:

- The first thing to be done with the illegal dependencies should simply be to optimise the imports in the system. Redundant imports are not part of the code base, but are still references. Several tools exist that can automate that process.
- Second, move methods, classes and modules that are placed in the wrong subsystem. Moves like these often give major results. Of course, one must give attention to clients and interface changes before moving public API related modules.
- Third, standard refactoring and redesign techniques must be used to remove the last illegal dependencies. This part is naturally the most risky, but may result in major gains for the system such as reusable frameworks.

Being Cynical. When working on the third and most complex part, our advice is to start at the most fundamental and risky element. Having that part separated out gives confidence, proof of the theory and will probably give the greatest gains for the organisation. The rest of the subsystems will then be much easier to separate out. The Cosmos Radar may continually give you the complete picture of how the system compares to the legal dependency graph. When you are done the path is clear to implement an incremental build configuration and you have a highly more flexible and maintainable code base.

3.4   Code Rot

Problem. Developers often associate complexity with spaghetti code. Spaghetti code comes in many forms but is often caused by illegal dependencies. Hence, to be precise we define code rot as code with bad smells [5] caused by high complexity. Attacking this problem has been an extensive area of research, and today refactoring [5] is a well accepted practice. In light of that, we focus here on practices for discovering the most immediate problems in a large code base.

Solution. Identifying code rot is a task that depends on the nature of the system. Still, some problems are universal, two of these being high method complexity and duplicated (copied and pasted) code. We present our ways of identifying these, all supported by the Cosmos Radar.

Here we define a method complex if it has a high McCabe metric for Cyclomatic Complexity [4]. This metric simply is a count of the number of paths a call to a method can go. One typically counts each conditional in a method and out comes the magic number. Usually one sets the threshold on this to 10. All methods with a value above 10 should in time be refactored. The reason to this is that such code has reduced readability and testability. The result is less maintainable code. The metric can be found by static analysis of the code base.

Copying and slightly modifying code are results of quick wins for the short term. Such an act results in duplicated code [1]. For maintenance such code becomes a nightmare, especially if the copying and pasting continues on the originally copied code.

In our experience measuring copied and pasted code can be done in two ways:

- There exists several free tools that can statically analyse the code and find equal sequences of code in the same code base. Such an approach gives fast discoveries.
- The other method is to group all methods in the code base according to the method names and cyclomatic complexity. This measurement is a little more error prone compared to the previous but is often very effective. The theory is that methods with similar names and cyclomatic complexity have been copied. It has been our experience that this is usually true for methods with a CC larger than 10.

Being Cynical. After having done analysis of the code, you want to make a choice on which parts to focus on. One typically makes a list of code that is overly conditionally complex and/or copied and pasted. Maybe another code measurement has been crucial for your system, and violating code to this measurement has also been added to the list. What should you start with?

Prioritise the refactoring based on a very important dimension: Historical activity on the code base. Luckily, this measurement is easily obtainable from the source control system. Most of these systems have an API that one can program against to obtain the maintenance metrics on the code files. If, for instance, you have a list of classes in your system where code rot is a critical, prioritise them according to how much source control activity these have been involved in. The assumption is that the most historically maintained classes will likely continue to be maintained. Hence, the greatest benefit is achieved if you refactor and write unit tests on these classes first.

3.5   Prioritisation

When doing a reengineering project, your success is measured. Hence, even though your heart tells you to attack a certain problem you discover, it is not necessarily the right thing to do compared to all the other activities that are lined up. The philosophy should be to attack the problems that give the greatest benefits to the company on both the long and short term. We have used the following approach with success:

- It is strongly recommended to start by deleting obsolete code since the results are easy to obtain and it reduces the amount of code for the rest of the tasks in the project.

- After that, attack the illegal dependencies. You will not be able to save the typical mature and neglected system without having focus on this aspect.
- Last, pure code rot removal should be focused on. The risk will be minimized when you have a clearly defined and followed dependency graph. Furthermore, such work takes an immense effort to produce small results in a large system. From a project perspective, code-refactoring work usually does not defend the investment. The proposal is not to neglect code rot. Analyse the problems as suggested above and produce a prioritised list of the problems. The list should be attacked as part of continual maintenance after the reengineering project finishes.

Lack of dedicated maintenance was our reason why the system needed to be reengineered. We believe no reengineering projects will succeed if this knowledge is neglected by the organisation. It is time the system starts to continually pay back its technical debt.

4   Cosmos Radar

The Cosmos Radar is a batch processing application developed as a response to the Pareto project's needs. It gets results from more 8 open source projects and a couple of in house grown projects and presents the results as massive unified html/svg reports. The architecture is based on java, xml and xsl. Presently it only supports Java, but there are plans to produce plug ins for other leading languages. [6] presents the Cosmos Radar in detail.

Although developed as a corporate tool, it has been decided to make it open source (at the time of writing, the URL has not been established, but it will be given during the paper presentation). It heavily relies on open source products, and in this way we can give something back.

Measurements. As default, the Cosmos Radar gives measurements on standard software metrics such as package metrics and dependencies, code size and complexity, coding violations and code-style violations.

Data from unit test metrics and code coverage are also integrated, but must be obtained running the test suites on the system while doing monitoring. We have also integrated even more measurements such as from source control, performance metrics and SQL procedures. Similar plug ins will be made available for the public once we have produced a common generic API.

Reports. The Radar is available in two forms. Cosmos Radar Statics gives reports on the current build of the system. The other form, Cosmos Radar Dynamics, includes the time dimension and views the historical and present versions along the time axis. The Dynamics version relies on a set of two or more Statics runs of different system releases to work properly.

5 Conclusion

Based on our experience with reengineering a large component based system, we have presented a method for attacking such systems in general. The method is based on software metrics and quantitative measurements. The various symptoms and approaches for their resolution have been discussed in relation to the typical objectives of a reengineering project - objectives with a mandate in a business case. The methods goal is to get the old system technically ready for typical agile practices. The results of using the method have been very good. A future paper will present the hard results.

As a means of performing such reengineering work we have presented the community a new open source tool, the Cosmos Radar, that has been developed in parallel with the methodology. The tool is based solely on other open source projects. It can be used to measure all the various symptoms on a system as discussed.

Our viewpoint here has only had focus on the system challenges. When adapting a system to agile practices it is just as important to focus on the human side, methodology and process. The organization and process involved in maintenance of such a system needs a major shift in order to take out the potential resulting from reengineering. One does not want the system to go back to its old sins.

References

1. Hunt, A., Thomas, D.: Pragmatic Programmer, from Journeyman to Master (2000)
2. Martin, Robert C.: Agile software development, Principles, Patterns, and Practices (2002)
3. Beck, Kent: Extreme Programming Explained: Embrace Change (1999)
4. Fenton, Norman E., Pfleeger, Shari L. : Software Metrics: A Rigorous and Practical Approach, Revised. (1998)
5. Fowler, M., Beck, K., Brant, J., Opdyke, W., Roberts, D.: Refactoring: Improving the Design of Existing Code (1999)
6. Kvam, K., Lie, R., Bakkelund, D.: A Tool for Cynical Reengineering (2004) Presented at the rOOts 2004 conference

The Characteristics of XP Teams

Hugh Robinson and Helen Sharp

Centre for Empirical Studies of Software Development
The Open University
Walton Hall
Milton Keynes MK7 6AA UK
{h.m.robinson; h.c.sharp}@open.ac.uk

Abstract. What is special about XP teams? Adopting XP involves social change as well as technical change, but what characterises a successful team? What happens when a team takes on the 12 practices and four underlying values? This paper contributes empirical findings that help answer such questions. We expand on previous work that suggested four characteristics of an XP team by analysing the data from both the previous study and from a further study of another mature XP team. While there are clear differences between the two teams in terms of operating environment, their detailed implementation of the 12 practices and the team's overall character, we find that the four characteristics are present in both teams. The paper describes the characteristics in detail and discusses how those characteristics are embedded in the detail of the practices of XP as observed in the two particular settings.

1 Introduction

The practices of XP, as given by Beck [1], are carried out by teams of individuals working in particular settings. Teams and the characteristics of teams are central to XP: Beck [1, p35] asserts 'If members of a team don't care about each other, XP is doomed'. Indeed, XP is as much about human values as about technical values. Interviewing Beck, Highsmith [2] observes that his 'important vision is about changing social contracts, changing the way people treat each other and are treated in organizations' and quotes Beck's response to an article that attempted to revise XP: 'I was furious that someone would strip out all of the social change and still call it XP.'

But what is special about XP teams? What does a successful XP team look like? What effect does XP have on a team when the 12 practices and the underlying values are put into practice? While authors have discussed specific aspects of team interaction (e.g. [3]) and have reported on XP team activity (e.g. [4]), no reported work has focussed on the characteristics of mature XP teams. A team's character is determined in part by the individuals who are its members and the organisational and cultural setting within which they operate. However the claim from XP proponents that successful adoption involves social change suggests that the 12 practices themselves might sustain and be sustained by a common set of team characteristics that go beyond the documented practices and values.

This paper is about the characteristics of XP teams and how those characteristics are sustained by the detail of XP practices. We expand on the results of an earlier

J. Eckstein and H. Baumeister (Eds.): XP 2004, LNCS 3092, pp. 139–147, 2004.

empirical study of a mature XP team [5,6] that suggested four characteristics of XP teams, using an additional empirical study of a second mature XP team operating in quite a different environment. We first describe our empirical approach and then give some details of the setting for each of the two studies. We then move to an analysis of how team characteristics are embedded in the detail of XP practices, and finally discuss our findings and conclusions.

2   Empirical Approach

Our empirical approach was qualitative and emphasized understanding the reality of practice. Each team was studied by a researcher for a period of a week, complemented by follow-up visits to discuss findings. A different researcher was used for each study. Each week-long study involved the researcher immersing themselves as far as possible in the day-to-day business of XP development, and actively taking part in that business where possible. The detail of practice was documented via a range of means that included contemporaneous field notes, audio recordings of discussions and meetings, photographs/sketches of the physical layout, copies of various documents and artefacts, and records of interviews with practitioners.

Our approach was one of observing as far as possible the natural setting of practice without any form of control, intrusion or experiment. Our analysis sought to understand the practice we observed in its own terms, minimizing the impact of our own backgrounds, prejudices and assumptions. We placed emphasis on attending to the taken-for-granted, accepted and un-remarked aspects of practice, deliberately not discounting any feature of practice and explicitly considering the totality of practice with all its 'messy' characteristics. This observational and analytic approach is an *ethnographic* approach – a rigorous and non-subjective approach from the social sciences that has been used successfully to study software development (see [7-9] for example).

In both cases, the start of the study coincided with the start of an iteration and all 12 practices were observed.

3   Teams and Their Settings

3.1   Team A

Team A were part of a small company developing web-based intelligent advertisements in Java for paying customers. The team has used XP right from start-up, uses all 12 practices and is mature in its use of XP. At the time of the study, there were eight developers in the team, one graphic designer and one person who looked after the infrastructure. Iterations were three weeks long and the only documentation support tool was a wiki site where the team captured details of each iteration such as the identifier of the stories planned, those completed, those removed or added, and the team's velocity. Stories, indeed anything that was written down, were captured on 4" by 6" index cards, which were then discarded once they had been used for their purpose. The company employed four marketing people who determined what was required in collaboration with clients. Marketing were regarded as being, in effect, the on-site customer.

Each member of the development team apart from the graphic designer had experience of traditional software development methods. As a team they had only ever used XP, and while the membership of the team had expanded and contracted over its lifetime (two and a half years at the time of the study), the individuals involved had remained stable.

The setting for the XP team was a long rectangular first-floor office organized so that it was both open but also had distinct areas. There was an area where pair programming took place, with desks shaped specifically for programmers to sit two to a machine. The wall in this area had a notice board devoted to the active story cards. There were also four 'to do' lists on the board headed by a picture of Anton Chekhov and one of Pavel Chekhov. These lists were checked-off to signal certain events, and the area was known as the Chekhov Board. This is where stand-ups took place. There was a separate area for the Planning Game, with tables, chairs and a sofa. Adjacent to this area was the machine used to release modified and tested code into the main system. The marketing team was located at one end of the floor; each person had their own desk. The infrastructure support person and the graphic designer also had their own area. There was a well-equipped kitchen that was used extensively and it had a homely and personal feel to it.

3.2   Team B

Team B were part of a company producing software products to support the use of documents in multi-authored work environments. They have 3,500 accounts worldwide and over half a million users. Software is produced by two development teams: one in Capetown, South Africa, and the other in London, UK. We studied the latter team. They adopted XP in early 2001, as a result of problems with a conventional, but unstructured, approach. The team adopted all 12 XP practices. At the time of the study, there were 23 people working in the team, including three programme managers (who took the role of the on-site customer), two testers, a technical author, a development team coach (who also managed the development team and pair programmed) and 16 developers. Within each iteration (which lasted two weeks), the development team organised itself into sub-teams oriented around the various software products or related issues. For example, during the week's study, a sub-team of a dozen or so individuals (developers, programme managers, testers) worked on stories in connection with an up-coming release of the company's most recent software product.

The team developed software in C++. They used a custom-built computer documentation tool to record, communicate and progress stories, rather than index cards. The tool was a significant medium of communication in that it captured the detail of each story: the estimate, a brief description, the customer acceptance test, who was working on it, progress through development, integration, pre-quality assurance testing, etc.

The development team occupied the whole of the first floor in a converted warehouse. The space was large and open-plan with seven rectangular tabled areas. Each tabled area had four workstations in twos, back to back, organised for pair programming. There was considerable space between each tabled area and there were also two separate round tables for discussions or small meetings. Adjacent to this open area was a partitioned conference room. The whole effect was of an open, airy working environment. On the ground floor was a modern dining area and kitchen with everything that was needed for making drinks or light snacks.

3.3 Team Differences and Similarities

The main similarity between our two teams is that they had both been using XP successfully for a number of years at the time of our studies. They both had found and continued to find difficulties in using XP but were committed to finding solutions to any problems they encountered. Apart from this, they were different in many ways: some cultural, some technical, and some operational.

They had two distinct organisational cultures working in different application domains. Team A was part of a very small company that had only been in existence for two and a half years, while Team B were in an SME that had been in business for over seven years. The overall atmosphere for Team B was considerably more intense and solemn than in Team A. This may have been a result of the differences in pair programming. When Team A were programming they were focused on their work and became intense, but they took common breaks, and so there were also times when the mood lightened. For Team B, however there were no common breaks, and so at any time of the day there would be pairs programming intensely. The pairs in Team B also appeared to be different in character, being on the one hand more rigid insofar as individual pairs often paired for more than one day and sometimes for a whole iteration, but also more flexible in their approach to coding. This flexibility was evident by the ease with which a pair might be interrupted, for example growing easily to be a threesome or indeed a group of people all working on one issue, and if one of the pair was absent for a while the partner would continue to work alone.

Team A would celebrate their successes, e.g. making a little box on top of the release machine 'moo' whenever a new piece of code was released. Team B however showed no such celebrations. Even within the pair, it was sometimes difficult for the observer to be sure that an issue had been settled because this may be signalled by something as small as a sigh and leaning back in the chair, or by nothing discernible at all.

Technical differences included the development languages and the software and support environments they used, while operational differences were evident in the manner in which they carried out the XP practices, including iterations, stand-ups, planning game, and organisation of pairing.

In the next section, we will illustrate how the two teams exhibit a set of four common characteristics. However we shall also note how the detail of practice varies between them, to underscore that although they are comparable, they are certainly not the same.

4 Team Characteristics and Their Relationship to Practices

Our earlier study [5,6] suggested that the characteristics of XP teams are that:
1. both individuals and the team are respected;
2. both individuals and the team take responsibility;

3.　　both individuals and the team actively encourage the preservation of the quality of working life;

4.　　both individuals and the team have faith in their own abilities to achieve the goals they have set themselves, which is constantly re-validated and re-affirmed.

In the following we provide an expanded description of these characteristics, and explain how they are embedded in the detail of XP practices as deployed in the two settings. This detail has both commonalities across the two teams and differences, and the explanation is based on observations from our empirical studies.

The first two of our characteristics deal with respect and responsibility. These are closely related in terms of our analysis and we therefore discuss them together.

4.1　Respect and Responsibility

Respect is Beck's underlying core value and he describes the importance of members of the team respecting each other and caring about the project [1, p35]. Our characteristic includes these two aspects of respect, but also includes some other aspects. The simple way we have stated the characteristic obscures these different facets and it is worth unpacking them explicitly before we describe how they manifest themselves in each team. In our context, respect involves three main parties: the individual, the team and those outside the team. What we have found is that individuals within the team respect each other in a variety of ways, individuals within the team respect the goals and desires of the whole team, the whole team respects each individual within the team, and those external to the team such as customers respect the team.

In both teams under study, the individual is respected and takes responsibility in a variety of ways, which centre around what work they do and how they carry out that work. Work was not allocated to individuals, with an allotted time in which that work must be completed, for their passive acceptance. Rather, individuals actively agreed their responsibilities. Individuals clearly felt that they had the respect of their fellow team members and were therefore empowered to take on responsibility in this way.

The daily business of pair programming continued this emphasis on an individual's respect and responsibility. Within the overall scope of the iteration, pairing was a process that acknowledged the individual, each person self-electing to work on a particular piece of the system. This self-election might be on the basis of particular expertise but equally it might be on the basis of a desire to become more familiar with a particular area of the code base. Within a pair, the process of programming was conducted as a conversation between equals with snippets such as 'I'm not sure about that. Can we go back and look at ... ?' being typical. Much effort was expended on understanding code and it was demonstrably important that this understanding was shared between the pair. Similarly, the process of writing code was a negotiated process between two individuals: one perhaps writing code, the other correcting it. In both teams, no-one dominated the process or monopolized control of the keyboard. Developers were quite happy to take (and relinquish) responsibility when one of a pair wanted control of the keyboard following a particular insight.

Respect for the individual permeated the other practices associated with producing working, released code. There was no sense of frustration or a lack of understanding of a common purpose. For example, in Team B, testing typically required the tester to discuss some issues with the developers. This discussion was not conducted as a planned, formal meeting but involved the tester initiating the discussion with a casual interruption of the work of developers. There was no sense of an unwelcome or irritating interruption: the need to discuss was accepted and welcomed.

Similarly, in both Team A and Team B, the team was respected and took responsibility. Whilst the individual actively accepted responsibility for work, the nature and significance of that work was embedded in the team activity of the Planning Game and the negotiation of what work was to be done and how the team organized themselves to achieve that work. The Planning Game we observed in Team A was an unusually (for them) protracted process, for a variety of reasons, but everyone accepted that it was important that the team took whatever time was needed to get the iteration off to a good start. Similarly, estimates were discussed and revised in Team B until consensus was achieved. For both teams, team decisions were respected and upheld by members of the team and were accepted by customers. For example, in Team A, the developers' decision that a technical story took priority was accepted unquestioningly by the customers.

Team B offered an interesting insight into the relationship between respect and responsibility. Each sub-team actively agreed responsibility for work and respected the similar action of the other sub-teams. When we questioned a member of one sub-team about a crucial release date for a software product that was vital to the company's plans the reply was 'Don't know: I'm not working on that.' This does not show indifference, but trust in the sub-team that was working on that software product, and focus on the developer's own responsibilities. It is worth noting that we found evidence that developers in Team B did not offer trust automatically, since they displayed a rather more critical attitude to the other XP team based in South Africa.

4.2   Preservation of the Quality of Working Life

Observations of Team A and Team B showed both individuals and the team actively encouraging the preservation of the quality of working life. This manifested itself most strongly with the atmosphere of calmness that was prevalent in both teams. The Planning Game was notable for the absence of adversarial or confrontational exchanges and for the presence of shared discussion where risks and other factors were carefully considered. Stand-ups for both teams were opportunities to share and facilitate achievement as opposed to any monitoring of progress against plan. The organization of work via pair programming oriented to the quality of working life insofar as pairing took account of the wishes and needs of individuals as well as the purpose and priorities of the team.

Both teams adhered to the 40-hour week practice but as a rule around which to orient working life rather than as a rule to govern working life; working hours were organised to take account of the individual. Evidence for this included, in Team A, an acceptance by all when one developer needed to leave early because he had a long way to travel that night, and in Team B when one of a pair needed to take time away for a medical appointment. In neither case, did this disrupt the rhythm of the day. The overall impression from both teams was that of the skillful and accomplished achievement of a productive, sustainable and enjoyable working life via their shared responsibility for, and ownership of, the work product, and of control over how the work was achieved. The end result was to make development sustainable in its human dimension.

Within this overall context there were clear differences between the two teams, although both exhibited this characteristic. Team A seemed more overtly concerned about the quality of working life with a range of activities that contributed explicitly and implicitly to it. For example, regular and communal breaks were taken in the morning, afternoon and at lunchtime, particularly during the Planning Game. These regular breaks were perceived as being important by all members of the team, and one developer took it upon himself to remind people to take them. Other indications were the blue stress ball that sat on the Planning Game table, the instigation of 'gold cards' (two days a month when a developer could pursue something on his/her own) and the identification of an 'exposed pair' (to protect pairs from customer interrupts).

In contrast, Team B did not have any such activities. For example, meal breaks were not taken together. Indeed, on one occasion we witnessed a pair who stopped for lunch with one of the pair going to the ground floor dining area where they ate their packed lunch, whilst the other continued work as a singleton, reviewing code. Short breaks for tea, coffee, etc. were usually taken by pairs at the workstation: one or both of the pair would descend the stairs, make their drinks, and come back up to continue work. We detected a desire to stay in the immediate area of the workstations even when an impromptu meeting took place, such as a discussion between a pair, a customer and a tester. Despite there being two convenient round tables close by the workstations, such discussions were always carried out around the workstation even though some participants had to stand. It was clear that this way of working was not imposed by management since the development coach commented that he wished developers would take more breaks away from the workstations.

Despite these differences, Team B valued the quality of working life in a similar, albeit sometimes different, fashion. The discussions took place as and when needed and there was no sense that they were a distraction. Indeed, they seemed a vital part of working life and we speculate that they gave a similar rhythm to the day as that of the regular and communal breaks of Team A. Neither should the situations where a pair became a singleton be seen as some diminishment in the quality of working life. This would occur at mealtimes but also at both ends of the day and it was clear from the way in which a pair discussed this singleton work that it was viewed as a natural continuation of the main activity of pairing to produce work in which shared pride could be taken. In addition, the development team coach had an orchestrating and support role, always being aware of the pulse of the team and actively intervening and supporting where needed. For example, we observed a particularly intense bout of pairing which lasted without a break all afternoon. In subsequent conversation it became abundantly clear that both the team coach and other members of the team had noticed this and were monitoring it; in the end, the coach intervened to provide the necessary break and support.

4.3   Faith in Their Own Abilities

In both teams, faith in their own abilities, and the sense of re-validation and re-affirmation of those abilities flowed through working life: from the agreement of work in the Planning Game, through the acceptance of tasks in pair-programming allocation, the reporting of progress in the stand-up, and the desire for creating quality code. It is worth emphasising here what is remarkable about XP practices in terms of creating quality code: faith in the customer to know what is required, faith in the team to estimate appropriately and faith in two individuals who have self-elected to work together to produce code. This faith in their own abilities had no sense of heroism or arrogance; indeed, it had two aspects: both believing that they were capable of achieving the tasks they set themselves, but also understanding where their limitations lay. It was a natural part of this process to involve others, maybe to go to the customer for clarification or to seek out expertise of another developer outside the pair.

So, for example, in Team A the sense of competence and cool belief in their own abilities did not mean that the team were over-confident – they brought in outside expertise when faced with a situation they had doubts about. Issues were carefully discussed and alternatives considered, but once the team had agreed the course of action, it was carried through with certainty. Their abilities were re-validated and re-affirmed through feedback from the code (which executes successfully), the customer (who is happy with the software) and each other (who provide solid support and encouragement to each other).

4.4   A Fifth Characteristic: Trust

In working through the detail of our observations of XP practices we were forced to the conclusion that there was a fifth characteristic which pervades the original four: that of trust. Trust has been identified explicitly as a key attribute of relationships between customers and the development team (e.g. [10]) but from our detailed empirical observations, it is also clear that trust is required within the team. Trust is complementary to the four characteristics discussed above, and is needed in order for them to flourish throughout the team's activities.

For example, trust underpins the Planning Game, so that the four characteristics necessary to enable the active agreement over what work was to be done and what estimate of resource was required, could be effective. Without trust, the sense of respect, responsibility, concern for the quality of working life and faith in ability would not be as strong, and developers would not be sure that their colleagues, nor the team as a whole, could deliver what they promised.

Similarly, the activity of pair programming depends on a relationship between two individuals which demands trust, so that they may respect what each brings to the encounter and have faith in their abilities as a pair and as a singleton. The nature of the trust relationship here transcends the immediate business of two individuals pairing and is persistent. It also applies across pairs (and sub-teams), with each pair trusting the others to do their part, and it extends beyond the detail of the 12 practices, so that, for example, respect of the need for interruptions shows trust that the interruption wouldn't happen unless the interrupter thought it important enough.

5   Discussion

In our previous work, we identified four characteristics of a mature XP team. In this paper we have deepened our analysis, included a second team, and have introduced a fifth characteristic: trust. We have found that both of the teams studied show evidence of having these characteristics, despite being different in nearly all other aspects apart from their use of XP.

What do we therefore claim? It is tempting to simply say that we have shown that carrying out the practices of XP gives rise to teams with these characteristics and that we have uncovered a causal relationship. However, reality is not that simple and we do not make such a claim. We are mindful of the fact that both the organisations in which the teams were situated had their own culture and values and, broadly, those organisations were open and positive in their attitude. It is therefore not a surprise that the characteristics and values we have described exist in such organisations. Similarly we do not claim that we have shown all teams carrying out software development in these organisations will have these characteristics. Rather we suggest that there is a reflexive relationship between characteristics and practices that is mediated by the detailed setting in which activity takes place. That is, the practices actively and continuously sustain and are actively and continuously sustained by the characteristics we describe and that the detailed setting influences this process.

Acknowledgements. We would like to thank our collaborator companies, Connextra and Workshare for their support and co-operation during the studies reported here.

References

[1] Beck K. eXtreme Programming Explained: embrace change. In: Beck K, editor. The XP Series. San Francisco: Addison-Wesley, 2000.

[2] Highsmith J. Agile Software Development Ecosystems. In: Highsmith J, editor. The Agile Software Development Series. San Francisco: Addison-Wesley, 2002.

[3] Pentecost K. XP and Emotional Intelligence. IT Cutter Journal 2003;16 (2):5-11.

[4] Roodyn N. Dear Diary: the making of an XP team. IT Cutter Journal 2003;16 (2):18-25.

[5] Sharp H, Robinson HM. An ethnography of XP practice. Proceedings of the Joint Conference on the Empirical Assessment of Software Engineering (EASE) and the Psychology of Programming Interest Group (PPIG). Keele University, 8-10 April, 2003. pp. 15-27.

[6] Robinson HM, Sharp H. XP culture: why the twelve practices both are and are not the most significant thing. Proceedings of the Agile Development Conference. Salt Lake City, Utah, 25-28 June: IEEE Computer Society Press, 2003. pp. 12-21.

[7] Singer J, Lethbridge T, Vinson N, Anquetil N. An examination of software engineering work practices. Centre for Advanced Studies Conference (CASCON). Toronto, Ontario, 1997. pp. 1 - 15.

[8] Sim SE. Evaluating the Evidence: Lessons from Ethnography. Workshop on Empirical Studies of Software Maintenance. Oxford, England, 1999.

[9] Robinson HM, Segal J, Sharp H. The case for empirical studies of the practice of software development. In: Ciolkowski M, editor. Proceedings of the ESEIW Workshop on Empirical Studies in Software Engineering. Rome Castles, Italy, 29 September, 2003. pp. 99-108.

[10] Sharp H, Robinson HM. Customer collaboration: challenges and successes in practice (Technical Exchange session). Agile Development Conference. Salt Lake City, USA, 2003.

The Oregon Software Development Process

Till Schümmer[1] and Robert Slagter[2]

[1] Computer Science Department, FernUniversität in Hagen,
Universitätsstrasse 1, 58084 Hagen, Germany
Till.Schuemmer@fernuni-hagen.de
[2] Telematica Instituut, P.O. Box 589, 7500 AN, Enschede, The Netherlands
Robert.Slagter@telin.nl

Abstract. User participation is still a difficult topic in software development. Based on the results of the Oregon experiment in construction we propose a novel development process – the Oregon Software Development Process. The process focusses on patterns to empower end-users so that they can make well-informed design decisions and tailor their environments. The four core principles of the process – participation, piecemeal growth, patterns, and diagnosis – are discussed and first anecdotal usage experiences are provided.

1 Introduction

Although many technical problems in software development have been solved over the last twenty years, we still observe a lack of support for end-user participation. While most modern software development processes highlight the importance of considering all different stakeholders, it is still a difficult task to actively involve the end-user. Especially the knowledge transfer to end-users is difficult. We therefore propose the adaptation of a design process known in construction as the Oregon experiment.

This design process combines aspects that are typically left unrelated. To give an overview, these aspects are:

End-user participation, as it is present in a participatory design approach [12],

Piecemeal growth in short iterations, which is proposed by most iterative processes [5], especially the eXtreme Programming methodology [4],

Adaptability that is typically achieved by composing software out of independent functional building blocks (software components [15]) that are plugged into a framework,

Pattern oriented application design, which is represented by design patterns [9], and

End-user tailorability that is proposed by recent literature to handle the changing needs and personal preferences [11].

This paper first summarizes how the design process worked in the Oregon experiment. It will then compare the process with the XP methodology as one representative for agile processes.

J. Eckstein and H. Baumeister (Eds.): XP 2004, LNCS 3092, pp. 148–156, 2004.
© Springer-Verlag Berlin Heidelberg 2004

We will show that aspects from the Oregon process are used in current agile processes, but that there is still no holistic approach that includes all aspects of the Oregon experiment. We propose a combination of several up-to-now unrelated design activities to fill this gap for end-user centered design. The resulting development process is denoted as the Oregon Software Development Process. The paper ends by briefly reporting on experiences with the process in a research development project.

2   Summary of the Oregon Experiment

The Oregon experiment was based on the vision of the architect Christopher Alexander, stating that every user of a building or a place should have the freedom to shape the environment in a way that it suits his needs and personal preferences. This vision was institutionalized in the planning process of the campus of the university of Oregon – the Oregon Experiment [2]. The process defines six basic principles: *organic order, participation, piecemeal growth, patterns, diagnosis,* and *coordination.* Organic order and coordination – as applied in the Oregon Experiment – are very specific to the context of town planning. We therefore concentrate on the remaining four principles, explain their application in the Oregon experiment, and investigate how to apply them to software development. Coordination returns as an important aspect when software design decisions impact various participants.

Participation ensures that the end-users will be part of the planning process and therefore participate in shaping their environments. Alexander defines participation on different levels, ranging from acting as a client for an architect to actually building their environment. ([2], p. 39)

In the Oregon Experiment, participation led to a very successful campus design [14]. The university established a user group with students, faculty members, and staff. The user group decided, which projects should be built in the next phases. In a refinement phase, special focus groups (users with specific interests) concentrated on one aspect of the building. In both user group and focus groups, the prospective users started thinking about the various parts of the space and how each part should be improved.

Piecemeal growth. By concentrating on one part at a time, one follows the principle of piecemeal growth. This includes identifying one concrete problem and finding a solution for this problem.

Patterns. To empower the end-users so that they can find working solutions, they necessarily need a way of accessing established proven solutions. By means of patterns, one can describe expert knowledge in the form of rules of thumb. These rules include a problem description, which highlights a set of conflicting forces and motivate a proven solution, which helps to resolve the forces.

In this manner, patterns can serve as an educational resource in the user group: they make the core of the problem and the solution explicit by explaining what happens to the inner forces.

Additionally, patterns are the essential language applied in the user group: the patterns (taken from a pattern language [1]) act as a basis to communicate on a high level of abstraction the key properties of design. Although patterns are proven solutions, they are not static. Users are encouraged to enhance, adapt, or correct the patterns. Changed patterns will be incorporated in the community pattern language, as long as the community agrees with the adaptation.

Diagnosis is the process of analyzing the existing campus regarding aspects that work and aspects that do not work. This includes a phase of reflection: during the use of the environment, users are encouraged to step back and ask themselves, whether or not the environment serves their needs. If not, they are asked to mark the deficits and thus state change requests for the environment. The planning committee uses a map to catalogue all patterns that are not working (and the places where patterns are working well).

All the mentioned principles are in use at the university of Oregon for nearly 30 years, where new patterns are still brought in by the users.

3   Comparing the Oregon Process with XP

The principles of the Oregon process partially map to the principles of XP [4]. We can observe the following equivalences and differences:

Participation takes place in the planning game of XP and in the principle of the on-site customer. Compared to the Oregon process, agile processes argue for a more light-weight integration of the customer (without formal user groups).

Piecemeal growth corresponds to the principle of small releases. It is implicitly present in the principle of simple design. Every change in the environment should just be as large enough to reach the goal of the small release.

Patterns become more and more common in software development. They can be considered as a general development technique for developers but they are not explicitly mentioned in the practices of XP. One could argue that patterns and simple design are contrasting concepts: Patterns provide proven solutions to common problems. These solutions are reusable and thus comply with the counter-example for small releases stated in [4]: "Implement for today, design for tomorow" (p. 57).

Diagnosis is the process of adapting the software to changing needs. It is one of the core assumption that underlies all XP practices: requirements are changing and the process should be flexible enough to suit the users' changing needs. we find the process of diagnosis and repair in the practice of refactoring.

The core difference between the two processes is the role of patterns. In the Oregon process, patterns inform the other principles.

Participation uses patterns as a common language and as a means for educating end-users so that they can actually shape their environment as experts would do. With this respect, patterns bridge the gap in the communication between end-users and professional software developers. At least for less technical users, this means that the patterns have to be understandable by non-software developers. This is often not true for technical design patterns (as collected for instance in [9]). As we discuss later, we need patterns for end-users that are closer to the prosaic style of Alexander.

Piecemeal growth always focusses on one pattern at a time. Compared with story cards in planning games, patterns have the advantage that they explicitly name the different interacting forces and the consequences and trade-offs involved. This empowers the end-user to make more responsible decisions.

Diagnosis is always supported by means of patterns. The patterns indicate possible problems and help to find out, why a specific part of the environment does not work. Moreover, patterns provide hints on how to repair the problematic aspects. Actually, the 72 refactorings in [8] are such patterns that help to improve the quality of source code – although they focus on the developer.

In summary, the comparison of the Oregon process with XP highlights the importance of patterns and the need for empowering the end-user to make well-informed design decisions. To satisfy these needs in an agile process is the goal of the Oregon Software Development Process proposed in this paper.

4   The Oregon Software Development Process

The Oregon Software Development Process (OSDP) intends to foster end-user participation, pattern-oriented transfer of design knowledge, piecemeal growth in form of short iterations, and frequent diagnosis or reflection that leads to an improved application.

Figure 1 shows the different phases of OSDP. It suggests three different kinds of iterations, denoted by the three circles. In the following paragraphs, we will explain the different iterations (numbers refer to the step number in figure 1). In the actual execution of the OSDP, each iteration may be executed many times.

Throughout all iterations, the users participate and work with a shared software pattern language. This language consists of patterns on two levels with different target groups: High-level patterns describe issues and solutions typically targeted at end-users. Low-level patterns describe issues and solutions typically targeted at software developers on a more technical level. A large number of low level patterns and several high level patterns have been collected by the design patterns community – cf. www.hillside.net.

High-level patterns aim to provide end-users with profound design knowledge. This empowers them to act as a designer and solve some issues, without having to escalate them to a designer. In cases, where high-level patterns can be implemented by adding functions (without the need of changing software code), the end-users can perform these tailoring actions themselves.

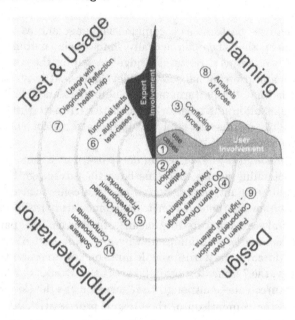

Fig. 1. The Oregon Software Development Process.

The innermost *inceptive iterations* comprise the activities of (1) use-case analysis and (2) the selection of appropriate patterns. First, the users describe the intended system use with simple use cases. These can be stories (for users, who are not familiar with formal use-cases) or success scenarios, which describe the use-case's story in a more formal but still prosaic way [6].

The use-cases then drive the selection of initial patterns from the software-patterns catalogue, which serve as starting points for exploring the different forces in the area. During the inceptive iterations, the end-users will be highly involved. In most cases, there will be technology experts present to support the users in writing stories and pointing the users to appropriate sets of patterns. One result of inceptive iterations is a common pattern language, which then eases the communication within the design team. The other result is a set of initial user requirements.

The second set of iterations is made up from (3) the detection of conflicting forces, (4) a pattern-driven object-oriented design, (5) the implementation of this design using object-oriented development technologies like frameworks or low-level components, and (6) functional tests. We call these iterations *development iterations* since they form the part of the process, where software engineers develop the application.

The user first identifies the conflicting forces. Developers will assist the user in this task, by structuring the discussion. Together with the user, the developer then looks for low-level design patterns to solve the issue.

Developers typically implement a pattern by means of application frameworks or developer-centered component frameworks. This may involve the development of new software components. Such components can be built using frameworks or other base technologies. To ease the implementation, each software-pattern can have technology recipes that show, how the pattern is implemented with a specific technology (using the cookbook style that was described in the Assembly Cookbook pattern [7]).

The result is tested using as much automated tests as possible (note that it is often better to exchange steps 5 and 6 as it is done in XP's test first practice). Steps (3) to (6) require a software developer to be involved. The user still makes an important contribution to the design because he participates in steps (3) and (4) and provides test data in step (6).

In the *tailoring iteration*, end-users use the application for the desired purpose. While using the system, end-users with pattern-based groupware design knowledge are encouraged to (7) reflect on their activities. This reflection in action [13] reveals actions that complicate or hinder the work process. If the users want to remove these difficulties, they start a tailoring iteration.

They first analyse the forces that are in conflict. High-level groupware patterns (8) help in this process by describing frequently occurring issues, the various forces and a proven solution in a way that is appropriate for tailoring end-users. These patterns are typically written fully in a natural language. We have gained good experiences with patterns that include a concrete usage scenario. Such scenarios can be easily understood by the end-users and empower them to learn, what needs to be changed to solve the pattern's problem.

The tailoring environment supports the tailoring end-users in the process of (10) selecting and composing appropriate functions. The prosaic nature of the stories in the patterns helps the tailor to make a well-informed selection of this functionality.

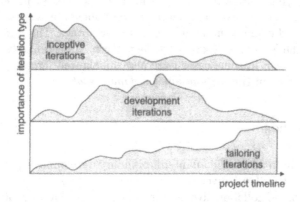

Fig. 2. Frequency of iterations during the project.

During project life, the different kinds of iterations will be executed in different frequencies as shown in figure 2. It is not intended to prescribe exact frequencies over time. The frequencies rather evolve over the project life cycle. At project start, inceptive iterations are the most important iterations. Prototypical development accompanies the gathering of use cases and patterns in development iterations. While the project evolves, the frequency of development iterations grows, while inceptive iterations are not as important anymore. Since the development iterations produce more sophisticated prototypes, users will start using the system more frequently and reflect on their system use. Thus, the number of user-triggered tailoring iterations increases towards the end of the project while the other two kinds of iterations become less important.

4.1 Pattern Structure

We have argued that patterns are the core of the OSDP. The OSDP advocates to represent patterns in an manner that is appropriate for end users as well as software designers.

We argue to use an extended Alexandrian pattern form [1]. The *pattern name* is followed by other possible names for the pattern (*AKA*), the *intent*, and the *context* of the pattern. All these sections help the reader to decide, whether or not the following pattern may fit into his current situation.

Then follows the core of the pattern composed of the *problem* and the *solution* statement in bold font separated by a *scenario* and a *symptoms* section. The *scenario* is a concrete description of a situation where the pattern could be used, which makes the tension of the *problem* statement (the conflicting forces) tangible. The *symptoms* section helps to identify the need for the pattern by describing aspects of the situation more abstract again. The section lists observable forces that are unbalanced before the pattern was applied.

After the *solution* section, the solution is explained in more detail (*participants, rationale, danger spots, known uses*) and indications for further improvement after applying the pattern are provided (in the *related patterns* section). The *participants* section explains the main components or actors that interact in the pattern and explains how they relate to each other. The *rationale* section explains, why the forces are resolved by the pattern. Unfortunately, the application of a pattern can in some cases raise new unbalanced forces. These counter forces are described in the section labelled *danger spots*.

5   Experiences

The OSDP has been applied in an interdisciplinary development project that ran for 9 months at the FernUniversität in Hagen. The goal of this project was to develop a web-based collaborative learning environment for students distributed throughout Germany. The system is currently in production state. More information on the goals and design of the system can be found in [10]. We report on our survey based on informal interviews and observations with the involved project members.

In the *inception phase*, we invited students, university teachers, and software developers to develop scenarios of system use. In addition, we presented a set of groupware patterns (to be exact, the prosaic stories of these patterns, the problem statements, and the solutions) to the members of this group. Since the group members were not aware of the current state of the art of groupware development, they appreciated this informative phase. As a result of the inception phase, the group identified five different learning scenarios that should be supported by the learning environment. Implicitly, the group members also selected patterns (they used the pattern names in their description of learning scenarios) that were considered relevant for the future development iterations.

In the *development iterations*, the users developed more detailed story cards together with the software developers. Again, patterns played an important role here. They served as metaphors for talking about the software system and helped the users to focus on one aspect at a time for each story card. The developers implemented the stories with help of the patterns (since the patterns were already mentioned on the card, the development was quite straight-forward). In parallel with the development, automated tests were created. Regarding the tests, one must note that the test coverage decreased in the last third of the project, since the project schedule was far too optimistic and the developers tended to neglect writing tests. But, as XP would suggest, this behavior caused even larger problems by the end of the project and a more complete test coverage is one of the first tasks for the follow-up project.

After the first development iteration (approx. 2 weeks of development), the users (teachers) started to use the system. They did functional tests (of the first prototypes) and requested new functionality (informed by their knowledge of system design that was based on groupware design patterns). They also started to reflect on their activities following the principle of diagnosis.

In the early phases of the project, these requests were escalated to the developers. In the later phases, the users could start to tailor the environment using the provided mechanisms for tailoring. These mechanisms included the composition of communication and collaboration technology as well as the tailoring of collaboration spaces (the creation of a virtual environment for collaborative learning). In the last third of the project, approx. 300 students started to use the system. They were asked to participate in development iterations (using the system itself to report feature requests by means of story cards) and in tailoring iterations (students were allowed to create their own learning environment).

In all phases of the development, the patterns (and especially the stories from the patterns) were very helpful for participating users and developers. The main problem with the patterns was that we did not yet have an comprehensive pattern catalogue (only few areas of groupware design are described by means of patterns by now). The other problem was that the system showed errors in the production phase for those parts that had a low test coverage. This is yet another indication, how important the test phases are in the process.

6   Conclusions

This paper addressed the issue that the involvement of end-users is often still problematic in software development projects. We proposed a development process that heavily involves end-users and fosters the reuse of existing knowledge – the Oregon Software Development Process, which is based on the results of the Oregon experiment in construction. It combines the four principles of participation, piecemeal growth, patterns, and diagnosis.

Patterns play a key role in this process. But to be easily understood by end-users, they have to be written in a more prosaic way than many technology oriented patterns. We have gained good experiences with patterns that include prosaic descriptions of situations, where the problem occurred and of how to apply the pattern. To increase the usefulness of the process, an extensive catalogue of such patterns is needed, which is an indication for future work.

References

1. Alexander, C.; Ishikawa, S.; Silverstein, M.; Jacobson, M.; Fiksdahl-King, I.; Angel, S.: "A pattern language", New York: Oxford University Press, 1977.
2. Alexander, C.; Silverstein, M.; Angel, S.; Ishikawa, S.; Abrams, D.: "The Oregon Experiment", Oxford University Press, 1980.
3. Alexander, C.: "The timeless way of building", Oxford University Press, 1979.
4. Beck, K.: "eXtreme Programming Explained", Addison Wessley, 1999.
5. Boehm, B.; Hansen, W. J. (Ed.): "Spiral Development: Experience, Principles, and Refinements", Spiral Development Workshop, CMU/SEI-2000-SR-008 - http://www.sei.cmu.edu/pub/documents/00.reports/pdf/00sr008.pdf, 2000.
6. Cockburn, A.: "Writing Effective Use Cases", Boston: Addison-Wesley, 2000.
7. Eskelin, P.: "Assembly Cookbook Pattern", http://c2.com/cgi/wiki?AssemblyCookbook: 1999.
8. Fowler, M.: "Refactoring: Improving the Design of Existing Code", Addison-Wesley, 1999.
9. Gamma, E.; Helm, R.; Johnson, R.; Vlissides, J.: "Design Patterns: Elements of Reusable Object-Oriented Software", Reading, MA: Addison-Wesley, 1995.
10. Haake, J.; Schümmer, T.; Haake, A.; Bourimi, M.; Landgraf, B.: "Supporting flexible collaborative distance learning in the CURE platform", Proceedings of HICSS-37, Hawaii, 2004.
11. Kahler, H.; Mørch, A.; Stiemerling, O.; Wulf, V.: "Tailorable Systems and Cooperative Work (introduction)", in: Special Issue of Computer Supported Cooperative Work, vol. 9, no. 1, 2000.
12. Muller, M. J.; Kuhn, S.: "Participatory design", in: Communications of the ACM, vol. 36, no. 6, 1993, 24-28.
13. Schön, D.: "The Reflective Practitioner. How Professionals Think in Action", New York: Basic Books, 1983.
14. Snider, J. R.: "User Participation and the Oregon Experiment as Implemented with the Esslinger Hall Recreation and Fitness Center", http://darkwing.uoregon.edu/~jrsnider/esslinger.htm: 1999.
15. Szyperski, C.: "Component Software: Beyond Object-Oriented Programming", Addison-Wesley / ACM Press, 1998.

Roles in Agile Software Development Teams

Yael Dubinsky[1] and Orit Hazzan[2]

[1] Department of Computer Science, Technion, Israel
[2] Department of Education in Technology & Science, Technion, Israel

Abstract. One of the key elements in describing a software development method is the roles that are assigned to the members of the software team. This article describes our experience in assigning roles to students who are involved in the development of software projects, working in Extreme Programming teams. This experience, which is based on 25 such projects, teaches us that a personal role for each teammate increases personal responsibility while maintaining the essence of the software development method. In this paper we discuss ways in which different software development methods address the place of roles in a software development team. We also share our experience in refining role specifications and suggest a way to achieve and measure progress by using the perspective of the different roles.

1 Introduction

Agile software development methods (SDMs) are composed of several elements, such as practices, values, roles, techniques, and tools. Different agile SDMs differ in their role specifications. In fact, one way by which an SDM may emphasize its main principles is through the roles that it specifies.

In order to achieve personal responsibility of all teammates when guiding Extreme Programming (XP) projects in the academia, we add personal roles to the original XP roles. By having a personal role, developers are expected to perform their development tasks as well as the tasks related to their personal role. Thus, no teammates are merely developers. As it turns out, the two activities have a mutual positive influence, and consequently, the collaboration between the team members is enhanced. For example, let us assume that one of the teammates is a developer who also has the role of the tester (and as such is in charge of testing activities, such as writing unit tests and guiding other teammates in the writing of tests). This responsibility leads the teammate to write more tests for his or her own development tasks. These tests can, in turn, serve as examples that illustrate to other teammates how unit tests should be written. Another example is when a teammate, who is a developer, also has the role of the customer. On the one hand, telling customer stories leads to an awareness of these stories when developing ones own tasks; on the other hand, the development work may inspire the definition of acceptance tests that are to be defined by the customer. This "changing of hats" is possible as long as everyone is aware of which hat is appropriate for each situation. In other words, each team member plays two

J. Eckstein and H. Baumeister (Eds.): XP 2004, LNCS 3092, pp. 157–165, 2004.

roles and switches between them according to the situation; other teammates comprehend these switches and refer to the appropriate hat depending on the relevant context.

In this paper we elaborate on the roles in a software development team, share our experience in adding roles and refining role specifications, and suggest a way to achieve and measure progress by using the perspectives of these different roles.

2   Role Experience

This section describes the evolution of possible XP roles. The description is based on the experience of guiding the development of XP projects in five different one-semester courses, in which 25 projects were developed by about 325 students. Main lessons are highlighted.

Summer 2002 Semester. Our first experience with XP projects was in the "Projects in Operating Systems" course given by the Department of Computer Science at the Technion, Israel. The course is a project-based capstone course. Since the Summer 2002 semester, XP has been implemented in the course on a regular basis. The students work in groups of twelve, and each group is guided by an academic coach. Each group has a dedicated equipped Studio (see [4]) for the project purposes.

In the said semester, four XP projects were developed. Every student of every team was required to select one special role out of six possible roles - *assistant coach, tracker, tester, on-site customer, release presenter* and *iteration presenter* - and to fill that role for a period of half a semester. The grading policy took the personal XP role into consideration; therefore, each student was required to have a role. In this first semester we decided that the academic coach would play the role of XP coach and would act as the main on-site customer. The role of assistant coach was defined as that of the XP coach but was supervised over by the academic coach. We identified the continuous integration practice as a technical obstacle, especially in an academic environment in which students meet only once a week. Accordingly, during the semester, the *responsibility of continuous integration* was added to that of the release and iteration presenters.

Lesson 1. A personal role helps to increase teammates' involvement in and commitment to the software development process.

Lesson 2. Role performance improves during the second half of the semester due to the learning that takes place during the first half of the semester.

Winter 2003 Semester. In this semester, the second in which the "Projects in Operating Systems" course was offered, we continued with 2 projects, using the same 6 roles used in the Summer 2002 semester. In addition, XP was also introduced, this semester, into a course dealing with operating systems concepts and the teaching of such, which was attended by 30 prospective computer science teachers. The class, working as a single team, developed a single XP project. Roles were assigned in this case as follows: two students were *trackers*; two students were *responsible* for the different stages *of the continuous integration*, and the others were developers.

Lesson 3. The academic coach does not have to be the XP coach in order to evaluate the team's work. Therefore, the role of XP coach should be given to a student.

Lesson 4. An XP project can be developed by 30 students, but they will not all be involved in the actual development process. In addition, those students who *do* have specific roles tend to feel that they deserve bonus points for their extra work.

Spring 2003 Semester. Some changes were made in the roles assigned in the four projects that were developed in the "Projects in Operating Systems" course. The number of roles was increased to seven, since there were some groups with 13 students. The roles were: *coach, assistant coach, tracker, person in charge of continuous integration, tester, person in charge of presentations,* and *person in charge of documentation.* In this semester, the academic coach was no longer the XP coach. We cancelled the on-site customer student role, assuming that this role would be the focus of the academic coach. We added a documentation role that handles the documentation of the development process, as well as the user's guide and installation manual. We also separated the topic of continuous integration from the presentations.

Lesson 5. We realized that we could not do without the on-site customer student role, but that we could give up the assistant coach role since the role of XP coach was now played by one of the students. The appropriate steps were taken at the second release developed later in the semester.

XP was also introduced into two other courses that were held this semester. The first course was on object-oriented concepts and on the teaching of this topic, and was attended by 30 prospective computer science teachers. Special roles were not assigned to the students during this first semester, and the students developed a single project, working as a single team. Similar to our experience the semester before, we found that in this way, too, an XP project can be completed, but again many students were not involved in the actual development process. The second course into which XP was introduced was a course on software engineering methods attended by 22 mathematics major students. In this course, the seven aforementioned roles were assigned, but several roles were performed by more than one student.

Lesson 6. The upper limit for the group's size should be about 12 students. The assignment of personal roles solves the problem of lack of involvement in the actual project work.

Summer 2003 Semester. During the fourth semester, we had 4 project groups in the "Projects in Operating Systems" course with no more than 12 students in each group. It was in this semester that the list of six roles that we then considered to be an optimal list was reached: *coach, tracker, tester, person in charge of continuous integration, on-site customer,* and *person in charge of presentations.* The documentation task was added to the role of the team member who was *in charge of presentations.*

Winter 2004 Semester. During the fifth semester of the "Projects in Operating Systems" course we again had four project groups and the same list of six roles was used as in the previous semester. In addition, XP was used in two other courses. The first of the two dealt with operating systems concepts and the teaching of such, and was attended by 18 prospective computer science teachers. The second course was on object-oriented concepts and was attended by 25 mathematics major students. In both courses, the class was divided into two project groups of 9 to 13 students each.

Students were asked to offer topics for projects that were related to the course topics, and then voted on the different subjects until only two subjects remained. From previous experience we had learned that projects that are developed in the framework of courses that are not project-based courses should be based on a single release that is composed of two iterations. Thus, we assigned 13 roles in the largest group; one role per student for the entire duration of the semester. The roles were assigned after several meetings, when the students had become acquainted with each other. Each group was asked to decide on the best way to assign roles to students. This way, each student had a single role to learn, to guide the other teammates accordingly, and to support on-going related activities during the semester.

The roles, on which we will elaborate in the sequel, were *coach, tracker, person in charge of unit testing, person in charge of functional testing, person in charge of continuous integration, on-site customer, person in charge of presentations, person in charge of documentation, person in charge of design, person in charge of code standards and tools, end user, person in charge of installation shield,* and *person in charge of code correctness and efficiency.*

Lesson 7. In the coming semester (Spring 2004), which will be the sixth semester in which we will implement XP in the "Projects in Operating Systems" course, one XP role will be assigned to each student for the entire duration of the semester. This lesson is observed clearly if we examine the learning curve of these roles, and is based on the positive experience expressed in the other courses (see Winter 2004 Semester).

Note: In parallel to the above gradual clarification and refinement of the student's roles, the academic coach role was continuously refined as well during the last five semesters. We began by assuming the roles of the team coach and the customer to the academic coach, and underwent several phases through which the responsibility of this role was transferred to the students. A framework for coaching XP projects in the university is presented in [3].

3 Roles in XP Teams

In the Appendix[1], we describe the roles defined by the different agile software development methods [5,1,2]. Clearly all agile SDMs have roles that aim to enhance communication and produce a better product. Differences among the methods result mainly from the different emphasis of the SDM itself.

When guiding a software project in the academia, an equal academic load should be assigned to all students. Therefore, according to the number of stu-

---

[1] You may contact *yael@cs.technion.ac.il* for the full version including the appendix.

dents in the project team, some roles are split or, alternatively, several roles are combined into a single role. Indeed, a relevant question that should be asked now is how different roles are split or combined. We have found that *all of the roles together should cover as many as possible of those practices that we wish our students to implement throughout the project development*. The importance of this principle is illustrated by the following example. Teammates may be aware of the importance of continuous integration and may appreciate working at a sustainable pace. These practices may, however, be applied properly (in most of the cases) only if one of the team members actively pushes the team in these directions. Accordingly, we refer to *roles* as *practice representatives*.

In Section 2, we explained the process that led to the formulation of the different roles. In total, we identified 13 roles, which are described and grouped into four major groups in Table 1. The first is the *leading group*, which consists of the coach and tracker. The second is the *customer group*, which consists of three roles. This group of roles focuses on providing the customer with the required product. The third group of roles is the code group, which is composed of five roles and focuses on those aspects of software development that are directly related to the design and to the code. The fourth group is the *maintenance group*, which comprises three roles and focuses mainly on the external presentation of the product. In addition to this grouping, some of the roles support the communications between the four groups. For example, the team member who is in charge of continuous integration is also in charge of communications with the customer group.

4   Using Roles to Achieve and Measure Progress

This section presents an analysis of data that was gathered in a qualitative research during the five aforementioned semesters. The data were gathered from videotapes of the meetings of one team in each semester, interviews with students and academic coaches, students' electronic forums and reflections, project presentations, and the impressions and periodical summaries of the various role holders. This data helps us illustrate how roles can be used to achieve and measure the progress of the software project.

The progress is examined from the following three perspectives: endowing XP values, learning XP practices, and increasing awareness to the human aspects of software development. Measurement of progress using roles is executed by examining the adherence to the time schedule and to the customer stories.

We found that the XP values establish a valuable framework for teamwork. Having a role causes each teammate to become more involved and much more communicative with other team members. For example, it is not possible to motivate one's teammates to write unit tests or to write according to specific coding standards without extensively communicating with them. Courage is required in order to take on additional responsibility besides being a developer, to accomplish the required work and to urge the other teammates to follow one's instructions within a specific area of responsibility. Feedback is provided

Table 1. Roles in an academic XP team

Role	Description
Leading Group	
Coach	Coordinates and solves group problems, checks the web forum and responds on a daily basis, leads some development sessions.
Tracker	Manages the group diary, measures the group progress with respect to the estimations and tests score, manages and updates the boards.
Customer Group	
End user	Performs on-going testing of the software as an end user, contacts real end users to test the software, collects and processes the feedback received.
On site customer	Tells customer stories, makes decisions pertaining to each release and iteration, provides feedback, defines and develops acceptance tests.
In charge of acceptance testing	Works with the customer to define and develop acceptance tests, learns the topic of first-test development and instructs the others on the subject.
Code Group	
In charge of unit testing	Learns about unit testing, establishes an automated test suite, guides and supports others in developing unit tests.
In charge of design	Maintains current design, works to simplify design, searches for locations in the software that need refactoring and ensures proper execution of such.
In charge of code standards and tools	Establishes and refines group code standards, searches for development tools that can help the team, guides and supports in the maintaining of standards and use of tools.
In charge of code effectiveness and correctness	Guides other teammates in the benefits of pair programming, enforces code inspection in pairs, searches for places in the code whose effectiveness requires improvement.
In charge of continuous integration	Establishes an integration environment including source control mechanism, publishes rules pertaining to the addition of new code using the test suite, guides and supports other teammates in the integration task.
Maintenance Group	
In charge of presentations	Plans, organizes and presents version presentations, demos, and time schedule allocations.
In charge of documentation	Plans, organizes and presents the project documentation: process documentation, user's guide, and installation instructions.
In charge of installation shield	Plans and develops an automated installation kit, supports and instructs other teammates as to the appropriate way to develop software for easy and correct installation.

to others and received from other's concerning one's role and performance. In turn, this feedback increases communication. When assuming responsibility for a specific topic related to the development of a software project, one wants it to be as simple as possible in order to easily establish and maintain it. Simplicity naturally leads to the assuming of the appropriate scope of one's responsibility. Table 2 presents students' feeling about their roles with respect to XP values.

Table 2. Students' feeling about their roles with respect to XP values

Role	XP Values	Students' expressions
Tracker	Simplicity	We do it the simplest way because we have tons of other things to do and we aren't looking for unnecessary complications.
Coach	Courage	First of all, I don't have the characteristics of a manager; I'm quite shy, not charismatic...
In charge of continuous integration	Communication	It's also hard to urge everyone to do their part ... All of this is of course understandable, and I believe I handled it well ... together with the hard work on the project.
In charge of documentation	Communication and feedback	This role is recommended for people who like to interact with other people, whether if it's in the presentation, the making of the presentation, the coding documentation or the project's working process report. If you don't like these things too much - take another role. If you do, I recommend ... Make sure from the start that people ... It is very important that they get used to doing it during the entire process of coding, and not just at the end, because ... Pay attention to the fact that people are used to ... so you have to be tough...
Customer	Feedback	As a customer, I wrote customer stories and decided... and gave feedback.
Tester	Communication	I continuously pushed them and asked them to write testing for their units and publish it on the forum. The main problem was that some of the team members didn't finish ... and in some cases I asked the coach for help in obtaining the test code.
Coach	Courage	I would say that a substantial part of the coach's duty was rendered superfluous due to the effort made by the entire group to work as a team.

The need to learn the XP practices leads to an on-going refinement of role definitions. Students performed their roles while learning the XP practices. Gradually, they became practitioners. Following are students' expressions of their feelings with respect to their perception of the different XP practices.

Customer: I had to follow and see that during implementation time people were working according to my stories.

In charge of unit testing: I published two documents that explain the testing subject. I published a request that teammates send me their planned tests for each module... I gave a short lecture about software testing...

Coach: I provided the team with the applications and operating systems, I tried to coordinate and make people move fast...

In charge of documentation: I published a documentation guidelines that also deals with coding techniques, and checked the team's code to see if they played along.

The human aspect of software development is a broad area. In this paper, we focus on students' feelings and awareness with respect to their roles, as expressed by them during the development process. Satisfaction on the part of the students in being role holders was observed, as well as in being able to obtain a global view of the project in additional to the accomplishment of specific development tasks. Most of the students reported that they handled this additional responsibility well and enjoyed it. Following are students' expressions of their feelings about their role handling.

Customer: The role gave me a "real life" feeling, not that we have a predefined task and we just perform it. This is very real, a customer with requirements,...

In charge of continuous integration: I enjoyed seeing that everything was integrated...

In charge of unit testing: I didn't enjoy the role at all ... it caused me a great deal of nervousness in the past two months...

In charge of documentation: So *I* wrote the documentation that *he* was supposed to write...it didn't kill me, but I consider it as a personal failure.

Measuring the development progress is usually a complicated task. As it turns out, by using roles we can obtain information on many of the elements of the progress of a software project in the form of narratives expressed by role holders. We used three narrative tools: stand-up meetings, periodical summaries by roles holders, and role holders' web expressions and reflections. An analyzed collection of the narratives information at every stage gives quick glances on the status of the team, and when looking at them over time, the progress in the different aspects of the project is revealed. Following are quotes taken from role holders' summaries of a specific project. These summaries were written at the beginning of the project after one week of development and two weeks before the presentation of the first iteration of the first release.

End user: I worked with the customer. We met with the coach in order to discuss the graphical interface. We defined each button...

Coach: I met most of the teammates in order to coordinate... I worked with the tracker on the documentation and publishing of the development tasks...

In charge of installation shield: I'm going to search for installation software and try to learn it for future use.

In charge of unit testing: I learnt about the subject...

In charge of presentations: For now, no actions concerning my role were required, but there soon will be.

5   Conclusion

It is a well-known fact that software development is a complicated process. In practice, a very unique kind of teamwork is required in order to accomplish its many significant elements. This paper raises the question whether each teammate in a development team should have one major role in addition to his or her personal development tasks. It is suggested that when a teammate has a specific role, his or her personal responsibility and accountability with respect to that aspect of the software development process represented by the said role, increase. The total array of roles enables the accomplishment of all practices we wish to include in the development process and leads to a high involvement of all teammates in the development process. Although this article presents data analysis of XP projects conducted in a university setting, we suggest that the above conclusion need not be limited to the academia, but rather its implementations for the software industry should be considered as well.

Acknowledgements. This research was supported by Technion V.P.R. Fund – B. and G. Greenberg Research Fund (Ottawa).

References

1. Beck, K.: Extreme Programming Explained: Embrace Change. Addison-Wesley 2000.
2. Crispin, L. and House, T.: Testing Extreme Programming. Addison-Wesley 2002.
3. Dubinsky, Y. and Hazzan, O.: eXtreme Programming as a Framework for Student-Project Coaching in Computer Science Capstone Courses. Proceedings of the IEEE Int. Conf. on Software - Science, Technology & Engineering, pp. 53-59, 2003.
4. Hazzan, O.: The reflective practitioner perspective in software engineering education. The Journal of Systems and Software 63(3), pp. 161-171, 2002.
5. Highsmith, J.: Agile Software developments Ecosystems. Addison-Wesley 2002.

Empirical Analysis on the Satisfaction of IT Employees Comparing XP Practices with Other Software Development Methodologies

Katiuscia Mannaro, Marco Melis, and Michele Marchesi

DIEE, Department of Electric and Electrical Engineering, University of Cagliari
Piazza d'Armi,
09123 Cagliari, Italy
{mannaro, marco.melis, michele}@diee.unica.it
http://agile.diee.unica.it

Abstract. Job satisfaction has been studied by economists and psychologists. We believe this factor is very important in that it influences the effectiveness of the software development process. This paper reports the first results of a comparative analytic study on the job satisfaction of developers that use XP practices and others that do not use XP practices. By determining the factors that are highly valued by developers, the research can provide insight in currently practised software development processes, and help make changes that increase their strategic value.

1 Introduction

Extreme Programming (short XP) is a lightweight discipline of software development that became very popular in recent years. This paper reports the comparative results of a research study on job satisfaction of IT employees that use XP practices in their software development process and IT employees that do not not use them[1].

Many XP projects have been completed but to our knowledge no quantitative study, to point out the efficiency of this light approach objectively compared to others Non-XP practices, has been accomplished yet.

Job satisfaction involves any work area and job performance is strictly correlated with it. Organizations interested in job satisfaction that identify and measure the perceptions and opinions of their IT employees, will get a better return for the same investment on research. Consequently, it is important to study the effectiveness of software development methodologies from the viewpoint of developers.

The development of an effective, validated and reliable survey for evaluating job satisfaction is fundamental to this purpose. In this paper we describe the rationale and procedures for the developing a survey to assess the job satisfaction

---

[1] This study is part of MAPS research project (Agile Methodologies for Software Production) funded by the FIRB research fund (grant nr. RBNE01JRK8) of the Italian Government (MIUR).

J. Eckstein and H. Baumeister (Eds.): XP 2004, LNCS 3092, pp. 166–174, 2004.

of IT employees (Section 2 and Section 4); we explain how data are gathered to support validation and reliability of this survey (Section 3); finally we present its results (Section 5).

2   Method

At present in the field of software engineering research, there has been great interest in the explorative type of surveys. Understanding the factors affecting software development is one of the main goals of empirical software engineering, and explorative surveys are very useful to this purpose. Since our research interest is the opinions and perceptions of adopted software development methodologies, we have carried out an empirical study using a questionnaire, in order to gather quantitative data about the population of IT employees.

2.1   Web-Based Survey

After a careful study and an analysis of several survey typologies [2], we chose to perform an on-line Survey, using a commercially available web survey tool: Create Survey[2]. This tool helped us reduce time and development costs in carrying out the survey. Data can be directly entered by the respondents, avoiding the tedious error-prone tasks of manual data entry by an operator. A Web-based survey presents a number of advantages [4] compared to telephone, e-mail or other traditional techniques. For instance, in traditional paper-based surveys, questions can be passed over for lack of care, or other reasons. On the contrary, on-line surveys allow to answer a subsequent question only if the previous one has been answered. Moreover, we chose a web-based survey also because all the members of our sample population are daily web-browsers users.

2.2   Structure of the Survey

The research process has been carried out according to the following phases:

- Formulation of the problem by establishing study objectives and a research plan: GQM approach;
- Sampling by definition of population characteristics;
- Data gathering;
- Data processing and data analysis;
- Research report.

GQM approach. To structure our research, we followed the Goal-Questions-Metrics (GQM) approach, the well known paradigm proposed by Victor Basili [3]. Our purpose in this survey is to understand the feelings and satisfaction of XP users (XPers) and non-XP users (Non-XPers) about their software development process. A secondary goal is to evaluate how Non-Xpers consider XP practices

---

[2] www.createsurvey.com

and their possible adoption. The GQM framework of the research is shown in Table 1.

Once the goals have been defined, a set of questions is used to achieve a specific goal, while a set of metrics may be associated with every question. We developed two questionnaires, one for persons using XP practices and one for those not using XP practices.

Table 1. GQM Approach

Goal	Purpose	Evaluate
	Issue	the job satisfaction related to
	Object	the software development process adopted
	Viewpoint	from the viewpoint of XP and Non-XP software developers.
Question	Q1	Is there a difference in background and application sector between XP and Non-XP developers?
Metrics	M1	Background Questions: age, gender, level of education completed, kind of product/service developed,...
Question	Q2	What is the job satisfaction and the team's work productivity as perceived by XP Users and Non-XP Users?
Metrics	M2	Assessment of quality of life and quality on the job of the developers, on the basis of the adopted software development method.
	M3	Productivity rating by the developers on the basis of the adopted software development method.
Question	Q3	How are XP practices evaluated by XP developers and Non-XP developers?
Metrics	M4	Subjective evaluation by the IT manager and IT developers.
Question	Q4	How willing are non-XP developers to adopt XP practices?
Metrics	M5	Subjective evaluation by the Non-XP developers.

3 Data Gathering

In order to avoid biases and ensure greater homogeneity in the answers, the period of data collection was limited to the Autumn-Winter 2003-2004.

The quantitative survey uses a non-systematic sampling approach. Though a probability sample was not drawn, the significance of the sample is guaranteed by the fact that the respondents have been recruited in many and very different ways, including mailing lists, newsgroups, interpersonal relations, and by self-recruiting (many developers spontaneously found the questionnaire on our website and decided to answer).

It is impossible to eliminate survey errors completely, but we have taken special care to avoid obvious errors. A sample survey is subject to four major sources of error [2]. In this survey we have taken the following steps to obviate them:

Coverage Error. We believe coverage error is low, because the analyzed population is a population of Internet users. This makes sample bias a non-concern in this population.

Sampling Error. The web-based survey has been carried out using a sample of available and volunteer respondents.

Measurement Error. We cannot check the results of inaccurate responses, because we do not know whether the respondents understood the questions correctly. However, some questions have very similar goals, and are written in several ways. So a check was made on the answers to these questions in order to eliminate incoherent responses.

Non Response Error. Respondents can only go on to the next question after having answered the previous one.

4 Design of Questionnaire

We have developed 69 questions for XPers and 57 questions for Non-XPers. For the sake of brevity we cannot report every question. The full questionnaires are available on our web site.[3]

Background Questions. We organized the questionnaires in various sections. This first and last part of the survey include questions about personal data, providing several data capable of classifying XPers and Non-XPers.

Satisfaction Rating Questions. The second section proposes the questions about satisfaction which are quite similar in the two questionnaires. Job satisfaction is analyzed by comparing the effects of variables on satisfaction with overt behaviors. We related some economic variables with subjective variables and we adopted a scale from 1 to 6, where 1: *"I Strongly Disagree"* and 6: *"I Strongly Agree"*.

A major determinant of our survey is the empirical analysis on job satisfaction. By combining the rating of generic questions with the rating of specific questions on satisfaction, it is also possible to evaluate the job productivity of the sample. Some of these questions are: *"The adoption of XP practices/the development process adopted by my team has favoured a better management of my time"*; *"The co-ordination among the team members taking part in the project work is satisfactory"*; *"The team developers are highly motivated towards the present software development method"*.

Satisfaction on XP practices Rating Questions. A third section, included only in the XPers questionnaire, was needed to estimate their level of satisfaction in the use of XP practices in the project. We adopted a scale from 1 to 5, where 1: *"Very Dissatisfied"* and 5: *"Very Satisfied"*. Examples of questions are: *"How satisfied are you with Pair Programming?"*, *"How satisfied are you with On-site Customer?"*.

---

[3] http://www.agilexp.org

Potential XP User Rating Questions. Finally, we included a fourth section only in the Non-XPers questionnaire. These questions help to estimate the propensity of Non-XPers to use XP practices. We adopted a scale of 1 to 5, where 1: *"Potentially Not at All Desirable"* and 5: *"Potentially Very Desirable"*. Some of these statements are: *"The project is directed by the customer,who is available to answer questions, set priorities, and determine project requirements any time"*; *"Every developer may be free to modify any code".*)

5   Results

Q1: Structure of the Population Sample. The population sample is made up of 55 XPers and 67 Non-XPers. In this section, we report some significant results about the answers received. We characterized our sample by studying the answers to the two questionnaires and the cross-correlations between them.

We found no significant statistical demographic difference between the two groups in terms of gender (91% male), age (a significant 75% of the respondents is aged between 26 to 40 years), and level of education (the majority has a bachelor's degree). Respondents by country are structured as follows:

- **XPers:** 64% Europe, 24% America, 2% Oceania, 9% Asia, 2% Africa
- **Non-Xpers:** 69% Europe, 20% America, 7% Oceania, 4% Asia.

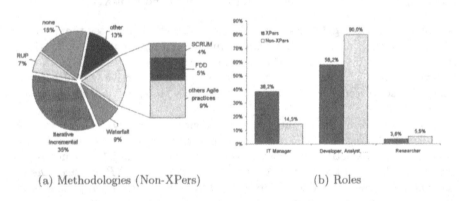

(a) Methodologies (Non-XPers)   (b) Roles

Fig. 1. Methodologies and Roles of the population sample.

In Fig. 1(a) we report the subdivision of Non-XPers respondents in relation to the particular software methodology adopted and (Fig. 1(b)) their professional role. It can be seen that among the Non-XPers respondents, 35% use an Iterative Incremental process, 9% the more traditional Waterfall process, and 7% RUP. Eighteen percent use agile methodologies such as *Scrum, Feature Driven Development* or other agile customised processes, while 18% of the Non-XPers declare: *"We do not use any specific development process".*

In Fig. 2 we characterize the population sample comparing the role with the experience gained with software development.

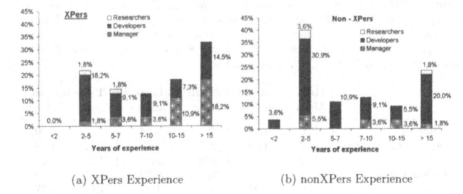

(a) XPers Experience   (b) nonXPers Experience

Fig. 2. Distribution of the population sample in relation to the Experience and the Role.

Q2: Job/Life Satisfaction and Productivity. The variables representing personal/familiar sphere, which cause an improvement in life quality, have shown a significant difference between XPers and Non-XPers (Table 2).

The adoption of XP practices seems to have a significant effect on job quality. In Table 3 the number of the variables representing job quality are been reduced to 6 macro areas:

1. the development process adopted favours the relationships and communication with colleagues (TC);
2. the job environment is pleasant and comfortable (JE);
3. the development process adopted has reduced the amount of perceived stress (RS);
4. the development process adopted has significantly increased the team's work productivity (P);
5. the developers are very motivated and have a positive attitude towards the project (M);
6. how respondents are willing to adopt the current development process again (W).

We have defined a *Team Productivity Index. Agree/Disagree* variables with statements related to team productivity have been weighted in the following way:

- Concentration (10%)
- Work Attitude (10%)
- Productivity (40%)
- Team developers' high motivation towards current development process(10%)
- Release Planning (15%)
- Time spent to supply the first version of product since the beginning of the project (15%).

Using this index, we found that 78% of XPers versus 57% of Non-XPers believe the adoption of the adopted process methodology has increased their team

Table 2. *"The adoption of the adopted methodology has Reduced the perceived Stress during my job"* (ReducedStress); *"My job does not interfere with my Family Relationship and/or with the management of my spare time"* (FamilyRelations); *"The development process adopted by my team favours a better management of my time"* (TimeMngmt). 1=Strongly Disagree, 6=Strongly Agree

	ReducedStress		FamilyRelations		TimeMngmt	
	Mean	StdDev	Mean	StdDev	Mean	StdDev
Waterfall	2,8	1,10	2,6	1,14	2,2	1,30
Incremental Iterative	3,47	1,43	2,79	1,47	3,32	1,34
RUP	3,00	1,41	3,25	2,06	2,25	1,89
Agile practices	3,64	1,03	2,64	0,92	4,27	1,42
other	4,00	1,41	3,67	1,37	4,17	1,17
none	3,60	1,43	2,90	1,29	2,80	1,14
XP	4,51	1,35	3,71	1,36	4,27	1,22

Table 3. Results (Mean and Standard deviation) regarding satisfaction on: Team Communication (**TC**), Job Environment (**JE**), Reduced Stress (**RS**), Productivity (**P**), Motivation (**M**), Willingness (**W**). 1 = Strongly Disagree, 6 = Strongly Agree

	TC	JE	RS	P	M	W
XPers	4,12 (1,25)	4,33 (1,39)	4,51 (1,35)	4,75 (1,12)	4,54 (1,15)	5,35 (0,96)
NonXPers	3,46 (1,38)	3,96 (1,26)	3,49 (1,30)	3,78 (1,39)	3,79 (1,25)	3,47 (1,51)

productivity. In this connection we can say that the former percentage is very important and significant in this survey, while the latter is not very significant because the sample of Non-XPers is very heterogeneous on account of the adopted methodology.

Q3, Q4: about XP practices. Of the XPers respondents, 85.5% claim that they have a medium to high knowledge of XP practices. We analyzed their satisfaction on the 12 XP practices, which were rated on a scale from 6 (*Very satisfied*) to 1 (*Very dissatisfied*). The average values and standard deviations are reported in Fig. 3(a).

Of XPers respondents, only 22% has had some difficulties adopting XP practices (see Fig. 4(a)) and 53% did not adopt the Metaphor practice (this result confirms previous empirical studies [6]) while 65% of those adopting the Metaphor practice are satisfied with it(Fig. 4(b)). We also found that the same percentage of XPers respondents (27,3%) do not adopt the *Planning Game* and *On Site Customer* practices. All the remaining XP practices are adopted with satisfaction by the majority of XPers .

Pair Programming is felt to positively affect job satisfaction and quality: 72,7% claimed that Pair Programming speeds up the overall software development process.

We have measured the assessment of some XP elements, from the Non-XPers viewpoint, which was rated on a scale from 5 (*Very desirable*) to 1 (*Not at all*

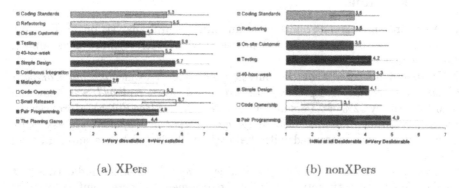

Fig. 3. Level of satisfaction of XPers on XP practices and propensity of Non-XPers to adopt XP practices (Mean and Standard Deviation).

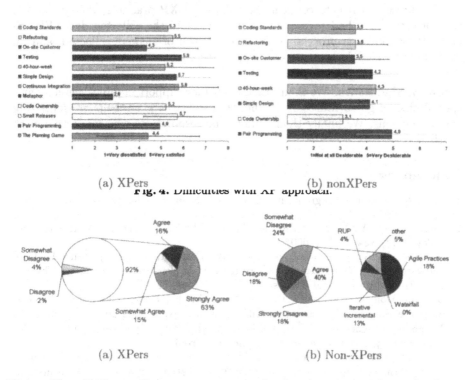

(a) XPers   (b) nonXPers

Fig. 4. Difficulties with XP approach.

(a) XPers   (b) Non-XPers

Fig. 5. "I would like my Company to carry on adopting the present software development method".

desirable). The average values and standard deviations are shown in Fig. 3(b). We can highlight a positive attitude toward Pair Programming practice.

6   Conclusions

We have presented some results from an experimental analysis on IT Employees Satisfaction by comparing XP practices with other software development methodologies.

It should be noted that the question whether *"I would like my Company to carry on adopting the present software development method"*, was answered with *"Agree"* by 92% of XPers and 40% of Non-XPers (see Fig. 5). Moreover the question whether *"I think I will adopt our current development process again in the future"*, was answered with *"Agree"* by 96.4% of XPers and 54.6% of Non-XPers.

Clearly, there is a very favourable feeling about XP practices, indicating that they ensure more satisfaction, the job environment is more comfortable and productivity increases. The tendency of Non-XPers towards XP core practices is positive and usually they are not very satisfied with their software development process.

The presented results confirm the validity of XP practices, though for the sake of brevity we had to present only a subset of the collected data. We are currently working on processing the whole bunch of answers collected, and on extending the sample.

Acknowledgements. We thank Elena Sensi for support in job psychology and special thanks go to Marco Abis and Davide Carboni for help in identifying contact persons. We finally thank the online respondents who made this work possible.

References

1. Beck, K.: Extreme Programming Explained: Embrace Change. Addison Wesley, Boston (2000)
2. Dillman, Don A.: Mail and Internet Survey: The Tailored Design Methode. John Wiley (eds), New York. (2000)
3. Basili V.: Applying the Goal/question/metric Paradigm in the Experience Factory. Software Quality Assurance and Measurement: A Worldwide perspective, Chapter 2, pp 21-44, International Thomson Computer Press (1995)
4. Dillman, Don A., Phelps, G.,Tortora, R., Swift, K., Kohrell, J., Berck, J. (ed.): Response Rate and Measurement Differences in Mixed Mode Survey: Using mail, Telephone, Interactive Voice response and the Internet. Paper available from http://survey.sesrc.wsu.edu/dillman/papers/ Mixed
5. Punter,T., Ciolkowsi,M., Freimur,B., John, I. (ed.): Conducting On-Line Survey in software Engineering. Proceedings of 2003 International Symposium on Empirical software. IEEE Computer Society, Los Alamitos, California (2003)
6. Rumpe, B., Schroeder, A.: Quantitative Survey on Extreme Programming Projects. Proceedings of XP2002 Alghero (Sardinia), May 2002. Available at http://www.xp2002.org
7. Succi, G., Marchesi, M.,Pedrycz, W., Williams L.: Preliminary Analysis of the Effects of Pair Programming on Job Satisfaction. Proceedings of XP2002 Alghero (Sardinia), May 2002. Available at http://www.xp2002.org

Agile Processes Enhancing User Participation for Small Providers of Off-the-Shelf Software

Christina Hansson[1], Yvonne Dittrich[1,2], and Dave Randall[3]

[1]Department of Software Engineering and Computer Science, Blekinge Institute of Technology, Sweden, {christina.hansson, yvonne.dittrich}@bth.se
[2] IT-University, Copenhagen, Denmark, ydi@itu.dk
[3]Department of Sociology, Manchester Metropolitan University, United Kingdom, D.Randall@mmu.ac.uk

Abstract. To survive in today's competitive software market, software developers must maintain contact with their customers and users and adopt a flexible organization which allows response to feedback and the changing requirements from the use-context. This also requires a software development that enables change proposals and error reports to be acted upon quickly. The present article uses a case study of a flexible development practice which so far has proved to be sustainable and successful to reconsider user involvement and software development practices of small software providers from an agile perspective. Implementing an agile process may allow for competitive flexibility without necessarily jeopardizing quality.

Keywords. Agile software development, user participation, qualitative methods

1 Introduction

During a research project focusing on e-government,[1] the manager of a one-stop shop in one of the municipalities involved pointed to a program for booking premises as the most useful and well-designed system they use. To our surprise, the provider was not a major company, but a small one, consisting of six people in a small town in southern Sweden. The company is known as Idavall. They allowed us to study their software development practice and how they co-operate with their customers and users; the aim is to improve their product called FRI.

What we observed can be regarded as a user-driven agile software development practice, although Idavall did not use the term "agile". The combination of use orientation and agile software development is a sustainable one: Idavall celebrated its 15th anniversary this year and users continue to be satisfied with the product

This article presents the software development practice and user involvement we observed. We discuss the possibility of small companies implementing agile processes as a way of involving users and customers in the improvement of their product,

---

[1] *Design of IT in use - supportive technologies for public services* (DitA), funded by the Swedish Agency for Innovation Systems VINNOVA, April 2000 – December 2002. The project leader is Dr. Sara Eriksén. The partners are five municipalities, two software consultancy firms, a Call Center and researchers at Blekinge Institute of Technology.

J. Eckstein and H. Baumeister (Eds.): XP 2004, LNCS 3092, pp. 175–183, 2004.

and if this can be done, what methods should be implemented. For small software and application service providers, the practices observed could provide a starting point for rethinking their software development processes. This case also provides examples of how to systematically gather feedback from users and how to make use of the feedback in the development process.

The article starts by taking up our research methods and is followed by a discussion of user participation and agile processes. Section four provides a 'rich' description of Idavall's practices; this provides the basis for our discussion. We take up what needs to be taken into account when users play a central role in the development process. The risks entailed with such a development practice are also discussed. We finish with a conclusion based on our findings.

2 Research Methods

The research we describe here was mainly based on a pragmatic approach which we might loosely term 'ethnographic;' we used qualitative methods. The latter were complemented by a quantitative questionnaire.

The fieldwork at Idavall began in January 2002. We visited Idavall regularly during the spring. Specific methods used included semi-structured and open-ended interviews, participatory observations at the company, field notes and analysis of documents. We also participated in a couple of user meetings and training courses. In the fall 2003 we returned to Idavall to follow up our previous fieldwork. The questionnaire was prepared in cooperation with Idavall. Most of the questions were of the multi-choice type and gave additional space for personal comments. Some questions were so-called open ones which gave space for individual comments. We sent out 787 e-mails and received 121 answers. The purpose of the questionnaire was to support our qualitative fieldwork and be able to find nuances among the overwhelmingly positive responses in our earlier interviews with users.

By using multiple ways of collecting data and combining different kinds of methods it is possible to support one finding with the help of others. It is also possible to find new information, i.e. to acquire additional information which can complement the overall picture. This method of evaluation is called *triangulation* and is a valuable and widely-used strategy. [14] We validated our impressions from the fieldwork by constantly referring back to, and cross-checking against various informants. This member checking is also a form of triangulation. [Ibid]

3 User Participation and Agile Processes

Usability and the usefulness of software are still problematic issues for software engineers. One of the reasons is possibly that use qualities are not attributes of the software only: they originate in the interaction between software and its use context. Use practices are not the product of design but are rather responses to the designed software. [5,10] As this response cannot be anticipated, constructive measures have been proposed to promote a useful outcome: participation of users during design and development of software [9], co-development of software and work practices, and evolutionary development allowing for feedback [7].

Mainstream software engineering addresses a somewhat different set of concerns. The aim is to control lead time, development costs, product qualities such as low number of errors, or certain real-time attributes, as well as the relation between the software development process and these variables. [1,12] The required control over development practices, decision processes and communication results in contradictory recommendations for the development process and increases the power of the developer's organization at the expense of user or customer control. [11]

Agile Software Development facilitates the discussion of user participation in software development in a new way. By introducing such concepts as community, amicability, joint decision-making, rapidity of communication, and connections to the interactions of individuals it is possible to facilitate user participation throughout development and obtain continuous user feed back. [4] The present article reports on observations of a software development practice in which the researchers did not make any direct contributions. We observed a company that combined close contact with their user community with a software development process that can be described as agile. The agile development practice allows the developers to react quickly to users requirements.

With respect to empirical work, agile development provides a different frame for understanding – and further developing – observed practices. A certain way of developing software can be regarded as a practice of agile development rather than constituting a chaotic development process. Such a perspective seems to fit software developing practices that emphasise usability and user participation. (See also [5].) The company whose development process is the subject of this article is a good example of this approach.

4 How Idavall Gets Users Involved

Idavall was founded in 1987. In the early years, the company developed a number of different programs, but from 1991 they have focused primarily on the booking system referred to here as FRI. Customers are widely dispersed, mainly in Sweden, but also in Finland and Norway.

FRI is one of the most frequently used booking systems in Sweden. Its most important users are the Swedish municipalities; a large number of different municipal administrations use the booking system. The software has a web interface that complements the basic program. The booking system is responsible for the administration of invoices, admission control and subsidies as well as bookings.

Idavall's avowed objective is to keep contact with the users of its program and to let their feedback guide future development of the system. By 'user' we mean the one who actually uses the program. When we use the word 'customer' we mean those who have money and the mandate to decide what to buy. Often, the user and the customer are not the same person. FRI was designed at the outset for one specific user. Since then the user community has expanded dramatically. This expansion has not altered the fundamental business concept employed at Idavall, which is to listen to users and develop software in a way that continues to keep customers and users satisfied. Gary, one of the employees, expressed his standpoint at a demonstration of FRI as follows: "The development is driven by our users, not by ourselves". In pursuance of this, representatives from Idavall meet their users by means of different kinds of activities. Following is a description of some of these activities. This description forms the basis of ensuing discussions.

4.1   User Meetings

Every year about 8 to 10 meetings for users and customers are held throughout Sweden, Norway and Finland. The meetings are informal, and their purpose is to disseminate news, discuss further developments, and answer questions about the booking system. For the users, user-meetings provide the opportunity to meet other users in the same area. User meetings thus offer an opportunity to create networks that make it easier to make contact with one other and thus co-operate on common questions or problems. Most of those who participate in user meetings (67%) think they are a good opportunity to learn new functions and meet other users and representatives from Idavall. Those who do not participate think that they do not need to, or feel that they do not have the time to attend. Some prefer to have individual teaching and support. One said "I do not want to listen to other users' problem; who is interested in listening to our problems?" Idavall's representatives encourage users to present proposals for new functionality and report errors. Every user meeting has its own link on the Idavall web site; participants are presented here as well as proposals, and failures are documented. This information is valuable to Idavall in the future development of FRI.

4.2   Support

One of the most important parts of Idavall's business philosophy is to offer adequate, friendly and professional support. According to the questionnaire, users think that the support service provided is very good. The majority think that they always receive quick and personal help. Explanations of problems are easy to understand. In addition to the user meetings, user support offers one of the most important ways of keeping informed about users' needs, wishes and proposals. Idavall claims that the objective is to talk to the user in exactly the same way that users normally talk, avoiding technical jargon. As one respondent said, 'no one should feel stupid or crazy when calling Idavall for support'. 86% of those who returned the questionnaire gave the highest or second highest score to the overall comprehension of the support service. However, it should also be mentioned that one desire was to have support service during the lunch break and in the evening. Many users work for associations and only use the booking-system after office hours. Support is given Monday to Friday between 8 am and 12 am. Everybody answers support calls, even the developers of the team. This in turn means that the developers receive first-hand feedback about problems with their product, thereby removing a reporting problem.

A call to the support service is initially generated when a problem arises. However, during the course of such calls proposals for new functionalities also appear. As a result, almost every phone call to the support service is logged in a searchable text database.

4.3   Courses

FRI can easily be tailor-made to specific requirements. How it is used depends on the customer; a higher level of knowledge is required than for using Microsoft Windows and Office^{tm}. Idavall offers courses where the use of different parts of the booking system is discussed and taught. In the questionnaire, users state that they consider it important to participate in courses. Besides learning about the booking system, they suggest they also get to know other users, which in turn makes it easier to share knowledge, e.g. by calling and asking how other organizations adapt the program to a specific task. They also like to come to Idavall and meet the developers. 'It becomes easier to call the support service when you know the face of a person'. Those who do not participate say that courses are too far away or too expensive. About 16% of those who returned the questionnaire say that they do not have enough time to take on extra responsibilities. Others remark that they teach each other at their place of work, or that they learn by doing.

5   Agile Development to Accommodate User Feedback

The development of FRI is an ongoing process. The system is continually being improved to satisfy the ever-evolving needs of users. How do the developers at Idavall manage to read and take advantage of all the error reports and change proposals sent in by their users? Despite the absence of a formal development process, the process can be seen as two different cycles. The faster and smaller on-going development cycle where errors are corrected and minor improvements continually take place is highly flexible. In the larger and slower long-term development cycle, major improvements take place. These cycles run simultaneously throughout the year.

5.1   Deciding What to Do

Before the implementation of new functionality starts, the proposals from users are reviewed and informally ranked by staff. Proposals are ranked according to their quality: Is the change generic? How would it affect other functionality? Is it useful for many users? How cumbersome would it be to implement the change? Ted, one of the developers, said that he preferred to implement many smaller improvements as opposed to one large one because many smaller changes make a lot of people happy. As every developer also has contact with users and customers, the users' perspectives are shared by many.

5.2   Daily Ongoing Development Cycle

The focus here is on implementation of users' proposals, refinement of existing functionalities, improvements in existing parts and correcting errors. Correcting errors has the highest priority. The code increases continuously since the functionality is growing. Sometimes code is written twice as a similar functionality is implemented. The developers must therefore re-factor their code regularly to make it easier to maintain. Jason tests all new code locally on his computer before he integrates it into the version on the common server. This means that the version on the server is always the latest tested version.

Programming takes place primarily in the afternoons, when the support service is closed. It takes between one and five weeks for a new version to be released on the website. This means that each release is quite small. A 'What's new' description is published for every version. This allows users to choose for themselves whether or not to download the most recent version. The system is designed so that not every change needs to be downloaded and installed. The idea is that every user shall be able to download and install a new version without the help of a technician. However, the questionnaire shows that new versions are in most cases installed by a technician; this is often because FRI is hosted on a server. 28% of the users returning the questionnaire download all versions while 18% only download the compulsory ones. Where this is the case, it is posted on the website and every user receives an e-mail.

5.3 Long-Term Development Cycle

The last major development took place in 1996, when a module was added that introduced steering number code locks throughout the system. Today, a new 32-bit version of FRI, which will replace the present 16-bit version, is being developed by Ted. The development of this new version normally takes place when the daily ongoing development cycles are relatively quiet. The new version will offer opportunities to add several new features. Today it is impossible to implement some of the change proposals in the present software due to an outdated implementation technique. The new version will accommodate the new improvements. The questionnaire shows that there is a great demand for the new 32-bit version.

A beta-version is already available to pilot-users. These users give feedback on the new version; this influences the ongoing development. The old version of the software will be maintained in parallel to the new version for an indefinite time.

6 Discussion

From a mainstream software engineering perspective the above-described practice could only be described as unorganized software development without any agreement on process. The success of the company argues against this perception: 15 years and a very satisfied and active user community is more than many companies achieve. So how can we make sense of what we observed? Idavall's practices are not a conscious implementation and adaptation of the ideas of the Agile manifesto [4] The company only came to know about agile processes through us. Applying an agile perspective [4], however, allows us to see our observations as a practice of agile development, and to understand how the necessary flexibility to react to user and customer feedback is achieved in a way that is sustainable for the developers as well as for the business. Instead of highlighting the shortcomings from a traditional software engineering perspective, we can understand how the developers at Idavall make things work and discuss their way of developing software.

6.1 What Is Needed to Take into Account User Feedback?

The decision as to whether to implement an agile process, and also which one should be implemented, is left to the discretion of each development organization. However, to use agile development to implement a user-driven software development process, additional measures are needed. Below we focus on what we see as the central factors behind a user-driven agile development process related to Idavall's way of developing FRI.

Communication is one of the main values in agile processes [2, 4]. The absence of communication or inadequate communication can jeopardize a project. Informal meetings between developers normally take place during the day and take the form of 'stand-up' meetings, i.e. people walk in and out of each other's rooms and discuss how to solve problems or what to implement next. Spatial arrangements are also important; Idavall's lunchroom, which is an open area, is located at the heart of the organization. A lot of discussions about design issues and problems take place here during coffee and lunch breaks.

Possibilities for direct communication between developers and users are also important. Arranging user meetings and courses around the country is one way to bring together users from a specific area and Idavall personnel. These activities also stimulate co-operation and mutual learning between users. An ongoing process of contributions and discussions in smaller groups would have a fruitful impact on the ongoing development of a system. These smaller groups can be compared to what Fischer (2001) called *Communities of Interests* (CoI). A basic challenge faced by the CoIs is developing a shared understanding of the task at hand. New knowledge is constructed through discussions and mutual learning. Participation shifts in such circumstances from designing a system to using and evolving it. User-meetings and courses are typical activities that bring users together and help to develop such CoIs.

Similar user communities can be observed in the computer game industry. [8] Expert users receive preview versions of new developments and become involved in designing new features. As the computer gamers feel at ease with electronic communication, the establishment of a website virtual community seems sufficient [3].

User meetings, user communities and courses are important arenas where developers and users can discuss problems and future developments. Nonetheless, the *support service* is the most valuable and most frequent way of keeping in touch with users since it is conducted on a daily basis. Such frequent user contact ensures that the 'right thing' is developed. It is important that developers man the support service on a regular basis. They also become aware of shortcomings in the booking system as well as users' requirements and needs. Through such frequent contact it is possible to react quickly and flexibly to new requirements. Close and continuous contact with satisfied users also stimulates the developers to do a good job.

It is necessary to *keep a record of feedback* and proposals arising from the support service, user-meetings and courses. Idavall runs the text database and web site mentioned earlier. Rittenbruch et al. [13] discuss their interaction with distributed users. They used an electronic system where users communicated their requirements, feedback and proposals via a web interface. These requirements were integrated into the design process in the same way as the requirements and proposals from Idavall's database and web site were integrated into Idavall's development process.

Working close to users requires a *technical as well as a social competence*. The developers work flexibly with different kinds of tasks. In addition to development tasks and support, they also teach and plan courses. Most of them also plan and participate in user meetings around the country. Their relationship to the users is friendly and relaxed. They must be able to talk to a technician using technical language and to the common user in non-technical language.

6.2   The Risks of Such a Development Practice

As proposed above, Idavall's practices successfully combine user participation with an agile-like software development process. Users are highly involved in the development process, and developers can react quickly to new requirements. But of course, one can find problems, and the development process has disadvantages and involves risks as well. These can have a serious impact on the development process and cause problems. We have identified the following potential problems.

The *prioritization process* is totally controlled by the developers at Idavall: users are only able to propose new functionality but have no impact on the prioritization process. This is a potential problem since wrong proposals may be implemented.

Relatively few users returned the questionnaire; this may mean that only a *few users might be active users* and bother to tell Idavall when problems arise or when new functionality is required. This means that only certain parts of the user community participate in the development process in the end and have any impact on the system. These users may not be typical users and may thus not be representative.

The informality of the development practice and the fact that only six people are employed at Idavall makes the process highly *dependent on the individual* person, and thus vulnerable. Every employee has his or her own specialties and cannot be easily replaced. It takes a long time to learn how the different parts of a booking system are built up and how to support them. According to Gary, it takes about one year before you are able to give FRI support in a proper way and on your own. If someone falls ill for a long period there would be serious problems.

Program developers at Idavall take care of support, develop the program, teach courses and participate in user meetings. To implement such a practice one must find employees who are able to rule out both the technical and social aspects of the work. It is difficult to *find the right person* for the job. Gary told us that the last time he had to find someone to employ it took him more than one year to find the right man.

Despite these potential problems, the case provides an example of how users and developers can work together on a daily process throughout the project.

7   Conclusions

This article describes a way of developing software where the users have a decisive impact on the process. Users steer developments in the sense that they give feedback on an existing program and make proposals for new functionality. Users and developers meet each other face-to face on a regular basis and in a variety of circumstances. Users also have a feeling that they are developing FRI in a co-operative way. This is made possible by a user-driven agile development practice. The agility of the process makes the development highly flexible and sensitive to the environment in which the software is used.

Small companies in particular could learn from this way of using agile development processes as a means of becoming more sensitive to customer and user requirements. They also could learn how to systematically gather user feedback and make use of it in the development process. We claim that this method of software development results in a product that satisfies both customers and users. The software is brought into line with customers' and users' needs.

Agile development provides a framework in which to understand existing software practices and an orientation for improvement that does not eliminate the flexibility that is necessary for responding to continuously evolving user requirements.

Combining user participation and agile development processes is our focus for future research, primarily in the area of computer support for municipalities.

References

1. Basili, V., Greeen, S.: Software Process Evolution at the SEL, IEEE Software, July (1994) 58-66
2. Beck, K.: Extreme Programming Explained: Embrace Change. Addison Wesley (1999)
3. Chang, A-M., Kannan, P.K., Whinston, A. B.: Electronic Communities as Intermediaries: The Issues and Economics. In: Proceedings of the 32nd Hawaii International Conference on System Science, IEEE Computer Society Press, Los Alamitos, CA, (1999)
4. Cockburn, A.: Agile Software Development. Addison-Wesley, UK (2002)
5. Dittrich, Y., Eriksén, S., Hansson, C.: PD in the Wild: Evolving Practices of Design in Use. In: Binder, T., Gregory, J., Wagner, I. (eds): Proceedings of the PDC 2002, Malmö, Sweden (2002)
6. Fischer, G.: Communities of Interests: Learning through the Interaction of Multiple Knowledge Systems. 24th Annual Information System Research Seminar in Scandinavia (IRIS'24), Ulvik, Norway (2001)
7. Floyd, C., Reisin, F.M., Schmidt, G.: STEPS to Software Development with Users. In: Ghezzi, G., McDermid, J.A. (eds.): Software Development and Reality Construction. Springer Verlag, Berlin (1989) 48-64
8. Henfridsson, O., Holmstrom, H.: Developing E-commerce in internetworked organizations: A case of customer involvement throughout the computer gaming value chain, Database for Advances in Information Systems 2002 vol.: 33 issue: 4 (2002) 38-50,
9. Kensing, F., Blomberg, J.: Participatory Design: Issues and Concerns, Computer Supported Cooperative Work 7, (1998) 167-185
10. Lehmann, M.: Programs, LifeCycles, and Laws of Software Evolution. In: Proceedings of the IEEE 68, (1980) 1060-1076
11. Nørbjerg, J., Kraft, P.: Software Practice is Social Practice. In: Dittrich, Y. Floyd, C., Klischewski, R. (eds.): Social thinking – Software practice. MIT Press, Cambridge Mass, (2002)
12. Paulk, M C., Curtis, B., Chrissis, M B., Weber, C V.: Capability Maturity Model, Version 1.1., IEEE Software , July (1993) 18-27
13. Rittenbruch, M., McEvan, G., Ward, N., Mansfiels T., Bartenstein, D.: Extreme Participation – Moving Extreme Programming Towards Participatory Design. In: Binder, T., Gregory, J., Wagner, I. (eds): Proceedings of the PDC 2002, Malmö, Sweden, (2002)
14. Robson, C.: Real World Research. Blackwell Publishing, (2002)

Self-Adaptability of Agile Software Processes:
A Case Study on Post-iteration Workshops

Outi Salo[1], Kari Kolehmainen[1], Pekka Kyllönen[1], Jani Löthman[2],
Sanna Salmijärvi[2], and Pekka Abrahamsson[1]

[1] VTT Technical Research Centre of Finland,
P.O. Box 1100, FIN-90571 Oulu, Finland
{Outi.Salo; Kari.Kolehmainen; Pekka.Kyllonen;
Pekka.Abrahamsson}@vtt.fi
[2] Department of Information Processing Science,
P.O.Box 3000, FIN-90014 University of Oulu, Finland
{Jani.Lothman; Sanna.Salmijarvi}@oulu.fi

Abstract. None of the agile methods are claimed to fit all development situations. A team should attempt to adapt the methods and practices to fit their specific needs. For that reason agile principles call for self-reflection on a regular basis in order to identify where and how to make improvements. While some systematic approaches on how to execute this self-reflection process effectively have already been proposed, little empirical evidence currently exists. This paper reports empirical results based on a study where a project team conducted a self-reflection process called "post-iteration workshop" in order to improve and optimize the adopted practices in an XP project. Both qualitative and quantitative data were collected from four 1-2 hour workshops. The results show that with less than 4% effort it is possible to hold post-iteration workshops that significantly help to improve and optimize practices and enhance the learning and satisfaction of the project team.

1 Introduction

Agile methodologies and principles [see e.g., 1] place emphasis on incremental software development with short iterations, adaptation to changing requirements, close communication, self-organizing teams, and simplicity [2]. While all of them are challenging to implement in practice, relying on self-organizing teams is an ambitious goal in itself.

Agile proponents have noted that "each situation calls for a different methodology" [2, p. 184]. Thus, one of the principles behind agile manifesto (www.agilemanifesto.org/principles.html) suggests that the team should regularly reflect on how to become more effective, and fine-tune and adjust its behavior accordingly. Cockburn refers to "the mystery of how to construct a different methodology for each situation without spending so much time designing the methodology" [2, p. 184]. Some systematic approaches have been proposed on how to execute this self-reflection process

J. Eckstein and H. Baumeister (Eds.): XP 2004, LNCS 3092, pp. 184–193, 2004.

effectively. Cockburn [2] suggests a methodology-growing technique including a team reflection workshop after each iteration. Furthermore, Dingsøyr and Hanssen [3] have suggested a learning mechanism called postmortem reviews to be used as an extension for agile software development methods. It works towards making good use of the experiences of project participants at the end of iteration to enhance the development process. In agile software development, one iteration may last from one to four weeks [4]. In terms of knowledge management, post mortem reviews could be described as a method that targets "dynamic interaction that facilitates the transformation of personal knowledge into organizational knowledge" [5, p.14]. The idea of postmortems in software development projects is not a new one. In recent years different postmortem techniques have been used in traditional software development approaches [examples 6, 7]. They suggest that each project should conclude with postmortem review to analyze our shortcomings in order to learn and improve [7]. Postmortem reviews have been found to be effective as a tool for organizational learning and productive from the software process improvement (SPI) point of view [example 8]. However, they are not suitable, as such, to an agile software development environment since they focus on traditional software development approaches involving long durations, rich and detailed documentation and large projects [see example 7].

However, little empirical evidence on using either team reflection workshops or the lightweight postmortem reviews in agile software development exists. This paper presents empirical results from a case study (eXpert) where a project adopting Extreme Programming (XP) method systematically reflected its practices after each increment in a session that combined elements from both the Cockburn's team reflection workshop [2] and the lightweight postmortem review technique suggested by Dingsøyr and Hanssen [3]. This technique, as presented here, is referred to as a post-iteration workshop. The case study presented here is the first among an ongoing series of Agile case studies conducted at the Technical Research Centre of Finland.

This paper is composed as follows. The following section presents the research design including the method, the research target and settings. The paper continues with the results, experiences of the post-iterations workshops and conclusions. The paper concludes with final remarks.

2 Research Design

In this section, the research method, data collection, the post-iteration workshop technique (i.e., research target), and the research setting are described.

2.1 Research Method and Data Collection

The research method used in this study was action research [9] that can be seen as one form of case study. The focus is more on what practitioners do rather than what they say they do [10]. The resulting knowledge should guide the practice [11]. In action research, the modification of reality requires the possibility of researcher intervention [12]. In the post-iteration workshops the researchers' acted in the role of a moderator and participated in the generation of positive and negative findings and enhancing the process with the project team. However, they did not participate in the actual software development work, but acted more as a support team for the developers.

Quantitative and qualitative research data was collected on a) effort used on workshops, b) quantity of findings and c) their content and, d) quantity and e) content of suggested and actual process enhancements (i.e. action points). Furthermore, developers maintained diaries to record their negative and positive perceptions on the process. A final interview was also held for the project team at the end of the project.

2.2   Research Target: Post-iteration Workshop Technique

The research aims to study how a short iterative reflection session is suitable for self-adapting the practices during an Agile software development project. The existing reflection techniques (i.e. lightweight postmortem review and team reflection workshop techniques) were examined beforehand. The aim was to combine and adopt these techniques in order to attain effective self-adaptability with minimal effort and high impact. As a result, a post-iteration workshop technique was constructed.

As suggested in the postmortem review technique, the problem-solving brainstorming method called KJ method [6] was adopted in the post-iteration workshops. It was used for *generating experiences* from the project team and collecting and structuring this data. As a result, the project team generated positive experiences, i.e. the practices that should remain the same, on post-it notes and placed them individually for display on a flip chart with clarifying comments. The findings were then grouped and the groups were labeled to simplify the discussion on the emerged topic areas. Similarly, the negative findings were placed on display and grouped in order to identify the problem area. The reason for using KJ for generating experiences in post-iteration workshops instead of more free discussion, as suggested by Cockburn [2], was its controllability and effectiveness as a result of strict procedures.

Both techniques suggested prioritizing the negative findings and analyzing only the most important ones. However, in post-iteration workshop technique all the findings were considered to be equally important (whether positive or negative) and were included in further discussion. Furthermore, the amount of post-it notes was not limited in any way, as reported to be in the case of the lightweight postmortem review technique [3]. Moreover, a root cause analysis technique called the Ishikawa diagram for analyzing the underlying causes, as suggested in lightweight postmortem review technique, was considered but not included. As an alternative, the Cockburn's suggestion of analyzing the negative issues and collecting improvement suggestions along with discussion was followed using the organized flipchart of negative findings as a guide.

The post-iteration workshops ended with the generation and agreement on the improvement actions for the next iteration, i.e. list of action points. Finally, the list of action points from the previous workshop was revised to find out what improvements had actually taken place and which ones were not implemented for whatever reason.

2.3 Research Setting

The case study was conducted in a software development project (eXpert) where a team of four developers implemented an intranet application for managing the research data obtained over years at a Finnish research institute. The project lasted eight weeks and the size of the resulting product was 10000 lines of code (see more details in [15]). The development team followed the XP process as suggested by Beck [4]. The team consisted of experienced university students to confirm comparability to practitioners in industry as suggested in [13]. The development team worked in a co-located environment with an on-site customer (a representative of a management organization), as suggested in XP practices [14].

The project members were novice on using agile software development methods. They were guided to adopt all the central XP practices including planning game, small releases, metaphor, simple design, testing practices, refactoring, pair programming, collective ownership, continuous integration, 40-hour week, on-site customer, and coding standards [4]. However, the project had the freedom to adapt the practices based on their experiences from the first iteration onwards. The decisions concerning process enhancements were to be made in the post-iteration workshops.

The project team worked a 24-hour week in four days, in other words from Monday to Thursday. As proposed by the 40-hour week rule, no overtime was recommended. The possible overtime was compensated in the following iteration. The project consisted of five iterations during the eight-week period. The first four iterations were the actual software development iterations and the last one was a corrective iteration. The first three iterations lasted for two weeks and the last two iterations for one week each. A post-iteration workshop was held after each of the iterations. Only the first four workshops are comparable and as a result included in the analysis presented in this paper. The last workshop can be regarded as post-project workshop that concentrates on the experiences from the entire project instead of the previous iteration. It is a valuable part of software process improvement (SPI) in an Agile organization and will be reported thoroughly in the near future.

3 Case Study Results

In this section, the results of the post-iteration workshops are presented and interpreted. Each post-iteration workshop concentrated on the experiences gained from the previous iteration. At the end of this section, the perceptions of the project team are summarized.

3.1 Post-iteration Workshop Findings

Table 1 presents the costs of post-iteration workshops in terms of effort usage. The data includes the effort of the four software developers. Results show that the effort spent reduced from iteration to iteration. In other words, the duration of a workshop went down from over 2.5 hours to less than one hour per session. It should be noted that due to the shorter duration of the fourth iteration (i.e. one week) the proportion of effort rises even though the actual effort spent is lower. Also, one factor that presumably increases the duration of workshop in the eXpert case study is the fact that the amount of findings was not limited and all of the findings were considered equally important (i.e., no prioritization).

Table 1. Cost of post-iteration workshop

Iteration	Effort on post-iteration workshops (in hours)	Total project effort (in hours)	Effort spent on post-iteration workshops (%)
1	10,7	195,4	5,5 %
2	7,3	189,7	3,8 %
3	4,0	193,7	2,1 %
4	3,7	110,7	3,3 %
TOTAL	**25,7**	**689,5**	**3,7 %**

In Dingsøyr and Hanssen's [3] study, the effort spent on lightweight postmortem reviews was around 4.7% and the duration of one workshop was roughly 1.4 hours per person (calculated from their data). Cockburn [2] estimates a minimal duration from two to four hours. In this study, the average effort was 3.7% and the average duration of the workshop was 1.6 hours. The percentual effort spent on post-iteration workshops may seem somewhat high. However, it should be noted, that in eXpert the project team worked a 24-hour week which increases the percentual effort proportion comparing to a "normal" 40-hour week.

Findings of the post-iteration workshops are shown in Figure 1 including positive and negative issues, and how many improvement actions they were followed by.

The four post-iteration workshops resulted a total of 93 positive and 52 negative findings. Figure 1 shows the declining trend in both positive and negative findings. The positive findings decreased from 38 to 11 and negative from 25 to 8 findings per workshop. Furthermore, the implemented process changes lessened during the project. This finding is in-line with that of Cockburn [2], who argued that the changes needed in the process will be much smaller after the second and subsequent increments.

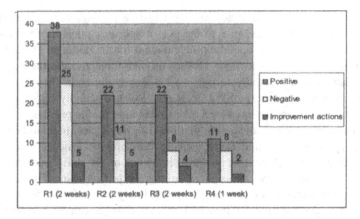

st-iteration workshop

o influence the decline
:ame more accustomed
ı have been taken for
granted. Moreover, as the post-iteration workshops were relatively close to each other
(from one to two weeks apart) the team did not find it necessary to repeat the findings
except for the most disrupting ones. However, the repeated positive and negative
findings were recorded also in the subsequent workshops.

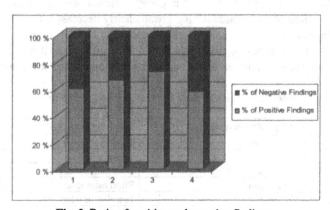

Fig. 2. Ratio of positive and negative findings

Figure 2 illustrates how the satisfaction of the project team evolved during the
project by examining the ratio between positive and negative findings. During the
first three iterations, the proportion of positive findings rises from 60% to 73%
indicating increased satisfaction. In the fourth post-iteration workshop the proportion
of positive findings dropped by 15%, while the amount of negative findings remained
the same. The trend of three first iterations suggests that the process actually
improves as a result of post-iteration workshops. However, this analysis is not yet
strong enough to draw any conclusions. Furthermore, the closer examination of

research data reveals that the topics causing negative findings became fewer during the project. The "topics" here refer to the post-it note groupings made according to the KJ-method to identify the specific problem areas for the findings. The data reveals that the criticism of the project team focuses on nine topic areas at the beginning of the project and declines rapidly to only two issues at the end. This analysis again supports the assumption that the XP process practices had actually self-adapted to the needs of the project team, i.e. increased their satisfaction for the process.

To explain the growing satisfaction that the data implicates, it should be reported that all except one suggestion for enhancing the software process practices were actually implemented. Alone, this power to influence on the daily working practices is likely to raise the positive atmosphere among the project team. Furthermore, the rapid and visible effect of the process changes is likely to satisfy the developers. The spread between the negative findings and process changes can be explained by the fact that several of the negative findings needed no actions but were rather misunderstandings or other issues solved by learning through discussion during the post-iteration workshops.

Table 2 demonstrates the top five positive and negative findings during the entire project. Interestingly, the top positive finding was the controversial pair programming practice. It continued to appeal to team members during the entire project. Noteworthy is also the fact that all of the top five positive topics belong to the practices of XP. The top negative finding was time tracking. Due to the research character of the project, the collection of measurement data was heavy and time tracking detailed. Testing only became a negative issue towards the end of the project when the motivation of the outside testing group clearly decreased. Code commenting and time estimating findings generated mostly from the lack of proper standards and instructions. Test-driven development was found to be difficult as it was the first time the project team had encountered it and an experienced coach was not available.

Table 2. Top five of the positive and negative findings

	Top 5 positive findings	Top 5 negative findings
1	Pair programming	Time tracking
2	Short iterations	Testing
3	Continuous integration	Code commenting
4	On-site customer	Effort estimation
5	Refactoring	Test-first development

Table 3 presents a summary of the improvement suggestions and actions on the top 5 negative issues to provide an overview on what kind of enhancements arose from the post-iteration workshop in the eXpert case study. The lines in an *italic* font indicate suggestions that were not implemented during the project as the others are the actual action points for the next iteration.

Table 3. Process improvement suggestions

Practice	Improvement Suggestions/actions
Time Tracking	• New column to project hours-table for dump task (PM2) • Own task for refactoring comments (PM2) • Developing personal process for time tracking (PM3) • *Tool support for time tracking (PM5)*
Testing	• Internal audits (code reviews) (PM2) • Pre-release testing (PM1)
Code Commenting	• Refactor old comments (PM2) • Commenting on test code also (PM2) • Coding standards needed (PM2) x3 • *Improve commenting: do immediately and in detail (PM5) x3* • *Coding standard should be agreed at the beginning (PM5) x2*
Time Estimating	• Improve task descriptions: More exact tasks (PM3) • *Analyzing time estimates of previous releases (PM3)*
Test First	• Modify test cases to find errors (PM2)

3.2 Developer's Perceptions

The project team felt that the post-iteration workshop technique was an effective and convenient way to learn because it summarized the previous iteration and forced each team member to think about its difficulties and negative aspects. This way each member was able to learn and improve their own actions and pay attention to negative issues even if they were not always written down as improvement suggestions. In addition, post-iteration workshops were seen as an efficient and honest way to improve the process because they actually forced the process to take a better direction. The project team found it very creative to discuss experiences and solutions in a group and to criticize the things that were done sloppily or could have been done better. The issues were brought to light and the improvement actions turned out to be successful, according to the project members. As an example, pre-release testing was brought as a new practice to the process and relieved the actual release testing with customer.

The opinion of the project team was that the post-iteration workshop, as applied in eXpert, didn't take too much effort yet still improved the weak aspects of the process significantly. When the development was done in short cycles the things agreed in post-iteration workshops stayed clear in the mind and the effects of improvements were noticeable in the following iterations. All developers were confident that post-iteration workshop was a way to get better outcome from the development process. All also favor using this technique in future projects when applicable.

4 Conclusions and Further Work

Agile software development relies on self-organizing teams and the Agile principles suggest that the team should regularly reflect on how to become more effective, and fine-tune and adjust its behavior accordingly. While some systematic approaches have been proposed on how to execute this self-reflection process effectively, little empirical evidence exists as yet. This paper has served for this purpose. Two known self-reflection approaches were combined and 4 post-iteration workshops were held on an XP project. The case study presented (eXpert) is the first in an ongoing series of Agile case studies conducted at the Technical Research Centre of Finland and provides a baseline for further replications for the progress of the post-iteration workshop technique.

Based on our experiences, the KJ method (see section 2.2. for details) proved to be an effective tool in adapting practices in an XP project, as was suggested by Dingsøyr and Hanssen [3]. The quantitative and qualitative findings from the case study support the assumption that with less than 4% effort it is possible to hold post-iteration workshops that concretely help improving and optimizing practices, and enhance the learning and satisfaction of the project team. The empirical data from the case study shows that the post-iteration workshops fine-tuned the development process and increased the project team's satisfaction. A strong indication of the benefit of the post-iteration workshop was the positive remarks made by the developers.

However, this study lacks evaluation of the effects of process improvements on, for example, the effectiveness of the process or quality of the product. One reason for this is that the existing project level SPI techniques, including the post-iteration workshops, lack a detailed procedure for the follow-up of software process improvement actions, as well as their support with, for example, measurement data. Furthermore, the existing techniques lack important aspects in enhancing the extensive learning in the future projects. As a result, the post-iteration workshop technique has been evolved and is currently being applied for further evaluation in a third XP case study (bAmbie).

References

[1]   P. Abrahamsson, J. Warsta, M. T. Siponen, and J. Ronkainen, "New directions on agile methods: A comparative analysis," presented at International Conference on Software Engineering (ICSE25), Portland, Oregon, 2003.

[2]   A. Cockburn, *Agile Software Development*. Boston: Addison-Wesley, 2002.

[3]   T. Dingsøyr and G. K. Hanssen, "Extending Agile Methods: Postmortem Reviews as Extended Feedback," presented at 4th International Workshop on Learning Software Organizations (LSO'02)), Chicago, Illinois, USA, 2002.

[4]   K. Beck, *Extreme Programming Explained: Embrace Change*: Addison Wesley Longman, Inc., 2000.

[5]   I. Nonaka and H. Takeuchi, *The Knowledge-Creating Company*, 1995.

[6]   R. Scupin, "The KJ Method: A Technique for Analyzing Data Derived from Japanese Ethnology," *Human Organization*, vol. 56, pp. 233-237, 1997.

[7]   B. Collier, T. DeMarco, and P. Fearey, "A defined process for project post mortem review," *IEEE Software*, vol. 13, pp. 65-72, 1996.

[8]   M. J. Tiedeman, "Post-mortems-methodology and experiences," *IEEE Journal on Selected Areas in Communications*, vol. 8, pp. 176-180, 1990.

[9]   J. B. Cunningham, "Case study principles for different types of cases," *Quality and quantity*, vol. 31, pp. 401-423, 1997.

[10]   D. Avison, F. Lau, M. Myers, and P. A. Nielsen, "Action Research," *Communications of the ACM*, vol. 42, pp. 94-97, 1999.

[11]   P. Oquist, "The epistemology of action research," *Acta Sociologica*, vol. 21, pp. 143-163, 1978.

[12]   G. I. Susman and R. D. Evered, "An Assessment of the Scientific Merits of Action Research," *Administrative Science Quarterly*, vol. 23, pp. 582-603, 1978.

[13]   M. Höst, B. Regnell, and C. Wohlin, "Using Students as Subjects - A Comparative Study of Students and Professionals in Lead-Time Impact Assessment," *Empirical Software Engineering*, vol. 5, pp. 201-214, 2000.

[14]   K. Beck, "Embracing Change with Extreme Programming," *IEEE Computer*, vol. 32, pp. 70-77, 1999.

[15]   P. Abrahamsson, "Extreme Programming: First Results from a Controlled Case Study," presented at 29th Euromicro Conference, Belek-Antalya, Turkey, 2003.

Enterprise Continuous Integration Using Binary Dependencies

Mike Roberts

ThoughtWorks, Ltd., Peek House, Eastcheap, London, UK
mroberts@thoughtworks.com

Abstract. Continuous Integration (CI) is a well-established practice which allows us as developers to experience fewer development conflicts and achieve rapid feedback on progress. CI by itself though becomes hard to scale as projects get large or have independent deliverables. Enterprise Continuous Integration (ECI) is an extension to CI that helps us regain the benefits of CI when working with separately developed, yet interdependent modules. We show how to develop an ECI process based upon binary dependencies, giving examples using existing .NET tools.

Keywords: Continuous integration, scalability, tools and techniques, .NET

1 Continuous Integration – A Review

Kent Beck defines Continuous Integration (CI) by stating '*No code sits unintegrated for more than a couple of hours. At the end of every development episode, the code is integrated with the latest release and all the tests must run at 100%*' [1]

Automated CI [2] takes much of the CI effort away by running an automated build every time a developer commits a change to version control (see 'Ubiquitous Automation' [3]) Automated CI is implemented by using a dedicated CI build server tool like CruiseControl [4] or CruiseControl.NET [5].

Both of these processes assume you have a single source tree which is developed as one advancing 'code line' [6].

Unfortunately, there can be scalability issues with this. While describing CI, Kent Beck states '*If integration took a couple of hours, it would not be possible to work in this style ... You also need a reasonably complete test suite that runs in a few minutes*' [1]. For a medium to large sized project (e.g. upwards of 5000 classes) a full build can take an hour to complete when compilation, unit testing and acceptance testing are included. This is long enough to significantly break up the development flow of a project using CI.

There can also be business concerns with forcing a large development effort onto a single source base with unified build and release timelines. Consider a client/server application that has a server layer communicating not only with the client GUI but also with other external applications. The release schedule for those external applications places requirements on the server code that do not exist for the client code. Thus, there is a need to decouple the GUI and server development efforts. However, if the client code needs the server code to compile, the client build must be able to find and reference the server code for each of its builds. Finally, you may decide to break up your application into different 'bounded contexts'[7] when it makes sense to have semi-independent domain models within your application.

J. Eckstein and H. Baumeister (Eds.): XP 2004, LNCS 3092, pp. 194–201, 2004.

All of these issues point to the same thing - sometimes the ideal approach of developing with one tightly bound source tree doesn't work out and we need to introduce extra processes to help.

2 Breaking up the Build by Introducing Binary Dependencies

One way to start addressing the above issues is to separate out the source tree into different modules, each with their own independent build and CI processes. Each module uses pre-built binary versions of any other modules it depends on.

We're going to use the client/server decoupling example from section 1 as a common example thread throughout the rest of this paper. We'll start resolving it by applying this binary separation idea.

Assuming the application has a layered architecture [8], its source code should be easily split into client, server and 'common' code. We can decouple the development of the client and server layers by moving the source that is specific to the client into a separate module in version control, leaving the common and server code in the original module (which we call simply the server module from now on.)

The client code requires the server code in order to compile. As a 'first cut' implementation to get the client building, we can include a pre-built binary version of the server module in the client's version control tree. We also setup **separate** CI servers to build each of the 2 modules.

This technique by itself is nothing new, but we now consider how we can extend Continuous Integration techniques to such separated projects.

3 Enterprise Continuous Integration

By itself, the above separation process has a flaw. With the separated client and server modules, as soon as a developer commits code to the server module, the client module is building against an old version of the server code. In other words, the new server code has not been integrated with the client code. Despite not having a unified build and source tree, we can still apply the principles of Continuous Integration to the complete application.

We define **Enterprise Continuous Integration (ECI)** as the process of integrating 2 separated but dependent source trees whenever code changes in either of the 2 trees.

ECI allows us to continually integrate separated modules as if they were developed as one module.

3.1 Designing an Enterprise Continuous Integration Process

Reviewing our client/server example:

- We have 2 separated modules in version control, one for the client and one for the server
- Each module has its own CI process that builds the contents of version control and produces a versioned binary distribution

- The client source tree includes a built version of the server module

The next step is to add an Enterprise Continuous Integration (ECI) process that will attempt to build the client module with the latest binary version of the server. This is **in addition** to the existing CI process that just builds what is specified by the client's build script.

3.1.1   Specifying Dependency Versions

To setup such an ECI process we need a way of varying which version of the server module the client is to build against. The first step to implementing this is to **publish** the built versions (or distributions) of the server module to a file server. It needs a structured directory layout, including the ability to locate distributions by both version number, and *latest* logical tag.

We can now update our client build to fetch a specified version of the server module from the build server before building, rather than keeping a fixed copy within the version control tree. The version of the client build script checked into the source tree would always default to use a *last-known-good* version of the server that we have successfully integrated with the client. However, the ECI process **overrides the server version to *latest*.**

We'll see concrete examples of all of this later on.

3.1.2   When to Integrate

The next question is when do we integrate? With normal CI, we perform an integration run whenever the source code changes, since that is the only changing input of our integration process. However, our client build now has a 'latest server build' that can also change, so we should perform an ECI run whenever there is a change in either the source code we are integrating, or the binary dependencies upon which the source code depends.

3.1.3   What to Do on a Successful ECI Build

The client's standard CI build is already responsible for producing a release-ready distribution and corresponding source label, so what can you usefully do with a successful ECI build? It's always good to know when everything is working together, so marking the client source with an appropriate label is a good practice. You can automate it so it's zero effort, and in most modern Source Control systems labeling is a cheap, and fast, operation.

However, you know that the client build now passes all of its tests against a new version of the server, so it's also useful to **automatically update** the client's *last-known-good* server version so that developers, and future client builds, are up-to-date with the server version.

3.1.4   What to Do on a Failed ECI Build

There are 2 possible causes of an ECI build break:

- The source module (the client module in our example) is internally broken.
- There is a discrepancy between the source module and the latest versions of the dependencies.

The first of these should also be picked up by standard CI processes. If an ECI build fails in this way we should check that the standard CI process has failed in the same way.

Breakages of the second kind are the feedback that ECI provides beyond single-module CI. There are various reasons why such a situation can have occurred:

- A compilation error may indicate a change in the interface of the server module. In this event, the development team could consider using deprecation cycles to avoid breaks between modules.
- A breaking test could indicate that the client code was relying on 'accidental behavior' of the server code. In this case the client code should be updated.
- A breaking test could also expose an untested part of the server code. In this case the server module would need updating, preferably including a new test that would simulate how the client code had broken the old code.

3.2   Versioning

So far we have made a few assumptions with respect to versioning:

- We do not need to worry about the versions of *chained* dependencies (e.g. the dependencies of the server module itself.)
- Versions of the server module increase linearly, with no branching of versions.
- If the server module is branched, it is always appropriate for the client to build against the *trunk* version of the server, rather than against a stable branch.

The first of these is a complicated area beyond the scope of this paper. A solution to it would allow us to perform binary dependency-based ECI for scenarios where we'd like any module in a complex dependency tree to cause an integration attempt for all dependent modules.

The second two points do not require assessment if dependency modules are never branched, but if they are we have some decisions to make. We'll have an introductory look at this area in the rest of this section.

3.2.1   Aside: Continuous Integration and Branching

Extreme Programming steers towards a model of continual release, and source tree branching is not required in such an ideal model. However, due to business concerns many agile development projects can't release to the actual customer at the end of every iteration (especially if iterations are 1 or 2 weeks long.) Typically a development team will construct a release branch for fixing any bugs that may appear in the release, but still be able to carry on continual development on the trunk.

In such a case, it is worth using the same CI process on the release branch that is used on the trunk, e.g. to use the same automated build, testing, and distribution techniques. However, if the CI process publishes distributables and performs labeling, how do we perform CI for both the trunk and the branch in a non-conflicting manner?

A good answer is to do the following:

- Use different CI instances for **each** code line.
- Use an appropriate **version numbering scheme** so that the distributables and labels produced by each CI instance are distinguishable from each other.

3.2.2   Targeting a Project at a Branched Dependency

In our ongoing example, it may be necessary to target the client code at a branched version of the server module. When branching the server, we would implement 2 standard CI processes (one for the branch and one for the head.) The branch CI process should publish a *'branch-latest'* distributable and the ECI process for the client module should be updated to use this branch-specific version, rather than the latest trunk version.

3.2.3 Ranged Versions and Published Interfaces

What we have done above is to create a **ranged version.** E.g. if the branch of the server defined the *1.2* version range of the module, we are saying that the client module should be able to build against *1.2.** (any 1.2 version) of the server.

The server trunk could now be considered the *1.3* version range. The differences between 1.2 and 1.3 may include an update of the 'published interface' [9] of the module.

4   Example – Implementing Enterprise CI in .NET

Now we have a design for ECI, how do we implement it? For Java and .NET the tools already exist since we can use standard CI and build applications. In .NET specifically we can use *CruiseControl.NET* [4] and *NAnt* [10]. There are various other .NET build and CI tools (*Draco.NET* [11] and *Hippo.NET* [12] are alternative CI tools, and *MSBuild* is an alternative build tool to be released as part of .NET 1.2)

We will follow on with the client / server example and will assume that the client depends on a '1.2' branch of the server. We use *NAnt* and *CruiseControl.NET* as our build and CI tools.

4.1   Defining the Distribution File Server Directory Structure

We are implementing ECI using binary dependencies, so let's start off by setting up our dependency distribution file server structure. Below is a directory tree that would be created by the 3 individual 'atomic' CI instances (1 for the client, 1 for the server's *1.2* branch, and 1 for the server's *1.3* trunk).

```
\\DistributionFileServer\
+--> Server
|      +--> 1.2.455
|      |      +--> server.zip      distribution file
|      +--> 1.2.456
|      +--> 1.2.457                the last successful 1.2 build
|      +--> 1.2.latest            always the last successful 1.2 build
|      +--> 1.3.20
|      +--> 1.3.21                 the last successful 1.3 build
|      +--> latest                always the last successful trunk build
|
+--> Client
       +--> 1045
       |      +--> client.zip      distribution file
       +--> 1046                   the last successful client build
```

4.2   The Client Build Script

We now setup a *NAnt* build script for the client. NAnt uses *targets* to define actions to happen during the build. Our build script needs a target to retrieve dependencies (*get-dependencies*), and a main target (*all*) that makes sure this happens before the rest of the build occurs. The *server-version* number is specified in a *property*, and this can be overridden by the environment calling the NAnt script. The *server-version* property enables us to specify exactly which server distribution file to use.

```
<project name="client" default="all">
    <property name="server-dist-location"
value="\\DistributionFileServer\Server"/>
    <property name="server-version" value="1.2.456"/>
    <property name="server-dist-name" value="server.zip"/>

    <target name="get-dependencies">
        <mkdir dir="dependencies\server"/>
        <unzip zipfile=="${server-dist-location}\${server-
version}\${server-distname}" todir="dependencies\server" />
    </target>

    <target name="all" depends="get-dependencies, compile, test,
deploy, dist"/>
    <!-- .. Other targets would go here.. -->
</project>
```

4.3   The CruiseControl.NET Config File for the ECI Build

Now we can create a *CruiseControl.NET* instance for our ECI build. We do this by setting up a configuration file like the following. It has 2 critical sections:
1. A *sourcecontrol* section which defines where to check for modifications. We look in 2 locations – on the *filesystem* to check for server version 1.2 changes and in *cvs* to check for client changes.
2. A *build* section which defines what to build when a change is detected. It runs the NAnt build tool, and specifies the client project's build directory and build script (which configured in the previous section). Importantly it overrides the *server-version* property to always use the *latest* version of the server.

It is the check of the server distribution directory, and the override of *the server-version* property that would differentiate this from the client's normal configuration.

```
<cruisecontrol>
  <project name="ClientECI">
    <sourcecontrol type="multi">
      <sourceControls>
        <filesystem>
<repositoryRoot>\\DistributionFileServer\Server\1.2.latest</repositoryRo
ot>
        </filesystem>
        <cvs>
          <executable>c:\tools\cvs-exe\cvswithplinkrsh.bat</executable>
<workingDirectory>c:\localcvs\myproject\client</workingDirectory>
        </cvs>
      </sourceControls>
    </sourcecontrol>
```

```
    <build type="nant">
<executable>c:\localcvs\myproject\client\tools\nant\nant.exe</executable
>
    <baseDirectory>c:\localcvs\myproject\client</baseDirectory>
    <buildArgs>-D:server-version=1.2.latest</buildArgs>
    <buildFile>ccnet.build</buildFile>
    <targetList>
      <target>build</target>
    </targetList>
    </build>

    <!-- Other CCNet config would also appear as normal -->
  </project>
</cruisecontrol>
```

5 Other Solutions

5.1   Continue to Use Atomic Code Lines

Our motivations for Enterprise Continuous Introduction were 2 possible issues that can occur in medium-large development projects:

- Build process too slow
- Requirements for separated delivery of different components

The best solution, if possible, may well be **not** to separate out code lines. Enterprise Continuous Integration adds extra process to your team and so if (for example) you could actually shorten your build times by reworking your tests, etc., then this would be preferable. We use several techniques for this in ThoughtWorks. One related technique is to have 2 separate CI builds for one code line: one an 'express build' that just runs unit tests to give a basic idea of the success of an integration; another a longer 'full' build that actually runs database processes, acceptance tests, deployments, etc.

5.2   Enterprise Continuous Integration Using Separated Source Code Lines

A very different approach that some of my colleagues at ThoughtWorks have used successfully on large teams is to not separate out the project into binary dependencies, but instead to give different teams separated source areas (either on separated branches or in separate source control servers.) Each team has its own CI process for the code they are working on, but there are also ECI processes that attempt to integrate the entire project's code (both into and from each team's code line.)

A similar approach is Gump [13] which tries to build the latest source versions of various projects against each other.

6 Further Work

We have seen a design and corresponding implementation in .NET for Enterprise Continuous Integration which will work for many scenarios. However, we have not addressed the issue of 'chained dependencies', and specifically what happens when the versions of chained dependencies change. This area requires further work. .NET supports ranged assembly version specification, so it is possible that this may be of use in a .NET implementation.

Other areas affecting versioning that are worthy of investigation include:

- Is it worth thinking about the difference between build- and run-time dependencies?
- What is a convenient way of expressing versioned dependency requirements in build scripts and deployment artifacts?

Maven [14] includes some solutions towards these problems. It offers a way for projects to define their structure and dependencies, and from this definition 'builds' the project to produce various artifacts. It also publishes and downloads built projects using well structured, versioned repositories.

Apart from versioning, we could also address the following:

- For projects consisting of lots of separated modules, would it be worth introducing modules just for the basis of integration?
- What tests should we run in an ECI build? Can we optimize the ECI build by only running specific tests based on which dependencies have changed?

7 Summing Up

Extreme Programming defines a very useful set of practices and values that can be used throughout agile software development, including the practice of Continuous Integration. In this paper we have explored one way to solve scalability issues with Continuous Integration by splitting up a project into several modules, and then using Enterprise Continuous Integration (implemented with existing tools) to still gain the feedback that single-project CI provides.

References

1. Beck, K.: Extreme Programming Explained, Addison Wesley (2000)
2. Fowler, M., Foemmel, M., : http://martinfowler.com/articles/continuousIntegration.html
3. Hunt, A., Thomas, D.: The Pragmatic Programmer, Addison Wesley (1999)
4. CruiseControl: http://cruisecontrol.sourceforge.net/
5. CruiseControl.NET: http://ccnet.thoughtworks.net/
6. Berczuk, S., Appleton, B.: Software Configuration Management Patterns, Addison Wesley (2003)
7. Evans, E: Domain-Driven Design, Addison Wesley (2004)
8. Fowler, M.: Patterns of Enterprise Application Architecture, Addison Wesley (2003)
9. Fowler, M: http://martinfowler.com/ieeeSoftware/published.pdf
10. NAnt: http://nant.sourceforge.net/
11. Draco.NET: http://draconet.sourceforge.net/
12. Hippo.NET : http://hipponet.sourceforge.net/
13. Apache Gump : http://jakarta.apache.org/gump/
14. Apache Maven : http://maven.apache.org/

Agile Project Controlling

Stefan Roock and Henning Wolf

it-wps GmbH, Vogt-Kölln-Str. 30,
22527 Hamburg, Germany
{stefan.roock|henning.wolf}@it-wps.de
http://www.it-wps.de

Abstract. Agile methods like eXtreme Programming (XP, cf. [2]) are grass rooted. They derive from practicioneers and focus on their needs. Therefore, at the beginning, project controlling was not in the focus of agile methods. The paper shows how to integrate simple mechanisms for project controlling. These mechanisms address both developers and management needs.

1 Introduction

Project controlling covers the processes and rules within project management to ensure that the project goals are met. One key idea of project controlling is to measure the current state of the project. From this base it is possible to create a prognosis of the project future. Will the project be able to reach its goals in time on budget?

Often it is assumed that a complete requirements specification and an architecture definition is needed to do this kind of project controlling. Every time a requirement is fulfilled, the project leader can close it. Tracking closed vs. open requirements gives an idea about

the velocity of the project

the progress of implementation

a prognosis for the deadline

Agile methods claim that in most cases a complete requirements specification is an illusion. Instead the requirements specification is incomplete, inconsistent and continuously changing. These moving requirements have lead to the perception that agile projects are uncontrollable. Since project controlling needs a stable frame for data a *classic* requirements specificiation is indeed not suitable for controlling agile projects. This paper introduces hierarchical decomposition of requirements for controlling large agile projects.

J. Eckstein and H. Baumeister (Eds.): XP 2004, LNCS 3092, pp. 202–209, 2004.

2   The SCRUM Way

In the SCRUM methodology (cf. [3]) development is scheduled for so called sprints, each with a duration of 30 days. Programming tasks (*stories* in XP speak) are assigned to sprints at the beginning of the sprints. During the sprint the assigned stories must not change.

On the stable base of the assigned stories tracking is done for each single sprint. A typical diagram is shown in Figure 1.

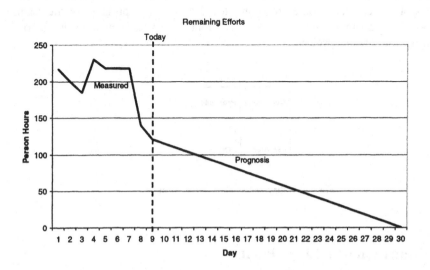

Fig. 1. SCRUM Sprint Signature

Based on such diagrams it is possible to control the development during a sprint. If the prognosis shows that the developers are not able to implement all stories, stories are removed from the sprint. If the developers work faster than expected, additional stories are assigned to the sprint.

This kind of tracking is effective for short time frames like the SCRUM sprints. But it doesn't scale up to large projects since normally it is impossible to know all stories of the whole project: The tracking base becomes instable again.

3   Hierarchical Tracking

While it isn't possible to have a complete set of all stories for medium to large size projects, it is always possible to have the *big picture*. Depending on the project size the big picture could be:

for small projects: the set of all stories

for medium size projects: the set of all features (a feature is a set of stories)

for large projects: the set of all subsystems (a subsystem has a set of features)
The elements of the big picture can be used for project tracking as long as the sets
are stable and small (should be less than 100). Figure 2 shows the possible
subsystems of a large project.

The subsystems are not detailed upfront, but on demand. When the developers start
to work on a subsystem the feature set is specified. Then the developers go on with
detailing features into stories.

The subsystems can be linked via the features to the stories and therefore to the tasks
of the developers. Whenever a story is completed it can be computed how many
stories of the current feature are completed. Knowing the progress of the features
allows us to compute the state of the current subsystem which leads us to the
progress of the whole project.

Fig. 2. Subsystems of a large project

4   Estimation with Effort Points

Counting stories, features and subsystems may be too rough for project controlling.
The efforts needed to implement two stories may vary a lot. The same applies to
features and subsystems. Therefore we use *effort points (EP)* to weight the
complexity of items. Stories are weighted with *story effort points (step)*, features with
feature effort points (feep) and subsystems with *system effort points (syep)*[1].

The estimation by effort points defines the complexity of items of the same level
(subsystem, feature, story) relative to each other. A subsystem with 3 *syep* roughly
needs three times the effort of a subsystem with 1 *syep*. In our it is quite easy to
estimate this relative complexity. After estimating the complexity of the subsystems
of a project we go on estimating the features of a few subsystems and then the stories
of a few features. With simple mathematics we get formulas for transforming *syep*,
feep and *step* into each other. Thus we get an estimation of the whole project without
knowing most of the features and stories. Figure 3 shows an example with the
subsystems *Customer, Order, Accounting* and *Production*.

---

[1] Using abstract measures is well known from Function Point Analysis (cf. [1]).

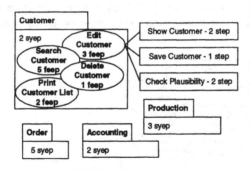

Fig. 3. Estimation with effort points

The figure shows that the *3 feep* of the feature *Edit Customer* relate to *5 step* (for the three stories). Therefore *1 feep* computes to *5/3=1.67 step*. In the subsystem Customer *2 syep* relate to *11 feep*, which means that *1 syep* computes to *11/2=5.5 feep*. In summary *1 syep* computes to *5.5*1.67=9.19 step*.

When we know how much effort we need to implement a *step* we can compute estimated efforts for features, subsystems and the whole project. Assuming *15 person hours (peh)* for a *step* in the example above we can compute that we need *15 peh * 1.67 = 25 peh* per *feep* and *25 peh * 9.19 = 230 peh* per *syep*. Since the whole project has *12 syep* the complete project effort is *230 peh * 12 = 2,760 peh*.

The effort needed to implement a step may vary. The basis for the effort calculation in the given example are 3 stories with 5 step for just one feature of one subsystem. We just finished *75 peh* of *2,760 peh* for the whole project, that represents just 2%! If we assume *20* instead of *15 peh* for a *step*, our result would be 33% higher (*3,671* instead of *2,760 peh*). Evidently a brighter basis leads to a better confidence in our estimation. It is helpful to implement stories of different features and even different subsystems at the beginning. In many cases knowledge, conditions, requirements and used technology vary a lot between features and subsystems. Our first estimations might be fuzzy, but they give an idea about the dimension of the project. The better our basis, the sharper our estimation becomes.

5 Putting It All Together

Starting up a new project we sketch the big picture. In larger projects we will end up with a list of subsystems. We identify a few subsystems which we investigate further for their features. Few of the features are then broken down into stories.

During the initial *exploration phase* we implement some of the stories to compute the initial velocity of the team. Based on the computation scheme described above we give a rough estimation for the whole project.

Agile projects normally don't implement subsystems and features sequentially. This would conflict with the idea of short releases. For a usable release one would need some features of several subsystems. This is similar for most features. In the beginning the users only need a part of each feature. Therefore we count *completed* stories and compute the completion percentage of features and subsystems (see Figure 4).

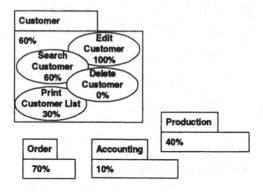

Fig. 4. Project completeness in agile projects

SCRUM-like diagrams show us the progress of the project on different levels. An *iteration completion diagram* shows progress for the current iteration. For this diagram type we simply count open *step* every day. The *release completion diagram* shows the progress for the current release. Depending on the length of the release we count open *step* or compute open *feep*. Usually this diagram is updated every week. The *project completion diagram* shows the progress on the level of subsystems. It is updated every week or every few weeks.

In most cases all project participants including customer and all developers get the information. This is especially necessary in situations where the estimation must lead to reactions like skipping some of the stories or features. In some cases when our customers insist of making fixed-price projects we only use the information internally.

6 Experiences

The concepts described so far have to be adapted to the project situation at hand. We have made following experiences with the presented practices:

- Most business sectors have well established concepts of organising systems – often oriented at departments. While the relationships between legacy systems often are tangled, the division into subsystems proved stable. In most cases it is possible to get a complete list of all subsystems of the project in short time.
- Business analysts and experienced developers mostly have a good understanding of the complexity of the subsystems. Therefore estimating the subsystems with system effort points becomes quite easy.

- The used levels for hierarchical estimation and tracking have to be adapted to the project situation. For a lot of projects stories and features are sufficient and the subsystem concept must not be used.
- Some project trackers prefer to track remaining efforts in person days directly and not in effort points. This is the original SCRUM way of tracking but leads to instability when the productivity of the team varies. Estimations based on effort points are not influenced by varying productivity, estimations based on person days are.

There are limitations to the approach presented in this paper. The following prerequisites are essential:

- You need to create a rather complete and stable list of subsystems for the project.
- You need to be able to measure or estimate the productivity of your team. If you can't, your project is still in the exploration phase.

6.1 The Project Beaker Experience

Project Beaker was running several years when we joined in. The main problem of the project was that nobody really knew the exact project state. The only thing clear was that once again an important deadline was exceeded.

Although the project wasn't agile, but had a waterfall-like style, the project controlling instruments presented in this paper proved useful. We collected all known open requirements and discovered three types: change requests, use cases and subsystems. We interpreted change requests as stories and use cases as features. Then we estimated the efforts with effort points for the three levels and calculated the remaining effort of the project in effort points.

The fact that the project was active for quite a long made it possible to analyse the previous productivity. We estimated a representative set of completed change requests and use cases to compute the needed hours per effort point (result: 11 person hours per effort point). Based on this analysis of the previous productivity we created SCRUM-like completion diagrams. While programmers and management had severe communication problems these diagrams enabled effective communication. The first time during the project the management saw a visualisation of the project state and discussions between management and programmers about the future directions of the project became possible.

Based on the discussions several actions were proposed to get the project back on the timeline. The idea of introducing new programmers into the team was controversial: While management assumed a linear growth in productivity the project team suspected that it would take a very long time for new programmers to become acquainted with the system. In this complicated situation the completion diagrams again proved useful. We assessed the effects of introducing new programmers to the teamusing a worst a best case scenario. Based on these worst and base case effects of introducing new programmers (and some other actions) we created new completion diagrams. Figure 5 shows the new completion diagram with releases R1 to R4. Since each release has its set of stories the remaining efforts increase after every release.

Obviously the gap between best and worst case increases with time but it became clear that there was a *chance* to meet all deadlines. It also became clear that the risk of failing to meet some or all of the deadlines was high. By-and-by it was possible to check the assumptions of our prognosis: We included the measured productivity into the diagram and compared it with the computed best and worst case productivity. (Side note: Our assumptions were right that the real productivity was in between best and worse case and it was closer to the best case.)

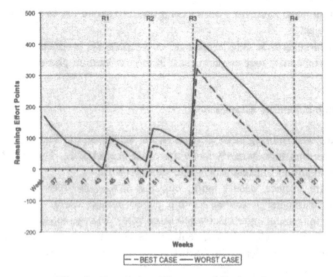

Fig. 5. Completion Diagram of Project Beaker

6.2 The Project Bear Experience

Project Bear is organized in 2 phases. Currently we stand at the beginning of phase 2 and have just fixed the contract. Phase 1 was a long exploration phase and produced a lot of prototypes. Phase 2 is a fixed-price project with variable scope. We defined requirements that are "feature size" and made them part of the contract. During development the customer may change requirements as long as the sum of feature points isn't increased.

Due to the long exploration phase our estimation basis was quite stable. We used our experiences in finishing features for this customer. The project consists of four big systems for four different organisational units. Experience tought us, that the effort to finish a feature is different for each organisational unit. This had a strong impact on our project estimation.

We started out with a first rough estimation for the project based on the idea of hierarchical effort points described in chapter 4 above. This only took a few days of discussions with customers to end up with a dimension of 4,000 person days for the whole project. Unspecified circumstances led to an arrangement that limited the effort to 2,800 person days. In discussions between customer and software developers the feature lists were reworked to give full particulars and better estimations.

The hierarchical tracking is now to be installed to track the project progress. Hierarchical structures were also necessary to do the iteration and release planning so that reasonable releases will be delivered to the customer.

Of course we are not certain, if our estimation of extra effort for producing productive software instead of prototypes is appropriate. Fortunately we made some experiences with 2 smaller systems we delivered in phase 1 which led to noticable additions to the effort estimation.

References

1. Albrecht, A.J..: Measuring application development productivity, in: GUIDE/SHARE: Proceedings of the IBM Applications Development Symposium. Monteray. 1979.
2. Beck, K.: Extreme Programming Explained. Addison-Wesley. 1999.
3. Schwaber, K. , Beedle, M.: Agile Software Development with Scrum. Prentice Hall. 2001.

Leading Fearless Change—Introducing Agile Approaches and Other New Ideas into Your Organization

Linda Rising and Mary Lynn Manns

The authors of the forthcoming patterns book on introducing innovation into organizations present their work in a dialogue about the trials and tribulations of introducing agile approaches into an organization.

J. Eckstein and H. Baumeister (Eds.): XP 2004, LNCS 3092, p. 210, 2004.
© Springer-Verlag Berlin Heidelberg 2004

Automated Generation of Unit Tests for Refactoring

Bartosz Walter and Błażej Pietrzak

Institute of Computing Science, Poznań University of Technology, Poland
{Bartosz.Walter, Blazej.Pietrzak}@cs.put.poznan.pl

Abstract. The key issue for effective refactoring is to ensure that observable behavior of the code will not change. Use of regression tests is the suggested method for verifying this property, but they appear to be not well suited for applying refactorings. The tests verify the domain-specific code relations, and often neglect properties important for the given refactoring or check the ones that actually change. In the paper we present a concept of generic refactoring tests, which are oriented toward the refactorings rather than the code. They can be generated automatically, are able to adapt to changes introduced by refactorings and learn the specifics of the tested code.

Keywords. Refactoring, unit testing, automation

1 Introduction

Software refactoring is a key to agile software maintenance [1]. It not only helps to find bugs more easily, but, what is more important, to keep it readable and ready for changes [3]. If applied regularly, it benefits in shorter learning curve and easy accommodation of possible changes. However, the necessary condition for effective refactoring is to ensure its correctness. Any modification that may introduce new bugs to the software is more dangerous than untidy code: it requires additional time wasted on debugging the formerly working code.

Unit testing [2] is commonly suggested as the primary method of verification for refactoring. Typical test cases are used to check if domain-specific relations in the code persist and bug has been re-injected . Refactorings, however, aim at different goal. Although they have to preserve the software functionality (and the regression tests as well), but they also introduce new, independent from the business domain properties that must be satisfied or break some of some existing ones. Effectively, many of ordinary test cases fail after refactoring, and some other need to be created. The considerable effort required to adjust the testing suite at every single refactoring indicates that unit tests are inappropriate for refactoring. There is a need for tests suited exclusively for refactoring that would fix the deficiencies of unit tests.

In the paper we present a concept of refactoring tests, which are intended to ease the process of testing the refactorings. These tests are created exclusively for the refactoring purposes and check the properties specific for the transformation being applied. In subsequent sections we describe the requirements for them and their suggested implementation.

J. Eckstein and H. Baumeister (Eds.): XP 2004, LNCS 3092, pp. 211–214, 2004.

2   Concept of Refactoring Tests

Unit testing plays an important role in refactoring. It comes from the observation that the testing suite collected during the everyday development is a powerful tool preventing from unwanted functional changes[1]. According to the *green bar rule* [2], all tests must run every time they are executed, so they act like anchors: protect the ship (code) from drifting out. Since XP assumes that tests are developed along with code, refactoring based on them should be relatively inexpensive and error-resistant.

Unfortunately, it is not always the case. The belief is based on an optimistic assumption that the testing suite is complete and consistent. Actually, it is not the number of tests that matters; it depends rather on the invariants being tested.

There are a few reasons why ordinary test cases are not well suited for refactoring:

- **They are developed for the code**, and therefore are focused on retaining relations specific to that code and, consequently, are closely related to it. Refactorings, however, may require different properties from those in the business area.
- The primary use of unit tests is to protect the code from injecting regressive bugs. In other words, every test **remains unchanged and verifies the same invariant** forever. Refactoring, while preserving some code properties, breaks other, and also break the unit tests. This is misleading for programmers.
- Unit tests used for refactoring purposes are assumed to **run both before and after the change is made** to verify if a given property still exists. However, in two cases the tests are legitimate to fail after the code is refactored: either the tested property is changed or removed, or is expressed now in a way that breaks a test.
- **Unit tests usually do not change**. On the other hand, refactoring enforces changes in the code (and in tests as well) not only to accommodate simple renames or replacements, but it may also introduce semantic changes.

These deficiencies show that there is a need for tests suited exclusively for refactoring, which would overcome some of the limitations mentioned above. The requirements for the proposed *refactoring tests* follow:

- **Refactoring tests should be related to a given refactoring**, not to the code. They represent invariants and properties resulting directly from the transformation.
- **They are logically independent from the ordinary, domain-oriented test cases, and are executed only while applying the refactoring**. Obviously, the refactoring tests can be later used for regression testing, but it is not the primary use of them.
- However, **their interface should be compliant with unit tests**. It allows running all tests in the same environment.
- **Refactoring tests may change during the transformation**. Unit tests are expected to run regardless from the code changes, and the refactoring tests should also comply with that rule.

The aim for the refactoring tests is to support the code analysis in verifying correctness of the source code transformations. Several preconditions for many refactorings cannot be proved statically, and the gap may be filled by refactoring tests. Obviously, they only provide support for detecting functional changes, but usually it appears sufficient for effective programming. Among refactorings provided by Fowler there are a few that can be verified with a well-known, fixed sets of tests [5]. Refactorings of that group are intended beneficiaries of the proposed refactoring tests.

3   Test Adaptation Mechanism

Although refactoring tests verify well-known, fixed properties in the code affected by the transformation, it is still the programmer who is responsible for writing them, which requires considerable effort.

Fortunately, it can be significantly minimized. A refactoring test actually builds up on two pillars: (1) a property it verifies and (2) actual code-related data: class names, methods, interfaces etc. Such generic, code independent tests are called *test templates*. Unlike an ordinary test, a test template has to be implemented once only and later can be reused for generating actual, code-specific tests.

The need for tests adaptation is another issue. As an example, let's consider *Encapsulate Collection* refactoring [3]. It replaces direct access to a collection with delegate methods provided by the collection owner. After the refactoring is complete, the destructive methods on the collection are disabled. Instead, newly created delegating methods become available. A test case for *add()* method, although syntactically correct, would therefore fail for the refactored code. To avoid this, the refactoring tests should seamlessly adapt to the changed interface.

The proposed mechanism assumes that a single refactoring test is actually composed of two test case sets: *pre-tests* and *post-tests*, executed before and after the change is made, respectively. Since they also can be expressed as test templates, the doubling the number of tests is meaningless. The subtests are invisible from outside: the refactoring test implements the *Strategy* pattern [4] and chooses one of them for execution, depending on the phase of refactoring.

It is important to notice that the multiplicity of the pre- and post-tests may differ from 1:1. Coming back to the *Encapsulate Collection* example, a pre-test for *add()* method checks if an object is successfully added to the collection. The refactoring, however, is expected to disable direct *add()* calls on collection and produce a new method *addClass()* in the owner class, that will take its responsibility. Thus, two post-tests are required: one for the existing *add()* method (that should leave collection unchanged) and another for a newly created method *addClass()* (which should succeed).

4   Learning Tests

The test templates are sufficient for generating simple tests. However, some properties of the tested code that may lead to differences in results of pre- and post-tests, are related to the specific implementation. They cannot be hardcoded in templates and must be determined at runtime. To avoid running the software, a new kind of pre-tests is introduced: *the learning tests*.

Unlike other pre-tests they are not required to pass. Their sole responsibility is to learn specific implementations by sampling the code if it behaves in a particular way. A failure is not an error indication, but a source of information about the code. The acquired results are used for generating post-tests that better fit the code internals. Learning tests help to ensure that the post-tests will expect the same behavior as the one that program presented before the transformation.

Again, the *add()* method in *Collection* interface will serve as an example. Different implementations of that interface may vary, and the programmer does not need to know how particular *add()* method in the code acts. S/he rather expects the code to preserve the behavior after the refactoring is complete. To make the post-tests immune from possible failures at inserting *null* values, a learning test checks if the collection accepts *null*s. Depending on the result, the post-test considers the failure of the same operation as an error (if pre-test succeeded) or a success (if it failed before).

The overall algorithm for using the refactoring tests is following:

1. Programmer generates pre-tests and learning-tests from existing templates for that transformation. The tests are then executed and their results are stored.
2. Programmer refactors (manually or automatically) the code.
3. The post-tests are generated and executed. The results are compared to the pre-tests footprint and evaluated. Any difference indicates that refactoring was incorrect.

5 Conclusions

The presented concept of refactoring tests has been developed as a plug-in for Eclipse platform for *Encapsulate Collection* refactoring. It is a step towards automation of refactoring in the area that previously was subject to manual-only manipulations. They are created and executed for the sake of a given refactoring, not for regression purposes, which makes them different from ordinary unit tests. They exploit the idea of test templates, which relax the programmer from coding them. Refactoring tests act like proxies for pre-tests and post-tests, which allow keeping them working regardless of the changes resulting from a refactoring. And finally, they can learn the program specific implementation and adapt to its expected behavior. Thanks to these features, testing the refactorings can be easier and less error-prone.

Acknowledgements. This work has been supported by the Polish State Committee for Scientific Research as a part of the research grant KBN/91-0824.

References

1. Beck K.: Extreme Programming Explained. Embrace Change. Addison-Wesley, 2000.
2. Beck K.: Gamma E.: Test infected: Programmers love writing tests. Java Report, 3(7), 1998, pp. 51-56.
3. Fowler M.: Refactoring. Improving the Design of Existing Code. Addison-Wesley, 1999.
4. Gamma E. et al.: Design Patterns. Elements of Reusable Object-Oriented Software. Addison-Wesley, 1995.
5. Walter B.: Extending Testability for Automated Refactoring, in: Succi G., Marchesi M. (Eds.): Extreme Programming and Agile Processes in Software Engineering, Lecture Notes in Computer Science 2675, Springer Verlag, 2003, pp. 429-430.

XP: Help or Hindrance to Knowledge Management?

Hans Dermot Doran

Starscions,
Im Ahorn 22,
8125 Zollikerberg,
Switzerland.
hans.doran@ibhdoran.com

Abstract. Whereas XP has established itself in the project managers' repertoire, there are still many issues concerning the administrative implications surrounding XP teams and the organisations within which they operate, Knowledge Management being one of those issues. This paper examines the interplay between XP and KM principles and seeks to show that while "pure" XP is incompatible with KM, agile KM can be achieved with few modifications to the XP process.

1 Introduction

"Software developers possess highly valuable knowledge relating to product development, the software development process, project management and technologies" [2].

Arguably, if this were the case then papers like this wouldn't need to be written and conferences on the subject mater wouldn't need to be held. But in technology organisations, the growth and maintenance of skills in these areas are vital to their success; the ability to prove that knowledge and skills can be efficiently utilised, provides a unique selling proposition for investors and customers alike. This allows management to view the acquisition, realisation and commissioning of development projects as a strategic exercise, abstracting, if necessary, the value drawn from such a project from the original projects aims and target industry.

From a project manager's point of view, XP is the tool of choice to develop innovative projects, read high-risk high uncertainty, precisely the kind of projects that are of strategic interest. However XP suffers from the perception of lacking transparent and definable milestones and other means by which management can; measure, in their terms, the progress of the project; fulfill their duty of supervision; have at their disposal enough material to enable founded discussions on what strategic gain has been achieved by the project results and the manner in which they were achieved.

The benefits from effective Knowledge Management (KM) are clear, for the project manager it is a risk reducing resource, for management it is a tool that allows them to consolidate and articulate their employees specific skills, further enhancing the value of the company and its position on in the market. Yet, traditional KM

J. Eckstein and H. Baumeister (Eds.): XP 2004, LNCS 3092, pp. 215–218, 2004.
© Springer-Verlag Berlin Heidelberg 2004

conjures an image of heavy investment, expensive tools and dedicated staff, as far removed from the concept of an agile methodology in the operative, and lean management in the strategic, as one may wish to get. Indeed it is only recently that experts are beginning to develop KM solutions aimed specifically at the software development industry rather than simply modifying classic techniques [1].

We shall review some knowledge relevant concepts, examine the intrinsic support, and its limitations, that XP has for KM and then draw some conclusions.

2   Concepts of Knowledge

It is generally accepted that there are at least two categories of knowledge. Explicit knowledge, that which can be articulated, written and described, and implicit or tacit knowledge that hidden quantity, embedded in the singular or collective memory and infrastructure of the company. The relationship between information and knowledge can be described by:

"Information becomes knowledge once it is processed in the mind of an individual, which then becomes information once it is articulated and communicated to others. The receiver can cognitively process the information so that it is converted back into tacit knowledge."[2]

This statement carries several important implications; tacit knowledge can only be reproducibly stored as information and the quality of tacit knowledge is both dependant on the quality of information and the cognitive abilities of the receiver. In other words the provenance plays a part in the quality of knowledge. In contrast, explicit knowledge has generally undergone the scientific process; its provenance is, or should be, irrelevant.

Data underlies all information. Data is converted to information by means of any combination of normative or cognitive analysis, it being important to understand the distinction and limitations between and of the two.

3   XP and KM

As indicated above, software engineering knowledge spans development methodologies, product development, technologies and project management. XP blurs the distinction between a software development methodology and a project management tool allowing it to be viewed as one. In fact, since XP is a collection of best practices [4], which are in themselves an articulation of knowledge, XP may be considered an example of tacit structural knowledge. That is: a collection of best practices, the peer accepted results of experience structured into a methodology, allow the initial project management to benefit from this knowledge without having to actually acquire it. Documented best practices are also examples of tacit structural knowledge. For example coding conventions that enable the programmer to accelerate his understanding of a program by structuring the way it looks and is described. It sounds obvious but lots of programmers learnt the value of coding conventions the hard way. Placing this knowledge in an open document as a collection of recommendations allows people to benefit from past experience [3] without having to think about the reasons why certain things are done in a certain way; their work is structured more efficiently.

The principles behind XP actively encourage its own mutation, enabling the integration of newly gained process knowledge back into the process, thus continuously maintaining the structural knowledge.

The primary function of the on-site customer is to contribute to the growth and utilisation of knowledge concerning the problem domain. This is then captured in the solution architecture; the residue, in the histographical sense, of the planning game and assorted other pieces of paper. The KM relevant effect of using XP is to make implicit much of the problem domain knowledge as the learning-by-doing system slowly integrates this knowledge into the product. This enables a much higher quality of problem domain knowledge than achieved by working from a specification but it is by definition implicit.

The growth and maintenance of technology knowledge, at least that demanded by the project, is also well supported by XP practices. The test first practice can be applied to external libraries and frameworks just as easily as to ones own code and the policy of small iterations allows for efficient forays into unknown territory.

At this point it is clear that XP, if carried out in the intended spirit, strongly supports implicit knowledge management without placing any extra burden on the developers. It does require an active management to recognise and guide this knowledge growth and it must be realised that this knowledge gain is wholly contained within the scope of the project. There are no intrinsic mechanisms available to transfer this knowledge to the rest of the organisation. At this point specific KM measures must be utilised.

One none KM-specific approach is to use the post mortem to determine knowledge gained, now accepted as another industry best practice [5]. Such a session can be used to articulate what is considered to be the growth in all forms of relevant knowledge types. It is not fully suitable for this purpose as a post mortem is an effectively post-hoc and quasi-canonical summation, which makes objective re-interpretation in the light of later experience difficult.

A final note on maintenance; the issue of traceability, the ability to link between requirements and code structures, is not given in an XP project. Taking the line that: since all solutions are the simplest and that the solution is it's own documentation, therefore this is not an issue, is both logically and practically untenable. Logically because the word simple requires context, and if the context is not known, there is always a simpler solution. The author experienced the practical failure of this approach, a product specification had to be created post-hock before maintenance and feature extension could be achieved with functional consistency *regardless* of the state of the code. Whereas maintenance can proceed using XP practices [6,7], there is a clear need to explicitly interface knowledge gained during development to the maintenance crew.

4   Conclusion

The XP methodology is a framework, which acts as an *a priori* knowledge base, continuously maintained by its use and modification. The knowledge gain is restricted to the scope of the project. We have shown that XP also acts as a framework within which problem domain knowledge can be generated and preserved, sometimes of exceptionally high quality. Like process knowledge, it is largely tacit with salient items embedded in the program and its architecture. There are question marks over the quality and usability of knowledge stored in this way.

Likewise, project relevant technology knowledge is facilitated by XP practices, this knowledge being embedded in the interfaces to this technology and the method of its implementation.

We have touched on the fact that the ability to articulate unique knowledge can be important for the development and self-identity of a company or team. We have also indicated that a re-interpretation of assumptions concerning company knowledge may be beneficial in the light of later experiences but this process can only be fully successful if there is original information and data available. This is not given, due to the lack of proscribed project documentation, so this important process is hindered by the XP methodology.

In theory, KM can be totally implicit within the scope of a project, since there is no method to transfer this implicit knowledge intact out of the project scope, some of this knowledge must be made explicit. As post-mortem is only partially suited to this, it is recommended that this knowledge be continually articulated during the development process. There is therefore an urgent need for the XP community to revise its philosophy on tools and documentation. This echoes the calls by those attempting to certify XP development teams according to ISO9000 [8].

[9] Discusses some experience on these matters with references to simple tools.

References

1. Managing Software Engineering Knowledge. (Eds.) Arum A., Jeffry, R., Wohlin, C., Handzic, M., Springer Verlag, Berlin Heidelberg 2003.
2. Preface. Ibid.
3. Lindvall, M., Rus, I. Knowledge Management for Software Organizations. Ibid
4. Beck, K., Extreme Programming Explained. Addison-Wesley, Reading, Massachusetts. 2000.
5. Birk, A. Dingsoyr, T., Stalhane, T., Postmortem: Never Leave a Project without It. IEEE Software 19:43-45 May/June 2002.
6. Doran, H.D., XP: Good for Anything other Than Software Development? (Eds.) Marchesi, M., Succi, G., Proceedings 4th International Conference XP2003. Springer Verlag, Berlin Heidelberg 2003.
7. Poole, C. Huismann, J.W., Using Extreme Programming in a Maintenance Environment. IEEE Software 18:42-51 November/December/ 2001.
8. Marchesi, M., Agile Methodologies and Quality Certification. Keynote Speech XP2003. Genoa. 2003.
9. Doran, H.D., Poster Session. 5th International Conference on eXtreme Programming and Agile Processes in Software Engineering XP2004. Garmisch-Partenkirchen. 2004.

Test Driven Development and Software Process Improvement in China

Kim Man Lui and Keith C.C. Chan

Department of Computing
The Hong Kong Polytechnic University, Hung Hom, Hong Kong
{cskmlui, cskcchan}@comp.polyu.edu.hk

Abstract. Developing areas in China are attracting increasing investment in manufacturing. This has increased the local demand for software and, consequently, demands on local software teams. Such teams, typically small, inexperienced and suffer high personnel turnover, often produce defective products. As software process improvement models are unsuitable for such teams, research was conducted applying a test-driven development (TDD) approach. TDD quickly improved the overall team performance. Our findings are applicable in other Asian developing countries.

1 Introduction

Time pressure makes software teams reduce testing cases, or postpone part of them so that the program can be promptly released. This affects software quality even if the system is developed by talent programmers. The situation gets worsened if the system is developed by inexperienced software teams as such team members are generally not skilled at time estimation or quality assurance, and do not quickly learning from their mistakes. As China is a world factory, many manufacturing plants are built in developing areas and they are the source of a strong demand for custom-made commercial software. Consequently, the number of software teams there has increased exponentially. These teams are local, small, inexperienced and suffer from high staff turnover. But, the demands of product quality and customer satisfaction require that these teams improve their software processes. Unfortunately, heavyweight models like CMM may not be appropriate for software development that uses such small, high turnover software teams. Test Driven Development (TDD) [1] casts light onto the software process improvement for inexperienced software teams .

2 Software Development in Developing Areas in China

In developed cities in China, well-trained and experienced developers are readily available for software projects. However, China has many developing cities. The trend in active rural industrialization is that manufacturing plants move from many more-developed regions to the less developed so as to exploit lower-cost land, labor and distribution channels. Consequently, numerous small local software teams, either

J. Eckstein and H. Baumeister (Eds.): XP 2004, LNCS 3092, pp. 219–222, 2004.

in-house or software house, have been established to provide system solutions. The teams composed of local people are very greatly influenced by the local environment. The gap between less-developed town and well-developed cities is huge in China. Indeed, the difference is widening because developed cities have advanced themselves much faster than developing towns. We summarize the environmental characteristics of developing areas.

- Programmers are not good at English, which hinders them from gaining new technical information on English-language web sites.
- There are few books on software methodology available in translation. Most books are about tools (e.g. Dreamweaver) and computer languages (e.g. Java).
- Active industrial developing areas can be within 250 km of the modern cities. This encourages people to seek opportunities in the nearby developed cities.
- There are a number of small computer companies. Their business is mainly on the hardware side. Generally, 80% of business is to provide hardware support.
- IT education is focused on practical tools and computer languages, rather than on software process engineering, software engineering, etc.

Managing local IT teams in such regions, we encounter a number of different problems including a lack of experienced programmers and an extremely high personnel turnover. Often, once inexperienced programmers gain valuable development experience, they would like to advance their career in developed cities. This leads to high personnel turnover rates and frequent job handovers [5]. Whether the software teams are in-house or external to a company, they have common properties.

- They are not well trained
- They are low-cost. Month salaries range from USD 62.5 to USD 312.5.
- They have fewer than eight members
- They have a high proportion of inexperienced programmers
- They have a high turnover of good members
- They rarely consider trying new ways of solving old problems
- They prefer step-by-step guidance when learning and applying new skills
- They are willing to work long hours (as much as 50-55 hrs/wk)
- They are willing to accept comments about their mistakes, yet are prone to repeat the same kind of mistake.

Software process improvement (SPI) models like CMM is not practical for those software teams because (i) cost cannot be justified as it takes time to train people and to implement the model, and (ii) for a high turnover small team, a document driven process does not seem to be a promising approach. Besides, SPI models emphasize software capability and process maturity, instead of aiming at the problem of how to manage inexperienced teams developing better software. The SPI models take a top-down approach, starting at a process level such as project planning, and only later considering the many lower level tasks. But, for inexperienced programmers, a bottom-up approach could be much more effective. Adopting practices directly related to programming like automated test cases quickly improves overall team performance and hence the teams have a better chance of running software projects within budget, on time and of producing quality work. We intended to adopt TDD to manage inexperienced teams. From an SPI perspective, TDD enhances visibility and quality.

It is practical as it is driven by a tool (XUnit), not by bureaucratic procedures. TDD promotes self-discipline. All these contribute to software process improvement in inexperienced teams. As TDD is a programming model more than an SPI model, many important process areas are not addressed. However, TDD delivers values to inexperienced teams and significantly improves system development in a shorter time, at lower cost and for small high-turnover teams.

3 Test-Driven Development and Software Process Improvement

This section discusses the adoption of TDD by inexperienced software teams in China. In 2003, we assisted two software teams from two companies in developing areas in China to implement TDD to improve their system development. The performance of the two teams adopting TDD and the other three non-TDD teams were compared. We found that TDD greatly improved the following four areas.

(1) Task Estimation: usually, inexperienced people wrongly estimate resources they need to complete their tasks. In particular, inexperienced programmers tend to underestimate time and, as a result, they have to cut down on testing. In some extreme cases they spend very little time on testing their code, with ratios as great as four days coding to two hours testing. This has a substantial impact on task planning. The situation greatly improved after the adoption of TDD. The reason is that it is easier to estimate how long it takes to write unit cases than how long it takes to write a piece of code. The estimation in their minds is divided into two steps: (i) think of what they need to write for unit cases and estimate the time, and then (ii) estimate the programming effort. This helps inexperienced teams better estimate the time need to complete a task. Having the unit test first establishes a specific goal; the programmers can better estimate the effort that will be required to write a program to pass the unit test (i.e. to reach the goal).

(2) Progress Tracking: there is little value in the report of an inexperienced programmer that his or her team has completed 40% of its coding. There are a number of reasons for this: (i) the code cannot be executed since it is incomplete; (ii) even if the 40% of code were completed in four days, that isn't to say that the remaining 60% can be completed in the next six days; (iii) the inexperienced programmers are not sure of how many lines the program will ultimately require, so the 40% is just a guess; (iv) the report does not include the progress of testing, so even a report of 100% done is not useful as the code still has to be tested.

After the adoption of TDD, the programmers report in a completely different dimension. They can report how many unit cases have been written and what functionality they have covered. In addition, all written code has been tested and each piece of code has its corresponding unit test. Now the programmers can provide an objective assessment of their programming progress. Although this does not tell us how long the developers will need to complete the program, it does help software managers oversee their activities. In a word, TDD provides managers with better visibility than before.

(3) Discipline: inexperienced programmers do not follow consistent practices and even where written guidelines are clearly established, they tend to work in an undisciplined way (i.e. their own way). After the adoption of TDD, the ability of inexperienced programmers to conform to standard practice greatly improved. A number of factors account for this: (i) writing unit tests is just as the same as writing code. TDD does not require the production of documents or program comments. (ii) XUnit provides an excellent tool for automating their testing. (iii) Programming activities in TDD are easily tracked with an XUnit tool. If owing to personal indiscipline or TDD misinterpretation the developers do not follow the framework, they can be quickly identified and counseled.

(4) Software Quality: after inexperienced teams have adopted TDD to develop software, has software quality improved? As the different teams were writing different commercial systems it is not possible to analyze defects on the same baseline, however, we have collected some equally interesting defect-related data. We compared how long programmers took to fix defects reported by users during user acceptance testing and production operations. In total, collected 643 defect cases from by non-TDD teams and 212 defect cases from TDD teams. Further, as Figure 1 illustrates, while non-TDD teams were able to fix only 73 % of their defects in one day, in the same time, TDD teams were to fix 97% of theirs. In short, TDD teams produced many fewer defects and fixed them much faster.

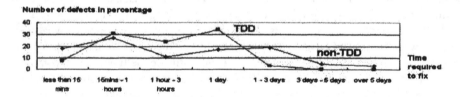

Fig. 1. Time required fixing defects by two kinds of inexperienced software teams

4   Contributions

This paper contributes to understanding how and why TDD can help small-inexperienced software teams. TDD – as agile software process improvement – does indeed improve their work processes. The lesson we learnt in this investigation may be applicable in developing Asian countries, such as Thailand and Malaysia, which share many characteristics with less developed areas in China.

References

1. Beck, K. *Test-Driven Development by Example*, Addison-Wesley, (2003)
2. Lui, K.M. and Chan, K.C.C. Inexperienced Software Team and Global Software Team Edited by Gunasekaran, A., et al, *Knowledge and Information Technology Management: Human and Social Perspectives,* Idea Group, Hershey, PA, pp 305-323, (2003)

Project Management and Agile Methodologies: A Survey

Michela Dall'Agnol, Alberto Sillitti, and Giancarlo Succi

Center for Applied Software Engineering
Free University of Bozen
I-39100 Bolzano, Italy
{mdallagnol, asillitti, succi}@unibz.it

Abstract. This paper examines analogies and differences derived by the adoption of Agile Methodologies (AMs) in a set of software companies from the point of view of project management techniques. Data come from questionnaires filled in by twenty-one managers. The analysis of these questionnaires shows that managers using AMs focus on people and process more than the other managers do. The adoption of AMs seems to be a good starting point for improving software development and customer satisfactory.

1 Introduction

Surveys covering over 8000 projects [1] indicate that the major sources of software project failure lies less with shortfalls in formal methods skills and more with shortfalls in skills to deal with stakeholder value propositions.

Five of the top six reasons of failure are related to communications among developers and customers [2].

The updated Standish Group study, conducted in 2000, identified 10 software success factors. The second most important factor is *user involvement* and the third is *experienced project manager*. This means that many projects fail due issues related to people and project management rather than technical [3].

Several recent studies [4] indicate that project managers are learning how to become more successful at managing IT projects.

The aim of this work is the investigation of the main problems in software development and the adopted solutions from the point of view of managers. The investigation is based on 21 interviews with software managers.

We adopt the Petroski's views [5]: *analyze the causes of failures can do more to advance knowledge than all the successes in the word.*

The main goal is to find out differences and analogies in software management techniques derived by the adoption of Agile Methodologies (AMs) and their effectiveness in the improvement of the software production.

This paper is organized as follows: section 2 and subsections describe the structure of the research activity performed; section 3 shows the analysis of the data; finally, section 4 draws the conclusions.

J. Eckstein and H. Baumeister (Eds.): XP 2004, LNCS 3092, pp. 223–226, 2004.
© Springer-Verlag Berlin Heidelberg 2004

2 The Structure of the Investigation

2.1 Design of the Experimentation

This research can be classified as a pre-experimental design, according to classification of Campbell and Stanley [6], in particular it is a statistic group comparison.

The study considers two groups of managers: the former using AMs and the latter not using them. The adoption of AMs is the experimental variable, the effects of which have been measured. Interviewees have been selected among managers involved in the NAME project (Network for Agile Methodologies Experience) [7] or other projects of the Center for Applied Software Engineering of the Free University of Bozen.

The pre-experimental design has two limits. The former deals with the selection: the two groups could be affected by how the two groups have been selected; in particular, the involvement in the NAME project could have influenced managers.

The latter limit is the mortality: some differences in groups are due to the lack of answers to the questionnaire. This limit does not affect the data collection because all the managers have filled in the questionnaire.

Table 1. Main topics of the questionnaire

1.   Firm's general information
2.   Main software problems
3.   Planning and organization of the software development process
4.   Relationship with customers
5.   Planning and feasibility of a project
6.   Developer's characteristics
7.   Agile Methodologies
8.   Firm and interviewee's personal data

2.2 The Questionnaire

Questionnaires are always subject to loss of information and lack of integrity of the collected data [8]. A typical solution to these problems is the collection of massive number of questionnaires [9].

The questionnaire is intended for managers of software companies, whose time and availability is usually very limited. For this reason, a low number of respondents was expected.

The questionnaire has been built according to the psychological criteria of Converse and Presser [9] and its soundness has been checked according to the principles of Marbach [8].

The questionnaire consists of four parts:
1.   the first analyzes the interviewee's status, main problems in software development and the adopted solutions;

2. the second deals with the planning and the organization of the software development process;

3. the third evaluates the relationship with the customer;

4. finally, the fourth assesses the knowledge, the actual use of AMs and the vantages and disadvantages of their use.

It includes several multi choice questions alternated with some open questions. Topics included in the questionnaire are listed in Table 1.

3 Analysis of the Result

All the companies interviewed have been exposed to changes in their software production process.

The motivations are clear: 43% because of changes in customer requirements, 48% because of technological changes, and 9% because of failure with the previous software development process.

According to 71% of the managers, delivering software with all functionalities in time is the main problem in software development. There is no significant correlation between the main problems in software development and the adoption of AMs in the software process. A survey, made by the Standish Group on 8000 projects in the 1999, shows the same result: only 26% of the development projects were completed on time, on budget, and with all the originally specified functionalities.

Most of managers focus on process and people in order to improve the performance of the company, according to the results of Standish Group [1] and Thomsett [3].

For the managers that are using AMs, an improvement in the software development planning produces also an improvement in the customer satisfaction. This result is in accordance to the principles of the Agile Methodologies [10]. AMs highlight the importance of planning and organization in projects.

The adoption of AMs is correlated with the importance of teamwork. The importance of high individual abilities is negatively correlated with the adoption of AMs and with the importance of teamwork.

These results are in accordance to Schumpeter's principles [11]: innovations are new combinations of existing knowledge and incremental learning. The sharing of knowledge facilitates the transfer of knowledge within a group and it makes easier the development of new ideas. These results are also in accordance to the principles of AMs [10], Thomsett [3], and to the outcomes of the Standish Group [1].

AMs consider teamwork, in particular pair programming, essential in software development in order to improve the communication and the transfer of knowledge within the organization.

Interviewed managers have adopted several solutions to improve developers' skills, such as continuous training, regular communication, and involvement.

4 Conclusions and Further Research

This paper is a first analysis of the differences and the analogies derived by the adoption of AMs in twenty-one software companies from the point of view of project management.

Methods used to improve software are different but most of the managers adopt solutions focused on people and process. AMs focus on people in a number of different ways, this orientation is also confirmed in the collected data.

The correlation between the adoption of AMs and the preference for teamwork among developers is another good strategy based on people. Teamwork is useful to improve knowledge transfer, communication and coordination within an organization. Knowledge sharing within a group makes easier its transfer and the development of new ideas.

The analysis presented in this paper is a quite preliminary one and further investigation is required.

Acknowledgements. We would like to thank the interviewed software managers for their useful help in our research.

References

[1]   J. Johnson, "Turning Chaos into Success", Software Magazine, Dec. 1999, pp. 30-39, available at http://www.softwaremag.com/archive/L.cfm?Doc=archive/1999dec/

[2]   B.B. Boehm, "Six Reasons for Software Project Failure", IEEE Software, Sep. 2002, pp. 97.

[3]   R. Thomsett, Third Wave Project Management upper Saddle River, Yourdon Press, NY, 1993.

[4]   D. Philips The Software Project Manager's Handbook Principlea that Work at Work, IEEE Computer Society Press, 1998.

[5]   H. Petroski, To Engineer is Human: The Role of Failuer in Successful Design, Vintage Books of Random House, Inc., New York, 1992.

[6]   D. T.Cambell and J. C. Stanley, Experimental and quasi-experimental designs for research, Houghton Mifflin Company, Boston, 1966.

[7]   NAME project – website: http://name.case.unibz.it/

[8]   G. Marbach, Le Ricerche di Mercato, Utet, Torino, 1996.

[9]   J. M. Converse and S. Presser, Survey Questions: Handcrafting the Standardized Questionnaire, Sage, Beverley Hills, 1986.

[10] K. Beck, Extreme Programming Explained, Addison Wesley, Amsterdam, 2000.

[11] J. Schumpeter, The Theory of Economic Development, MA: Harvard University Press, Cambridge, (published in 1911; republished in 1968).

Evaluating the Extreme Programming System – An Empirical Study

Panagiotis Sfetsos[1], Lefteris Angelis[2], Ioannis Stamelos[2], and Georgios L. Bleris[2]

[1] Department of Information Technology, Technological Education Institute,
54101 Thessaloniki, Greece; sfetsos@it.teithe.gr
[2] Department of Informatics, Aristotle University,
54124 Thessaloniki, Greece; {stamelos,lef,bleris}@csd.auth.gr

Abstract. In this paper we discuss an empirical study about the success and difficulties 15 Greek software companies experienced applying Extreme Programming [1] as a holistic system in software development. Based on a generic XP system including feedback influences and using as a research tool a cause-effect model including social-technical affecting factors, the study statistically evaluates XP practices application by the software companies. Data were collected from 30 managers and developers, using the sample survey technique with questionnaires and interviews, in a time period of six months. Practices were analysed separately using Descriptive Statistics and as a whole by building up different models using stepwise Discriminant Analysis. The results have shown that companies, facing various problems with some practices, prefer to develop their own tailored XP method and way of working-practices to meet their requirements.

Keywords. eXtreme Programming System, Cause-effect Model, Feedback, Empirical Study, stepwise Discriminant Analysis (DA).

1 Introduction

Systems thinking is a discipline for seeing wholes rather than tiny things focusing on relations and behaviours in complex systems [3]. It was first Beck and Jeffries who defined XP as a system [1] [2]. The implementation of the XP practices involving managers, customers and developers, strengthen the properties of the XP system. Practitioners communicate, interpret, decide and act on the basis of their skills and experience affecting the feedback control. The most significant properties of a feedback system are negative and positive feedback influences. A cause-effect model, on which a generic XP system builds up, incorporating feedback influences, was developed and used as our research tool. This model was used in evaluating the practices along two dimensions: small companies versus large companies and managerial versus development staff.

J. Eckstein and H. Baumeister (Eds.): XP 2004, LNCS 3092, pp. 227–230, 2004.

2 The Cause-Effect Model

In this preliminary XP cause-effect model, moreover values and practices, we added a new aggregated variable-type named *"factors"* (for details see Appendix A in [5]), including skills (e.g. Efficiency in programming, Work in team), interactions or hidden dependencies between practices, other pre-conditions (in the form of 'needed factors', e.g. Customer collaboration, Partnership relations) and post-conditions (in form of reflective positive results, e.g. Tacit knowledge transfer, Quick software development) (see figure 1).

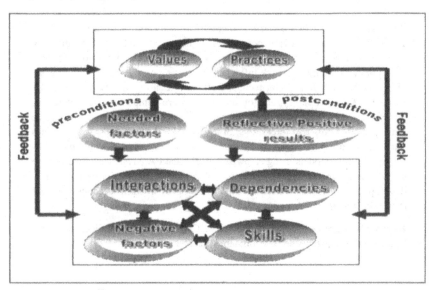

Fig. 1. The structure of the XP cause-effect model

3 Methodology – Data Analysis

The research study has been carried out between September 2002 and February 2003, investigating fifteen software companies that apply the XP-practices in Northern Greece. The selected companies, sized from five developers up to 200 developers, are an active part of the software production industry. Fifteen developers and fifteen managers were thoroughly interviewed using the sample survey technique with questionnaires and *semi-structured* [4] interviews (see Appendix B and C in [5]). Data analysis was completed in two separated statistical procedures. In the first procedure, data selected for each practice were analysed separately, using Descriptive Statistics (DS). DS application includes counts, percentages and various graphic displays (see Appendix D in [5]). In the second procedure, data were analysed using the stepwise Discriminant Analysis (DA). DA was used for the 15 responses for each practice (separately for managers and developers) in order to find (a) whether there are differences between the two company groups (large and small) and (b) if there are differences, which are the variables – questions that can distinguish the two groups.

4 Results

Different opinions have been expressed by the four categories of interviewees about the importance of certain factors. These factors are reported per practice.

Planning Game. MSC[1]: organizational issues, facility in software development, interaction with practice – testing, difficulties with big and complex projects. **DSC:** human - cultural and organizational issues. **DLC:** missing experience.

Pair Programming. **MLC:** distributed developers, bad working conditions or relations among staff. **MSC:** efficiency in modifying code. **DSC:** develop SW easily, SW less expensive to develop. **DLC:** distributed developers.

Testing. **MSC:** developer collaboration, interaction with refactoring. **MLC:** interaction with sort release cycles. **DLC:** system simplicity. **DSC:** developer collaboration.

Refactoring. **MSC:** efficiency in using tools, developer collaboration. **DSC:** efficiency in using tools, interaction with the practice - continuous integration.

Simple Design. **MSC - DSC:** efficiency in programming, efficiency in modifying, documentation in distributed developers.

Common Code Ownership. **MLC:** transfer ideas faster, organizational obstacles in large companies. **MSC:** interaction with the practice - testing. **DLC:** develop software easily. **DSC:** limited access to code.

Continuous Integration. **MSC:** OOA (drive by analysis), human - cultural factors. **DLC:** code quality, develop software easily. **DSC:** human-cultural factors.

On Site-Customer. **MSC:** increase experience, interaction with the practice - metaphor. **MLC:** flexibility. **DSC:** increase experience, kind of the project. **DLC:** less expensive software development.

Short Release Cycles. **MLC:** quick software development, less expensive software development. **MSC:** developers efficient in decomposition. **DLC:** less expensive software development, problems with big projects. **DSC:** efficiency in programming.

---

[1] MLC=Managers from Large Companies, MSC=Managers from Small Companies, DLC=Developers from Large Companies, DSC=Developers from Small Companies.

40-Hour Week. MLC - DLC: organizational obstacles. **DSC:** time-to-market pressure.

Coding Standards. MSC: missing experience, interaction with the practice-refactoring. **DLC:** develop software easily.

Metaphor. MSC: develop software easily, manager satisfaction, human-cultural factors, the practice as is in theory. **DLC:** transfer ideas faster, missing experience. **DSC:** interaction with practice planning game.

5 Evaluation and Conclusions

Results have shown that both small and large companies, facing various problems with some practices, prefer to develop their own tailored XP method and way of working. Problems with pair programming concern the kind of project and the distribution of the developers. On-site customers were provided only in big projects leading companies to invent different and simpler ways to communicate with customers when it was needed (telephone, internet etc.). Large companies tended to break 40-hour week and to prevent the involvement of the developers in both common code ownership and metaphor for different reasons. Small companies strongly demanded skilled and experienced developers but at the same time they applied 40-hour-week in a more relaxed time – schedule, if needed. Managers and developers asserted that the interaction between practices contributed to their success. The lack of a detailed description for some practices such as simple design, coding standards and metaphor affect negatively the implementation of the practices. Pairing and testing were found to be the most significant success factors for the rest of the entire XP system. Finally, communication and synergy, starting in planning game, are other significant success factors. This study is an initial attempt, aiming at the characterization of current state-of-the-practice in one software industry, as a starting point for further research. The cause-effect model may be seen as the first step towards an XP system dynamics model, that will be able to simulate and predict XP application.

References

[1]   Beck, K., Extreme Programming Explained: Embrace Change. Reading, Massachusetts: Addison-Wesley, (2000).
[2]   Jeffries, R., A. Anderson, and C. Hendrickson, Extreme Programming Installed. The XP Series, ed. K. Beck. Upper Saddle River, NJ: Addison Wesley, (2001).
[3]   Senge, P.M. Fifth discipline- The art and practice of the learning organization, Double-day, New York, USA. (1990).
[4]   Taylor, S.J., and Bogdan, R. Introduction to Qualitative Research Methods. New York: John Wiley and Sons, (1984).
[5]   http://sweng.csd.auth.gr/htmls/publications.html

A Comparison of Software Development Process Experiences

Robert Gittins[1], Julian Bass[2], and Sian Hope[3]

[1] School of Informatics, University of Wales Bangor, UK.
rgittins@informatics.bangor.ac.uk
[2] Business Agility UK Ltd, UK
Julian.Bass@business-agility.com
[3] School of Informatics, University of Wales Bangor UK.
sian@informatics.bangor.ac.uk

1 Introduction

Commercial pressures to produce faster and more dependable software prompt management initiatives to improve software practices. Technical solutions such as CASE tools, 4GLs, Interactive Development Environments and more recent modeling notations and tools have made some contribution. This article concentrates on the introduction of new development methodologies that are shown to have a positive on software development practices.

We examine data collected from verbatim transcripts of interviews taken in three small software development companies; other data from non XP adopting companies is published elsewhere. The first company consists of four developers and one manager, using an exploratory prototyping software development process. Both of the other companies were studied during the adoption of an Extreme Programming (XP) methodology. We examine the impact of introducing XP on developers and managers and highlight the factors they stated had influenced their work.

Typical changes that adopting XP brought about were the introduction of pair programming where by the action of regularly rotating partners spread knowledge throughout the team. Companies B and C found that communication was improved by pair programming and pair programming helped develop collective (rather than individual) code ownership, designed to improve maintainability. Pairing had a mixed reception from developers; some were encouraged by the way it improved their skills and gave them support through difficult problems, as well as providing an increased social interaction, taking them out of isolation. Other developers preferred to work alone, or had problems harmonising their skills with others. Some experienced developers saw this practice as a threat to their position and future prospects.

XP Planning Games bring together developers, managers and customers to determine project release dates and requirements planning through the use of story cards. An important change that XP provides is the close collaboration with the customer on-

J. Eckstein and H. Baumeister (Eds.): XP 2004, LNCS 3092, pp. 231–236, 2004.

site, clarifying requirements stories and making decisions quickly to eliminate information bottlenecks.

We chose to focus on two categories in this paper; pair programming, and planning games, to reveal the variation in attitudes of developers and managers in the two companies adopting XP.

2   A Brief History of XP

Recent evolution of software practices since   [1],[3],[11], have brought about a reaction to bureaucratic and heavyweight methodologies in the form of more lightweight or flexible methodologies.   Trial and error using simplified, lightweight methodologies brought together various advocates culminating in a manifesto and the formation of the 'Agile Alliance' [5]. Since 2000, lightweight software methodologies like XP, so called 'Agile methods', have emerged as a response to heavily document-reliant traditional methods, an Agile strategy is designed to reduce the cost change throughout a project.

XP was developed by Kent Beck [1] and others while actively involved in commercial OO software development. In this regard, XP is different to many other approaches in that it is practitioner led. XP is built around four core values; communication, simplicity, feedback and courage. The XP values are supported by five principles and twelve practices that rely on small release cycles to achieve early business value, through small steps that are easily manageable and therefore less difficult to change. Practitioner led conferences report improvements with Agile software engineering and there is increased interest from the broader software engineering community [4] [9].

3   Research Approach

Several research methods and data collection techniques were used in this research. The choice of data collection methods is determined by the needs of a given research project and, in particular, by the research questions confronted. Broadly, data collection techniques can be classified as quantitative and qualitative. These methods are complementary rather than mutually exclusive approaches. Each set of techniques has their particular strengths and weaknesses [8]. Quantitative survey techniques were used, for example, to obtain a frequency count of developer preferences for the adoption of XP practices. Tape-recorded one-to-one interviews and questionnaires were conducted to elicit the experiences and views, of developers and their managers. Open-ended interviews were adopted to understand the world as seen by the respondents [8]. The approach sought to avoid predetermining imposing views through prior selection of questionnaire categories. The interview transcripts provide a wealth of information in which interviewees explain, in their own words, their perceptions and defend their point of view. When reviewing notes from interviews it was evident that the spirit of the interview had been lost. Problems with note-taking during interviews (Opinions succinctly and concisely stated during the interviews are inadequately recorded in writing) are avoided using tape-recorded interviews. Question variation from interview to interview raised some difficulties, when it came to comparing responses, as it was felt important to refine the interview questions in response to feedback. The "interview guide" approach [8] consists of a set of issues outlined in advance for each interview. The cycle was completed when transcripts of the recorded interviews were carefully compared and correlated during analysis, and interviewee names were changed to protect confidentiality in subsequent reporting of the results.

4 Company Profiles

The three companies (A, B and C), presented three distinct approaches to managing their software development environment, dictated to a large degree by their size, resources and their adopted approaches to software development. Questions targeted the software development process, XP practices, and both managerial and behavioural effectiveness. Company A was a small traditional company without any distinct development process methodology. Company B was a medium sized rural based software development company of 9 developers, which included a developer manager who reported to senior management. Resources were amply provided from the budget of the multiple projects the company turned over. There were two rounds of questionnaires and two rounds of interviews conducted six months apart, four developers missed the second round of questionnaires and four developers missed the second round of interviews. Company C were a large city based software development company of 36 developers, one developer manager and two active senior managers. Resources were plentiful, provided from the prestigious projects. The recent development methodology adopted was XP, which influenced environmental changes. Eight Company C team members were interviewed in one round of interviews and eight developers filled in questionnaires three weeks following the interview.

5 Pair Programming

The lack of informal day-to-day meetings at Company A was recognised as impeding communications.
"The water cooler ...where main decisions are made around a water cooler in the corridor ...that's not happening!"
                    Alan, Developer Manager, Company A, Interview, May 00.
The contrast between the nature of communications at company A with no pair programming activity and team communication difficulties and those of companies B and C who adopted stand-up meetings, pair programming and planning games was revealed in the interviews. One developer contrasts her pair programming experience at Company C with an earlier job.
"I'd much rather be swapping around with different people – its made the whole process a lot more sociable, ...whereas if I came to the office four weeks ago everybody was sitting at their desks ...it was much less social."
                    Susan, Developer, Company C, Interview, March 01.

As soon as pair-programming started it appealed to some developers immediately.

"A few weeks back we started doing pair programming ... I hadn't had as much fun in ages!"

Robin, Developer, Company C, Interview, April 01.

The responses of many developers show that the benefits of the technique depended on the balance of abilities between the paired developers. The technique works most effectively when there is a harmony of skills and temperament between the paired developers.

"It's tedious for the person who has to watch someone who is experienced on a given subject type-away."

Robert, Developer, Company B, Questionnaire, January 01

"When two are of roughly the same understanding on subject, language and method, then pair programming works brilliantly."

Robert, Developer, Company B, Questionnaire, January 01

"It depends on the task, sometimes it's absolutely deadly, and sometimes it's worthwhile- when you know something about the task and they do, both contributing."

Edward, Developer, Company B, Interview, April 01.

Developers also find that social compatibility affects experience with pair programming.

"There are probably 1 or 2 people I prefer not to pair with, when you're having a conversation they're always trying to get one up on you."

Albert, Developer, Company C, Interview, March 01.

"... the biggest problem is personality clashes. Generally most people here are very amenable. ...I have found myself preferring to partner with some people as opposed to others, just generally because we get on a bit better, and work in a similar way."

Susan, Developer, Company C, Questionnaire, April 01.

Several of the developers demonstrated that the goal of collective code ownership was worth the difficulties encountered using the technique.

" I would prefer to work independently, but I believe that pair programming is essential to XP as it drives collective code ownership, coding standards, and code style. ...pair programming helps me learn new things, ... I learn from my partner."

Robin, Developer, Company C, Questionnaire, April 01.

"It is not a panacea but a very effective method for producing coding."

Mark, Developer, Company C, Questionnaire, April 01.

"I feel that pair programming can be very taxing at times."

Mat, Developer, Company B, Questionnaire, October 00.

Less confident or inexperienced developers can be exposed by pair-programming. It takes courage to adopt the pairing approach when lacking confidence.

"Sometimes you do think - actually I'm not sure what I'm doing and I don't want to do it in public!"

Susan, Developer, Company C, Interview, March 01.

6   Planning Games

Planning games are perhaps the key management process of the XP methodology [7] [2], requirements gathering, strategic planning and manager, developer and customer communications are used in an iterative process to determine requirements, prioritise work and receive customer directives on scope and time through the course of a simple organisation process. Organisation time wasting figured strongly in the criticisms voiced by developers.

"We need to be more ruthless about sticking to the agenda. This is especially important if the meeting has lots of people... since more time is wasted. Meetings are not effective if there are too many people at the meeting. Time is often wasted if an individual misunderstands a point or gets confused, or decides to wander off on a tangent."

Mat, Developer, Company B, Questionnaire, February 01.
"Planning games seem to take up too much time. It is not clearly defined."

Robert, Developer, Company B, Questionnaire, October 00.
"I think that the meetings often go into too much detail about tasks. Also tasks agreed at the meetings do not always relate to the work that is done afterward.."

Mat, Developer, Company B, Questionnaire, October 00.
Managing meetings takes skill and experience otherwise frustration sets in, evident from a comment by one of the company C developers.
"I find the free-for-all task allocation reminiscent of MacDonalds and thus stressing because of uncertainty."

Mark, Developer, Company C, Questionnaire, April 01.

Not surprisingly for such a pivotal activity, planning games presented organisational problems that frustrated developer activity.   Variation in the organisation and interpretation of planning games rests with the developer manager, how he interprets the XP practice and then how local factors influence their successful implementation and evolution.

7 Conclusions

A combination of quantitative and qualitative research methods has been used to explore development methods used in three companies. Quantitative methods provide statistical results but shed little light on the underlying explanations for developer experiences. Qualitative methods, in contrast, seek to provide additional insights through the detailed analysis of confidential interview transcripts. The interviews provide a vehicle for developers to explain in their own words the strengths and weaknesses of the techniques they are using.

Developers expressed enthusiasm for the socially rewarding benefits of several of the XP practices. Pair programming brought fun back into software development for some. However, the collaborative nature of agile methods, such as XP, can make it difficult for experienced developers to gain leadership positions in projects. This lack of a distinctive architectural role could be seen as undermining the professional development required for career progression. Pair-programming appears most effective when both developers are contributing a broadly similar level of expertise. Pair programming can be advocated for mentoring. A careful approach to coaching is required to avoid this being reduced to a tedious observation of an expert in performance of their art [10] [9].

Clearly, developers are having great difficulty with how and when to add functionality. The temptation of experienced developers to program flexibility into their code at an early stage is deeply ingrained. Using flexible architectural subsystems, such as those advocated by the design patterns [6] community minimizes risk. Planning games must be facilitated carefully to avoid time wasting. Morale is adversely affected when considerable periods of time bring little tangible benefits, from the developer's perspective.

Based on the evidence presented here, and from studies reported elsewhere [8] the authors conclude that XP was helpful because it offered the chance of support to otherwise isolated developers. It improved communications through pair programming and raised the morale of some developers but concerned some developers who felt XP undermined their status. XP held the prospect of better customer relations, which was appreciated by developers. Not everyone bought-in to simple design and from the evidence of this limited study, it would suggest that this practice calls for a re-evaluation.

References

[1] Beck.K. 'Extreme Programming Explained : Embrace Change': Addison-Wesley, 1999.
[2] Beck, K. & Fowler M. 'Planning Extreme Programming.' Addison-Wesley, 2001.
[3] Cockburn, A. 'Selecting a Projects Methodology.' IEEE Software 17(4), pp 64-71, 2000.
[4] DeMarco, T. & Boehm B. 'The Agile Methods Fray', IEEE Computer, 35(6), pp 90-92, 2002.
[5] Fowler, M. 'The Agile Manifesto: Where it Came From and Where it May Go.' http:www.martinfowler.com/articles/agileStory.html .
[6] Gamma, E,. Helm R,. Johnson, R. and Vlissides J. 'Design Patterns' Elements of Reusable Object-Oriented Software.' AddisonWesley, 2000.
[7] Jeffries, R., Anderson, A. & Hendrickson, C. 'Extreme Programming Installed.': The XP series, Addison-Wesley, 2001.
[8] Patton, M. Q. 'Qualitative Research & Evaluation Methods.' SAGE Publications, 2002.
[9] Sharp, H & Robinson H. "An Ethnography of XP Practice." Proceedings of The Joint EASE and PPIG Conference, Keele University UK , pp. 15-27, 2003.
[10] Williams, L. A. Kessler R. Cunningham W. & Jeffries R. 'Strengthening the Case for Pair Programming.' IEEE Software, July/Aug 2000.
[11] Williams, L. A. & Kessler R. R. 'The Effects of Pair Pressure and Learning on Software Engineering Education.' Thirteenth Conference on Software Engineering Education & Training.' 2000.

Abstract Test Aspect: Testing with AOP

Robert Wenner

Port25 Solutions, Rathaus-Allee 10,
53757 St. Augustin, Germany
robertport25.com

Abstract. This article shows how to use AspectJ to create an Abstract Test Aspect, that makes sure objects respect their basic contracts given by base classes or implemented interfaces. The approach presented is an aspect-oriented alternative to Abstract Test Case.

Keywords: AOP, aspect-oriented programming, AspectJ, Java, unit testing, Abstract Test Case

1 Basic Object Duties

Design by contract [6] is often mentioned as one of the 'classic' fields of aspect-oriented programming [3]. Aspects help a lot when checking the contract for a hierarchy of classes, where derived classes have to honor their parent's contract according to the Liskov Substitution Principle [4]. This is especially true for such basic requirements as those inherited from `Object`.

The Abstract Test Case pattern [2] defines a hierarchy of test cases matching the hierarchy of classes under test. The Abstract Test Case defines those tests that all derived classes' objects must pass.

For demonstration purposes we will look at the equals contract. As documented in [1] each `Object` descendant that overwrites `equals` has to honor the general equals contract. The `equals` method must be reflexive, symmetric, transitive, consistent, and must return `false` if the given object is `null`.

2 The Abstract Test Case Way

Using Abstract Test Case, one derives test classes from `AbstractEqualsTest` for example, which defines methods like `testReflexivity` and an abstract method to obtain an object to check with. Derived tests implement the abstract method and return an object to be checked with whatever `AbstractEqualsTest` considers check-worthy.

This fails for lots of the equals contract tests, because these can not do their checks with only one object. The transitivity check needs at least three objects. The abstract test case can define three abstract methods that do provide three different objects. Alternatively, it can define a method for each check, e.g. `provideSymmetricEqualObjects` which may return a collection of objects that

J. Eckstein and H. Baumeister (Eds.): XP 2004, LNCS 3092, pp. 237–241, 2004.

should pass the equals transitivity check. Unfortunately, this requires the derived test to fill in lots of blanks, which is almost more work than rewriting the test. Furthermore, the test setup gets hard to understand.

3   Abstract Test Aspect: An Aspect-Based Approach

3.1   Picking Test Objects

A pointcut is the aspect way of identifying so-called join points in the execution of a program, e.g. object creation or method calls. For the equals test, the pointcut picks objects created in regular tests as test objects, and uses an abstract pointcut, seesInterestingObject, to allow customizing the code. One derives from the abstract aspect and defines what points in the flow of the program are considered interesting by implementing the abstract pointcut.

Listing 1.1. Abstract Test Aspect

```
public abstract aspect AbstractTestAspect {
    pointcut testedObjectCreation ():
        within(junit.framework.TestCase+)
        && !within(AbstractTestAspect+)
        && !call(java..new(..))
        && seesInterestingObject ();

    public abstract pointcut seesInterestingObject ();

    after () returning(Object object): testedObjectCreation () {
        takeTestObject(object);
    }

    protected abstract void takeTestObject(Object object);
}
```

Associated with the pointcut is an (**after returning**) advice: code that is called after the join point is met. It calls an abstract method takeTestObject for each object obtained at the pointcut. The test code may store it in a collection or do some tests right away.

Naturally, the equals contract example pointcut considers anything derived from Object interesting. It picks interesting objects upon their creation. Other checks may choose other pointcuts, e.g. when a certain method is called.

Multiple pointcuts, each in its own aspect, can exist in one project independently from others. They may even be triggered by the same control flow.

3.2   Storing Test Objects

A concrete variant of the abstract `takeTestObject` method in the equals check places the object in a vector for later use.

Storing in a vector means storing a reference to the object. The original code, that created the object, will do something with it, and we end up with a vector of different objects. This 'collect all' approach is likely to obtain a wide range of objects to test with. Assuming the 'normal' tests cover a broad range of possible objects for the class under test, chances are at least one of the collected objects will fail a test, if the class does have a problem.

Storing the objects is a little tricky, because JUnit runs tests independent from each other. The test runner creates a new instance of the test class and calls the test method on it. Thus the vector for the test objects must be static, or all tests would have their own vector, which would be lost after the test was run. The concrete aspect itself is static, too, because AspectJ allows only static inner aspects, and inside the test class is the best place for it.

3.3   Running the Tests

Once the derived aspect is written, the tests are written in the test suite as usual, as public void testXyz methods. JUnit collects and runs the tests. If derived abstract tests go in the end of the suite, other test can provide test objects[1].

Coming back to the equals contract testing example, a possible test method may make sure **equals** behaves symmetrically. It checks all objects collected in its vector and throws after the made assertion fails for the first combination of collected objects. This is fine, because one failure is enough to show there is a problem with the code under test.

The code in a derived aspect may as well chose to not collect the objects but rather perform the desired tests right after it got hold of an object. To achieve this, the derived aspect simply does the test in `takeTestObject`. This saves the overhead of storing various objects for later use. Test failures occur faster, for example, a non-reflexive equals implementation fails with the first instance of the faulty class, rather than at the end of the suite. If more than one object is required for a test (e.g. checking equals for symmetry), one can access the objects collected until now. As above, this is the fastest way to signal a failure. However, this bends the rule that tests are independent of each other. That test fails, which creates the second object of the faulty implementation. The test suite becomes dependent of the order in which tests are run. To be clear on this: the failure is detected anyway, but its location may vary, if the test cases are re-arranged. With meaningful failure messages this should not be a problem, though.

---

[1] Though JUnit does not guarantee the order of test execution, this approach seems to work fine.

4 Summary

The presented Abstract Test Aspect is similar to the Abstract Test Case that both make sure that derived / implementing classes follow the extended / implemented behavior. However, the approach is quite different.

Abstract Test Case requires implementing the methods to obtain objects to test. These objects are collected automatically in the Abstract Test Aspect.

The Abstract Test Aspect is more flexible. Once the pointcut is defined, one does not have to remember all implemented interfaces in the test suite. If another interface is added to a class, the pointcut will automatically take the newly found objects into account. If an interface is removed from a class, the joinpoint will not be triggered and the test suite for the interface is automatically excluded from the class' tests.

A drawback? With the test aspect, it may not always be obvious, that there is in fact code that does this test. This is common to all advised code. In my opinion this is just like having methods. You usually do not know in what context (beyond the scope of the object) they are called or who overwrites them. However, nobody has a problem with this, because methods work independently from each other. If a method must be called from a special context, it may be private or protected, or the requirements are documented. The same holds true for aspects. An aspect should be independent from the code it advises, and no code should make any assumptions on what aspects may work on it.

Is there a problem with keeping the test objects around longer than the advised test expects? It shouldn't. Two possible problems come to mind. First: relying on the finalize thread in the test, i.e. waiting for the object under test to do something on being garbage collected. Due to the unpredictable behavior of the finalize thread, it is no good idea to use it anyway. Second: the object under test holds scarce resources like file handles or database connections. Well, usually these will be replaced by (not scarce) mock objects, anyway [5]. And if you *can not* allow objects living longer, just move the tests to their own class, which is not picked by the seesInterestingObject pointcut.

4.1 Conclusion

The test aspects are usable even if the project does not want to use AOP in production in general. The aspects are isolated and have little coupling with the code they work on. This makes them easy to use and easy to adopt to different situations.

References

1. Anonymous. Java API overview. *Sun Developer NEWS*, 1(1):10, 11, "Fall" 1996.
2. Eric George. Abstract test cases. http://c2.com/cgi/wiki?AbstractTestCases.
3. Gregor Kiczales, John Lamping, Anurag Mendhekar, Chris Maeda, Cristina Lopes, Jean-Marc Loingtier, and John Irwin. Aspect-oriented programming. In Mehmet Aksit and Satoshi Matsuoka, editors, *11th Europeen Conf. Object-Oriented Programming*, volume 1241 of *LNCS*, pages 220–242. Springer Verlag, 1997.

4. Barbara Liskov. Data abstraction and hierarchy. In *Proceedings of the ACM Conference on Object-Oriented Programming Systems, Languages, and Applications*, December 1987.
5. T. Mackinnon, S. Freeman, and P. Craig. Endotesting: Unit testing with mockobjects, 2000.
6. Bertrand Meyer. Applying design by contract. *Computer (IEEE)*, 25(10):40–51, 1992.

XMI for XP Process Data Interchange

Sandro Pinna and Nicola Serra

Dipartimento di Ingegneria Elettrica ed Elettronica, Universitá di Cagliari,
Piazza d'Armi, 09123 Cagliari, Italy
{pinnasandro, nicola.serra}@diee.unica.it
http://agile.diee.unica.it

Abstract. In this paper[1] we present an XML based format for XP
process data collection and interchange. This format is based on a XP
Metamodel that can be easily extended to other agile methodologies. XP
process data conformant to the metamodel are represented in an XML
format according to OMG XMI specification. Our research group has
developed an XP process supporting tool that uses this format to collect
and interchange process data.

1 Introduction

As a research group working in the field of Extreme Programming and Agile
Methodologies, we developed a tool - named XPSwiki - to support an XP
development process [2] . The main purpose of the tool is to track the process
and to collect process data. Thus, it is essential to define a format to save and
represent data. The need to define a specific process data format is also due to
the necessity of making XPSwiki able to communicate with other external tools
or specific development environments (IDEs). In this way, our initial problem
of saving and managing process data turned on the more general problem of
interchanging data among different contexts.

A lot of tools supporting an XP process have been developed in the last years.
Like XPSwiki, the great part of these tools essentially support planning and
requirement gathering activities. For example, they allow to write user stories,
assign them to iterations and track the project advancement by computing useful
metrics. Each tool uses its own standard to store and export process data. As
a consequence, interoperability among different tools is very hard. The need to
support interoperability among tools is not the only reason that lead to the
definition of a unified way to manage data relative to XP and Agile Processes.

There is a growing demand from academic and scientific community for a
standard that easily allows to collect and manage data produced across agile
processes in order to gather experience and knowledge on agile methodologies
to quantitatively assess their effectiveness.

Starting from the above observations, we defined an XML based format for
data interchange.

---

[1] This study is part of MAPS research project (Agile Methodologies for Software
Production, funded by FIRB research fund of MIUR.)

J. Eckstein and H. Baumeister (Eds.): XP 2004, LNCS 3092, pp. 242–245, 2004.

The proposed format is based on the OMG XML Metadata Interchange (XMI) specification and an XP metamodel defined using the Metamodel Object Facility (MOF), the OMG language for representing metamodels.

It's not our purpose to propose a definitive XML standard for data gathering and interchange. Indeed, it's our intention to highlight this need and to propose a possible starting point.

In section 2 we describe XMI and in section 3 the XP Metamodel.

2   XMI

XMI is the OMG standard for mapping a metamodel into a Document Type Definition (DTD), which is in turn the basis to validate XML documents describing specific instances of the same metamodel. A metamodel describes the abstract syntax to build and specify a model, that is an instance of the metamodel. A generic metamodel is typically specified using the Metamodel Object Facility (MOF), the OMG language for representing metamodels. The MOF Model is the abstract language for defining MOF metamodels. The MOF Model and the core of the UML metamodel are close enough in their modeling concepts to allow UML notation to be used to express MOF-based metamodels. XMI provides two different sets of rules:

- The XML DTD Production Rules for producing XML Document Type Definitions (DTDs) starting from a MOF-based metamodel specification.
- The XML Document Production Rules for encoding metadata into an XML compatible format. In practice, XMI defines precise rules for generating XMI documents starting from an instance of a given metamodel. These rules are represented in EBNF notation and can be found in the XMI specification.

3   XP Metamodel and Generated XMI DTD

In this section we present our metamodel for XP processes. The metamodel is not meant to be definitive or exhaustive, indeed it should be considered as a starting point for future evolution.

This metamodel and the derived XMI DTD are the XPSwiki basis for data collection and management. The main part of the DTD has been automatically generated following the OMG XMI specification rules for mapping metamodel elements into DTD declarations.

The metamodel consists of a set of UML diagrams representing the elements of a generic XP process and the relationships among them.

The main diagram (fig.1) is the inheritance tree class diagram representing the core classes of the metamodel and the main attributes of these classes. The metamodel is based on a root class called XPProcess and all the remaining classes are children of this class. There are two main subtrees, the first represents the people involved in the project, the second the elements composing the planning phase. The diagram is structured in order to be easily extended. Extensibility

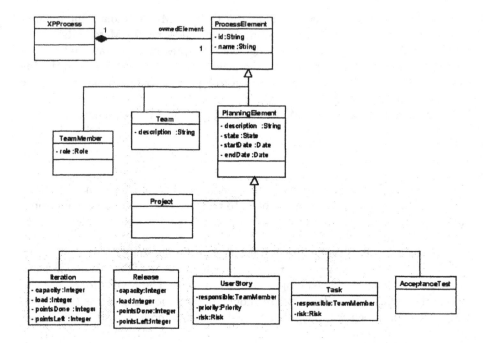

Fig. 1. XP Tree

is provided by the class PlanningElement which is the root class of all other
classes representing specific parts of the process (Project, Iteration, Release,
etc.). The addition of new concepts to the metamodel (i.e. Activities, Events,
etc.) is provided by subclassing the PlanningElement class.

3.1   XMI Production Rules

In this section we give an example of a XMI document which represents an instance of the XP Metamodel. We focus our attention on a simple XP Metamodel
instance represented by a Project with an Iteration named Iteration1 and two
Stories named Story1 and Story2. The following code shows the portion of the
XMI file related to the Iteration.

```
<XP:Iteration xmi.id = 'itr1' name='iteration1'
   id ='it01' capacity='70'>
   <XP:Iteration.story>
     <XP:Story xmi.id = 'str1' name='story1'
       id='st01' iteration='itr1' >
       <XP:Story.startDate>
         <XP:Date xmi.id='dt1' year=2004
         month='January' day='23'>
       </XP:Story.startDate>
```

```
        <XP:Story.endDate>
          <XP:Date xmi.id='dt2' year=2004
          month='January' day='23'>
        </XP:Story.endDate>
      </XP:Story>
      <XP:Story xmi.id = 'st2' id='st01'
      iteration='lsm:1c794cc:f9eadd539c:-7fc1'>
        <XP:Story.startDate>
          <XP:Date xmi.id='dt3' year=2004
          month='January' day='23'>
        </XP:Story.date>
        <XP:Story.endDate>
          <XP:Date xmi.id='dt4' year=2004
          month='January' day='23'>
        </XP:Story.endDate>
      </XP:Story>
    </XP:Iteration.story>
  </XP:Iteration>
```

4   Conclusions

The definition of a unified format for storing, managing and sharing data derived from a development process is the starting point to provide a large knowledge base about agile methodologies. In this paper we have proposed an XML format supported by XPSwiki, a tool supporting the requirement gathering and planning activities within an XP process.

Our format is based on the OMG XMI specification, which is the de-facto standard for metadata interchange. In order to define an XMI based format, we developed a metamodel describing the main entities of an XP process and the relationship among them.

The XP metamodel may easily be extended to other Agile Methodologies.

It would be useful to create a task force of both industrial and academic partners to evolve this rough model, and to push it toward a standard specification proposal.

References

1. Beck, K.: Extreme Programming Explained: Embrace Change. Addison Wesley, Boston (2000)
2. Pinna, S., Mauri, S., Lorrai, P., Marchesi, M., Serra, N.: XPSwiki: an Agile Tool Supporting the Planning Game. In: Proceedings of XP2003, Italy, May 25-29, 2003. Lecture Notes in Computer Science, Vol.2675. Springer-Verlag, Berlin Heidelberg New York (2003) 215–224
3. MOF, an adopted standard of the OMG. http://www.omg.org
4. UML, an adopted standard of the OMG. http://www.omg.org
5. XMI, an adopted standard of the OMG. http://www.omg.org

Analyzing Pair-Programmer's Satisfaction with the Method, the Result, and the Partner

Uuno Puus[1], Asko Seeba[2], Priit Salumaa[3], and Sven Heiberg[4]

[1] Post-graduate student, University of Tartu
Head of Laboratory, Cybernetica
+372 5142594, Uuno.Puus@cyber.ee
[2] Post-graduate student, Helsinki University of Technology
Software Development Manager, Cybernetica
+372 5105744, Asko.Seeba@hut.fi
[3] MSc student, Software Systems Engineering, RWTH Aachen
+372 55571484, Priit.Salumaa@ut.ee
[4] Research Engineer, Cybernetica
+372 5059627, Sven.Heiberg@cyber.ee

Abstract. This paper gives an overview of a programmer satisfaction survey in pair-programming experiment. The experiment took place at Institute of Computer Science, University of Tartu (UT), Estonia. The paper includes the problem statement, description of the questionnaire, and the survey results.

1 Introduction

Pair-programming is programming technique according to which two programmers are working together on the same task at one computer [10]. Pair-programming satisfaction is important aspect discovered in most surveys and experiments as a reason of success of pair-programmers. In experiments usually the programmers were filling the questionnaires about working process and explain theirs satisfaction (or dissatisfaction). This satisfaction shows how the people enjoy working (paired or non-paired) process. Although in most cases pair-programming (as working method) was preferred [1], [5], [8], [9], implementing the actual pair-programming is sometimes difficult. For example one of the obstacles occured in Norwegian XP projects [6]. It was "the resistance to work together as a pair".

Authors of current paper analyzed the structure of satisfaction with pair-programming as a part of pair-programming experiment in University of Tartu. The main goal of the experiment was to measure, how pair-programming affects the programmer's productivity. The result about productivity are described in [4]. The goal of this paper is to describe the results of the satisfaction survey. The satisfaction survey objective was to explain more precisely the structure of satisfaction.

J. Eckstein and H. Baumeister (Eds.): XP 2004, LNCS 3092, pp. 246–249, 2004.

2   Satisfaction Survey

2.1   Three Types of Satisfaction

Pair-programming satisfaction has different meanings in different investigations.

Usually satisfaction is considered as satisfaction with working method (organisational aspect). In [10] it is declared that programmers are satisfied with pair-programming, because pair-programming collaborators keep each other on the disciplined track. In [7] satisfaction helps "with increased communications between developers, speed of communication of design changes, and organization of meetings". In [3] satisfaction is also explained as satisfaction with method ("how satisfied are you with the way you and yours partner worked together on this assignment?") and with work ("how you spent your time in this assignment?").

The second important aspect is satisfaction with result (with program or assignment). It's first of all motivational apsect and shows how confident are the programmers in their solution. So is it declared in [9] and [1]. Increased confidence in results is giving more satisfaction with pair-programming result.

Satisfaction with partner is not specially surveyed. Some results are described in [5]. There were discovered no correlation between partner's gender and satisfaction. "Only men reported significantly higher enjoyment than the women regardless of whether they partnered with a woman or a man." Nevertheless satisfacton with partner is an important social aspect in pair-programming. Disagreeable pair-programming partners may drive all the pair-programming benefits to zero.

So, it is reasonable to distinguish three different types of satisfaction:

- satisfaction with method – organisational aspect;
- satisfaction with result – motivational aspect;
- satisfaction with partner – social aspect.

2.2   Satisfaction Questionnaire and Data Analysis

In addition to analyzing the pair-programming productivity in a pair-programming experiment as described in [4] the programmers satisfaction was also analyzed in the same experiment. There were two phases with different assignments[1]. At end of the each phase programmers (OO Programming course students in University of Tartu) filled in the satisfaction questionnaire.

The satisfaction questionnaire contains 36 questions. For each type of satisfaction the positive and negative questions were designed to neutralize the effect of temptation to answer questions positively. For example a positive question about satisfaction with partner is "Partner affected my result positively", and negative question is "I did'nt communicate much with my partner".

After Phase1 of the experiment satisfaction questionnaire was filled by 97, and after Phase2 by 82 students. Total amount of questionnaires analyzed was 176 (data of 3 students was incomplete).

---

[1] Detailed design of the experiment is described in paper [4]

Factor analysis [2] was used to analyze the collected data. Factor analysis is a method of statistics to reduce the number of variables. In our case we try to reduce the 36 answered questions to 3 types of satisfaction. Factor analysis divides the questionnaire into three parts according to three types of satisfaction described above. According to factor analysis the three-types of satisfaction affect the medium result by 18.4% of total variety of results.

3   Discussion

Average satisfaction with result was statistically significantly different for pair and non-pair programmers: -0.16 and 0.22 accordingly (the range of types of satisfaction is from -3.7 to 3.7[2]). It means that, contrary to some other investigations ([10],[1]), pair-programmers are less satisfied with their result than non-pair-programmers.

Assignment for Phase 2 of the experiment was more complicated. Average satisfaction with result was statistically significantly different for Phase 1 and Phase 2 – 0.27 and -0.35 accordingly. More complicated assignment resulted with lower satisfaction with result.

Other authors also [3] discovered influence of assignment to the satisfaction. In this case also the complicated assignment drives to lower satisfaction (in pair-programming) – the satisfaction was not statistically significantly different between pair and non-pair programmers.

Satisfaction with partner (non-pair programmers had a partner also, but they worked at two different computers as an ordinary two person teams) between pair and non-pair programmers wasn't statistically significantly different.

Satisfaction with method between pair and non-pair programmers also wasn't statistically significantly different. But the complexity of assignments affected the satisfaction with method similarly as in satisfaction with result. Average satisfaction with method was 0.051 (for Phase 1) and -0.35 (for Phase 2, more complex assignment).

4   Conclusions

To analyze the satisfaction in (pair-)programming it is reasonable to have exact imagination what type of satisfactions we consider. In this paper authors analyzed the satisfaction that consists of three types – satisfaction with result, satisfaction with partner and satisfaction with method. In other studies [3], [10] satisfaction with pair-programming usually means satisfaction with method.

Authors of the paper have not found any works analyzing specifically the satisfaction with partner.

Significant differencies were discovered in satisfaction with result (pair programmers were less satisfied with result than nonpair-programmers). Satisfaction

---

[2] Answers to negative questions contributed to negative values, and positive questions contributed to positive values

with result is usually called as confidence in other works ([5], [10], [3]). If assignments are more complicated the pair-programming method doesn't give more satisfaction. It confirms the same result from [5].

5   Future Work

While the satisfaction with result gave us statistically significant results in this experiment, it is not clear whether the relationship between programming method and satisfaction with result remains intact when changing complexity of the assignment. The complexity of the assignment affects the satisfaction with result, but it is not clear whether the impact differs for different programming methods.

Acknowledgements. Authors of the paper would like to thank all the people who helped to reach the point so far and the students of OOP lecture who acted as the selection.

References

1. Cockburn, Alistair; Williams, Laurie; "The Costs and Benefits of Pair Programming", XP2000, 2000.
2. Gorsuch, R. L. "Factor Analysis", Hillsdale, New York:Erlbaum, 1983
3. Hanks, Brian; McDowell, Charlie; "Program Quality with Pair Programming in CS1", www.cse.ucsc.edu/ brianh/papers/ ProgQualHanksMcDowell.pdf
4. Heiberg, Sven; Puus, Uuno; Salumaa Priit; Seeba Asko; "Pair-Programming Effect on Developers Productivity"; Proceedings XP 2003
5. McDowell, Charlie; Werner Linda; Bullock, Heather E.; Fernald Julian; "The Impact of Pair Programming on Student Perfomance, Perception and Persistence", www.cse.ucsc.edu/ charlie/pubs/icse2003.pdf
6. Sharifabdi, Kamran; Grot, Claudia; "Team Development and Pair Programming - tasks and challenges of the XP coach", www.agilealliance.com/articles/articles/ Sharifabdi-Grot–TeamDevelopmentandPairProgramming.pdf
7. Succi, Giancarlo; Marchesi, Michele; Pedrycz Witold; Williams Laurie; "Preliminary Analysis of the Effects of Pair Programming on Job Satisfaction", collaboration.csc.ncsu.edu/laurie/Papers/Succi-Pedrycz– PreliminaryAnalysisoftheEffectsofPairProgramming.pdf
8. Williams, Laurie; Kessler, R. Robert; "All I Really Need to Know about Pair Programming I Learned in Kindergarten", Communications of the ACM, 2000.
9. Williams, Laurie; Kessler, Robert R.; Cunningham, Ward; Jeffries, Ron; "Strengthening the Case for Pair Programming", IEEE Software, 2000.
10. Williams, Laurie; "The Collaborative Software Process", University of Utah, 2000.

Literate Programming to Enhance Agile Methods

Vreda Pieterse, Derrick G. Kourie, and Andrew Boake

Department of Computer Science, University of Pretoria, South-Africa
vpieterse@cs.up.ac.za

Abstract. In this position paper, after explaining the essentials of literate programming, we argue that a literate programming style is consistent with the values espoused by agile software development; and that the application of literate programming in the context of an agile software development methodology is likely to enhance both the quality and lifespan of the final product.

Keywords: Literate Programming, Literate Extreme Programming

1 Literate Programming Essentials

Knuth [1] uses the term "Literate Programming" (LP) to describe his approach to program design. Rather than seeing the program as instructions to a computer that include comments to the reader, it should be seen as an explanation to a human with corresponding code between "code delimiters" [2]. For a program to be literate it should have the following attributes:

- **Literate Quality**: An artistic creation that explains the solution to a human by crisply defining its components and delicately weaving them together. [1]
- **Psychological Structure:** The program is organized in such a way that the reader is naturally led to an understanding of the decisions that shaped the code. [3]
- **Integrated Documentation:** Documentation of the program is seen as an integral part of the literate program that is developed around the code.
- **Table of Contents, Index and Cross References**: The document must have a table of contents, an index, as well as cross references between related modules within the program. The automatic generation of this information is important [4].
- **Pretty Printing:** Indentation, font styles text colours etc. should be judiciously applied to improve the readability and ease of understanding of code.
- **Verisimilitude:** The generation of executable code and the production of the human readable literate version of the program should be automatically extractable from the same source document. [5]

The first Literate Programming Environment (LPE) called WEB, was designed by Knuth [1] in 1984 at the advent of the procedural programming era. WEB used two processors called TANGLE and WEAVE to convert the original source document respectively into an executable program (which could be *executed* using a standard Pascal compiler), and into a publishable, human readable program (which was *printed* using TEX)

Soon a number of similar LPE's (such as those shown in table 1) evolved to support other programming languages or to produce documents using other typesetters.

J. Eckstein and H. Baumeister (Eds.): XP 2004, LNCS 3092, pp. 250–253, 2004.

Table 1. Some Early LPE's

LPE	Year	Language	Typesetter
WEB [1]	1984	Pascal	TEX
CWEB [6]	1986	C	troff/nroff
Literate Program Browser[3]	1987	SmallTalk-80	troff
FWEB [7]	1990	FORTRAN8X	TEX
APLWEB [8]	1993	APL	TEX

In 1990 van Wyk [5] commented that the general acceptance of LP would not be possible before a universal LPE could be marketed. In the light of the technology of the time, most developers accepted this as the death knell of LP. Some valiant supporters of LP however continued to build adaptable LPE's (such as those shown in table 2) that were able to support a variety of programming languages, and to produce documents in various specified formats.

Table 2. Some Language independant LPE's

LPE	Year	Languages used
LIPED [9]	1992	Assembler, Pascal, Clipper
CWEB [10]	1993	C, C++, ANSI C, Java
VizAuthor [11]	1996	APL, Pascal, C, C++, Java
Leo [12]	2002	Java, C, C++, Pascal, Fortran, Perl, Icon, Python, SmallTalk, Cobol, etc.

In the meantime object oriented (OO) development emerged. Commercial integrated development environments (IDEs) supporting OO implemented LP concepts, albeit without specifically supporting LP. Consequently:

- Pretty printing in editors has become a matter of course.
- Tools like javadoc in the JDK support integrated documentation and create hyperlinked documentation with an index and table of contents.
- Tools like Rational Rose show different views of program design, supporting psychological ordering of the program components.

2 Justification of Literate Extreme Programming

Coding done in a literate style promotes the values associated with agile methods.

- **Individuals and interactions over processes and tools**: LP is a communication-oriented programming method [13] and can aid communication better than the pure source code even though intention revealing.
- **Working software over comprehensive documentation:** LP supports comprehensive documentation without wasting time on synchronising documentation with the code. LP improves the chances of creating working software sooner. [1]
- **Customer collaboration over contract negotiation**. LP provides a more readable form of the program, facilitating better customer collaboration.

- **Responding to change over following a plan**: LP promotes simplicity of design by insisting on a psychologically friendly structure. Complete up-front analysis, design and documentation violate the LP concept of integrated documentation. Thus, LP shares with the agile methods the concern that too much planned up-front analysis and design limit the ability to respond to change.

Application of LP is likely to improve the product in terms of the following:

- **Communication:** Reenskaug and Skaar [14] experienced improved communication through written documents while applying LP in practice. XP on the other hand is designed to enhance verbal communication. These communication modes can potentially augment one another.

- **Quality:** Many authors have reported improved code quality when applying LP [2], [6], [15]. While not denying that XP may produce quality code, adding LP to XP is likely to further enhance the quality.

- **Documentation:** Much has been said about the advantages of having proper documentation for programs [16], [17], [18] and about the disadvantages of having documentation that does not match the system. [6], [16], [18]. LP emphasises these advantages and diminishes likelihood on incurring the disadvantages through better consistency between code and documentation [19]. When using LP, the XP team no longer has to minimize documentation to avoid its disadvantages. Instead, they are enabled to reap the benefits of its advantages.

Added benefits of applying Literate Extreme Programming include the following.

- **Retention of knowledge**: In an XP context, the knowledge about the system resides mostly in the memories of the team members. However, no-one remembers everything all the time. Information recorded in the literate program remains available to refresh a team member's memory when the code is revisited.

- **Accelerated distribution of knowledge**: Using verbal as well as written communication will improve the quality of the information that programmers retain. Access to the documented information can also save time later, because the learning curve to understand the code will be flattened by the presence of this information.

- **Newcomer Integration:** The improved quality of the code and the enhanced recorded documentation will help newcomers to be productive in the team sooner.

- **Customer confidence:** Because the knowledge about the system is recorded in ways that ensure continuity, the customer will enjoy greater peace of mind.

- **Outsourcing:** Applying XP in outsourced development is generally discouraged. Adding LP will allow the delivered project to be resumed by a different team. Inclusion of LP could therefore improve XP's applicability to outsourced coding.

- **Scalability:** The agile value set and practices are best suited to teams of less than 50 people who are engaged in projects that are not life-critical [20]. We feel that it will be possible to alleviate concerns about team size, project size and project character that are often associated with XP, by adding aspects of LP to it.

3 Conclusion

We have argued that LP is consistent with and supportive of agile methodologies. The incorporation of LP into a methodology such as XP will enhance communication and improve the software quality. We are cognizant of the commonly observed fact that programmers are not enthusiastic about documentation [18]. Nevertheless, given the cited evidence that LP improves both quality and communication, it seems worthwhile to pursue an empirical study to build a good LPE and to measure the extent to which it can find acceptability amongst extreme programmers. Work in this direction is under way.

References

1. Knuth D.E. *Literate Programming*. The Computer Journal, 27 (2) (1984) 97-111
2. Williams R. *FunnelWeb Tutorial Manual*. Online:
   http://www.ross.net/funnelweb/tutorial/intro_what.html visited 2003/01/05 (2000)
3. Beck K., Cunningham W. *Expanding the Role of Tools in a Literate Programming Environment*. Presented at CASE'87. Boston Mass. online: http://c2.com/doc/case87.html Visited: 2003-12-19. (1987)
4. Denning P.J. *Announcing Literate Programming*. Communications of the ACM, 30 (7) (Jul 1987) 593
5. Van Wyk C.J. *Literate Programming : An Assessment*. In: Literate Programming. Communications of the ACM, 33 (3) (March 1990) 361-365
6. Thimbleby HW. Experiences of 'Literate Programming' using CWEB. Computer Journal, 29 (3) (June 1986) 201-211
7. Avenarius A., Oppermann S. *FWEB: a literate programming system for Fortran8x*, SIGPAN Notices, 25 (1) (1990) 52-58
8. Dickey LJ. *Literate programming in APL and APLWEB*. APL Quote Quad, 23 (4)11.(1993)
9. Bishop J.M., Gregson K.M. *Literate Programming and the LIPED Environment*. Structured Programming. 13 (1) (1992) 23-34.
10. Levy S. Literate Programming and CWEB. Computer Language, 10 (1) pp 67-70. (1993)
11. Pieterse V., Bishop JM. *Visualization of Programs in Textbooks* Online:
    http://www.literateprogramming.com/visualze.pdf Visited 2004/01/08 (May 1996)
12. Ream E.K. *Leo Literate Editor with Outlines*. online:
    http://www.3dtree.com/ev/e/sbooks/leo/sbframetoc_ie.htm visited 2004/03/28, (Dec 2002)
13. Beck K. *Extreme Programming Explained*, Addison-Wesley, (1999).
14. Reenskaug T., Skaar AL. *An environment for literate Smalltalk programming*. OOPSLA 1989 Proceedings, New Orleans, (1989) 337-345
15. Lindsay D.C., Thimbleby H. *A File Difference Program*. In: Literate Programming. Communications of the ACM, 32 (6) (June 1989) 740-755
16. Kotula, J. *Source Code Documentation: An Engineering Deliverable* Online:
    http://csdl.computer.org/comp/proceedings/tools/2000/0774/00/07740505abs.htm   Visited: 2004/01/08 (2000)
17. Hyman M. *Literate C++*, Computer Language. 7 (7) (Jul 1990) 67-69
18. Parnas D. *Software Aging*. In: Software Fundamentals. Addison-Wesley, (2001)
19. Shum S., Cook C. *AOPS: an abstraction-oriented programming system for literate programming*. Software Engineering Journal, 8 (3) (May 1993) 113-120
20. Williams L., Cockburn A. *Agile Software Development: It's about Feedback and Change*, Computer, 36 (6) (June 2003) 39-41

Mockrunner
– Unit Testing of J2EE Applications –

Alwin Ibba

Lebensversicherung von 1871 a.G., Maximiliansplatz 5,
80333 Munich, Germany
alwin.ibba@lv1871.de

Abstract. A fast test – development cycle is absolutely mandatory when developing applications with agile methodologies. There are different approaches to overcome the sluggishness of in-container testing. One common technique is the use of mock objects or of stub objects. Mockrunner is a framework that simulates J2EE [1] containers. It simplifies unit testing of J2EE based applications. The application can be tested without changing the original code. Mockrunner is open source and can be downloaded from [2].

1 Introduction

Applications in the J2EE environment are often remarkable complex systems. They are usually running on different machines and are separated into multiple tiers. It's a really tedious and annoying process to deploy the components to the application server. Dozens of deployment descriptors have to be provided by the developer to configure the J2EE environment. There are development tools which support the development and deployment cycle of J2EE applications but it's still a lot of work to do besides the pure development of the business logic.

Testing the different components of a J2EE based application can be really bothering. Running the unit tests against an EJB [3] in the container really taxes the developers patience. This is especially true if there are many EJBs, perhaps with access to a database.

Besides the poor performance it is a lot of work to setup the test environment. Deployment descriptors and test database tables have to be created. This test data has to be clearly seperated from the production environment.

The main goal of Mockrunner is to provide a test environment for large J2EE applications without the need of a running application server or a database. Mockrunner is usually used in conjunction with a simulated EJB container called MockEJB [4] and can be used to test servlets, servlet filters, custom tags, EJBs and JDBC [5] code. Furthermore it includes a test framework for Struts [6] and for JMS [7]. Test frameworks for other J2EE related technologies will be included in future releases, especially for Java Data Objects JDO [8]. See [1] for a detailed description of the different J2EE technolgies.

J. Eckstein and H. Baumeister (Eds.): XP 2004, LNCS 3092, pp. 254–257, 2004.

Mockrunner extends JUnit [9] and requires Java 1.3 to run. It supports J2EE 1.3 and Struts 1.1.

2 Architecture

The core of the Mockrunner framework are different test modules. A test module is a simple Java class that can be used to setup the configuration for the different tests and it holds the state while running a test method. Usually the state of a test module is reset in the `setUp()` method of a JUnit test case. A test module provides verify methods to test the different conditions. A verify method throws a `VerifyFailedException` if a test fails.

Mockrunner is providing six test modules at the moment. The `ActionTestModule`, `ServletTestModule` and `TagTestModule` can be used for testing Struts actions and forms, servlets, filters and custom tag classes. The `JDBCTestModule` simulates a database and can be used to test JDBC code. The `EJBTestModule` utilizes MockEJB and is meant for EJB testing. The `JMSTestModule` is meant for JMS related tests. Of course the test modules can be combined. For example, the `ServletTestModule` can be used in conjunction with the `EJBTestModule` and the `JDBCTestModule`.

Usually a test module is created and used in a JUnit test case. For every test module there's also a `TestCaseAdapter`. For the `ServletTestModule` there exists a `ServletTestCaseAdapter` for example. The adapters just delegate to the corresponding modules. In difference the adapter itself is a JUnit test case, so the test case can simply extend the adapter. Since a Java class is limited to one base class, it's obligatory to use the test module approach, if multiple test modules are combined. If only one module is involved in the test it is easier to extend the corresponding adapter. Mockrunner handles the creation of the corresponding module in this case.

Mockrunner does not provide a reimplementation of a J2EE container. Functionality that is not necessary for unit tests or a normal application will not be simulated. In some cases the test modules differ from the real container, if the different behavior is more suitable for a test environment. In other cases you can switch between real container mode and test mode.

Mockrunner generally does not read any deployment descriptors or configuration files. All necessary setup is done using the Mockrunner API. So it is very easy to test all elements as reusable components regardless of the settings you use in one or another application.

3 Writing Tests with Mockrunner

J2EE applications are usually separated into three tiers, the web tier, the business tier and the integration tier. Mockrunner covers all three tiers. The three test modules for the web tier, namely the `ActionTestModule`, the `ServletTestModule` and the `TagTestModule` can be used to simulate a web container and the Struts infrastructure. It is possible to prepare the session, the request and the servlet context, to execute one Struts action or one servlet and to verify the changes of the request or session state at the end.

The result of a servlet or tag call usually is an HTML page. The corresponding test modules are providing the created HTML code in different formats, namely as text, as an `InputReader` or as a JDOM [10] or W3C [11] XML document. HTML often contains mistakes and is not wellformed in general. Mockrunner is using the NekoHTML parser [12] to overcome this issue and is usually able to provide a fixed XML document that can be used for further testing. For example, the XML document can be used as an input for an XML test framework.

EJB is the favorite technology for the business tier of a J2EE application. The EJB part of Mockrunner is based on the open source MockEJB framework. MockEJB provides a lightweight simulated EJB container with enough functionality for running EJBs in unit tests. Refer to the project page at [4] for details. MockEJB supports stateless and stateful session beans as well as message driven beans. Entity beans are not supported but probably will in future releases.

Mockrunner utilizes MockEJB. The `EJBTestModule` does not implement much functionality. Its purpose is to bring Mockrunner and MockEJB together. MockEJB usually works with a real database. The EJB is executed in a real transaction created by the application server. Mockrunner implements a simulated database and runs transactional code inside a simulated transaction. The simulated transaction keeps track of any commits or rollbacks.

The EJB test environment of Mockrunner manages the transaction and the simulated data source. Furthermore it offers some additional functionality for an easier to use and more convenient deployment mechanism.

Mockrunner provides two test modules for the integration tier, namely for JDBC and for JMS. The JMS framework implements all the JMS interfaces and simulates a message server. Messages can be sent to simulated queues and topics. They are forwarded to the registered receivers in the same way as with a real message server. The `JMSTestModule` can be used to test JMS based code, i.e. code that uses the JMS interfaces.

The `JDBCTestModule` simulates a database in order to test JDBC code without the need of setting up a real database. It implements all the interfaces of JDBC 3.0 and focuses on the functionality that is necessary for unit testing. The simulated environment is not a database and it does not execute any SQL statements. It is not able to store any data persistently. Its only purpose is to test the Java part of JDBC based applications. If the tests are all green it's still no guaranty that the application is working well with a real database. It may be necessary to test the SQL code itself by running it against a real database.

Mockrunner provides a `MockDriver` that registers itself for any incoming connection attempt. All database calls are intercepted and answered by the framework.

Since the simulated JDBC environment does not execute SQL code, it's necessary to specify the answers the database would provide when receiving different SQL statements. It's possible to setup MockResultSet objects for test queries and any other return value a database may provide. It is even possible to tell the mock driver to throw exceptions when receiving a specified statement. This feature can be used to test database failures.

The JDBCTestModule keeps track of all executed statements, returned results and update counts, thrown exceptions and closed connections, statements and result sets. It manages the transaction and counts commits and rollbacks. It does not matter if it is a JDBC transaction or JTA [13] transaction.

4   Conclusion

Mockrunner provides an easy way to write unit tests for J2EE based applications. It is very fast and it does not require to write the application code in a special way that makes it compatible with the test environment.

References

1. Sun Microsystems Inc., J2EE, Website, http://java.sun.com/j2ee
2. Ibba A., Mockrunner Project, Website, http://mockrunner.sourceforge.net
3. Sun Microsystems Inc., EJB, Website, http://java.sun.com/products/ejb
4. Ananiev A., MockEJB Project, Website, http://mockejb.sourceforge.net
5. Sun Microsystems Inc., JDBC, Website, http://java.sun.com/products/jdbc
6. Apache Software Foundation, Struts, Website, http://jakarta.apache.org/struts
7. Sun Microsystems Inc., JMS, Website, http://java.sun.com/products/jms
8. Sun Microsystems Inc., JDO, Website, http://java.sun.com/products/jdo
9. Beck, K., Gamma, E., JUnit, Website, http://www.junit.org
10. Hunter J., McLaughlin B., JDOM Project, Website, http://www.jdom.org
11. World Wide Web Consortium W3C, XML, Website, http://www.w3c.org/XML
12. Clark A., CyberNeko HTML parser, Website,
    http://www.apache.org/~andyc/neko/doc
13. Sun Microsystems Inc., JTA, Website, http://java.sun.com/j2ee/transactions.html

Application of Lean and Agile Principles to Workflow Management

Barbara Weber[1] and Werner Wild[2]

[1] Institute of Computer Science - Quality Engineering Research Group
University of Innsbruck, Technikerstraße 25/7, 6020 Innsbruck, Austria
Barbara.Weber@uibk.ac.at
[2] EVOLUTION Consulting
Jahnstraße 26, 6020 Innsbruck, Austria
werner.wild@evolution.at

Abstract. Today's dynamic and uncertain business environment requires quick reaction to change and frequent deviations from plans. Lean principles and agile methods address this need and have been successfully applied to software development. This paper shows how lean development and agile values can be applied to workflow management, as workflow modeling has strong similarities to software development. The required adaptability is enabled by the integration of workflow management and conversational case-based reasoning (CCBR) and is implemented by the research prototype CBRFlow.

1   Introduction

Workflow management systems (WFMS) are frequently used to control the execution of business processes and to improve their efficiency and productivity. Today's business is characterized by ever-changing requirements and unpredictable environments (e.g. due to global competition). A WFMS must therefore be flexible at run-time so that necessary modifications are possible when they arise.

The need for flexibility and adaptability in WFMS is addressed by adaptive workflow management research (e.g. [1], [2]). Weber [3] proposes an architecture for such an adaptive WFMS (CBRFlow). CBRFlow, a research prototype, integrates workflow management and CCBR to foster flexibility and supports an approach to workflow management which supports many of the principles advocated in lean [4] and agile software development [5].

2   Adaptive Approach to Workflow Management

CBRFlow [3] builds upon the idea of integrating CCBR and workflow management to provide the system with learning capabilities and to foster adaptability and flexibility. Its architecture allows an adaptive approach to workflow management and supports many of the principles advocated in lean and agile software development.

J. Eckstein and H. Baumeister (Eds.): XP 2004, LNCS 3092, pp. 258–261, 2004.

During workflow modeling an initial computerized representation of selected business processes is created. The control flow between activities is modeled by business rules. When run-time changes to the workflow model become necessary due to exceptions or changing requirements, the user annotates the workflow model with context-specific information in the form of cases. When this process knowledge becomes well-established, the workflow modeler abstracts these cases to rules, thus explicitly updating the underlying model (Figure 1). The system and the organization continuously learn how to better handle new situations as more and more experience is gained and the knowledge is readily available for reuse.

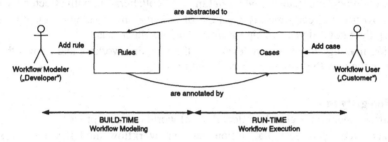

Fig. 1. CBRFlow's approach to workflow management

3   Application of Lean Principles to Workflow Management

Eliminate Waste
- cost of a complete workflow model often exceeds the potential business value
- covering too many details in the workflow model involves the risk of including rarely needed parts, not yet needed or even unneeded ones, thus creating waste
- focusing on core functionality allows to shorten the modeling period and allows for an earlier productive system

Amplify Learning
- business process management deals with wicked problems that cannot be planned in every detail; the *right the first time* approach does not work, but the selected solution has to be continuously improved
- WFMS must provide tight feedback loops (*model-execute-evaluate cycle*) and be able to handle modifications when they arise (i.e. short iterations); the gained knowledge can be immediately reused in subsequent workflow instances

Decide as Late as Possible
- initial workflow model covers only the details of a business process that provide an immediate business value
- detailed modeling is delayed until the company's needs are more clearly understood
- supporting just-in-time updates to the existing workflow model using the CCBR sub-system, additional knowledge is added during run-time in form of cases
- refactor knowledge encoded in cases into rules when it becomes frequently reused

Deliver as Fast as Possible
- only core functionality of the most valuable business processes is implemented in the first iteration to earn value form early on and to get feedback right away
- changes and new functionalities are added on demand (i.e. just-in-time)
- CBRFlow allows hot deployment of changes to the workflow model and does not require a restart of running workflow instances.

Empower the Team
- workflow modeler creates initial model in close collaboration with affected users
- workflow users directly modify the flow of activities by creating or adapting cases to keep the knowledge available for immediate and later reuse
- decision making authority is delegated to the frontline workers and allows them to improve the way they do their work on their own

Build Integrity in
- workflow model must closely reflect the real world business processes
- best achieved by close collaboration between workflow modelers and workflow users during build-time and by allowing modifications during run-time by the user
- workflow model is modified and tested directly by the user (customer test)
- the workflow modeler should create and run corresponding developer tests
- refactor when user acceptance drops (frequent case reuse) or duplication is found

See the Whole
- risk of sub-optimization is mitigated by monitoring workflow execution, as users directly modify the workflow even without a mental picture of the overall workflow
- metrics should cover the entire workflow or even the underlying business process

4   Application of Lean Values to Workflow Management

In this section we show how the core values described in the Agile Manifesto [5] can be applied to workflow management and how they are supported by CBRFlow.

Individuals and Interactions over Processes and Tools
- CBRFlow empowers the users to be problem solvers, not just process followers
- users are entitled to immediately respond to changes using the integrated CCBR sub-system without following a complicated or time-consuming process

Working System over Comprehensive Documentation
- CBRFlow brings a WFMS up and running fast and fosters learning from there
- feed-back from the frontline users is integrated immediately into the system and be made available instantaneously
- knowledge retained in the CCBR sub-system provides a concise documentation for later refactoring by the workflow modeler

Customer Collaboration over Contract Negotiation
- initial workflow model is developed in close and informal collaboration between the workflow modelers and the workflow users as they hold the knowledge of how the business processes are actually performed in the company
- permanent changes to the model are also done in close collaboration between the workflow modelers and those frontline workers who have entered the cases when deviating from the predefined workflow model

Responding to Change over Following a Plan
- the execution of a predefined model is not strictly enforced
- frontline workers can respond to changes immediately by entering a case, thus implicitly update the workflow model using the CCBR sub-system

5   Conclusions and Further Studies

The research prototype CBRFlow covers many of the lean and agile principles and values. The application of CCBR to workflow management relaxes the strict separation between build-time and run-time and supports just-in-time updates to the workflow model enabling to delay the decision how to model a business process precisely until the company's needs are more clearly understood. This immediate feedback resolves uncertainty, and permits to rapidly incorporate the results of the learning processes into subsequent workflow executions. Requirements are modeled when they arise and when their modeling provides a clear business benefit. Shortening the modeling period allows a sooner productive use of the system and enables earning business value from early-on.

References

1. Reichert, M.; Dadam, P.: ADEPTflex – Supporting Dynamic Changes of Workflows Without Loosing Control. In: Journal of Intelligent Information Systems, Special Issue on Workflow Management 10 (1998) 2, pp. 93-129.
2. Luo, Z.; Shet, A.; Kochut, K.; Miller, J.: Exception Handling in Workflow Systems. In: Applied Intelligence 13 (2000) 2, pp. 125-147.
3. Weber, B.: Integration of Workflow Management and Case-Based Reasoning: Supporting Business Process Management through an Adaptive Workflow Management System. Dissertation, Innsbruck 2003.
4. Poppendieck, M.; Poppendieck, T.: Lean Software Development: An Agile Toolkit. 1st edition, Addison Wesley 2003.
5. The Agile Alliance. Agile Manifesto (2001). Available at http://www.agilemanifesto.org, visited on December 27, 2003.
6. Weber, B.; Wild, W.: Agile Approach To Workflow Modeling. To appear in: Tagungsreihe Modellierung 2004.

Assistance for Supporting XP Test Practices in a Distributed CSCW Environment

Ibrahim Lokpo[1], Michel Babri[1], and Gérard Padiou[2]

[1] Institut National Polytechnique Félix Houphouet-Boigny,
Departement of Mathematics and Computer Science,
Yamoussoukro, Côte d'Ivoire, West Africa.
lokpo@hotmail.com,michel_babri@yahoo.fr
[2] Ecole Nationale SupéŽrieure d'Electrotechnique, d'Electronique,
d'Informatique et de Télécommunications,
Institut de Recherche en Informatique de Toulouse (IRIT-CNRS),
Toulouse, France.
padiou@enseeiht.fr

Abstract. One of the main requirements of eXtreme programming (XP) is to do unit testing be a critical task of the daily development routine of a programmer. Our work aims at contributing to make easier the actual practice of this requirement in the framework of distributed computer-supported cooperative work (CSCW) and in an education context. The proposed XP test environment is used as a basic mechanism for structuring the XP process in a distributed context. As an experimental prototype, we propose a Junit and JML based unit testing environment as an extension of the BlueJ Interactive Environment.

Keywords: XP-programming, Unit testing, distributed CSCW.

1 Introduction

XP[Bec00][SM01] aims at providing the software developers with a simple method that helps producting quickly high quality functionalitie. Since Unit testing has been included as an important part of XP methodology of software development, efforts have been made to encourage programmers to actually use it in their daily development routine[GB98]. Our work aims at contributing to assist the actual practice of this requirement in a distributed context. In this paper, we describe JUTE, a Junit[Bec01] and JML based unit testing environment that helps doing XP tests driving developpement and supports public ownership practices as an extension of the interactive BlueJ environment. Furthermore, the CVS tool is used to assist the versioning of test results in a distributed context.

In the next section we study the problem of unit testing and distributed CSCW in the framework of XP programming. Among these problems we choose to explore the assistance to distributed unit testing considering that unit testing is a basic and essential subject in Extreme Programming. More precisely,

J. Eckstein and H. Baumeister (Eds.): XP 2004, LNCS 3092, pp. 262–265, 2004.

we consider the test process as the basic structuring mechanism of deveopment interactions in a distributed context. In section 3, we focus on the implementation of such an environment. We describe how it combines assistant tools for testing, namely JML and Junit, a Java programming environment BlueJ and a distributed version control system CVS. Each of them provides its functionalities to carry out a distributed unit testing environment in an XP programming framework. This tool is a first step towards a distributed Java XP programming tool. In section 4, we outline the current step of our prototype.

2   Distributed XP Programming Based upon Distributed Unit Testing

Distributed eXtreme Programming (DXP) is eXtreme Programming with a relaxation on the requirements of physical proximity of the team members [BM02],[KJCL01]. Several aspects of distributed XP have been tackled through a lot of research projects. They have proposed differents concepts such as the notion of virtual team[Mau02],[SMMO+03]. Such approaches aims at providing a set of CSCW functionnalities in a distributed environment to enforce the close coupling of programmers. However, such an approach requires powerful underlying network resources too. We propose an other approach assuming minimal connecting resources. This requirement is implied by the context of our experiment : a low bandwidth connection between France and Côte-d'Ivoire. Therefore, we focus our approach upon a distributed unit testing assistance as a basic step towards loosely-coupled XP-programming and public ownership practices.

XP programming requires intensive and continuous unit tests[Bec00]. It appears clearly that software development following XP is driven by test. Furthermore, it has been shown that unit testing is helpful to the other XP practices[Gas01]. A very simple and useful assistance to unit testing in Java is provided by the Junit tool[GB98]. However, in a distributed context, it seems important to insure the gathering of unit tests so that no tests is overlooked. Therefore, our proposal involves the generation of a test suite including all unit tests modules in the file hierarchy of the project.

3   A Distributed Java Unit Testing Environment (JUTE)

Junit (http://www.junit.org) is a very popular tool to help programmers for this purpose in the framework of XP programming. The Junit tool forces both a strict methodology to write unit tests and a simple way to execute tests sequences. The interactive Java environment BlueJ [KQPR03,PKR03] (see also : http://www.bluej.org) integrates the Junit tool and allows to perform unit tests associated to different packages in a project.

However, unit tests must be written by programmers. A further assistance is provided by the JML project. The JML project (Java Modeling Language) aims at providing a specification language to specify behavior of Java modules.

It combines the approaches of Eiffel and Larch, with some elements of the refinement calculus. It involves several tools and, especially, a unit test generator (jmlunit). This tool generates Junit-like tests skeletons. These skeletons must be refined to obtain executable test suites. In this approach, basic test cases are automatically generated from specifications. JML requires a knowledge of logic-based specification languages to describe safety properties (invariants, pre and post-conditions).

The integration of this jmlunit tool in the BlueJ environment should provide a further facility to assist the development of unit tests in an teaching context for carrying out XP practices. Moreover, in the framework of XP programming, the unit tests of a whole project have to be launched in a systematic and regular way. If all the tests succeeds, a new current version of the project can be recorded and final users will perform acceptance tests upon it.

This task requires to develop a global test suite of all test suites in a project. We have written a generator to automatically obtain such a global test program. This program explores the project tree and generates a Java source program which gathers all test cases in a global test suite. Then, this generated program is compiled and the junit tool is launched to execute this global test suite.

An important assumption of XP is its continuous refinement process during software development. As nobody is able to predict exactly what functionality may be requested in the future, XP tends to produce a now useful software with possible adjustment when necessary. This flexibility meets that of BlueJ. On the other hand, CVS provides a means to overcome the colocation restriction the co-location restriction.

4 Current Work

The Junit package is plugged in the BlueJ environment as a basic but useful support for handling unit tests. We extend this capability and plug in two further tools : the Java Modeling Language (JML)[LRL+00] and the version control system CVS (Concurrent version System). The members access the repository via a secure connection and open their local copy of the project with Bluej. Then, they are allowed to perform all available operations : update the local copy, test a module, commit an updated module, etc. Furthermore, the gathering of all tests in a global suite has been implemented.

The project we are working on is located at Ecole National Supérieure d"Electrotechnique, d'Electronique, d'Informatique, d'Hydraulique et de Télécommunication (ENSEEIHT) in Toulouse (France). An other contributing team is located in Côte d'Ivoire at Institut National Polytechnique Félix Houphouët-Boigny(INP-HB) in Yamoussoukro.

5 Conclusion

This approach is a challenge with respect to the usual high level of locality and synchronous communication among XP teams. This requires to evaluate its actual feasability without invalidating the main features and pratices of XP programming. We believe that BlueJ, on one hand and frameworks such as JML(Java Modelling Language and CVS(Concurrent Version System) on the other hand, complement each other to improve distributed computer-supported cooperative work and to overcome the XP co-location constraint without loosing XP basic features and advantages.

References

[Bec00]   Kent Beck. *Extreme Programming Explained : Embrace Change*. The XP Series. Addison Wesley Publishing Company, 2000.

[Bec01]   Kent Beck. *Test-driven Development by example*. The Addison Wesley Signature Series. Addison Wesley Publishing Company, 2001.

[BM02]   S. Bowen and F. Maurer. Designing a Distributed Software Development Support System using a peer-to-peer Architecture. In *Proceedings of the Workshop on Cooperative Supports for Distributed Software Engineering Processes*. 26th IEEE Annual International Computer Software and Application Conference (COMPSAC), 2002.

[Gas01]   Peter Gassmann. Unit testing in a Java project. In Kent Beck, editor, *Extreme Programming Examined*, The XP Series, pages 249–269. Addison-Wesley Publishing Company, 2001.

[GB98]   Erich Gamma and Kent Beck. Test infected : Programmers love writing tests. *Java Report*, 3(7), July 1998.

[KJCL01]   M. Kircher, P. Jain, A. Corsaro, and D. Levine. Distributed extreme programming. In *XP2001 - eXtreme Programming and Flexible Processes in Software Engineering*. Villasimius, Sardinia, Italy, May 2001.

[KQPR03]   M. Kölling, B. Quig, A. Patterson, and J. Rosenberg. The BlueJ system and its pedagogy. *Journal of Computer Science Education*, 13(4), Dec 2003.

[LRL+00]   G. T. Leavens, K. Rustan, M. Leino, E. Poll, C. Ruby, and B. Jacobs. JML: notations and tools supporting detailed design in java. In *OOPSLA'00 Companion*, pages 105–106, August 2000.

[Mau02]   F. Maurer. Supporting distributed extreme programming. In Don Wells and Laurie A. Williams, editors, *XP/Agile Universe 2002, Second XP Universe and First Agile Universe Conference Chicago, IL, USA, August 4-7, 2002, ProceedingsXP/Agile Universe*, volume 2418 of *Lecture Notes in Computer Science*, pages 13–22. Springer, 2002.

[PKR03]   A. Patterson, M. Kölling, and J. Rosenberg. Introducing Unit Testing with Bluej. In *Proceedings of the 8th conference on Information Technology in Computer Science Education (ITiCSE 2003)*, 2003.

[SM01]   Giancardo Succi and Michele Marchesi. *Extreme Programming Examined*. The XP Series. Addison Wesley Publishing Company, 2001.

[SMMO+03]   H. Skaf-Molli, P. Molli, G. Oster, Cl. Godart, P. Ray, and F. Rabhi. Toxic farm: A cooperative management platform for virtual teams and enterprises. In *5th International Conference on Enterprise Information Systems ICEIS03*. Angers, France, April 2003.

Requirements of an ISO Compliant XP Tool

Marco Melis[1], Walter Ambu[2], Sandro Pinna[1], and Katiuscia Mannaro[1]

[1] Dipartimento di Ingegneria Elettrica ed Elettronica, Universitá di Cagliari,
Piazza d'Armi, 09123 Cagliari, Italy
{marco.melis, pinnasandro, mannaro}@diee.unica.it
http://agile.diee.unica.it
[2] Atlantis spa, via San Tommaso d'Aquino, 18
09134 Cagliari, Italy
walterambu@gruppoatlantis.it
http://www.gruppoatlantis.it

Abstract. In the last years, a few studies and experiences have been published about the compatibility between Extreme Programming and ISO 9001:2000 certification. The actual problem is not to demonstrate if it is possible to certificate an XP process but to explain how an XP process can maintain its agility in such a context. We think that the use of an appropriate tool that supports both XP practices and ISO 9000 standard can simplify this integration process. In this paper we will provide the essential requirements for a tool supporting such functionalities.

1 Introduction

Recent studies have shown that it is possible to achieve ISO 9001:2000 [3] certification in organizations using agile methodologies [4]. These studies are mainly concerned with the demonstration of compatibility between Extreme Programming practices [1] and ISO standard requirements. Furthermore, a few experiences have been presented in support of these ideas [5][1].

In order to achieve certification, ISO 9001 requires the organization to define specific procedures to establish how each significant activity in their development process is conducted. This means that the organization must always be able to show objective evidence of what is planned, what has been done, how it was done, the current status of the project and product, and it must be able to demonstrate the effectiveness of its quality system. The main problem that arises in practice is that the adoption of these activities could lead to an heavyweight process, in contrast with Agile philosophy. The adoption of a certified quality system is justified only whether it gives an added value to the whole organization. At the same time, a lot of tools supporting XP processes have been developed ([5], [6]). These tools mainly support requirements gathering and planning activities. It is our opinion that the use of such tools can be very helpful in order to manage software development processes. In this paper we will

---

[1] This study is part of MAPS research project (Agile Methodologies for Software Production) funded by the FIRB research fund (grant nr. RBNE01JRK8) of the Italian Government (MIUR).

J. Eckstein and H. Baumeister (Eds.): XP 2004, LNCS 3092, pp. 266–269, 2004.

provide the essential requirements for the development of a tool supporting XP project management and ISO 9001:2000 certification (section 2).

2   Guidelines for Validation of a XP Tool Supporting ISO 9001:2000 Certification

In this section we intend to give some guidelines helping to define those requirements that should be supported by a project management tool (*Tool*) to support ISO 9001:2000 certification [3]. From the ISO standard we have extracted those clauses that are involved in software development for which the *Tool* can be useful, giving some clue for its implementation.

ISO normative identifies 5 main process areas:
- Quality Management System ([3], sect. 4);
- Management Responsibility ([3], sect. 5);
- Resource Management ([3], sect. 6);
- Product Realization ([3], sect. 7);
- Measurement, Analysis and Improvement ([3], sect. 8).

In this section we only present *Design and Development* area of Product Realization.

2.1   Design and Development [D&D] ([3], 7.3)

Design and Development Planning (7.3.1). "The organization shall plan and control the design and development of product."
The *Tool* shall support the planning of the software development processes, such as definition of Releases and Iterations. Moreover it should support definition of relative responsibilities and authorities. In addition, it shall communicate results regarding these planning activities inside the organization as well as control the realization of planned activities.

Design and Development Inputs (7.3.2). "Inputs relating to product requirements shall be determined and record maintained. . . "
The *Tool* shall provide for recording these type of inputs and for maintaining relative records. It should supply information and suggestions gathered in previous similar projects.

Design and Development Outputs (7.3.3). "The outputs of D&D shall be provided in a form that enables verification against the D&D input and shall be approved prior to release."
The main outputs of a XP development process are the code and its relative tests (unit and acceptance test). By mean of the *Tool*, it shall be possible to automatically verify that output elements are suitable to satisfy input requirements: in practice, the *Tool* should allow the association of each output artifact with the correspondent input element and relative test. In this way, thanks to an appropriate interface with a testing application, it will be possible to verify requirement satisfaction.

Design and Development Review (7.3.4). "At suitable stages, systematic reviews of D&D shall be performed in accordance with planned arrangements." In an XP process, iteration meetings are a formal review of design and development. The report of this activity and the resulting outputs are records of the quality management system that shall be integrated in the *Tool*. Pair-Programming with refactoring and testing are other forms of design and development reviews. The *Tool* shall identify and record outputs of these activities (refactored code, test reports,...) to document and give evidence of the continuous review done in an XP environment.

Design and Development Verification (7.3.5).
"Verification shall be performed in accordance with planned arrangements to ensure that the D&D outputs have met the D&D inputs requirements. Records of the results of the verification and any necessary actions shall be maintained." In an XP project, design and development verification is continually done because of continuous integration and testing, but it can be formally executed in specific moments such as the end of iterations. It consists of verifying the effectiveness of outputs to satisfy input requirements. It can be mainly done by means of automatic acceptance tests. The *Tool* shall allow the execution of these tests each of which related to the appropriate User Story. Then it shall record outputs (test report) and identify each User Story correctly implemented as tested/verified.

Design and Development Validation (7.3.6).
"D&D validation shall be performed ... to ensure that the resulting product is capable of meeting the requirements for the specified application or intended use... Records of the results of validation and any necessary actions shall be maintained." D&D validation is a set of activities done by the organization, often with the customer, aimed to assess that product is compliant with customer requirements for the foreseen usage. In XP projects, validation is in charge of the customer (or his delegate). For this reason the *Tool* shall restrict the permission of modifying validation state of each entity of the process (User Story, Release,...) to the customer only (or to his delegate).

Control of Design and Development Changes (7.3.7).
"D&D changes shall be identified and records maintained. The changes shall be reviewed, verified and validated, as appropriate, and approved before implementation. The review of the D&D changes shall include evaluation of the effect of the changes on constituent parts and product already delivered." Agile methodologies accept continuous requirement changes. However, these shall be controlled and each entity/artifact involved in requirement changes shall be identified. With this aim the *Tool* can have a fundamental role thanks to its traceability feature: it can correlate every single User Story with the specific code and tests. These functionalities could be implemented thanks to the integration with a Configuration Management application. In this way it is immediate to find out all those entities involved in changes, identify the level of change then monitor and control all these activities. After a change the *Tool* shall re-activate

review, verification and validation processes for each involved entity. Moreover, it shall provide, by means of apposite distribution list, spreading of information related to the changes done.

3   Conclusions

Starting from a detailed analysis of ISO 9001:2000 normative we have identified those clauses that can be automatically supported by a tool. Moreover, for each of these clauses we have specified a set of requirements that shall be owned by such an ISO compliant tool.

By analyzing these requirements we can deduce that a lot of them are already implemented by several existing tools for XP project management. Other requirements are implemented by specialized applications commonly used in a XP software development context, such as testing and continuous integration frameworks.

We can conclude that the main requirement for the *Tool* we are defining is the ability to communicate with other existing applications in order to exploit and integrate their characteristics.

References

1. Beck, K.: Extreme Programming Explained: Embrace Change. Addison Wesley, Boston (2000)
2. European Committe for Standardization: Quality Management Systems - Fundamentals and Vocabulary (ISO 9000:2000). Europeanc Committe for Standardization (2000)
3. European Committe for Standardization: Quality Management Systems - Requirements (ISO 9001:2000). Europeanc Committe for Standardization (2000)
4. Nawrocki, J.R., Jasinski, M., Bartosz, W., Wojciechowski, A.: Combining Extreme Programming with ISO 9000. In: Proceedings of EurAsia-ICT 2002, Iran, October 29-31, 2002. Lecture Notes in Computer Science, Vol.2510. Springer-Verlag, Berlin Heidelberg New York (2002) 786–794
5. Wright, G.: Achieving ISO 9001 Certification for an XP Company. In: F. Maurer and D. Wells (Eds): XP/Agile Universe 2003. Lecture Notes in Computer Science, Vol. 2753. Springer-Verlag, Berlin Heidelberg New York (2003) 43–50
6. Pinna, S., Mauri, S., Lorrai, P., Marchesi, M., Serra, N.: XPSwiki: an Agile Tool Supporting the Planning Game . In: Proceedings of XP2003, Italy, May 25-29, 2003. Lecture Notes in Computer Science, Vol.2675. Springer-Verlag, Berlin Heidelberg New York (2003) 215–224

Going Interactive:
Combining Ad-Hoc and Regression Testing

Michael Kölling[1] and Andrew Patterson[2]

[1] Mærsk Mc-Kinney Møller Institute, University of Southern Denmark, Denmark
mik@mip.sdu.dk
[2] Deakin University, Australia
patto@deakin.edu.au

Abstract. Different kinds of unit testing activities are used in practice. Organised unit testing (regression testing or test-first activities) are very popular in commercial practice, while ad-hoc (interactive) testing is popular in small scale development and teaching situations. These testing styles are usually kept separate. This paper introduces a design and implementation of a tool that combines these testing styles.

1 Introduction

Testing always has been, and in all likelihood always will be, an important part of software development. Currently one of the most popular tools for supporting unit testing is JUnit [2].

JUnit is a small and elegant unit testing framework that supports organised regression testing for application units. It can be used both as a pure regression testing tool, as well as a test-first tool following the extreme programming methodology.

Ad-hoc testing is the interactive testing process where developers invoke application units explicitly, and individually compare execution results to expected results.

BlueJ is an integrated development environment that provides support for interactive execution of selected methods (ad-hoc testing) via a graphical user interface.

The work described in this paper consists of the design and development of a single system that combines a unit testing framework with ad-hoc testing functionality. This system is based on BlueJ and JUnit.

We demonstrate that the result is not only a side-by-side coexistence of ad-hoc testing and regression testing, but that new functionality emerges through the combination of the two, which was not previously available in either of the separate systems.

2 JUnit vs. BlueJ

JUnit has become a de facto standard for implementing unit tests in Java. With JUnit, programmers implement *test classes* by extending a JUnit class called *TestCase*. In

J. Eckstein and H. Baumeister (Eds.): XP 2004, LNCS 3092, pp. 270–273, 2004.

this class, they implement *test methods*, which can later be executed through the framework. Several assertion methods are available for use in test methods.

JUnit has been extensively described in the literature, so we will, for the remainder of this paper, assume that the reader is familiar with JUnit.

BlueJ provides support for ad-hoc testing – the interactive calling of individual methods and explicit inspection of method results.

Using the object interaction mechanism in BlueJ, a user can create the initial setup of a test phase by instantiating objects interactively and placing them on the object bench. Methods can then be tested by making a sequence of interactive method calls. Parameter values can be entered and method results are displayed.

No test harnesses or test drivers are required to execute the methods that have just been constructed. The call sequence can be created dynamically – the decision about details of the next call can depend on seeing results of the previous one. However, this testing is ephemeral. Objects are automatically removed if any change is made to their class or if the project is closed. More information about BlueJ can be found in [1, 3].

3 Integrating BlueJ and JUnit

To merge the functionality of BlueJ and JUnit, we have integrated the JUnit framework into the BlueJ environment. Possible interoperations between the two have been analysed to achieve more than a simple side-by-side co-existence of the two.

3.1 Recognising JUnit Classes

The most fundamental specific JUnit support can be provided by recognising JUnit test classes as a special kind of class type in the BlueJ environment and treat them differently than general classes. These differences may include:
- using a distinct visual representation for test classes;
- providing specific default source code skeletons;
- providing functionality for selective display, which hides test classes temporarily;
- association of specific test commands with the test class (see below).

Each of these enhancements can make working with test classes more convenient.

3.2 Executing Test Methods

BlueJ's test support allows the interactive invocation test methods in various ways: invoking single test methods, all tests from one class, or all tests in a project.

Single test methods can be executed by selecting them from a pop-up menu. Since JUnit test cases are individual methods, integration in BlueJ results in these methods being interactively and individually executable. These test method calls can be recognised as such by the environment, and success or failure be reported in an appropriate manner. (Using a standard interface like the SwingRunner GUI may not be appropriate to display the result of a single test method.)

All tests of a single test class may be executed using a specific „Test All" command provided in the class's context menu. This function is similar to a standard JUnit test run. An interface similar to the standard JUnit SwingRunner may be used to display results.

All tests in a project can easily be executed by providing a „Test All" function in the environment (e.g., as a toolbar button) Again, a SwingRunner-style interface may be used to present results.

3.3 Attached Test Classes

BlueJ presents class diagrams of projects, and interaction is heavily designed around using contextual menus on classes and objects.

This can be used for a further enhancement: Instead of creating test classes independent of other classes, they may be created in direct association with an exiting implementation class. For example, as class's context menu may have a 'Create Test Class' command, which creates a test class *associated with this specific class*. This association is semantic: It signifies that the purpose of the test cases in this test class is to test the associated class (which we term the *reference class*). The association can also be functional: The test class may have a 'Create Test Stubs' command, which automatically creates stubs for all public methods in its reference classes. Lastly, the association may be visual: We can visually attach the test class to the reference class in the class diagram to signify this association to the user. Dragging the reference class in the diagram on screen would automatically move the test class with it.

Attached test classes could be supported in addition to *free* test classes (those not attached to a specific class). Free test classes contain tests for multiple reference classes.

3.4 Recording Interaction and Asserting Test Results

Among of the biggest advantages of ad-hoc testing is that it does not require manual writing of test drivers and its action sequences can be decided dynamically: seeing the result of one test can determine the next course of action. One of the biggest advantages of written test drivers is that tests can be replayed multiple times in the future.

Merging BlueJ with JUnit allows us to combine both advantages. We can execute dynamic interactive tests, while recording the test sequence and automatically writing JUnit tests cases from that recording. This could be done by providing a „Create Test Method" command in a test class's context menu, which starts a recording process until it is explicitly ended by the user. At that time the recording is transformed into Java source text and written into the test class as a test method.

We also need to add a mechanism to specify assertions on results during the interactive test activity. The existing BlueJ method result dialog can be extended with an assertion panel, which may be shown only while we are in „test recording" mode. This assertion panel would

- provide the option to attach an assertion to the result;
- provide a choice of available assertions; and

- allow us to enter values for the assertion parameter.

Recording test cases interactively is an added functionality to the standard (manual) creation of test methods. Test methods may also be written by hand. In fact, both techniques could be combined: tests can be recorded first, and later modified by manual edit. There is nothing special about recorded tests: they are transformed to standard Java source code and can be treated and processed like other test methods.

3.5 Creating Text Fixtures from Interaction Objects

JUnit text fixtures correspond to a set of objects interactively created on the object bench in manual tests.

This relationship can be exploited to aid the creation of fixtures for test classes: we can create test fixtures by manually creating and preparing a set of objects, and then invoking an „Object Bench to Test Fixture" command from the test class's context menu. This command can create Java source code in the test class's setup method that creates objects identical to those currently on the object bench. This function thus corresponds to interactive test fixture creation.

The test fixture/object bench relationship can be exploited the other way around as well: Existing fixtures (whether created via recordings or manual writing) can be copied onto the object bench. There, they are available for interactive testing. This function could be made available to users via a „Test Fixture To Object Bench" command in the test classes context menu.

4 Discussion

The discussion in the previous sections demonstrate that combining JUnit and BlueJ's ad-hoc testing mechanism can result in something more than mere co-existence of two test paradigms. Elements from both test-worlds can be mixed and combined, resulting in a new quality of system interaction that can be useful for both original tasks: creating regression tests, and ad-hoc testing. Existing interaction styles are not negatively affected by this. The recording functionality can co-exist with manual test-first functionality, and code produced by each can indeed co-exist in a single source file.

All of the functionality described in this paper has been implemented, tested and made publicly available for free download with BlueJ version 1.3.5 [1].

References

1. BlueJ - The Interactive Java Environment, web site at www.bluej.org, accessed 03/2004
2. Gamma, E, Beck, K.: JUnit, website at http://www.junit.org, accessed January 2004
3. Kölling, M., Quig, B., Patterson, A., Rosenberg, J., *The BlueJ system and its pedagogy*, Journal of Computer Science Education, Special issue on Learning and Teaching Object Technology, Vol 13, No 4, (2003) 249–268

Complete Test Generation for Extreme Programming

Mike Holcombe[1] and Florentin Ipate[2]

[1] Department of Computer Science
University of Sheffield, UK
m.holcombe@dcs.shef.ac.uk
[2] IFSoft, Romania
www.ifsoft.ro
fipate@ifsoft.ro

Abstract. Test generation is a key part of the *Extreme Programming* approach. This paper describes a very powerful functional testing method that generates test sets which can detect *all* possible faults in a computer program, provided some design for test conditions are satisfied. The basis for this *complete test generation* method is the *X-machine*, a simple and elegant way of visualising the dynamics of a program.

Keywords: Functional testing, unit testing, acceptance testing, test set generation, X-machines

1 Introduction

Testing is a major part of software development and in Extreme Programming the generation of test cases is a vital part of the initial phases of a project. In this paper, we present a method for generating test cases that provides a well founded approach to the problem of detecting *all* faults. The method is based on the computational modelling with *X-machines*, a sort of extended finite state machines, and can be integrated into Extreme Programming in a simple and designer-friendly way. It is a generalisation of the original X-machine based method [3], [1] that extends significantly its applicability and simplifies the testing process [4]. This generalisation is called in what follows the *complete* X-machine testing method. As the original method, the complete method assumes that some *design for test conditions* are satisfied.

The original X-machine based testing method [3], [1]assumes that the basic functions of the system are correct. This can be checked by a separate testing process, an effective way of doing this is to apply a functional method such as category partition and boundary value analysis. The simplest scenario is when tried and trusted components are used, for example, functions that take a keyboard input and echo it to a screen or put it in a register or perhaps a function that accesses a cell in a database table. However, if this is not the case, the original method will implicitly assume that each basic function can be tested *in*

J. Eckstein and H. Baumeister (Eds.): XP 2004, LNCS 3092, pp. 274–277, 2004.
© Springer-Verlag Berlin Heidelberg 2004

isolation from the rest of the system. This is not always a realistic assumption since the implementations of the basic functions are not always distinct units of code (e.g. subroutines, modules, etc.) that can be separated from the rest of the system.

The complete testing method removes this condition and allows the testing of the basic functions to be performed along with the main testing process and the test cases generated for the basic functions to be integrated into the overall test cases generated for the entire X-machine.

2   A Simple Example

In order to illustrate the application of the complete testing method we use a simple customer orders database as described in [2]. We can identify a number of stories such as: entering customer details, editing customer details, placing orders, editing orders, etc.. Then we identify from these stories what is prompting change (inputs), what internal knowledge is needed (memory), what is the observable result (output) and how the memory changes after the event. From the diagram (Figure 1) one can see how the basic functions are organised. Each state, in this example, has associated with it an appropriate screen with buttons, text fields etc.

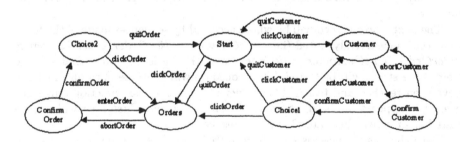

Fig. 1. The state transition diagram for the customer orders database

It is straightforward to generate a test set U_ϕ for each basic function ϕ using traditional functional methods such as category-partition and boundary value analysis. However, many of these functions do not fire in the initial state of the X-machine, so the context in which they are tested has to be taken into account as well, e.g. in order to apply the test set for *confirmCustomer*, one will first have to click the enter customer button and enter the customer details. Consequently the testing of a basic function will have to rely on the correctness of the functions that have been applied to set up the appropriate context, otherwise the testing results may be affected by the errors introduced earlier by these functions, e.g. when the test set for *confirmCustomer* is applied, one must assume that the correct customers details have been entered and recorded.

The solution to this problem is to test the basic functions in the order that they can be reached in the X-machine diagram. In this case, a basic function ϕ can always be reached by a sequence v_ϕ of other basic functions that have already been tested (and therefore been shown to be correct). Let us illustrate the process for our example.

We start with the basic functions that emerge from the initial state, $Start$. There are two such function, $clickCustomer$ and $clickOrder$. Obviously the sequence $v_{clickCustomer} = v_{clickOrder} = \epsilon$, the empty sequence, and the test sets $U_{clickCustomer}$ and $U_{clickOrder}$ can be applied straight to the initial state of the X-machine.

We look now for the states that can be reached from $Start$ by sequences made up only of the functions $clickCustomer$ and $clickOrder$. There are two such states: $Customers$ and $Orders$; $clickCustomer$ takes the X-machine from the initial state $Start$ to $Customer$, while $clickOrder$ takes the X-machine from $Start$ to $Order$. There are two functions, $enterCustomer$ and $quitCustomer$ that emerge from $Customer$. The sequence that reaches these functions is $v_{enterCustomer} = v_{quitCustomer} = customer\_button\_clicked$, where $customer\_button\_clicked$ is the event (or input) corresponding to the clicking of the customer button on the start screen, which triggers the function $clickCustomer$. In order to test $enterCustomer$ and $quitCustomer$, this input will be concatenated with the elements of $U_{enterCustomer}$ and $U_{quitCustomer}$, respectively. The two functions $enterOrder$ and $quitOrder$ are tested in a similar manner.

The next states visited will be whose accessed by sequences made of the functions that have already tested (i.e. $clickCustomer$, $clickOrder$, $enterCustomer$, $enterOrder$, $quitCustomer$, $quitOrder$) and the basic functions that emerge from those states will be tested. The procedure will continue until all functions have been reached and tested. It is sufficient to test a basic function only once even if it appears in the diagram many times, e.g. $quitCustomer$ will not be tested again when the state $Choice1$ is reached.

Once the basic functions have been tested and shown to be correct we can proceed to generate the test set for the whole system. This is done in the following way. We start at the initial state $Start$ with the initial memory value and the aim is to visit every state of the X-machine, e.g. in order to visit $ConfirmCustomer$, the sequence $clickCustomer :: enterCustomer$ is processed (Here :: means concatenation or sequence connector.) When we have reached a state we need to confirm that it is the correct state and this is done by following more simple paths from that state until we get outputs that tell us, unambiguously, what the state was.

Then we repeat the path to that state and check what happens if we try to apply every basic function from that state, some will succeed but some should fail. Have the correct ones passed and failed? This is then repeated for every state. Some example functions sequences are:

$$clickCustomer :: enterCustomer :: confirmCustomer,$$

$$clickCustomer :: enterCustomer :: clickOrder.$$

The first test has tried to apply a correct function (i.e. *confirmCustomer*) from the state *ConfirmCustomer* and should pass, the second has tried to apply an incorrect function (i.e. *clickOrder*) from that state and should fail. Now, this test set is not quite what we want since it is based on the set of functions which we cannot access directly, it needs to be converted to a sequence of inputs. So we choose suitable inputs that will trigger the correct functions as we trace through the diagram along the paths of functions, generating sequences of inputs which are our actual tests. The design for test conditions allow this to happen, the mathematical details and proof of correctness are in [4]. Thus we have the following test sequences corresponding to the sequences above:

customer_button_clicked :: customer_details_entered :: confirm_button_clicked,
customer_button_clicked :: customer_details_entered :: orders_button_clicked.

Of course, as this is a high level test set, the input *customer_details_entered* represents a more complex series of activities. e.g. entering the *customer_name*, *customer_address*, etc. Since all basic functions have already been tested and shown to be correct, at this stage the input that triggers a function can be chosen at random.

The test generation, which is fully automated, will generate all the input sequences needed to establish whether the implementation is correct, i.e. agrees with the X-machine model.

3 Conclusions

The use of smart test strategies in XP can provide substantial gains in quality. This paper is an attempt to explain how one of the most powerful test generation approaches, the complete X-machine testing method, could be put to use. The complete testing method generalises a previous X-machine based method by extending significantly its applicability and simplifying the testing process.

Further work for interfacing the method with XP is, however, needed. Ultimately we need to build smart test tools which interface naturally with the XP process. The development of such tools is currently in progress. The use of such tools will be reported in further papers.

References

1. Holcombe, M. and Ipate, F. 1998. *Correct Systems: Building a Business Process Solution.* Springer Verlag: Berlin.
2. Holcombe, M., Bogdanov, K., Gheorghe, M. 2001. Functional Test Generation for Extreme Programming *Proceedings of XP2001*: 109-113.
3. Ipate, F. and Holcombe M. 1997. An Integration Testing Method That is Proved to Find all Faults. *Intern. J. Computer Math.* **63**: 159-178.
4. Ipate, F. 2004 Complete Deterministic Stream X-machine Testing. *Formal Asp. Comput.*, to appear.

Story Management

Olaf Lewitz

microTOOL GmbH, Voltastr. 5, 13355 Berlin, Germany
Olaf.Lewitz@microTOOL.de

Abstract. Managing stories on cards lacks traceability and disables efficient management, if your organisation calls for comprehensive requirements storage. We developed and used a tool to track story state changes from ordered to done to verified. The transparency and traceability of our versioning project database containing stories, tasks, code, design and all relevant documents helps to meet the project goals as well as to involve and satisfy the customer.

Keywords. Story, project management, state management of stories, traceability, transparency, customer integration, project database, tool support

1 Motivation and Context

Writing stories on temporary index cards can have its disadvantages. Sometimes, it is compulsory to have all requirements documented and stored comprehensively. In this paper I would like to discuss how the management of users' requirements and the integration of the customer in the project can be improved through the use of a software tool suitable to manage user stories. I'm not just talking about storing the stories electronically; I mean managing states and dependencies and ensuring full traceability and transparency for developers, project managers and customers alike.

microTOOL GmbH is a German software development tool manufacturer in Berlin. We provide developers with tools for modelling software and managing projects. In one of our development projects, we began using agile methods in 2002. We started planning in iterations and used story cards, introduced unit tests, continuous integration and small releases. We quickly ran into communication problems with our stories and devised methods to mitigate them. In this paper, I'll share our experiences with emphasis on the tool we developed and used to manage our project.

I've been developing software professionally for some fifteen years now, doing programming, designing, architecting, controlling and project management. In 1999, I started reading about extreme programming and soon got an opportunity to put theory into practice when I was put in charge of a big development project in Hamburg, Germany. The team decided to use extreme programming as a process, to manage the "scope creep" and to ensure frequent, usable releases of the new product.

I joined microTOOL GmbH as a senior consultant in 2002. My area of responsibility is our process driven project management product, in-Step. As the central part of the microTOOL Suite, in-Step is the subject of this paper.

J. Eckstein and H. Baumeister (Eds.): XP 2004, LNCS 3092, pp. 278–281, 2004.

2   Stories Revisited

According to XP, stories are handwritten on index cards. This is revolutionary and it has its merits:

- Index cards are easy to change and manage
- They can be put on a table for the planning game
- They can be taken by the developer who signs up for the task

This approach is simple and easy. The whole idea behind agile methods is to be able to change the requirements. If a requirement is written on an index card, it is easy to write down, easy to change and easy to discard, if necessary. But is this really the case? Imagine you write an idea onto a card. The idea matures and you change the text on the card. You take some notes on the back when you talk to someone and gain new insight. Now you talk to the developers and you find out you need to split the story into three parts – it can't be estimated as it is. Where do you put your notes on the back? What if you need to know later on that those three new stories came from this one and want to record it?

Some teams record further attributes for the story, like priority or type (requirement, bug, idea, documentation). These have to be copied as well. Sometimes, someone might need the information on a card although they are working on another one, but someone else is using the card they need. The customer might want to take an in-depth look at the whole pile – but parts of the pile are sitting on the developers' desks while they are working on them. As you can see, there are some issues with cards along with the merits:

- Only one person (pair) can have a card at any one time
- Text cannot be copied and pasted
- Cards can get lost or torn

Of course, some of these things only affect you if you don't stick to XP as it is defined – if your stories are discarded once the acceptance test is written, you won't have these problems. But what if someone wants to check which new features went into Release X? And, more important, your organisation or your customer might not consider acceptance tests to be comprehensive requirements.

3   Always Know Where You Are

Why do we write down user stories? In XP, they fulfill two needs: The need to track the project's progress, and the need to capture the customer's and users' requirements. What does a story need to be useful in these two ways?

To capture the customer's requirements, the story needs to be written in natural language and easy to understand.

To enable efficient planning and to track the project's progress, stories need to be

- Estimated on a time scale
- Prioritized according to an agreed-upon scale
- Treated as an order or contract
- Assigned to someone responsible for implementing them
- Signed by the customer to acknowledge their acceptance

- Traceable to depending and dependent stories
- Stateful; you need to know if the story is ordered, done or tested
- Versioned; you'll want to be able to review the story's history

This list is not complete; it just touches on the main issues that make you want to store the stories in a database. In addition to these, you get a few nice features that make life in your project easier:

- All stories are accessible to anyone at anytime
- It's much easier to report the progress of your project
- Nothing ever gets lost
- You could put your design and code documents into the same database and interrelate everything
- You could store your resources and tasks in that database and have your project plan generated

Managing a project efficiently means always knowing where you are and where you want to be in the near future. If we choose to track our projects using small, simple stories, they need certain attributes in order to help us control the project. The only way to manage such a project is to make these attributes easily accessible and traceable in a database.

4   Agile Development at microTOOL – Stories First

Implementing a new process into a running project is certainly no easy task. This is why we decided to proceed in stages. In the first stage, we replaced big specification documents with stories and planned their implementation in iterations. The realisation of continuous integration marked the end of the second phase, which is beyond the scope of this paper. The length of an iteration started at two months; now it's down to three weeks. Our product manager took the customer role and broke down the required features into estimable stories, with the collaboration of the project manager. We found out, that planning was most accurate when all stories are roughly the same size – we try to keep them at or below five workdays. Learning to write those stories in a simple and concise way took a few iterations.

What was our experience in that phase? First of all, the level of detail and the quality of specification in our stories surprised us. We had assumed we'd lose some detail when we replaced detailed specification documents with small stories. The opposite was true. For a detailed estimate of the effort, the contents of the story need to be clear and precise. Since we try to keep the effort below five workdays per story, tasks have to be broken down into small pieces. These small pieces have to be prioritized by the customer – and for their business value to be assessed, the customer has to say exactly what he wants. Because the prioritizing process keeps a close and constant watch on all of the planned stories and these stories are treated like little contracts between the customer and the team, nothing irrelevant ever makes its way into any iteration. We build only what is needed, not what someone would like to have!

5   Tools and Techniques

We have a database tool to store all of the project data, stories, documents, models, build scripts and code, just to name the most important items. Everything is versioned and assigned a state; the possible states depend on the type of document. Stories can be *defined*, *postponed*, *rejected*, *ordered*, *verified* and *done*. They are *ordered* by the customer, assigned to a developer, *done* and, finally, *verified* by the customer. Every developer knows what she has to do; the manager knows who's doing what at all times. Planning is story-based, which means stories are assigned to an iteration, to a developer and the effort is estimated in workdays. The software calculates the amount of planned effort for an iteration, so we always know how much the team can do in one iteration. The build job writes the build number into every story assigned to the current iteration and marked as *done*. This makes it very easy to identify new features when a new build has to be tested.

Since the stories have some additional attributes, like category, priority etc., it is very easy to find out the things you need to know: which bugs were fixed in which iteration; have another look at ideas rejected in the past few months; look for the stories you originally posted... As we got used to this systematic approach, further possibilities were built into the system. The stories got a "documentation flag" to indicate that a story describes a product change that has to be documented in the help files, such as a new feature. The story form has an additional text field for the developer to jot down any hints specifically for the documentation team. The better our process became, the more we improved our tool support.

6   Summary

Where are we now? Planning and controlling became much easier with the new process. We always know where we stand because our software always shows the current state of things. Everyone just gets the information they need: The developer knows what to do next, the customer knows what to test and how many of his stories are already done or have been verified. Everybody has a good feeling that the project is delivering a lot of business value.

But this is only part of what we have. We not only defined the process and use it, we also have a tool environment that ensures it stays that way. Our project tool is the starting point of work for every project member. The customer writes stories with it, orders the stories for an iteration and signs them as accepted when they've been tested and verified. The project manager assigns developers to the stories, tracks their progress and generates project plans and reports. The developers have their To Do lists and full configuration management integrated into their IDEs. The build manager relies on the tool to pack our releases. So, we not only have a good process, we also have a process no one has to think about – that's what the tool is for!

"Did my story make it into our nightly build today?" I heard our product manager ask a developer the other day, when they met at the coffee machine. I think this is a good sign that people have really adopted a new method when they start using its technical terms in their everyday language.

Conditional Test for JavaBeans Components

Hironori Washizaki[1], Yuhki Sakai[2], and Yoshiaki Fukazawa[3]

[1] National Institute of Informatics, 2-1-2 Hitotsubashi, Chiyoda-ku, Tokyo 101-8430
washizaki@nii.ac.jp,
[2] NTT DoCoMo, Inc., 2-11-1 Nagatacho, Chiyoda-ku, Tokyo 100-6150, Japan
[3] Waseda University, 3-4-1, Okubo, Shinjuku-ku, Tokyo 169-8555, Japan
{yuhki, fukazawa}@fuka.info.waseda.ac.jp

Abstract. We propose a new conditional test suite that supports preconditions, postconditions, and class-invariants for any JavaBeans component, without the possibility of heisenbugs.

1 Introduction

Software components can essentially help to make software programs in the
rapid development process including eXtreme Programming (XP)[1]. Since components may be used in ways which their developers did not consider, the component developers should thoroughly test each component individually. XP approach relies on frequent unit testing. However, the unit testing is not enough
to ensure the behavioral correctness of software components.

The conditional test is a testing method which tests the logical correctness
conditions of the targeted Object-Oriented (OO) class to ensure the behavioral
correctness of the class[2]. The logical conditions tend to be embedded as assertions in class's implementation. There are some conventional techniques for
the conditional test; however, conventional techniques cannot be appropriately
applied to components composed of OO classes because of the following two
problems. First problem is the possibility of heisenbugs. None of the conventional techniques guarantee that the methods used in assertion expression do
not change the original program's state. The program error included in a test
script, which has side effects, is called a "heisenbug". Second problem is the
inseparability of program source codes and logical conditions.

2 Test Suite for Fine-Grained Components

We propose a new conditional test suite that supports preconditions, postconditions, and class-invariants for any JavaBeans component[3].

One JavaBeans component is composed of one or more Java classes, and
opens only one Facade class to the public. There are three important features of
any JavaBeans component: property, read method and business method. Properties are the named attributes, whose values can be read or written by invoking
the read/write methods. Read methods are methods to read the properties' values from outside of the component. Business methods are simply normal Java

J. Eckstein and H. Baumeister (Eds.): XP 2004, LNCS 3092, pp. 282–283, 2004.
© Springer-Verlag Berlin Heidelberg 2004

methods that can be invoked from outside of the component, except for the write/read methods. The following code fragment shows an example of a component. This component has one readable property named balance with one read method getBalance. The Facade class is Bank.

```
public class Bank extends Component { private int _balance;
    public int getBalance() { return _balance; } /* Read method */
    public void deposit(int i) { ... } /* Business method */ }
```

To solve the problems associated with conventional techniques, our conditional test technique is based on two concepts: (a) generating a subclass of the Facade class and (b) using a high degree of component observability.

(a) Our technique realizes the separation of a component's source codes and logical conditions by generating a subclass as a direct descendant of the Facade class of the target component, and embedding the necessary test scripts into overridden business methods of the subclass. Each test script acquires the necessary values, executes the original method implemented within the original Facade class, and tests the given conditions by using our runtime checker.

(b) Our technique realizes the exclusion of heisenbugs by limiting the invokable methods in conditions to read methods, and using our method inspector for the read methods. Values that can be specified in conditions are the original/current values of readable properties and the values of method arguments/return values.

All logical conditions are written in condition files separated from components. The following example shows the precondition and postcondition for Bank's business method deposit. The precondition specifies that the first argument value must be greater than zero when invoking deposit. The postcondition specifies that the value of the readable property (balance) after the method invocation must be equal to the value by which the first argument value is added to the original property value (@pre.balance).

```
Bank#deposit(int), pre : @argument.1 > 0
Bank#deposit(int), post: balance = @pre.balance + @argument.1
```

3   Concluding Remarks

We evaluated the test cost of our technique by testing several components. It is found that the total time for our technique has been reduced to 40% of that of conventional techniques. In our technique, component developers and users can easily and repeatedly change the conditions and execute the conditional test with high reliability (heisenbug-free) for the components.

References

1. A. Repenning et al.: Using Components for Rapid Distributed Software Development, IEEE Software, Vol.18, No.2 (2001).
2. S. Siegel: Object-Oriented Software Testing: A Hierarchical Approach, John Wiley & Sons (1996).
3. H. Washizaki, Y. Sakai and Y. Fukazawa: A Conditional Test Suite for Fine-Grained Software Components, Proc. of the 2nd ACIS International Conference on Software Engineering Research, Management and Applications (2004).

Agile Methods in Software Engineering Education

Christian Bunse[1], Raimund L. Feldmann[2*], and Jörg Dörr[1]

[1] Fraunhofer IESE, Sauerwiesen 6,
67661 Kaiserslautern, Germany
{Christian.Bunse, Joerg.Doerr}@iese.fraunhofer.de
[2] Fraunhofer Center – Maryland, 4321 Hartwick Road, Suite 500,
College Park, MD 20742, USA
rfeldmann@fc-md.umd.edu

Abstract. Agile methods such as extreme programming (XP) are becoming increasingly important for the rapid development of software applications. However, there is a tradeoff in using agile methods. Often they lack in providing a systematic guidance (i.e., a sound description of roles, artifacts, and activities), and thus, require disciplined and experienced developers. Are the promised benefits of agile methods still valid if they are applied by novice (student) developers? To gain some experience, we performed a study on teaching students agile software development with XP. Students performed a small software development project at the University of Kaiserslautern to collect some lessons learned. One result is that although agile approaches are easy to learn and quickly produce results, they are not the best starting point in training software development. The quality of the resulting system, at least in our experience, heavily depends on the discipline of the developers and their background and experience in software development.

1 Introduction

Today software organizations are under increasing pressure to timely develop their software systems, which is also reflected by the software-lifecycle models and methods applied. Agile software development methods become more and more popular due to their promise to dramatically increase the speed of development.

One such agile software development approach is eXtreme Programming (XP) [2][3]. XP is an approach to software development which emphasizes a tight cycle between code creation, testing, and debugging through the principle of 'lightweight traveling' (i.e., code is immediately integrated into the overall system after creation, and then subjected to serious testing). The expected benefits of such an approach include the rapid development of minimal systems, early creation of executable code, and low defect numbers. Despite its undoubted strengths, however, the XP approach has one major drawback: Lack of guidance. The success of an XP project heavily depends on the experience and discipline of the people in the team [13][14][15]. Therefore, detailed guidance is necessary, especially when dealing with novice devel

---

* Main parts of this work were conducted while the author was employed by the University of Kaiserslautern, Kaiserslautern, Germany.

J. Eckstein and H. Baumeister (Eds.): XP 2004, LNCS 3092, pp. 284–293, 2004.
© Springer-Verlag Berlin Heidelberg 2004

opers. Although many books and web representations exist on XP, it is not easy for a developer or project manager to set-up and run an XP project. One reason for this is that a concise and precise model of the XP process is often missing [15]. As a consequence, the development team has to define its own (implicit) rules and guidelines which is quite difficult for developers who do not have experience in software development. Thus, one major question remains: Can novice developers (e.g., students) successfully perform an XP project? This leads also to another, although related, problem: How can we train students in using XP?

In this paper we give an experience report of a practical course on XP, performed at the University of Kaiserslautern, Germany. Concerning teaching and training one might think of using a standard book from the shelf (e.g., [2][3]) to prepare a set of slides and lecture them to the students. However, XP is designed to be a practice oriented and lively approach. Thus, a 'simple' lecture would miss out the important practical part. Consequently, we chose a more practice oriented (i.e., programming and problem oriented) way of teaching XP. In the winter term 2002/2003 we organized a seminar 'Agile Software Development - Using XP as part of the official course program of the department of computer science at the University of Kaiserslautern. Eleven students participated in this extraordinary kind of seminar. In contrast to 'traditional' seminars that are more concerned with literature surveys, a small agile software development project was conducted by the students. In addition, we used the process model for XP, proposed in [15], as a limited form of guidance. Some of the practices of XP, were used during the project so that the students were able to gain own experience with the XP practices and formulate their own lessons learned. The students got information on all XP practices, but in the project they mainly used on-site customer, planning game, pair programming, common ownership, continuous integration, short increments, acceptance tests, programming standards, simple design and sometimes unit tests.

The remainder of this paper presents experience gained during the course. Section 2 presents background material on XP and software engineering education at the University of Kaiserslautern. Section 3 explains our approach on teaching XP. Section 4 presents an analysis concerning quality of the system developed during the course and discusses the effects the application of XP might have had. Section 5 discusses the subjective opinions and experiences of the participating students and supervisors. Finally, section 6 summarizes the paper and gives some conclusions.

2 Background

2.1 Agile Development and XP

Today, developers are under increasing pressure as organizations seek to gain competitive advantage from the timely development and deployment of software products and services. Agile software development [1], comprising many different methods such as XP [2][3], SCRUM [9], and Crystal [7] was introduced to address this problem by supporting the early and quick development of working code.

Introduced by Kent Beck in the late 1990's, XP was and is one of the most popular methods for software development. As an agile software development methodology, XP focuses on the principles of communication, simplicity, feedback, and courage. The goal of XP is to deliver software products within time and cost constraints (i.e., the rapid production of an executable system with a minimum of flanking measures, for instance, modeling, architecture evaluation, or measurement). As an agile approach, XP views a development project as the responsibility of a small team of developers, who intensively interact with the user or customer. Thus, in difference to procedural development strategies like the V-Model, XP uses a number of principles (e.g., *Test Firs*) for guidance.

The simplicity and light-weightness of XP makes it an 'ideal' candidate to practically teach students in software development. However, the required discipline of every developer and the lack of a documented process is a challenge to be mastered when teaching novices. This is discussed in more detail in the following.

2.2 Software Engineering Education at the University of Kaiserslautern

The department of computer science at the University of Kaiserslautern offers graduate students different types of exams in computer science (e.g., in applied computer science, for teaching at college preparatory schools, or a technically oriented exam with the focus placed on electrical engineering). Common to all exams is the fact that studies are split up into two parts:

*   A basic part, guarantees that all students get fundamental insights into the fields of technical, theoretical, and practical aspects of computer science. Basic Software Engineering principles (e.g., divide and conquer) are taught. To finish this part students usually need two years (split into four semesters).
*   Having successfully passed the exams of the basic part, students start the main part. Therefore, they have to choose different courses out of a set of lectures, exercises, labs, and seminars. Courses in software engineering or on specific aspects like requirements engineering, or product line engineering are offered. At the end of this part (usually five to six semesters) students will write a master thesis.

2.3 Requirements for Seminars at the University of Kaiserslautern

Seminars are an integral part of the main part of the students' studies. Topics of the offered seminars vary every semester. Usually, they focus on actual research topics, such as for instance, XP. All seminars have to fulfill several requirements. The most important is: Participating students have to learn, how to perform a literature survey and how to write a (research) paper. It is further required, that each student has to give a presentation on a topic investigated during the seminar. As a result, seminars traditionally are organized as follows: Chapters of a book or a set of up-to-date research papers are assigned to each student of the seminar. Based on this reading, students then have to do a literature survey to find additional material dealing with the addresses topic. The results are summarized as a survey report and presented to the other participants at the end of the seminar.

3 Our Teaching Approach

As outlined in the previous section our goals concerning the seminar described here are twofold. On the one hand, students should learn about agile development and especially XP. On the other hand, the seminar should allow examining whether XP can be successfully applied by novice developers, and the impact this has on the quality of the resulting system[1]. The following learning goals have been added to the requirements given by the department of computer science:

- Students should experience XP in practice and, thereby, get a feeling for the advantages and disadvantages of agile methodologies.
- Based on practical the experience, students should learn, how to formulate and document lessons learned.

In addition to the 'official' student learning goals additional, refined goals have been defined, which allow the investigation of novice developers applying XP in more detail. These goals are:

- To capture practical lessons learned in performing agile projects. Since the course system at the University of Kaiserslautern allows students to take different classes at different times during the main part of their studies, the students' degree of experience can vary at the time they are participating a seminar. This situation comes close to practice were some staff members will have rudimentarily knowledge while others are more experienced.
- To test a more practice-oriented form of teaching a seminar (i.e., based on the combination of a tutorial and a practical example in a lab environment).

The novice developer students must be able to compare XP with more traditional Software Engineering methods. Therefore, only those students who participated at least one of the lectures 'Software Engineering I' or 'Software Engineering II', and thus have a basic knowledge in software development, were allowed to participate. Concerning student motivation it has to be said that before the seminar started, students had the opportunity to choose between a traditional and the extraordinary way of conducting the seminar. They decided on the extraordinary way, even though this meant much more effort for them. Hence, the students can be described as highly motivated.

In order to teach students the basic principles, practices, and techniques of agile software development with XP, a full-day tutorial has been performed [4]. Furthermore, the students were told to use the book by Kent Beck [2] as an initial reference. After this introduction the students had to develop a system for planning and recording effort and time needed in a new project.

In order to be as close to practice as possible and to reflect XP's idea of early and continuous customer interaction all roles had to be represented. Since one learning

---

[1] To fully evaluate the impact of novices applying XP on system quality a controlled experiment comparing two groups of students (one applying XP and the other applying a more traditional approach) is needed. This was not the case in the described seminar. We decided to perform the seminar as a kind of pre-study to gain first experience before investing more effort for a future controlled experiment.

goal was to teach students in a practice-oriented form, it was decided to assign all XP roles to students, whereby the supervisors acted as an advisory board. The general rule being that the team has as much responsibility and freedom as possible. Therefore, the supervisors monitored the behavior of the students in the team and only intervened in case of serious problems (e.g., infrastructure problems, misunderstanding of an XP practice, etc., which did not happen too often.

The students had used the practice of on-site customer. Furthermore, the on-site customer and the developers interacted in the planning game as described in [2]. The students used pair programming and paired newly each day. The code was commonly owned and the students continuously integrated their changes to the code several times a day. In addition they used the practice of short increments, manual (i.e., not automated) acceptance tests, were issued programming standards, which they adapted for their needs, and used simple design in the sense that they did not include unnecessary code. For unit testing, JUnit 3.7 was used. The developer team had eight members. In addition, two students took the role of the on-site customers, and one student was assigned to the role of a tester and tracker in the sense of XP. As part of their role, the on-site customers had to analyze the project-planning system, and to determine the features to be implemented. In addition, the student assigned to the tester and tracker role was asked to help the on-site customers in writing acceptance tests, and to track the project status.

The project itself was scheduled and finished within four weeks. Each week the whole team worked eight hours (in two four-hour slots at different days of the week). For the development of the system three releases were planned. The first release was scheduled after two weeks, the other two releases followed after week three and four. Following the practical part the students were asked to write a report in which they shortly introduce one practice and then present their personal experience.

4 The Resulting System

The development project was scheduled and finished within four weeks, whereby three releases were planned in total. The releases were scheduled for weeks two, three and four, whereby each release had to produce an executable version of the system which was tested by the on-site customers in form of acceptance tests. Figure 1 shows a statistics of the passed and failed acceptance tests, which were derived from the user stories (at least one acceptance test per user story).

For the first release about 35% of the intended acceptance tests failed. This was not due to a misinterpretation of the on-site customer wishes or incorrect programming. This high number was due to many not implemented user stories for release one. The students were behind schedule for release one. It is interesting to see that even though there were only eight hours (one week) between release one and two, the students managed to get on schedule again. They managed to double the number of user stories, even though they had only half the time. There are two reasons for that: first, the students became more experienced with the agile development methodology. Second, the user stories for release one were estimated with too low effort because they were intertwined. It was hard for an inexperienced development team to estimate the user stories, especially the ones for the basic functionality. For release two and three, the failed acceptance tests were due to faults in the implementation of the user stories, i.e., the developers thought, they have implemented the story, but there were some faults in implementation or misunderstanding of the customer.

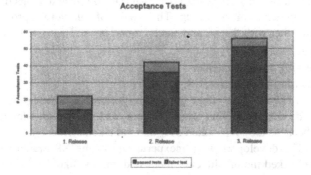

Fig. 1. Passed and failed tests

In the end, more user stories have been implemented in the system than originally planned in the planning game for the complete project. Neither the students, nor the advisors of the seminar thought that so much functionality could be integrated in such a small amount of time. It is even more surprising as eight out of eleven students were inexperienced with programming. To give an impression on the overall size of the developed tool, the source code contains about 2500 lines of code in 27 classes. Concerning the negative properties of the system, there are two major drawbacks. First, the system was judged to be hard to maintain by other people than the current team. Second, the usability of the system is quite bad. The bad maintainability was due to the fact that the size of the system was small enough that they easily managed to develop the software with a bad architecture. Little refactoring took place, as the developers were eager to integrate new user stories. The bad usability of the system is due to several reasons. First, students were not well trained in usability engineering. Second, developers sometimes tended to ignore or delay changes concerning comments of the customer regarding usability. This situation would be fatal in a real project, as usability is as important as functionality for a customer. More information can be found in [4] giving data collected by tracker. A software product was created that exceeded participants' expectations, but this functionality-focused development was at the expense of usability and maintainability.

5 Observations and Opinions

According to our outline of the seminar, the students were asked to formulate their lessons learned (LL) on practices of XP used in the conducted development project. The collected LL are based on the students' practical experience and their knowledge of more traditional software development methods, as taught in the prerequisite Software Engineering lectures. For documenting the LL, the participants used a given template (see [4]). Before the students finalized their statements, they came together and presented their LL to the entire group. Then, for each LL, the group voted if they had the same or a similar opinion, or not. This simple method was used to clearly identify whether a LL only reflected a personal (i.e., single and subjective) opinion or captured the experience of the group. The results of this voting process have been documented together with the LL and can be found in [4]. Examples are:

LL Example 1:
① *Name*: Guessing of requirements
② *Situation*: During implementation
③ *Symptom*: (A) Developers rather guessed requirements, although they could have asked the on-site customer. This caused rework, and (B) the on-site customers were disappointed because they felt skated over and not taken seriously.
④ *Diagnosis*: The developers were inexperienced in the XP practice of the on-site customer. They asked the on-site customers seldom, just like they were used to from other projects.
⑤ *Reaction*: Warnings were given during the standup meetings. However, they caused no direct reaction at the beginning of the project. After some time, through the gained experience in the project, the developers learned to use the customer more effectively.
⑥ *Recommendation*: Explain the advantage of the on-site customer and motivate to ask.

Based on the results of the voting process, the level of confidence in this LL can be regarded as high. For part (A) of the LL, all eleven participants expressed their agreement. For part (B), ten participants agreed and one student chose abstention from voting. A second LL, that may have influenced the first one, was recorded as:

LL Example 2:
① *Name*: On-site customer in a separate room
② *Situation*: During implementation
③ *Symptom*: The communication was not as good as it could have been.
④ *Diagnosis*: The on-site customers had their own, separate room.[2]
⑤ *Reaction*: No possibility to change something because of spatial environment.
⑥ *Recommendation*: Explain to the developers the advantage of an on-site customer and motivate them to ask. Make sure that on-site customers and developers are located as close together as possible.

For this LL the voting results have been recorded as: Agreement: nine / Abstention: one / Rejection: one. This LL may explain that at the beginning the on-site customers simply have been forgotten by the developers, since they were working in the next room and seemed not to be permanently present in person.

Another example for the importance of organizational issues in XP projects is reflected by our last example out of the collected LL:

---

[2] Due to space limitations, the onsite customers and the tracker were located in a separate room next to the lab.

LL Example 3

① *Name*: User stories (organization)

② *Situation*: During complete project

③ *Symptom*: (A) All user stories should be copied (i.e., exist two or more times). (B) Changed, spliced, or new user stories should be presented using color.

④ *Diagnosis*: Missing experience of tracker and in organization of XP projects.

⑤ *Reaction*: None in the project.

⑥ *Recommendation*: Use a color code for user stories, to identify changes.

This LL was reported by our tracker. The idea of two sets of user stories is based on the fact, that the tracker sometimes wanted to work with the user stories (e.g., sort or reorganize them for tracking purposes), while at the same time the developers wanted to read them. The voting results for part (A) read as: Agree: ten / Abstent: one / Reject: none. For part (B): Agree: ten / Abstent: none / Reject: one.

A complete list of all collected LL is further available as part of the CeBASE[3] [5] collection on XP/Agile Lessons Learned, available On-line @ [6]. One promising way is to compare our LL with LL of similar or other XP projects and classes conducted world wide. At the University of Maryland, for instance, Dr. Roseanne Tesoriero Tvedt taught an XP class in which LL were gained. A first exchange of our observations showed interesting results. A similar observation regarding the usage of the on-site customer (cf. *LL Examples 1* and *LL Example 2*) was made in this particular XP class at the University of Maryland. Again, students did not use the on-site customer intensively. Also the supervisors had some interesting observations:

- **Observation 1:** For an inexperienced team it is hard to give precise estimations regarding the complexity of a task and the effort needed for it's realization.
- **Observation 2:** Undisciplined and/or inexperienced development teams tend to ignore process restrictions and (methodological) requirements.

Of course these observations are not specific to XP projects. However, they issue a higher risk factor for a project when, as with agile methods, there is already a lack of guidance. Our observations seem to further strengthen the hypothesis from [12] that the success of an XP project heavily depends on the experience and discipline of the people in the team. We want to point out, that all of the stated LL and observations are based on our own, specific experiences. Therefore, they can not be regarded as valid. However, the collected LL may be used to trigger a series of empirical studies to gain more insights into XP and other agile methods.

6 Summary and Conclusions

The recent advent of agile software development and XP has shown the need for lightweight (i.e., flexible) approaches which allow the rapid development of software systems. However, lightweight approaches share one fundamental problem: lack of guidance. Although, often claimed that practices such as 'Pair Programming' are an ideal means for teaching novices, an agile project heavily depends on the discipline

---

[3] Center for Empirically Based Software Engineering

and experience of its developers [11]. Thus, although students can easily learn the practices of XP, it might be hard for them to successfully apply them.

This paper reports on the experiences made at the University of Kaiserslautern during a seminar on software development. Students, most of them novice developers, have been trained in XP and its practices before using them to develop a project-management system. The analysis of the developed system showed that although it runs and offers most of the required functionality it is hard to use and not easy to maintain. This is supported by the subjective experience of the participating students. They liked the way the system was developed, especially their freedom and responsibility during development. However, all of them believe that in future projects more attention has to be paid towards the customer concerning required functionality and usability. Another observation is that without technology experts (e.g., Java or databases) the project might have failed.

Overall the experience made during the practical course showed that agile development in form of XP is easy to teach and learn. However, it is not that easy to successfully perform an agile development project. The quality of the resulting system, at least in our experience, heavily depends on the discipline of the developers and their background and experience in software development [13] [14]. Although, the team managed to satisfy the customer needs concerning functionality, the quality of the resulting system concerning maintainability and usability was not satisfactory. Thus, a general conclusion is that although agile approaches are easy to learn and quickly produce results, they are not the best starting point in training software development for achieving high-quality software. Novice developers need the guidance and support of more predictive approaches in order to obtain the experience and discipline needed in agile projects. As our experience show novices tend to focus on functionality but tend to neglect other quality attributes such as maintainability or usability. One reason is missing experience, which can be provided by systematic guidance [13]. Therefore, we believe that software engineering education should focus on traditional approaches before teaching agile development. Students who first learn about traditional development can benefit from the experience incorporated in guidelines and rules [13] [14], and can use that knowledge in later agile projects. Currently, on the one hand, we plan to continue the seminar on agile development to give students a chance to learn about XP before working in real projects. On the other hand, we are planning a controlled experiment in order to compare traditional and agile approaches concerning novice developers and guidance.

References

1. Ambler, S.: Agile Software Development. Online @ www.agilemodeling.com, last visited February 2004
2. Beck, K.: Extreme Programming Explained: Embrace Change. Addison Wesley, 1999.
3. Beck, K., Fowler, M.: Planning Extreme Programming, Addison Wesley, 2001.
4. Bunse, Ch., Dörr, J., Feldmann, R.L. (eds.): Agile Software Development –Exemplified Using XP. Software Engineering Group, University of Kaiserslautern;
    On-line @ http://wwwagse.informatik.uni-kl.de/teaching/seminar/ws2002/results.html.

5. CeBASE: Center for Empirically Based Software Engineering. Online @
    http://www.cebase.org; last visited February 2004.
6. CeBASE XP Agile Lessons Learned Collection. On-line
    @ http://fc-md.umd.edu/agilell/index.asp; last visited February 2004.
7. Highsmith, J.: Agile Software Development Ecosystems. Addison Wesley, 2002.
8. Jeffries, R., Anderson, A.: Extreme Programming Installed. Addison Wesley, 2001.
9. Martin, R., Schwaber, K., Beedle, M.: Agile Software Development wit SCRUM. Prentice
    Hall, 2001.
10. Newkirk, J., Martin, R.C.: Extreme Programming in Practice. Addison Wesley, 2001.
11. Succi, G., Marchesi, M.: Extreme Programming Examined. Addison Wesley, 2001.
12. Turk, D, France, R., Rumpe, B.: Limitations of Agile Software Processes. Proceedings of
    the 3rd International Conference in Extreme Programming and Flexible Processes in
    Software Engineering, May 2002.
13. Briand,D., Bunse, C.,Daly, J.: A Controlled Experiment for Evaluating Quality Guidelines
    on the Maintainabilty of Object-Oriented Design Documents. IEEE Transactions on Soft-
    ware Engineering, 27/6, 2001
14. Briand,D., Bunse, C.,Daly, J.: An Experimental Comparison of the Maintainabilty of
    Object-Oriented and Structured Design Documents. Journal of Empirical Software Engi-
    neering, 2/3, 1997
15. Bunse, C., Pleayo, M., Zettel, J.: Out of the Dark: Adaptable Process Models for XP.
    Proceedings of the 3rd International Conference on eXtreme Programming and Agile Proc-
    esses in Software Engineering, Alghero, 2002

Extreme Programming in Curriculum: Experiences from Academia and Industry

Matthias M. Müller[1], Johannes Link[2], Roland Sand[2], and Guido Malpohl[1]

[1] Universität Karlsruhe, Am Fasanengarten 5, 76131 Karlsruhe
[2] andrena objects ag, Albert-Nestler-Straße 9, 76131 Karlsruhe

Abstract. Since the rise of the light weight software processes, the paradigm on how software should be developed has started to shift. Agile methods strive to supersede the traditional software process with its exhausting requirements elicitation at the beginning of a software development project, at least for smaller or younger companies.
The software engineering group at the Universität Karlsruhe has accounted for this shift and extended their offer of lectures by an Extreme Programming lab course held in cooperation with andrena objects ag.

Keywords: Extreme Programming, programming lab course, curriculum, experience report

1 Introduction

In the last thirty years, the inevitable necessity of exhausting requirements elicitation combined with an overall design at the beginning of a software development project has dominated software development. The exponential growing defect removal cost curve was the rationale behind this paradigm. However, since the rise of the light weight software processes, the paradigm on how software should be developed has started to shift, at least for smaller or younger companies. From this perspective, it is quite natural that students become aware of other possible software development processes which seek to account for a rapid changing business environment, and software companies discover the alternatives presented by light weight processes as well. In this changing environment, curriculum at universities should reflect the new possibilities for software development.

Since the summer semester 2000, the software engineering group at the Universität Karlsruhe has accounted for this change and extended their offer of lectures. While the new Extreme Programming (XP) lab course initially aimed at getting in touch with the new process, it is now an inherent part of the summer semester's lectures. The first experiences about this course were reported in [1]. In the last two years since the cooperation with andrena objects ag, the course settings have changed. The reason for change was the feedback from students and the views of andrena's XP professionals. The change with the most impact was the decision to issue a project week where the students had to work from Monday to Friday from 9 am to 5 pm instead of the weekly four hours programming

J. Eckstein and H. Baumeister (Eds.): XP 2004, LNCS 3092, pp. 294–302, 2004.

sessions scheduled previously. Consequently, the course was cut into halves. In the first part, introductory sessions presented the basic techniques of XP such as pair programming, test-driven development [2], refactoring, and the planning game. Along the way, students got to know supporting tools like JUnit and CVS. For the second part, the project week, students were divided into equal sized groups of six members each. Each group had to develop a WWW based movie theater seat booking system.

While the course settings changed, the students' preferences and problems concerning the XP practices kept the same. Pair programming was adopted from the very first session. This experience is consistent with others [3,4]. But, dividing the work into small increments and implementing them step by step in a test-driven fashion was difficult. However, the problems diminished over time and at the end of the course, even test-driven development was seen as a comfortable way of development by most of the students. Wilson [3] observed the same effect in his course: after the first difficulties were overcome students appreciated test-driven development.

The next section describes the programming course in detail. Motivation of the software engineering group and andrena objects ag for this course is given in sections 3 and 4, respectively. Section 5 accounts for the experiences.

2   The Programming Course

The course is presented from three different perspectives: the content, the organization, and the project.

2.1   Content

XP Practices. Introduction of the XP techniques alternated between lectures and programming sessions. Pair programming was introduced by andrena's XP professionals. After motivating the usage of pair programming, they exemplified pair programming with test-driven development by the development of an account class. During the presentation, the students got a first notion of how pair programming works and what development in small increments means. From the first session on, every programming task had to be solved in pairs with changing partners for every new task. The following sessions introduced test-driven development with JUnit, refactoring, CVS, the planning game, the basics of servlet programming, and HttpUnit.

Supplemental Techniques. Throughout the course, students used Java together with the *Eclipse* development environment. *Tomcat* was used as web server. It was managed by the Sysdeo Tomcat plug-in for Eclipse [5]. The choice for Tomcat was natural as the plug-in provides *start*, *stop*, and *restart* buttons for ease of use from within Eclipse. In the same manner, *JUnit* formed the testing framework. The integration of JUnit into Eclipse alleviated the adoption of test-driven development as the technical overhead was kept to a minimum. Version control was done with *CVS*. Committing local changes to the CVS server was synchronized by a CVS token. Each group could choose its token individually. Finally, Eclipse packaged with Tomcat, JUnit, and CVS did not make it necessary to leave the development environment during implementation.

Acceptance tests were written using the testing framework *FitNesse* [6]. The core of FitNesse is a wiki-server which has to be started in order to use the test framework. As everybody in the team had to work on the same set of acceptance tests, a separate acceptance test server was made available for every group to ensure consistency. Writing acceptance tests was allowed only at the server, though, every pair could execute them locally on their own computer. Using a dedicated server for the acceptance tests synchronized different pairs all wanting to enhance the tests. Although only one pair could work on the acceptance tests at a time the students did not complain on this bottleneck.

2.2   Organisation

In the summer semester, lectures at the university last for thirteen weeks. The introductory sessions were issued in the first and the last four weeks of this time frame. Figure 1 depicts an overview of the course schedule. The time from the

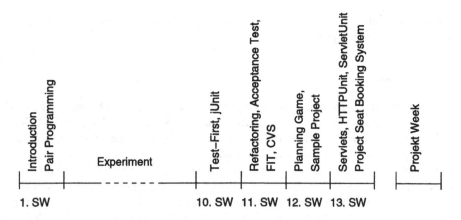

Fig. 1. Course schedule (SW = semester week)

second to the ninth semester week was reserved for a controlled experiment. Although the students had to participate in the experiment, the experiment did not add anything to the course topics.

The concluding project week was scheduled one week after the lectures. During the week, the students had to work from 9 am to 5 pm with about one hour lunch break. The project week was the largest change in the course settings as compared to previous years where the course had a weekly 4 hour schedule. We established the project week because students startup time in the weekly meetings to familiarize themselves with the new techniques were large. As a consequence, students had to less time during the weekly meetings for working on the scheduled programming tasks. During the project week, startup times appear only at the beginning of the week and then, they cease to exist.

For the project, the students were divided into three groups of six members each. The groups were selected according to students own performance ratings which they had to assess in the subject questionnaire of the experiment. Each group had its own coach and customer. The roles of the coach and the customer were taken on by the course organizers. Each organizer coached one group and played the customer in another group in a round robin fashion.

2.3 Project

Each group had to implement the same project: a theaters online seat booking system. The system should provide a customer and a box office portal. The groups started with a small skeleton of the seat booking system which implemented basic operations like movie selection and ticket ordering. The skeleton was provided to alleviate the beginning of the project by giving the students a basic software architecture to start with. We decided to provide the skeleton due to our experience in the preceeding year when student teams started from scratch. Since the students had little or no experience with setting up a web project it took them almost a day to have the first visible results, i.e. a simple dynamic web page deployed on the tomcat web-server. This experience left the students frustrated with what they considered hardly an accomplishment after a full day of work.

In order to familiarize the teams with the provided skeleton, each group had to work on the following fixed set of stories during the first day.

Story 1. Logout for theater's box office.
Story 2. The number of tickets for one order is limited by five tickets.
Story 3. Announcement of new movies and more halls.

The stories had to be divided into smaller tasks. For the first iteration, division of stories was done by the organizers as well. The following list sketches additional tasks. These tasks had to be done only once at the beginning of the project.

Task 1. Configuration of work places such that all provided tests run.
Task 2. Configuration of acceptance test server.
Task 3. Reorganizing the code base into two Java packages.

Arrangement of work places is necessary for every project, though, time consuming. Thus, configuration of work places and test server has to be recorded. Task 1 and 2 account for this project set up. During Task 3, the group should separate implementation concerns of the customer and the box office which were mixed up in the initial code base and presented some kind of code smell.

Although the groups got the same skeleton to begin with and the course organizers agreed on a set of stories, the three projects evolved in different directions concerning functionality. The different characters of the three projects were not caused by XP itself but rather by the different priorities and notions the "customers" had on the stories.

3   Motivation of Institute

The software engineering group came across XP in the winter of 1999. Initial literature [7,8] aroused our interest in the new process. Thus, we planned for a programming course to satisfy our curiosity. Our first aim was to get in touch with the process and to gather practical experience beyond the guidelines formulated in the literature. We focused on the promises made by XP. However, we were disenchanted with the process as there were lots of problems nowhere mentioned so far. The subsequent report [1] summarized our experience.

In the following time, we concentrated on the evaluation of XP. Focused on XP promises, we started to investigate the central implementation techniques. In order to achieve reasonable results, a better understanding of parts of the process and the process as a whole was necessary. We were triggered by the following questions:

- How can these techniques be modeled?
- Where are the pitfalls while evaluating them?

We started to educate students in XP and its techniques such that we could use them in experiments. Our results [9,10,11,12] show so far, that XP and its techniques are far from being the promised silver bullet, though, there are project settings where XP strengths come into full play and where XP is a reasonable choice.

Apart from the evaluation issues, the need for coaching experience grew because acquisition of background knowledge is a mandatory prerequisite for teaching compulsory lectures. And last but not least, presenting students alternative development techniques besides the conventional process is a welcome byproduct.

4   Motivation of Industry

andrena objects ag has been experimenting with XP since 1999 when the first online material became available on the Web. The main motivation for our interest was XP's focus on both quality and high flexibility. Some of the XP techniques were successfully adopted early on in in-house projects: test-driven development [2], pair programming, simple design, refactoring, continuous integration, short iterations and stand-up meetings. Other practices could not be realized as easily due to our customers' resistance, for example to provide a person who is full-time dedicated to support the development team. Moreover, we realized that familiarizing developers with test-driven design took lots of extra training and intensive supervision. Another difficulty we hit on was some developers' initial unwillingness to pair.

So our motivation to collaborate with the software engineering group was manifold:

- We wanted to gain experience in introducing XP to developers new to agile development practices. Sometimes we have to deal with beginners in Java or even programming who must be integrated into an XP team. Trying to teach students about XP and agile development seemed a reasonable way to practice teaching in a controlled and riskfree environment.
- In order to convince our customers' of doing XP we need enough empirical data and statistically relevant numbers to support XP's view of the development world. Helping researchers to gain insight into the subtleties and intricacies of XP is andrena's way to accelarate the appearance of relevant studies and publications.
- Since andrena objects focuses on high-quality individual software we are in need of developers who strive for a high standard in their development skills. Teaching at the University is one way to get to know future employees and to be visible for graduates looking for a job.
- Last but not least, giving lectures and courses about XP is a good means to "spread the word" and to make students acquainted with agile development.

Eventually, the management board of andrena objects decided to invest in student education by allocating two experienced developers to the XP programming course; so far, there have been no regrets.

5   Experience

Experience is shown from three different viewpoints: students' experience, software engineering group's experience, and andrena's experience.

5.1   Student's Experience

Pair programming was the technique the students' had the least problems to adopt to. This may be caused by the nature of the course itself because students subscribed voluntarily such that only those students took part who were willing to pair off for development. The "youth" of the students may be another reason for the fast adoption of pair programming. Most students are not coined by any software development paradigm. Thus, accepting new rules for implementation does not conflict with confirmed habits. And finally, pair programming causes a casual atmosphere on the sometimes boring development process.

When pair programming was the method adopted most easily, test-driven development caused the most problems. Breaking down the whole programming task into small steps was one problem. Implementing the small pieces in a test-first way was the other. At the beginning of the course the students asked for an idea on how to divide the problem. Later on, the answers switched over to on how

300 M.M. Müller et al.

this or that can be formulated in a test. But in the end, students felt comfortable with test-driven development. Work progresses step by step which reduces the mental task stack to a minimum such that the possibility of forgetting something is minimized. As a byproduct, automated tests were seen as helpful and the number of new written test cases was seen as some kind of productivity measure.

The Planning Game was taught in the fourth introductory session, see Figure 1. In the mini project part of that session, students had to estimate and implement small tasks of about five minutes duration each. From this session, they came to know that effort estimation even for small tasks is difficult. As a result, in the beginning of the project week, students were uncertain about their story and task estimates. Another problem for story estimation was lack of overview over and experience with the code base. However, as the project proceeded estimates became more and more accurate because analogies to existing stories could be found.

Another aspect of XP is team software development. Most students do not have any experience in team software development. Thus, the experience that the own piece of code depends on the proper implementation of others and that the own code only runs if others' code runs as well is an experience most students are not familiar with. Other experience concern the team feeling. Students were proud of finishing an iteration with all the assigned stories done. It was seen as success of the team. And on the other side, no pair was blamed on not concluding its tasks, even though the customer was unsatisfied with the team's progress. The problem was identified later on and the whole team sought for solutions.

Every team was assigned its own acceptance test server. The customer formulated its acceptance test and the team had to implement them. However, writing acceptance tests with FitNesse is HTML centered. A small change to the HTML skeleton of the project web sites resulted in a dozens of acceptance tests that had to be adapted as well, although the functionality has been retained unchanged. But after two days, the students found a means to modularize the acceptance tests thereby minimizing the necessary rework from iteration to iteration.

5.2 Institute's Experience

From a programming course organizer's point of view, teaching XP is simple: follow the given rules. However, practice looks different. The subtle discrepancies between what is written in literature and how it is put into life are challenging. As a result, there is almost no field which we can identify as *the* field we got the most new experience in.

Besides these differences, the way XP handles unit testing is refreshing. Although students subscribed and participated in a programming course with a strong emphasis on XP as a development process, they got a keen sense of what can go wrong within the code. The emphasis on the automated tests widens the way students look on their own code. However, we do not believe that it is really necessary to implement the tests *first*. But for the classroom, test-driven development is the means for teaching software testing, as it forces students to think on how the implementation task can be divided into small and testable parts.

5.3   andrena object's Experience

The most valuable effect for andrena was that we – professional developers but no professional pedagogues – could refine our teaching skills. Especially we learned that the time it takes to bring an XP newbie up to speed can differ widely, but most students managed the basic techniques in the end. In contrast to the institute's view we are convinced that taking the test-first road has a big advantage. In our experience most developers write less and worse tests when adding them after the fact. Many even start "forgetting" them completely after a few iterations. This is mainly a psychological problem: writing tests for functionality that already works is perceived as useless and tedious whereas writing tests beforehand can be much more of a challenge.

Another point we eventually had to accept is that decent programming knowledge is a must; students who fight with Java syntax cannot focus on the development process at all. Luckily, the students' programming skills were better on average than what we can usually expect from "professional developers" in industry.

Effort estimation is difficult and must be practiced to reach a reasonable accuracy. As for standard development tasks the students quickly learned to come up with realistic numbers. However, as soon as something fundamental changed, for example a new technology was introduced, estimations were yet again very inaccurate.

Finally, some XP practices which we had somewhat neglected in our professional work are well worth the effort. Especially automated acceptance tests can give the development team much more confidence in what they are doing than fine-grained unit tests alone.

6   Conclusions

In the summer semester 2004, the Extreme Programming lab course will be offered for the fifth time. While the first course aimed at acquainting the software engineering group with the new process, the course is now an inherent part of the summer semester's lectures.

The changes in the course settings with the most impact are as follows.

- We switched from a course setting with a weekly 4 hour schedule to a course which is held en bloc to reduce students startup time needed to familiarize themselves with the new techniques.
- A skeleton was provided to alleviate the beginning of the project and to provide the students with a basic software architecture.

By teaching XP, we made the following experiences:

- Reasonable Java programming skills are a must. Students who struggle with Java syntax cannot focus on the development process at all.
- Pair programming is the technique students' have the least problems to adopt to.
- Test-driven development causes the most problems. Breaking down the whole programming task into small steps and implementing the small pieces in a test-first way is difficult. But in the end, students feel comfortable with it.
- Students feel uncertain during story estimation but over time, estimates become more and more accurate due to the ability of finding analogies to existing stories.
- Most students are unfamiliar with team software development. It is a new experience that the own piece of code can depend on the proper implementation of others people's code.
- Teaching XP requires practical experience. An experienced XP practitioner cannot be replaced by the study of literature.

References

1. Müller, M., Tichy, W.: Case study: Extreme programming in a university environment. In: International Conference on Software Engineering, Toronto, Canada (2001) 537–544
2. Link, J.: Unit Testing in Java - How Tests Drive the Code. Morgan Kaufmann (2003)
3. Wilson, D.: Teaching xp: A case study. In: XP Universe, Raleigh, NC, USA (2001)
4. Fenwick, J.: Adapting xp to an academic environment by phasing-in practices. In: XP/Agile Universe. Volume 2753 of Lecture Notes in Coputer Science., Springer (2003) 162–171
5. Sysdeo Formation: Sysdeo eclipse tomcat launcher plugin. (http://www.sysdeo.com/eclipse/tomcatPlugin.html)
6. Martin, R., Martin, M.: Fitnesse. http://www.fitnesse.org/ (2003)
7. Beck, K.: Extreme Programming Explained. Addison Wesley (1999)
8. Beck, K.: Embracing change with extreme programming. IEEE Computer (1999) 70–77
9. Müller, M., Padberg, F.: On the economic evaluation of XP projects. In: Joint European Software Engineering Conference and Symposium on the Foundations of Software Engineering (ESEC/FSE), Helsinki, Finland (2003) 168–177
10. Padberg, F., Müller, M.: Analyzing the cost and benefit of pair programming. In: International Symposium on Software Metrics (Metrics), Sydney, Australia (2003) 166–177
11. Müller, M., Padberg, F.: About the return on investment of test-driven development. In: International Workshop on Economics-Driven Software Engineering Research (EDSER), Portland, Oregon, USA (2003)
12. Müller, M., Hagner, O.: Experiment about test-first programming. IEE Proceedings Software 149 (2002) 131–136

Human Aspects of Software Engineering: The Case of Extreme Programming

Orit Hazzan[1] and Jim Tomayko[2]

[1] Department of Education in Technology & Science, Technion, Israel
oritha@tx.technion.ac.il
[2] School of Computer Science, Carnegie Mellon University, Pittsburgh, PA, U.S.A.
jet@cs.cmu.edu

Abstract. As with to other agile methods, which value "Individuals and interactions over processes and tools" (http://agilemanifesto.org/), Extreme Programming (XP) cares about the interaction among the people involved in software development processes. The four XP values and its twelve practices inspire this feeling as well. Accordingly, and not surprisingly, in a course that we teach about human aspects of software engineering and in a book that we are writing about the topic [7], we find it illuminating to highlight human aspects of software engineering incorporated in XP. This article gathers these illuminations into one place.

1 Introduction

If you ask a group of software engineers what software engineering is, you would probably come up with more than one definition, each definition emphasizing different aspects of the discipline. This phenomenon is reflected also in the definitions of software engineering described in the professional literature. Indeed, software engineering is a multifaceted discipline. The rationale for the course described in this article stems from the fact that though recently the human aspects of software engineering get more and more attention, in our opinion they do not get yet the attention they deserve.

The beginning of the awareness of the human aspects of software engineering appeared in Brooks's book *The Mythical Man Month* [3]. In the preface to the 20th Anniversary Edition, Brooks writes that he is surprised that *The Mythical Man-Month* is popular even after 20 years. Such a statement indicates how difficult is to apply lessons that had been learnt with respect to software development to future software development projects. This difficulty may be explained by the multifaceted nature of the discipline and the uniqueness of software development processes. The course described in this article addresses this complexity as well.

As has been mentioned above, the importance of the human aspects of software engineering becomes acknowledged recently. For example, many failures of software systems can be explained by human factors. Taking into the consideration the complexity of the topic, the course described in this article focuses on social and cognitive aspects of software engineering, and addresses topics such

J. Eckstein and H. Baumeister (Eds.): XP 2004, LNCS 3092, pp. 303–311, 2004.

as teamwork, customer - software-engineer interaction, and learning processes in software development.

Since the agile approach in general and Extreme Programming (XP) in particular are about humankind, we find it appropriate to illustrate human aspects of software engineering by the agile approach in general and XP in particular. The next two sections describe the rationale for the course and how some of its main messages are illustrated by XP.

2   Human Aspects of Software Engineering

As it is well known, the more the software world is developed, the more it is accepted by the software engineering community that the people involved in software development processes deserve more attention, not the processes themselves or technology. This fact encapsulates the rationale for the introducing of the agile approach to software engineering and may explain the relatively rapid acceptance of the agile approach by software developers. In this spirit, the course presented in the article attempts to highlight the world of software engineering from the perspective of the main actors that are involved in software development processes: the individual, the team, the customer, and the organization. Needless to say, the code and technology are main actors in this process as well. Indeed, they are also discussed in the course. However, when code and technology are addressed, the discussion is conducted from the human perspective.

The course aims at increasing students' awareness of the various facets of the human aspects of software engineering. The idea is neither to cover all the available material about the human aspects of software engineering nor to supply a full, comprehensive, and exhaustive list of references about the topic. Rather, the course aims to illustrate the richness and complexity of the human aspects of software engineering and to increase the learners' awareness of problems, dilemmas, questions, and conflicts that may be raised with respect to the human aspect of software engineering during the course of software development.

3   Extreme Programming Illuminates Human Aspects of Software Engineering

In this section we describe how XP serves as an illuminating example for human related topics that are addressed in the course. Specifically, in what follows we review the course lesson by lesson, and illustrate how we highlight the human aspects of software engineering by using XP.

Lesson 1. The Nature of Software Engineering: This introductory lesson sets the stage for the entire course. Both the agile approach and the heavyweight approach to software development are introduced. Yet, the terms (agile and heavyweight) are not yet introduced at this stage. Alternatively, instead of describing these two approaches, we tell a story of two software developers: One works in a software house where development processes are guided by the heavyweight approach; the second developer works in a software house that its software production is guided by the agile approach. Students are asked to compare the two environments and to formulate their preferred environment for software development. These two approaches are introduced in the second lesson of the course.

Lesson 2. Software Engineering Methods: In this lesson different software development methods are described. Naturally, one of them is XP. In general, it is explained that agile methods are more tied to the human aspects of software development. A special attention is given to the meaning of the adjective *extreme*.

Each of the four XP values and each of the dozen XP practices is examined from the human perspective. For example, it is discussed with the students how the value of communication is expressed by the practices pair programming, metaphor, simple design, on-site customer, the planning game and coding standard. It is also explained how the "40-hour week" (or, sustainable pace, or no extended overtime) is based on the assumption that tired programmers make more mistakes. It is highlighted that communication subsumes many of the XP practices. Indeed, this is not surprising since communication is very much a human characteristic of software engineering.

In addition, roles in XP teams are explained and their contribution to the software development process is outlined. Sensitive human issues in software development, such as load balancing among individuals, are highlighted as well.

Lesson 3. Working in Teams: After several central roles in software teams are described, their implementation by different methods (such as the Personal Software Process - PSP) and different team structures (such as hierarchical teams) are explained. One of the discussed approaches is the agile paradigm. It is explained that a team using agile processes probably functions better as a democratic team, since there are no layers in between the manager and the engineers, and communication, valued by many of the agile processes, is enhanced.

With respect to XP, it is illustrated how the XP practice of collective ownership ensures the democratic approach. Particularly, with respect to XP teams, the human related topic of small ego that is necessary for any democratic is emphasized. In addition, it is discussed how the XP practices may increase trust among team members.

Lesson 4. Software as a Product: This lesson examines the human aspect of software engineering from the perspective of the customers - the people that use software products. It focuses on how users and developers deal with defining software requirements in a way that fulfill customers' needs. Indeed, the process of defining customer's requirements is viewed in this lesson as a process in which both the customer and the developers participate.

When the topic is illustrated by XP, it is explained that XP advocates that if a software team wishes to produce the software that the customer needs, the customer should be able to give the developers on going feedback. For this purpose the customer should be on-site. In addition, XP outlines a very specific process (the Planning Game) for defining the customer requirements (here called 'customer stories').

Lesson 5. Code of Ethics of Software Engineering: In this lesson the focus is placed on the notion of ethics in general and the Code of Ethics of Software Engineering[1] in particular. The discussion focuses on the main ideas and the essence of the Code of Ethics of Software Engineering and students analyze scenarios taken from the software engineering world. The idea is to guide the students in the formulation of personal ethical behavior. This is a personal process that each practitioner should go through individually. In this sense, this lesson is different from the other lessons of the course since it raises more questions and philosophical dilemmas than it provides answers.

XP is discussed in this lesson by focusing on the practice of test-driven-development. Since the source of many of the ethical issues in the world of software engineering stems from the fact that software systems are not tested properly, it is found illuminating to describe how XP bypasses these ethical dilemmas by including the test-driven-development practice among its core practices. Students are asked to learn about the XP way of testing and to explain how this approach ensures that tests will not be skipped or diminished. It is also discussed how this approach towards testing may help developers avoid many of the ethical dilemmas, such as those that deal with how to tell customers that due to time pressure some tests are skipped.

Lesson 6. International Perspective on Software Engineering: In this lesson the field of software engineering is examined from an international perspective. The focus is placed on the community of software engineers and what is examined is expanded beyond the team and the organization frameworks. Specifically, in this lesson the influence of certain events on the global high-tech economy and the nature of software engineering in several places on the globe are explored. In addition, the topic of gender and minorities in the hi-tech industry is discussed.

Since the agile approach in general and XP in particular represent a new paradigm in the evolution of software development methods, we find it appropriate to discuss in this lesson the fitness of XP to different cultures and to women's management and communication style.

Lesson 7. Program Comprehension, Code Inspections, and Refactoring: One of the main messages of the course in general and of this lesson in particular is that the development of software is based on an iterative process through which the code structure and functionality are improved gradually. It is discussed that different software development methods deal differently with these gradual improvements. XP serves in this lesson as a suitable example since it includes refactoring [4] as one of its twelve core practices.

To connect this topic to the previous lesson (International Perspective on Software Engineering), it is discussed with the students that in a way similar to other human beings' habits, one would refactor or not pending on the culture one lives in and one's attitude towards refactoring. Accordingly, for an XP team, refactoring is one of the method's practices, it is accepted naturally, it is part of the development routine and it stops feeling like an overhead activity.

---

[1]   The URL of the code of ethics is http://www.acm.org/constitution/code.html.

Furthermore, refactoring is tightly connected to the other XP practices, such as unit testing and continuous integration.

In addition, it is illustrated how several IDEs (Integrated Development Environments) offer Refactoring menus which include actions such as Extract, Rename, etc. Two such Java IDEs are IntelliJ IDEA (*http://www.intellij.com/idea/*) and Eclipse (*http://www.eclipse.org/platform*). This inclusion of refactoring in IDEs is a clear sign that refactoring has become part of the profession of software engineering. At the same time it is highlighted that though refactoring has so many advantages, there are cases where refactoring should not be carried out. One of these cases is when the code is a mess and it would be better to start its development from the beginning. In fact, even this act can be viewed as some form of refactoring.

Lesson 8. Learning Processes in Software Engineering: This lesson is largely based on [6]. Specifically, together with the students we discuss how a reflective mode of thinking may be interwoven is software development processes in general and in XP environments in particular.

The reflective practice perspective was introduced by Sch?n, mainly in the context of certain kinds of professional fields such as Art and Architecture [8,9]. Generally speaking, the reflective practice perspective guides professional practitioners (such as architects, managers, musicians and others) towards examining and rethinking their professional creations during and after the accomplishment of the process of creation. The working assumption is that such a reflection improves both proficiency and performance within such professions. Analysis of the field of software engineering, the kind of work that software engineers usually accomplish, and the XP practices, support the adoption of the reflective practice perspective to software engineering in general and to XP development environments in particular. Specifically, it is suggested that a reflective mode of thinking may improve the application of some of the XP practices. In this lesson this possible contribution is examined.

Specifically, we aim to construct, together with the students, ladders of reflection. Ladders of reflection are described by Schön in the following way:

We can [...] introduce another dimension of analysis [for the chain of reciprocal actions and reflections that make up the dialogue of student and coach in the architecture studio]. We can begin with a straightforward map of interventions and responses, a vertical dimension according to which higher levels of activity are "meta" to those below. To move "up", in this sense, is to move from an activity to reflection on that activity; to move "down" is to move from reflection to an action that enacts reflection. The levels of action and reflection on action can be seen as the rungs of a ladder. Climbing up the ladder, one makes what has happened at the rung below an object of reflection. [9] (p. 114)

The ladder of reflection described in this quote refers mainly to student-tutor dialogue in the *architecture* studio. [5] expands the ladder of reflection presented by Schön to a student-coach dialogue in a *software* studio and with respect to an individual work. The idea in both cases is to illustrate how one may increase the level of abstraction of one's thinking when reflection is interwoven in software development processes.

In this lesson we construct ladders of reflection with respect to different software development situations in general and with respect to XP-based cases, such as a pair programming session, a planning game session and a refactoring process, in particular. These cases illustrate how a ladder of reflection may promote one's comprehension of the relevant development process and may lead to insights that eventually may save time and money. Figure 1 presents one of the tasks presented in this lesson.

In what follows two situations are describes. For each of them:

- Identify potential topics for reflection.
- Construct a ladder of reflection.
- Describe what lessons you have learnt from this experience.

Case 1 - Testing in eXtreme Programming: In eXtreme Programming [1] programmers write tests before they write the code. This approach is called test-driven-development (TDD). Write a class Student according to the TDD approach.

Case 2 - New developers join your team: You are a team leader. You are asked to accept to your team two software engineers who have developed software that can be integrated into the project that your team works on. You ask your team and the two new developers to meet in the meeting room to discuss how to merge their code successfully.

Fig. 1. A Task in the Human Aspects of Software Engineering Course: Construction of Ladders of Reflection

Lesson 9. Different Perspectives on Software Engineering: In this lesson we aim to illustrate how the profession of software engineering is shaped and that different approaches may influence the way it is eventually organized and established. Among other dual perspectives towards software development we introduce the agile paradigm vs. the heavyweight approach. Naturally, XP is mentioned among the other agile methods. It is explained that the agile approach towards software development has emerged in the last decade as an answer to the unique and typical problems that characterize software development processes.

In this lesson it is also illustrated how different approaches address failure and success of software projects. Among other approaches we cite Kent Beck who refers to the conceptual change towards software project success and failure that both developers and customers should adopt when they decide to use XP as their project development method [2]. Indeed, the question of what a successful software project means invites many debates. It is emphasized that one agreement has been reached, though, among the entire community of software practitioners. They mostly agree that software projects should meet customer's needs.

Lesson 10. Abstraction and Other Heuristics of Software Development: This lesson examines different kinds of activities that are carried out during software development processes that are, in fact, heuristics (or ways of thinking) that one employs when one performs other activities. One of these ideas is abstraction.

With respect to XP, the students are asked to review the different XP practices and identify those practices that guide software developers to think in terms of different levels of abstraction when appropriate. It is suggested that developers' familiarity with the big picture of the developed application may improve their performance in the development of their specific tasks. One way to achieve this familiarity with the entire picture of the developed application is by the Planning Game. Though each developer is responsible for specific tasks, they all participate in the Planning Game. Their participation in the Planning Game enables them to become familiar with the entire picture of the developed application. In later development stages, when they have to make decisions related to different parts of the application, this kind knowledge may be useful. The main message of this part of the lesson is that the ability to think in terms of different levels of abstraction throughout the development process may contribute to and support software development processes.

Lesson 11. Characteristics of Software and the Human Aspects of Software Engineering: This lesson examines software characteristics from the developers' perspective and illustrates that even software characteristics that seem to be connected only to the software itself, cannot be isolated and detached from the software developers. Specifically, the focus is placed on communication issues related to programming style. Figure 2 presents sample tasks discussed in this lesson which are connected to XP.

Example of a preparation task:
In Lesson 2 (about Software Development Methods) we discussed three software development methods: Spiral Model, Unified Process, and eXtreme Programming. Analyze each of these methods according to the software characteristics that each of them guides its production.

Example of a summary question:
Simple design (one of the eXtreme Programming practices) is a software characteristic.

- What does it require from the software developers to produce code according to this practice?
- Discuss connections between simple design and refactoring.
- How do these two practices support the eXtreme Programming values of communication and simplicity?

Fig. 2. Tasks about Characteristics of Software, the Human Aspect of Software Engineering and XP

Lesson 12. The History of Software Engineering: In this lesson the history of software engineering from its early days in 1968 is outlined. One phase in this history is the entry of the agile methods in general and of XP in particular to the software engineering world. The uniqueness of XP - the specification of practices that implement values - is explained.

Lesson 13. Software Project Estimation and Tracking: It is well known that many software projects are late and over budget. This lesson explores the effects of overtime on programmers. In addition, it presents several methods of estimating and tracking time on task, so that the students will have additional tools to avoid being part of another late project. One of these tools is The Planning Game. Its main steps are described and the potential contributions of its different stages to software project tracking are examined and discussed with the students. When there is enough time, the Planning Game is played in detail for one iteration of a specific software tool according to the students' choice.

Lesson 14. Software as a Business: This lesson is about software as a business. It consists of two main parts: a brief account of how software became profitable, and more recent stories of making money with software. With respect to XP, its explicit attention to returning value to the customer with each release is highlighted.

4   Conclusion

In this paper we outline how in a course about human aspects of software engineering we use XP as an example of a software development method that emphasizes human aspects of software engineering. Specifically, we explain how XP is connected to each topic discussed in the course.

At the end of the semester the students discuss and analyze case studies related to the human aspect of software engineering. These activities aim to increase students' awareness, sensitivity and analysis skills when they participate in software development environments. The analysis of the case studies is based on theories that have been learned in the course. Not only students are presented with case studies. Rather, they are also asked to present case-studies from the professional literature or from their own experience in software development. The appearance of XP in these cases is optional. When XP does appear, its human aspects are highlighted.

References

1. Beck, K.: Extreme Programming Explained: Embrace Change. Addison-Wesley 2000.
2. Beck, K.: Extreme programming: an interview with Kent Beck. The Cutter Edge. *http://www.cutter.com/research/2002/edge020903.htm*, 3 September 2002.
3. Brooks, P. F.: The Mythical Man Month: Essays on Software Engineering. Addison-Wesley 1975, revised in 1995.

4. Fowler, M.: (with contributions by Kent Beck, John Brant, William Opdyke, Don Roberts). Refactoring: Improving the Design of Existing Code. Addison-Wesley 2000.
5. Hazzan, O.: The reflective practitioner perspective in software engineering education. The Journal of Systems and Software 63(3), pp. 161-171, 2002.
6. Hazzan, O. and Tomayko, J.: The reflective practitioner perspective in eXtreme Programming. Proceedings of the XP Agile Universe 2003, New Orleans, Louisiana, USA, pp. 51-61, 2003.
7. Hazzan, O. and Tomayko, J.: (in preparation). Human Aspects of Software Engineering. Charles River Media 2004.
8. Schön, D. A.: The Reflective Practitioner. BasicBooks 1983.
9. Schön, D. A.: Educating the Reflective Practitioner: Towards a New Design for Teaching and Learning in the Profession. San Francisco: Jossey-Bass 1987.

Extreme Programming in a University Project

Roger A. Müller

University of Münster, Leonardo Campus 3, D-48149 Münster
piromu@wi.uni-muenster.de

Abstract. Extreme programming is a light weighted software engineering process – too lightweighted to handle technically and algorithmically complex problems? This paper describes the problems encountered when engineering demanding and complex software systems on the example of a software engineering project at the University of Münster.

Keywords: Extreme Programming, Experience Report

1   Introduction and Scenario Description

The information system curriculum in the University of Münster contains a course devoted to a student's project averaging six month of full time work. This course is usually taken by a small group of students, which makes it ideally suited for the use of extreme programming (XP) as a process model.

As it turned out, XP was very useful for the project, but both the project team and the course's tutors encountered difficulties with the usage of XP, as the target system had a high technical and algorithmical complexity, both of which had impact on several XP practices.

The course was held in the summer term of 2003 at University of Münster, Germany. The setup of a "student's project course" is similar to a practical training course, where students get the chance to employ and test their knowledge regarding software or information system projects on a self organized basis. The aim of the presented course was to implement a symbolic Java virtual machine that can be used for test case generation (see [ML03] for a details). The sought goal was not a set-up specifically for the seminar, but the seminar was organized to implement the virtual machine – i.e. a real customer situation existed. Each of the four participants was a graduate student, all of them had experience in Java programming but no prior exposure to XP. Thus, before the start of the project, the students familiarized themselves with XP.

The actual beginning of the course was marked by the planning game for the first iteration. In the first two and a half weeks the students settled into their new work environment and familiarized themselves with the technical ideas behind the project. The second iteration marked the real start of the project. From this point on most of the story cards were not to be fulfilled on an assiduity basis, but some research and study on the topic had to be conducted by the students' team. For the whole project which lasted for six iterations, the students teamed up for pair programming. The tutors did not get involved in the actual programming

J. Eckstein and H. Baumeister (Eds.): XP 2004, LNCS 3092, pp. 312–315, 2004.

process even when a team member was missing due to other commitments. As noted above the instructors also acted as customers and project managers. Both fitted really well in the real situation, as the instructors really were the customers for the project and the tutoring usually performed by an instructor comes pretty close to the project management and mentoring tasks necessary for an XP project.

The following paper will present the course set-up, the problems with XP in this very project will be discussed in detail and the found solutions will be presented and, finally, summarized.

2 Lessons Learned

2.1 Tool Selection

The project plan, i.e. the iteration management was done electronically using XP-Web, a tool which simply provides the user with web-version of the story and task cards. Some other features can be supported by this tool as well, but only the card management and the metaphor management was used to any noteworthy extend, and only the story and task card part showed notable effect, as it offered the following advantages over the usual planning game. On the one hand the customer could easily follow the progress of the different story cards. Also, and probably more importantly, he could check the different task cards that were made up by the students and – as some problems only got clearer when programming was started – changed over time. On the other hand the students could check early, what would await them in the next iteration and prepare themselves for the next iteration period. In fact, the new iteration was entered into the system on Fridays, so the weekend could be used for considering the tasks and familiarization. In fact, this proceeding proved invaluable for the success of the project, as it was firstly employed after the first iteration's planning ended nearly disastrous as the students did not know enough about the virtual machine to discuss it in the needed depth – several little post-meetings had to do the job.

As a basis for communication a wiki system was selected. As such a system offers an anarchistic kind of content management, topics can be discussed fitting to the flat hierarchy in XP projects.

The other software used were JRefactory for refactoring NetBeans as an IDE with integrated CVS and JUnit support. It was chosen over more complex CASE-Tools, especially Borland TogetherSoft ControlCenter, as the team was already familiar with it and performance proved to be much better.

2.2 Simple Design and Iteration Planning

Simple design is the dogma for XP projects. Interestingly, none of the participating students had any notable problems with that, which is probably because of the offensive marketing involved for the course as an XP course and the resulting dedication of the students to XP. Another assumption may lie in the strategy used for the planning, i.e. the story cards. As it hopefully had become clear in the setup description the target program was non trivial in the sense, that the goal was easily describable but the way to that goal was at best clouded. As a result, the tutors gave design hints by the formulation of the story cards.

The acceptance tests differed from the usual ones as well. To test (in the sense of validate) for example, a virtual machine execution engine, a rather specialised set of tests is necessary. For this project this problem was solved by testing the program with a set of example code provided for a computer science lecture, as it was believed to represent most issues involved in programming in a compact way.

The test suite was continuously upgraded and expanded as the capabilities of the machine enhanced. Due to its complexity the construction processes for the suites made up story cards of their own, which seems to be a novel approach worth further studying.

One best practise of XP turned out to be too strict to handle, at least in a technical context: it was next to impossible to discard all user stories the team cannot finish in iteration time. Some user stories are critical not to the current iteration but to the success of the next. Though one might argue, that such a story could easily be postponed to a later iteration, this is not always true. If, for example, one iteration is concerned with programming a virtual machine that should be used in the next, the virtual machine has to be finished first, whatever XP says. It proved to be a good practise to start the next iteration with a story card "finish story cards x to y from the last iteration", just to make sure the critical parts of the project are implemented.

As it turned out the XP team had troubles to figure out where to start and how to plan their iteration. The cause for this was the complexity of the project. To counter this problem the tutors used the priorities of the task cards as a queue, which sometimes resulted in priorities differing from the real importance of the task. However, as the planning usually resulted in very well timed iterations, this did not turn out to be a problem. The approach of allocating the priorities to represent an order of the tasks instead of the real priority can be adapted to other, similar projects as well. However, the abnormal use of the priorities should be communicated to the project team, as only this ensures that the team can use the information in a suitable manner.

2.3 Pair Programming, Testing, and Refactoring

The project participants were asked to program in pairs. To underline this request, the team's room was only fitted with two computers and a server. The computers were connected to one monitor and one keyboard each. Despite the good reception of the pair programming, some parts like coding huge amounts of analogous coding or GUI implementation were conducted on a single person basis.

Another point discussed on a regular basis is the exchange of experience involved in programming in pairs. The participants described their learning curve in regards to the pair program as steep and later on flattened. From the tutors point of view, the anxiety usually associated with the more complicated parts of a project could not be perceived in this case, which might be easily associated with the pair programming.

Overall the pair programming was received very well, as the programmers felt more secure with the technically complex task, which kept a continuous discussion going throughout the whole project.

As with most XP projects JUnit was the natural choice for testing the system for both acceptance and unit tests. As described above it blended well into the chosen IDE and was easy to learn and implement. The test-first strategy was adapted with little problems, and was kept up throughout the project. The team adapted very early to the kind of testing and it bolstered the confidence in their project.

3   Related Work and Conclusion

Some related work has been conducted on the usage of XP in a university or R&D environment. For a pure R&D environment Boutin [Bo00] described the experiences made in his company when a change of both method and programming language was conducted. Classroom experience for introducing XP was described in the papers of Astrachan et al. [As02] and Sanders [Sa02]. Holcombe [Ho02] described a setting with a similar initial starting situation like the project described in this paper, but the set-up, project execution and the conclusion differ quite a lot.

To sum up, this paper has shown that XP is suited to deal with complex software systems. We have shown, that the complexity has to be broken down by the project manager, to enable the actual project team to estimate complexity and as simple things as a meaningful order of implementation. This is mostly because technically complex applications need some research in adavance. If the reasearch is conducted by a different group than the programmers, as it might usually be the case, the results learned have to reflect strongly on the project plan and the planning game, if that means, that the separation of customer and programmer has to be lifted to a certain extend. At last we discovered that pair programming takes some of the anxiety usually associated with complexity away from the team.

References

[As02]   Astrachan, O. L. et al. Bringing Extreme Programming to the Classroom, in: Marchesi, M. et al.: XP Perspectives, 2002 (237-250).

[Bo00]   K. Boutin. Introducing Extreme Programming in a Research and Development Laboratory, in: Succi, G. and M. Marchesi: XP Examined, 2000 (433-448).

[Ho02]   M. Holcombe et al. Teaching XP for Real: Some Initial Observations and Plans, in: Marchesi, M. et al.: XP Perspectives, 2002 (251-260).

[ML03]   R. Müller, C. Lembeck, and H. Kuchen: GlassTT - a SJVM using Constraint Solving Techniques for Test Case Generation, TR 102, Univ. of Münster, 2003.

[Sa02]   D. Sanders. Extreme Programming and the Software Design Course, in: Marchesi, M. et al.: XP Perspectives, 2002 (261-272).

Agile Methods: The Gap between Theory and Practice

Kieran Conboy

Dept. of Accountancy and Finance,
National University of Ireland,
Galway, Ireland

Abstract. Since the software crisis of the 1960's, numerous methodologies have been developed to impose a disciplined process upon software development. Today, these methodologies are noted for being unsuccessful and unpopular due to their increasingly bureaucratic nature. Many researchers and academics are calling for these heavyweight methodologies to be replaced by agile methods. However, there is no consensus as to what constitutes an agile method. An Agile Manifesto was put forward in 2001, but many variations, such as XP, SCRUM and Crystal exist. Each adheres to some principles of the Agile Manifesto and disregards others. My research proposes that these principles lack grounding in theory, and lack a respect for the concept of agility outside the field of Information Systems Development (ISD). This study aims to develop a comprehensive framework of ISD agility, to determine if this framework is adhered to in practice and to determine if such adherence is rewarded. The framework proposes that it is insufficient to just accept agile methods as superior to all others. In actual fact, an ISD team have to identify whether they need to be agile, and to compare this to their agile capabilities before deciding how agile their eventual method should be. Furthermore this study proposes that an agile method is not just accepted and used. Rather it may be selected from a portfolio of methods, it may be constructed from parts of methods, or indeed it may be the product of the ISD team's deviation from a different method altogether. Finally, this study recognises that agility does not simply come from a method. In actual fact, a cross-disciplinary literature review suggests that it is important to classify sources of agility, which could be the people on team, the way they are organised, the technology they use or the external environment with which they interact. A three phase research method is adopted, incorporating a set of pilot interviews, a large-scale survey and finally, a set of case studies. The survey is intended to produce generalisable results while the case studies are carried out to obtaining much needed qualitative information in an emerging field where little is currently known.

J. Eckstein and H. Baumeister (Eds.): XP 2004, LNCS 3092, p. 316, 2004.
© Springer-Verlag Berlin Heidelberg 2004

Correlating Unit Tests and Methods under Test

Markus Gälli

Software Composition Group
University Bern
gaelli@iam.unibe.ch

Keywords: Unit tests, methods under test, method examples, test scenarios, traits

Research Questions: What are the relationships between unit tests and between unit tests and methods under test? What can be gained by making this relationships explicit? How does the concept of *method examples* compare with other possible techniques to relate this entities?

Significant problems and current solutions: (1.) Missing explicit relationships between unit tests and methods under test make it difficult to trace which features are thoroughly tested and hinder navigability between unit tests and their methods under test. xUnit uses a naming convention which is brittle when it comes to renaming the methods and classes under test. (2.) Schuh *et al.* [1] introduce the concept of *ObjectMother* to compose complex test scenarios. (3.) Failing unit tests are presented randomly and not in a meaningful order. [2]

Definition: A *method example* tests a single method **and returns** the resulting receiver, parameters and potential return value of its method under test.

Approach: Show which kind of relations between unit tests and between unit tests and method under tests exist. Correlate the unit tests of the base system of Squeak by decomposing them into *method examples*. Show, that the single concept of *method examples* enables navigation and traceability between unit tests and methods under test, provides concrete types for the methods under test, fits well together with traits [3], and allows the composition of complex unit tests. Compare with other techniques to make this relationships explicit.

Achieved Results: Case studies show that a significant amount of the relationships between unit tests cover each other when one compares the sets of signatures of their called messages [2], and that the Squeak base unit tests can be successfully refactored to *method examples*.

References

1. Schuh, P.: Recovery, redemption and Extreme Programming. IEEE Computer **18** (2001) 34–41
2. Gälli, M., Nierstrasz, O., Wuyts, R.: Partial ordering tests by coverage sets. Technical Report IAM-03-013, Institut für Informatik, Universität Bern, Switzerland (2003) Technical Report.
3. Schärli, N., Ducasse, S., Nierstrasz, O., Black, A.: Traits: Composable units of behavior. In: Proceedings ECOOP 2003. Volume 2743 of LNCS., Springer Verlag (2003) 248–274

J. Eckstein and H. Baumeister (Eds.): XP 2004, LNCS 3092, p. 317, 2004.
© Springer-Verlag Berlin Heidelberg 2004

Exploring the XP Customer Role – Part II

Angela Martin

Faculty of Information Technology, Victoria University of Wellington
Wellington, New Zealand
angela@mcs.vuw.ac.nz

The Customer is the only non-developer role in eXtreme Programming (XP). Initial XP literature [1, 2] provided little guidance concerning this role; however Beck & Fowler did acknowledge the risk associated with the Customer role:

> *All the best talent and technology and process in the world will fail when the customer isn't up to scratch [1, p.17]*

Our research [4] is beginning to explore the practicalities of succeeding in the implementation of the XP Customer role. We have used interpretative in-depth case studies [3, 4] to explore our research questions within their natural setting; software projects. We have interviewed a total of 39 people across six projects in New Zealand and the United States, and in all cases have covered the spectrum of core XP roles. We found that the customer must shoulder several implicit responsibilities, including liaison with external project stakeholders, while maintaining the trust of both the development team and the wider business. The existing XP Customer practices appear to be achieving excellent results but they also appear to be unsustainable, and so constitute a great risk to XP projects, especially in long-term or high-pressure projects. We are continuing to analyse the data from these cases, as well as collecting data from projects in England & Europe, to further explore the issues encountered and successful and unsuccessful coping strategies utilised. The key contribution of our research will be to describe the essential characteristics and skills required in the customer role, and to identify the crucial practices and values to carry out the role successfully.

References

1. Beck, K., & Fowler, M. Planning Extreme Programming: Addison Wesley, 2001.
2. Farell, C., Narang, R., Kapitan, S. and Webber, H., Towards an effective onsite customer practice. in Third International Conference on eXtreme Programming and Agile Process in Software Engineering, (Italy, 2002).
3. Fitzgerald, B. Systems development methodologies: the problem of tenses. Information technology and people, 13 (3). pp. 174 – 185.
4. Martin, A., Noble, J., and Biddle, R. Proceedings of the Fourth International Conference on eXtreme Programming and Agile Processes in Software Engineering, Giancarlo Succi (Ed.), Being Jane Malkovich: a Look into the World of an XP Customer. Lecture Notes in Computer Science 2675, Springer-Verlag. 2003.

J. Eckstein and H. Baumeister (Eds.): XP 2004, LNCS 3092, p. 318, 2004.
© Springer-Verlag Berlin Heidelberg 2004

A Selection Framework for Agile Methodologies

E. Mnkandla and B. Dwolatzky

[1] Monash University, South Africa, Ernest.Mnkandla@infotech.monash.edu.au
[2] University of the Witwatersrand, South Africa, b.dwolatzky@ee.wits.ac.za

1   Introduction

Agile software development methodologies provide a significant improvement on the control and management of the software development process. Literature gives evidence of improvement in areas like development of software that meets the user requirements, delivery of the product on time and within budget. With the growing number of agile methodologies the selection of a methodology that is suitable for a particular project becomes a nontrivial issue. This research work aims at devising a mechanism that can be used by practitioners to select the most suitable agile methodology for a given software development project. The literature survey done so far reveals that whilst those who have used agile methods have made significant benefits, there is a lot of apprehensiveness and uncertainty about the use of agile methods in the IT industry. This uncertainty is due to the lack of literature on the representation of agile methods and the lack of empirical data on the use of agile methods. The literature also shows that due to these gaps there is also a lack of ways of selecting the appropriate methodology for a given project.

2   Significant Problems

1. Agile methodologies not well accepted in the IT industry:
   Solution: provide empirical data (through experimentation) on the gains made by agile methods.
2. IT professionals do not seem to accept change in their field that easily hence the delay in accepting software development methods that will bring positive change.
   Solution: Introduce the agile methods in the education system.

3   Proposed Approach

1. Design a framework for the representation of agile methodologies.
2. Conduct experiments on the use of some agile methods in teaching and also use existing data to show that the way developers choose a methodology depends among other things, on the way they were taught software engineering.

J. Eckstein and H. Baumeister (Eds.): XP 2004, LNCS 3092, pp. 319–320, 2004.

3. Design a framework for selecting the most appropriate agile method for a given project based on; the experience of the IT professional, the type and size of the project, and an algorithm (still to be designed) that suggests the best methodology given the different parameters that affect the success of the project.

4   Results Obtained So Far

We have found from a few software development companies in South Africa that a good number of them do not use any methodology at all in software development process. They just follow some way that gets things done.

Refactor Our Writings

Joshua Kerievsky

Industrial Logic
joshua@industriallogic.com,
http://industriallogic.com/

Abstract. Getting folks writing papers about useful information is good. However, a forest of ideas, with no organization, is bad. We would like authors and groups of authors come together to refactor older, related papers into new, consolidated pieces of literature that communicate comprehensive ideas on an important subject.
We need to encourage ourselves to refactor what we've written in order to produce excellent new pieces of literature.

1 Audience and Benefits

Everyone who is involved with or interested in writing, teaching and learning.

2 Content

The standard "Call for Papers" that gets announced before each of the XP/Agile conferences is good. It gets folks writing papers about useful information – techniques that have worked well, experiece using a process, etc. It is nice to see people from around the world contributing such papers to the various XP/Agile conferences.

However, I am now seeing what I saw in the patterns movement: a continuous stream of papers, with no refactoring of the literature. This is bad. It leads to a forest of ideas, with no organization and little practical value to a broad community that has not yet joined the XP/Agile community.

I would like to see authors and groups of authors come together to refactor older, related papers into new, consolidated pieces of literature that communicate comprehensive ideas on an important subject.

An example: At XP 2001, I submitted a paper to the conference called Continuous Learning. At the conference, I discovered that TimMacinnon? (sp?) had submitted a related paper. I also met Francesco Crillo (of XpLabs) who had lots of great ideas (and more important, practical experience) on the subject of Continuous Learning. I

J. Eckstein and H. Baumeister (Eds.): XP 2004, LNCS 3092, pp. 321–322, 2004.

remarked at the time that the three of us needed to consolidate our ideas to produce a more comprehensive piece of literature about Continuous Learning. That hasn't happened yet, though I am committed to making it happen.

I'd like this idea of refactoring our literature to spread to other authors. I don't want the conferences to limit the size of our consolidated papers. We need to encourage ourselves to refactor what we've written in order to produce excellent new pieces of literature.

The first step is to educate conference organizers about the need to refactor our literature, so that such an effort can be included as part of any "Call for Papers." Next, let's encourage this effort by suggesting some areas that we feel need to be refactored and consolidated. For example, I've read numerous papers on Teaching XP, Distributed XP, XP Testing.

3 Presenter

Joshua Kerievsky, a Senior Consultant with Cutter Consortium's Agile Software Development & Project Management Practice, began his career as a professional programmer at a Wall Street bank, where he programmed numerous financial systems for credit, market, and global risk departments. After a decade at the bank, he founded Industrial Logic to help companies practice successful software development. Kerievsky has programmed and coached on small, large, and distributed XP projects since XP's emergence. He recently pioneered Industrial XP, an application of XP tailored for large organizations. Kerievsky has been an active member of the patterns community and is presently completing a book entitled Refactoring to Patterns. He can be reached at consulting@cutter.com.

Be Empowered (That's an Order !) "Experience the Dynamics and the Paradoxes of Self-Organizing Teams"

Laurent Bossavit[1] and Emmanuel Gaillot [2]

[1]Exoftware,
laurent@bossavit.com,
http://bossavit.com/
[2]Independent,
egaillot@freesurf.fr

Abstract. "The best architectures, requirements, and designs emerge from self-organizing teams," argues the Agile Manifesto. Yet the opposite principle is built into the corporate model of collaboration: "someone has to be boss" – sometimes to the extent of attempting to mandate self-organization! Self-organization cannot be decreed from above, but conditions can be created which favor it; one such condition is that team members have experience with and can recognize self-organization. Drawing on lessons from the theatre, this workshop will provide just such an experience, as well as explore the conditions of self-organization.

1 Audience and Benefits

Participants will ideally have the experience of working in teams, or at least in groups; or of managing teams of groups.

- Participants and presenters will
- learn about the conditions under which self-organization can be expected
- experience achieving a purpose without the the need for a leader's direction
- generalize and extract insights from their own and each other's experience
- have fun

2 Content and Process

Extreme Programming does not define a "project manager" or a "team lead" role. It does have a "coach" role, whose responsibilities are to observe how the team is doing and reflect on that with the team – not to tell anyone what they should do. (Also, the coach is expected to fade away as the team becomes self-disciplining.) How can anyone expect a team to work without a boss – or at least a leader ? Yet if we are to pay more than lip service to the notion of "self-organizing" teams, we must understand how teams might function without externally imposed organization.

J. Eckstein and H. Baumeister (Eds.): XP 2004, LNCS 3092, pp. 323–324, 2004.
© Springer-Verlag Berlin Heidelberg 2004

This interactive and experiential workshop is meant as a point of departure for a collective investigation of self-organized teams in the context of agile projects. **Pre-workshop**, up to 20 participants (on a first-come, first-serve basis) will be invited to sign up and join in an exploratory Wiki conversation at
  http://selforganizingteams.com/

During the workshop, we will alternate theatrical exercises, inspired by the workshops run by director Anne Bogart; open discussion; presentation of some basic theoretical models; and exploration of regularities in participants' and presenters' experiences, leading to patterns, models or other insights applicable to the management of self-organizing teams. The workshop will run, in outline, as follows:

09:00-09:30	**Entry; informal and structured Q&A**
09:30-10:30	**Exercise: soft focus and the Circle**
10:30-11:00	Break
11:00-11:30	**Structured reflection – mental models of „team"**
11:30-12:30	**Fishbowl discussion – teams and self-organization**
12:30-14:00	Lunch
14:00-14:30	**Theoretical models – presentation & discussion**
14:30-15:15	**Exercise: a Sun Salutation** (no, Java isn't involved)
15:15-15:30	Break
15:30-16:15	**Exercise: a self-organized performance**
16:15-17:30	**Structured debriefing & writing up results**

After the workshop, results will be written up on the Wiki and conversation will continue, yielding results on a collaborative and self-organized basis. Hand-outs will be provided to guide individual exploration of relevant theoretical material.

3 Presenters

Laurent Bossavit is a developer with over 20 years of coding experience, 10+ of which on a professional basis. He has held positions from lowly tech writer to lofty project manager, but was most comfortable as just another coder. Laurent's new focus, originally as an employee and now as an external consultant, is on working with teams and keeping them supplied with the raw materials of change and effectiveness - clarity of purpose and a constant infusion of fresh ideas. Laurent stewards (but does not by any stretch manage) several communities in both real and virtual space, such as the French XP practitioner's group or the book-lovers' Wiki Bookshelved.

Emmanuel Gaillot is a software engineer, working both as an IT consultant and team facilitator in Paris, France. His areas of expertise and interests include Open Source Software in Corporate environments, and Extreme Programming. He is also an experienced designer (sound and light) for theatre and dance, and has adapted the principles and practices of XP for the theatrical production process.

How to Maintain and Promote Healthy Agile Culture

David Hussman[1] and David Putman[2]

[1]david.hussman@sgfco.com,
[2]dputman@exoftware.com

Summary: The workshop's aim is to raise discussion around the importance of creating and maintaining healthy culture on agile projects.

Abstract. Though agile development often works well initially, maintaining and nurturing a healthy culture is key to the success of any agile project. As a project's culture is affected by many forces, this challenge is often quite difficult. Varying skills sets, egos, schedules, and external project dependencies are just a few issues that must be addressed by those trying to promote or maintain the cultural health of an agile project. The intent of this workshop is to use shared experiences to create a list of tools and tactics useful in managing culture on agile projects.

1 Intended Audience

The ideal candidate would have lead or helped lead one or more agile projects. Candidates will need enough experience to write a short position paper which describes their experience helping to keep an agile project healthy. Candidates must be interested in sharing and learning about finding cultural smells that affect project cultures and solutions / tools that may help address the issues. Workshop attendees must not fear calling out that which has as well as that which has not worked on agile projects.

1.1 Benefits for Attendance

Workshop participants will have the chance to share and discuss successes and struggles as well as issues which may are be covered by the current body of agile writings. Through discussion in large and small group discussions, the participants should be able to find a set of common approaches to nurturing agile culture that have been successful for more than on project, company or culture.

J. Eckstein and H. Baumeister (Eds.): XP 2004, LNCS 3092, pp. 325–327, 2004.
© Springer-Verlag Berlin Heidelberg 2004

2 Workshop Overview

Workshop participants will create a collection of cultural smells they have encountered and capture this information on posters in a story like format. Small and large group discussion of how these issues affect a project's culture as well as solutions that addressed the issues will consume a large portion of the workshop. In an effort to learn from our mistakes, the group will discuss solutions that failed, and why. To further the importance of culture, as it relates to the communal nature of agile practices, the workshop to try to create some tangible output that can be used in the trenches by agile project leaders and project members.

2.1 Goals

1. Create a collection of cultural smells associated with agile projects and teams.
2. Drive out which issues have the least amount of coverage in the agile writings (as known to the participants).
3. Create simple discussion vehicles that represent the participant's experiences, which can be shared with the agile community.
4. Further the importance of culture and the way in which it relates to the success of agile projects (and the growth and adoption of agile practices).

2.2 Workshop Format

Pre Workshop - All participants read each others position papers and create a list of potential cultural smells.

First Half - Workshop participants discuss cultural smells and create a prioritized list of story titles for small group discussion. Each participant signs up for a story and takes this story out into small group discussions where more detail is added to each story.

Second Half - More story detail will be added as story owners take their story into a different small group discussion. Entire workshop regroups and story owners present their story to the group, adding or modifying the story content as per the large group discussion.

Post Workshop – The stories created during the workshop are posted somewhere at the conference. The workshop organizers create some publishable document which is posted on the workshop website and possibly published.

3 Organizers

David Hussman - A software geek for 10 years, David has developed in the following fields: medical, digital audio, digital biometrics, retail, and educational. Somewhere along the way, David moved toward an odd way of defining, communicating, and developing software. When someone organized a better version and started calling it XP / Agile, he felt right at home. Motivated to see IT folks succeed and smile, David has evangelized XP by working as developer, coach, customer, and manager on XP projects for 3.5 years. When David is not coaching, he is traveling with his family as often as possible.

David Putman – A music lover, David accidentally purchased a computer in the early 1980s and was immediately stricken by the programming bug. His deep interest and enthusiasm in the subject then lead to a lecturing position within the now University of East London (UEL). David also acted as the Officer with the Department of Trade and Industry working on the "Managing into the 90s" project.
Always a developer at heart, David lives in the Roman city of St Albans in the UK, with his partner, two step-daughters and the family feline. He has finally achieved his dream of owning a computerised music-studio - but now doesn't have the time to use it due the demands of his job as Senior Mentor at eXoftware.

Contact Information:

David Hussman
    p: 011-612-743-4923
    e: david.hussman@sgfco.com

David Putman
    p: 353-(0)1-410-0528
    e: dputman@exoftware.com

Customer Collaboration

How to Replace Our Old Semi-hostile Habits with Friendship and Rich Communication
Full Day Workshop

Proposed by: Ole Jepsen

Cap Gemini, Denmark
www.olejepsen.dk (mostly in danish – sorry)
ole.jepsen@capgemini.dk
Phone: +45 39778494

Abstract. Customer collaboration doesn't just happen because you want it to happen. There are many challenges that can bring the project into a negotiation climate rather than the collaboration climate, which works so well. A couple of examples of challenges are our own old habits – and organizational structures that support nothing but written contracts and detailed requirement specifications.

Audience

Project managers and developers, who have substantial experience with user interaction in development projects. Participants will benefit not only from others experiences – but also from a structured assessment of their own user interaction experiences. As an extra bonus they will learn a great technique for exchanging experiences.

Participants should have a fair amount of project experience, and should have been working on (or at least be conscious about) the working climate within the project team.

Benefits of Attending

After the workshop the participants will know some more of the usual challenges you often need to deal with, when you want to change the usual negotiation-like working-climate to a more friendly, open, efficient and collaborative working-climate.

Deliverables

The purpose of this workshop is to produce a number of no-nonsense, easy to implement, strategies for the art of making great customer collaboration happen. The notes taken during the workshop will – after a little extra writing – be the actual deliverable.

Process

The process is inspired by the „Los Altos Workshop on Software Testing" described at www.kaner.com/lawst.htm - and goes like this:

J. Eckstein and H. Baumeister (Eds.): XP 2004, LNCS 3092, pp. 328–330, 2004.

Step	Minutes	Remarks
-Welcome and agenda	15	Quick presentation of the purpose and unique technique for this workshop.
-Reflection	5	Participants think for themselves, select one specific experience – one story – they want to share, and take a few notes.
-Stories in pairs of two	10	Each participant tell his story to the other part. This is timeboxed – 5 minutes for each person.
-Stories in pairs of four	25	Each participant tell his story again – in 5 minutes. By telling the same story again, the story-teller starts reflection – and he gets better at telling the story. At the end the group selects the most interesting story.
-Presentation – participants	10	A brief presentation-round.
-Break	10	
-Exploring a story - A	5	The participants with a selected story tells it to all participants in the workshop – timeboxed – 5 minutes.
	25	Participants ask questions about the story – to explore the story for details that are interesting *to them*. Strictly questions. No suggestions or own experiences at this point.
	20	Participants ask more questions, share own experiences, and suggest actions that could have been usefull for the story-teller. During this part the workshop-leader takes notes on a PC with a projector, so everybody can see. Notes are about: „what have we learned from the story and from each other".
-Lunch	60	
-Exploring a story - B	50	Same as step 7 – but a different story
-Break	15	
-Exploring a story - C	50	Same as step 7 – but a different story
-Break	10	
-Exploring a story - D	50	Same as step 7 – but a different story

The above process and timescedule is designed for a group of 16 participants. However, the process will work with any number from 6 to 20 participants. A group of 4 or 5 participants will work fine as well, but should be limited to a half-day workshop.

Experience with Similar Workhops

I have been organizing and facilitating two workshops using the above process:
- One workshop was in collaboration with Ward Cunningham at JAOO Conference in Denmark in September 2003. A significant result of this workshop was the article „Improving customer developer collaboration" (www.bestbrains.dk/xpvip-jaoo2003-report.html). 14 people participated in this 7 hour workshop.
- An other workshop was in connection with a conference by the Danish „Teknologisk Institut". The subject was „Iterative development in fixed price projects". 4 participants – 3 hours.

After having tried this workshop process I will never use anything else for the purpose of exchanging experiences. It works SO well!!!

The subject of this workshop is somewhat similar to the first of the two above workshops. However - after having conducted the above workshop I have a strong feeling, that there is so much more challenges and experiences out there, just waiting to be uncovered and communicated...

Who Am I – Ole Jepsen

Ole Jepsen is a Principal Consultant with Cap Gemini – in the Accelerated Delivery Center (ADC). The key elements of the ADC is iterative development and intense collaboration between all parties in every development project. He has 20 years of project experience from a number of companies in Denmark, mainly banks and insurance companies, and two years of experience from various companies in Australia.

He values the substantial person-to-person face-to-face communication as the most important issue in system development projects.

Founder of „Danish Agile User Group".

Speaker at conferences like: Danish IT Association / "XP and Agile Software Development" – IEEE Joint International Requirement Engineering Conference - JAOO 2002 Conference – CONFEX/XP – JAOO 2003 Conference / „Stop the requirement war" – Danish IT Association / „Requirement specifications", etc.

Author of articles in english: „Time Constrained Requirement Engineering", „The project profiler", „Improving customer developer collaboration" – and a number of articles in Danish.

Assessing Agility

Peter Lappo[1] and Henry C.T. Andrew[2]

[1]Systematic Methods Research Ltd
Greylands House, Mallory Rd, Hove, BN3 6TD, UK
peter.lappo@smr.co.uk,
[2]Box River Ltd
Greylands House, Mallory Rd, Hove, BN3 6TD, UK
henry_andrew@yahoo.com

Abstract. A technique is described that uses goals to assess the agility of software development teams and shows how it can be used with some examples. The agile assessment can be used to make investment decisions and process alterations. Value stream mapping is seen as an important technique in analysing processes.

Keywords. Agile Goals, Assessment Technique, Value Stream Mapping, Net Benefit, Measuring Agility

1   Introduction

There seems to be a general feeling in the agile community that if you follow all the practices associated with your chosen method then you are by definition agile. While this may be true of agile methods such as XP [1] or Scrum [1] which have defined a set of practices that have emergent properties such that the team becomes agile as a result of the process. It is still possible to use XP or Scrum without gaining much in terms of agility.

There is much talk in the agile community of improving the software development process but most of the improvements are anecdotal. There have been attempts at measuring and proving the efficacy of agile software development methods versus traditional methods [3, 4]. These studies have shown that agile methods are at least as good as traditional methods. There is even some talk of metrics [5, 6] which some people unfortunately frown upon [7] because of the political connotations, but nevertheless metrics don't measure how agile you are. Williams et al [5] proposed an interesting set of agile metrics, but the metrics defined where not formalised.

This paper defines a technique to assess agility through goals and using some examples shows how to create agile goals. The technique won't compare you with other people, at least not directly, rather it is a means to measure your relative performance.

1.1   Comparative Studies between Traditional and Agile Methods

Comparative studies [3, 4] between traditional and agile methods are very difficult to do on a small scale because it is very hard to devise a controlled experiment that anyone trained in the theory of science can qualify as a valid scientific experiment.

J. Eckstein and H. Baumeister (Eds.): XP 2004, LNCS 3092, pp. 331–338, 2004.
© Springer-Verlag Berlin Heidelberg 2004

The problem is small scale studies are not repeatable primarily due to the human element.

The repeatability problem only disappears when large numbers of projects are compared and statistical techniques are used to correlate process features with outcomes. However, at this moment in time there is not enough data available to prove that agile methods are better than traditional methods. Although anecdotal evidence suggests that agile methods are more effective at delivering working solutions.

1.2   Relative Comparisons

The only practical way of determining whether agile methods actually make a difference to your software development process is by measuring your own process and seeing whether agile methods actually make a difference. The question is how to make the measurements and what to measure. Once these questions have been answered it is possible to have some clarity about what makes a difference in your environment.

While it is possible to use the technique proposed in this paper to compare yourself with other teams it is difficult as often you are not comparing like with like. However, other peoples performances are useful as a guide to what can be achieved.

1.3   Metrics versus Measurable Goals

There is a large body of work concerning software metrics. Most of this work is useful for the long term analysis of trends and comparative studies. Metrics are sometimes used during planning and bidding. However, metrics are not much use for assessing agility. This paper won't concern itself much with metrics as it is the belief of the author that most metrics are measuring artifacts of the process such as lines of code or code complexity.

Most environments the author has worked in collect some sort of metrics even if it is only hours spent on project tasks, requirements tested or defect rates. While these may be useful, especially the last two, the collection of hours on tasks is often a fantasy of the developer or manipulated by political necessities.

Rather than just gather metrics such as lines of code, code complexity, function point or quality metrics we need measurements that are related to business needs with an agile perspective. For instance, while code complexity analysis tells you how complex your code, it does not give you any idea whether this code is easy to change in practice and hence having the potential to be agile. You may also have code that is not complex, but you still may have difficulty being agile because of your process or because of the attitude or experience of the people working on the project. The point being that low level measurements of process artifacts don't necessarily mean anything at a higher process level.

Using the measurable goals described below it is possible to define a set of goals for your team that are directly related to agile principles such as frequent delivery of software. Goals differ from metrics principally in that they attempt to be free from the details of the process, so that a goal to be responsive to change, for example, doesn't care about metrics like lines of code or code complexity. The other reason to differentiate goals from metrics is because a goal implies thought about where you want to be rather than where you are now.

2   Technique for Defining and Achieving Goals

2.1   Goal Setting and Implementation

We simply define a set of measurable goals (see 2.3 below) for the process, environment, tools and software quality in conjunction with the project stakeholders (this includes developers). Then we determine what the current state of these goals are, agree a future value with the project stakeholders, and takes steps to achieve the agreed values.

The process of achieving the goals should of course be iterative, with regular reviews on progress and the goals themselves. The cost and benefit of change should also be considered thereby preventing over or under investment. You may of couse find that you are sufficiently agile using your current process.

The goals, ideally, should be method agnostic, that is, we shouldn't define goals in terms of particular practices used to achieve agility or in terms of the artifacts of the process as this will stop method innovation and cause a lot of argument about favourite best practices. But it should be possible to assess a particular practice in terms of the impact it has on agility. This however, this is beyond the scope of this paper.

2.2   Techniques for Achieving Goals

Numerous management techniques exist for improving processes, but perhaps the most interesting one to use at an early stage when you are investigating possible improvements is value stream mapping [8] as used by the lean community.

Value stream mapping produces a timeline for a complete process and determines those steps which add value to the process. Subsequent work entails eliminating steps that don't add value and eliminating process delays.

For example, the production release process is always an interesting process to examine. It may have a number steps that cause unreasonable delays which could easily be eliminated or automated.

2.3   Categorisation of Goals

It is useful to categorise goals to help define them and focus the mind on what goals are necessary. This paper proposes four categories as follows.

Process
Goals associated with the software development process and the process practices used.

Environment
Goals associated with the environment the process runs in. These are mainly organisational and people oriented goals.

Tools
Goals associated with the tools used to develop the software.

Software
These are goals associated with the design and quality of the software. How the software has been designed can have a big impact on agility and of course if the software is full of bugs or only manual testing is performed then again agility will be constrained.

2.4   Goal Definition

Goals are defined by the following attributes [9].
    Name
    Test
    Benchmark
    Now
    Worst
    Planned
    Net Benefit
    Planned Date
    Owner
    Notes

These are detailed as follows.

Name
This a short name for the goal to make it easy to remember and discuss. It is also used for cross referencing to other goals. For example, „Rate Of Change". Names are preferred over numbers as they are easier to remember and have more meaning. However, some people prefer to use numbers. We don't care what convention you use as long as it works.

Test
The goal needs to be measured in some way. This defines the test to measure the goal and its scale. The test is the most important parts of defining a goal.

Tests should be quantitative when possible, but it is appreciated that some things are difficult to measure, such as knowledge transfer, so qualitative assessments can be used.

For example, „Rate Of Change" could be measured by running a query on your change management system to determine how many changes have been released to production over a given period. The scale could be changes per month.

Benchmark
This is an actual measurement taken in the field. It could be data from within your own organisation but is more likely to be a measure taken from the best organisation in your line of business. In other words, it is the benchmark to compare yourselves against. This field is optional as the data may not be available or you have taken the „lean" approach [10] which is to strive for perfection and ignore benchmarks. However, you may find some data which is relevant to your situation.

Now
Now simply states what the current measurement is. For example, for the „Rate Of Change" goal could be 1 change released per month. This field is optional if data is unavailable. However, we don't recommend this because you won't know if you are making progress, so a rough guess is better than no data at all.

Worst
It is recognised that some goals may be difficult to achieve so this defines the lowest expected improvement in the goal. For example, the „Rate Of Change" goal could have a worst case improvement of 2 changes per month.

Planned
This is the planned level of the goal. For example, the „Rate Of Change" goal could have a planned value of 20 changes per month.

Planned Date
The planned date defines when you expect to achieve your planned or worst case goal.

Net Benefit
We'd rather you didn't implement any change to your organisation unless you have some idea of the net benefit of the goal. Where net benefit is the potential value of the goal minus its implementation cost.

Value is a difficult thing to define and measure and even more difficult to predict. It also dangerous as you may oversell the benefit of a goal and raise expectations too high. Some goals may have intangible values. In this case simply list the benefits and costs.

The cost of course is only an estimate as it is difficult to predict what the costs will be as you may incur unexpected costs. For instance, your new environment may not be suitable for some people and they may leave, forcing you to replace them and train their replacements.

You may find that some goals don't add much value or the cost of achieving the goal is prohibitive in which case the goal should be dropped. The net benefit serves as a means of checking whether its worth implementing this goal.

While this attribute is optional we recommend you attempt to quantify the benefits to your organisation. If nothing else it will help you justify what you are trying to achieve. One surprising result may be that the goal may cost virtually nothing. For example, implementing a daily build may simply require an entry into a Unix cron table, which, assuming you have you have the correct environment, may only take 10 minutes to implement.

For example, the „Rate Of Change" goal may bring the following intangible benefit: Ability to implement changes that previously had to be ignored because they weren't of a sufficiently high priority.

Owner
All goals must be owned by someone or if you prefer sponsored by someone, preferably this person should be in the management team or it could a steering committee. The owner is responsible for ensuring the goal is achieved but not necessarily implementing the goal, as this may be carried out by someone else.

Notes
This is simply further notes of explanation which can include a reference to further information that may be relevant. It is optional.

3   Agile Goals

This paper hasn't the space available to define a set of goals for a team as goals are dependent on business objectives and available investment so we shall just present a few sample goals to give you an idea of how to define them for yourselves.

3.1   Example Goals

If you read the agile manifesto one of its principles is to value working software over artifacts such as documentation. This leads us directly into the most obvious goals for your agile team, the **Frequent Delivery Of Working Software**. Of course your current process may be incapable of delivering this so you may set yourself another goal which could be **Quick Releases**, i.e. the ability to integrate, build and release your software in a timely manner.

On the environmental front you know key application knowledge is in the heads of a two or three individuals which is preventing the rest of the team from being productive, so you define a goal to **Share Knowledge**. How you do this is irrelevant to the goal, but some means of measuring is not be.

The tools you use are of course perfect and you are perfectly happy with vi (or so you think), so you don't define any tool goals. On the other hand you don't actually get your hands dirty with code, but when you hold a review with the project stakeholders your developers come up with their own goals, namely **Refactoring Support** as they know they are steadily creating an unmaintainable mess.

When it comes to the actual software you do know you have trouble, but you are convinced the QA testers are a bunch of slackers. Surely they didn't mean four weeks to regression test the system for such as small change? **Automated Acceptance Testing** seems the only way forward.

3.2   Formalised Goals

Rather than attempt to squeeze all the goals and their attributes on a single table we'll just look at a couple.

Name	**Frequent Delivery Of Working Software**
Test	Record the date when software is released to pre-production on a graph and measure the number of working days between each release measured in frequency in days.
Benchmark	10
Now	90
Worst	20
Planned	10
Planned Date	June 2004
Net Benefit	Each piece of automation will reduce the manual effort in processing the invoices and provide valuable feedback on how the users are adapting to the software and whether the software is meeting business needs. Reducing the delivery cycle to 10 days will require a large investment in test automation amongst other things. The expected net benefit is difficult to determine as it depends on the value of the changes being introduced at each cycle. However, if the system goes into operation earlier the company will start getting a return on its investment sooner.
Owner	Director of IT
Notes	None.

Name	**Share Knowledge**
Test	Amount of time spent pair programming in minutes per hour pre day.
Benchmark	unknown
Now	0
Worst	30
Planned	50
Planned Date	June 2004
Net Benefit	The team should be more productive as a whole as less experienced members won't have to waste time finding out things for themselves. Some reduction in key personnel productivity is expected. The actual net benefit is difficult to quantify.
Owner	Team Leader
Notes	This is difficult goal to measure and it is possible it should be divided into sub-goals.

4   Conclusion

With a little thought it is possible to define a number of measurable goals which will help you achieve greater agility, where of course agility is defined by your goals! Any number of management techniques can be used to achieve your goals with value stream mapping being particularly useful during analysis.

No longer will you have sleepless nights worrying whether you are doing all the recommended XP practices in order to be agile (whatever they are at the time). If your agile goals satisfy the project stakeholders then you are agile. You can of course look around and see what kind of agility scores your competitors are achieving and attempt to better them or you could take the lean approach [10] and simply aim to be the best.

The point is by measuring what you are doing and setting goals for the future you have an opportunity to achieve those goals. Without objective measurements you are in the same state as early philosophers that conjectured about our universe. You are guessing.

References

1.   Kent Beck. Extreme Programming Explained – Embrace Change, Addison-Wesley, (1999)
2.   Ken Schwaber. The Scrum Development Process (OOPSLA'95 Workshop on Business Object Design and Implementation (1995)
3.   John Noll and Darren C. Atkinson. Comparing Extreme Programming to Traditional Development for Student Projects: A Case Study. In Proceedings of the 4th International Conference of Extreme Programming and Agile Processes in Software Engineering, May 2003.
4.   Francisco Macias, Mike Holcombe, Marian Gheorghe. A Formal Experiment Comparing Extreme Programming with Traditional Software Construction. In Proceedings of the Fourth Mexican International Conference on Computer Science September (2003)
5.   L. Williams, G. Succi, M. Stefanovic, M. Marchesi. A Metric Suite for Evaluating the Effectiveness of an Agile Methodology. In Extreme Programming Perspectives. Addison Wesley (2003)
6.   William Krebs, Laurie Williams, Lucas Layman. IBM / NC State University XP Study Metrics. Workshop submission to XP Agile Universe, http://sern.ucalgary.ca/eeap/wp/bk-position-2003.html (2003)
7.   Tim Bacon, Steering With Numbers. XDay http://xpday3.xpday.org/slides/SteeringWithNumbers.pdf (2003)
8.   Mike Rother and John Shook, Learning to See. Lean Enterprise Institute (1998)
9.   Tom Gilb. Principles of Software Engineering Management. P133-158, Addison-Wesley,(1988)
10. James Womack and Daniel Jones. Lean Thinking: Banish Waste and Create Wealth in Your Corporation, Revised and Updated, Free Press (2003)

Designing the Ultimate Acceptance Testing Framework

Sean Hanly[1] and Malcolm Sparks[2]

[1] phone: +353 (0)1 4100526, shanly@exoftware.com, www.exoftware.com
[2] phone: +353 (0)87 9872004, msparks@exoftware.com,
www.exoftware.com, www.jcoverage.com

Abstract. The purpose of this workshop is to generate a prioritised set of features and user stories for the "Ultimate Acceptance Testing Framework".

1 Introduction

In recent times there has been a noticeable development in the body of knowledge around the concept of "Automated Acceptance Testing" as described by Extreme Programming. In particular frameworks have begun to evolve that address the needs of automated acceptance-testing. However, most if not all of these frameworks are in their infancy. The concept behind this workshop is to draw on participants experience to identify the features of such a framework were it to be fully mature i.e. the "Ultimate Automated Acceptance Testing Framework".

2 Intended Audiance

Candidates should have experience from either of two perspectives. Firstly, involved in the creation of automated acceptance-testing frameworks or secondly, users or desired users of acceptance-testing frameworks.

Benefits for Attendees

Audience participants will get a chance to see what the current state of the art is on the automated-acceptance testing front and what direction it is taking. In addition, participants will get a chance to share in others experience and see what they see as the required features for an automated acceptance-testing framework.

3 Workshop Outline

Theme

Presentation of current and desired acceptance-testing requirements with the desired goal of generating a prioritized list of features.

J. Eckstein and H. Baumeister (Eds.): XP 2004, LNCS 3092, pp. 339–341, 2004.

Goals

1. Give an overview of the current state of the art in terms of existing frameworks
2. Through an open and critical discussion discuss these and other desired features
3. Generate a prioritized list of features that would make up an idealized automated acceptance testing framework

Proposed Workshop Format

Pre Workshop — Have all participants read each other's position papers.

Part 1 — Participants will give a 5-minute overview outlining their solutions or requirements as the case may be. Participants are encouraged to bring along interactive demos, prototypes etc.

Part 2 — From this participants, through an open and critical discussion, will generate a list of possible features.

Part 3 — Participants will then be allowed to spend an amount of virtual cash on these features as means of generating a list of prioritized features.

Post Workshop — Publish the prioritized list as a feature request for "The Ultimate Automated Acceptance Testing Framework". The rational behind the decisions will also be published.

4   Participants

The audience will be open to all attendees with an upper limit of 15 participants. The organizers intend on soliciting participation from a number of people who have direct experience in this area.

5   Organizers

Sean Hanly: For the last several years, I have focused on promoting software process improvement in the European software sector through our company eXoftware. We specialise in XP/Agile methods and provide bespoke software solutions, and Agile training and mentoring services.

Through my work, I have organised and developed the Irish and UK Agile SIGs programmes (which typically get about 100 attendees per event and are run quarterly). I am also an active speaker at these events and am always looking for more interactive ideas for the SIGs. I am also an invited speaker to many IT events across Ireland and the UK and Europe. Most recently I gave presentations at XP Day Belgium and UK on the subject of "Creating an Automated Acceptance Testing Framework".

I have been instrumental in building Agile Alliance Europe, a programme under the auspicious of the Agile Alliance. The aim is to create a network that spreads Agility throughout Europe, and also acts as a repository for learning. I have also worked with the DSDM Consortium (UK) on its new release that brings XP and DSDM together. I am also currently involved with University College Dublin on a programme that brings together a public/private partnership under the government's Higher Education Authority, and will bring Agile thinking to Irish software developers.

Through my work with eXoftware I have lead transitions, analysed development environments and taught hundreds in XP. My previous 15 years of work experience has been as a Programmer, Team Lead, Technical Architect and Principal. I hold a Masters in Information Technology from the National University of Ireland, Galway.

Malcolm Sparks: Malcolm's first introduction to computer programming was on the ZX81 home computer, in 1981. In 1988, Malcolm started Vermin Software Design, a games label for Atari and Amiga computers. Since then, Malcolm has worked as a consultant, programmer, systems administrator and Oracle DBA, innovating solutions for Hoskyns, Cap Gemini, Littlewoods Stores, the Financial Times and IONA Technologies. As an undergraduate Malcolm won the Lucas Software Engineering Prize for an in-car navigation aid and received the President's Award for Innovation in 2002 while at IONA for software packaging technology. In 1997, Malcolm founded the Manchester Java Users Group and has spoken at a number of Java and XP related events, including JavaOne. Malcolm holds a Bsc(Hons) in Computer Science from the University of Warwick, and lives with his wife Sonya in Dublin, Ireland.

I was a co-founder of EJBHome, which produced the first publicly available implementation of the EJB 1.0 specification. More recently I have founded jcoverage.com, and I am the principal author of the jcoverage software.

More specifically to XP, I was the team lead for IONA's Xsume technology, and technical lead for IONA's software packaging team, which were both run as XP projects. Consequently, I have had a lot of experience in installing XP in a large organization, across multiple teams (IONA adopted XP across all its development teams globally about two years ago).

The XP Customer Role

Steven Fraser[1], Angela Martin[2], David Hussman[3],
Chris Matts[4], Mary Poppendieck[5], and Linda Rising[6]

[1]sdfraser@acm.org
[2]angela@mcs.vuw.ac.nz
[3]david.hussman@sgfco.com
[4]cjmatts@thoughtworks.com
[5]mary@poppendieck.com
[6]rising1@acm.org

Abstract. One of the core XP (eXtreme Programming) practices is that of the "on-site customer". In the words of Kent Beck (2000) in his book "eXtreme Programming Explained" the intent is that a "real customer must sit with the team, available to answer questions, resolve disputes, and set small-scale priorities" ... "someone who will really use the system when it is in production". This panel brings together practitioners and researchers to discuss and offer wisdom on the challenges and opportunities inherent in the practice.

Steven Fraser (sdfraser@acm.org) – Panel Moderator

Steven Fraser has been interested in the customer perspective in software engineering since his doctoral research on specification validation and his concern that software provides a solution to the "right problem" (validation) as contrasted to solving the "problem right" (verification). Steven Fraser is an independent consultant in Santa Clara California and serves as the Activities Co-Chair for XP2004. Previous to 2002 Fraser held a variety of diverse software technology program management roles at Nortel Networks including: Process Architect, Senior Manager (Disruptive Technology), Process Engineering Advisor, and Software Reuse Evangelist. In 1994 he spent a year as a Visiting Scientist at the Software Engineering Institute (SEI) collaborating with the Application of Software Models project on the development of team-based domain analysis techniques. Steve is an avid operatunist and videographer.

Angela Martin (angela@mcs.vuw.ac.nz) – *Challenges of the XP Customer*

At the end of Arthur Miller's "Death of a Salesman", the speech that passes for Willy Loman's eulogy includes the idea that:

> "For a salesman, there is no rock bottom to the life. He don't put a bolt
> to a nut, he don't tell you the law or give you medicine. He's a man way
> out there in the blue, riding on a smile and a shoeshine."

An XP customer is in much of the same situation as Miller's salesman. Customers don't write code or refactor it - developers do that; they don't make the key decisions

J. Eckstein and H. Baumeister (Eds.): XP 2004, LNCS 3092, pp. 342–346, 2004.

about the project - in any large business, rather more important managers will do that; nor do they tackle the key technical or process problems with the development - the XP Coach does that. Rather the customer "sells" the requirements of the business to the development team and then "sells" the products of development back to the business. XP practices support the development team in making the technical decisions that are their responsibility (Spike Solution, Once and Only Once, Merciless Refactor-ing, Do the Simplest Thing That Could Possibly Work). XP includes very few-practices that actually support the customer in their role - other than prescribing how they interact with the developers. In our research we have found that while the pre-scribed interaction appears to be achieving excellent results, it also appears to be unsustainable, and so constitutes a great risk to XP projects, especially in long or high pressure projects. The key contribution of our research will be to describe the essen-tial characteristics and skills required in the customer role, and to identify the crucial practices and values to carry out the role successfully.

Angela has over ten years of wide ranging information systems experience and has a firm grounding in all aspects of systems integration and development. She is a PhD Candidate at Victoria University of Wellington, New Zealand, supervised by James Noble and Robert Biddle. Her PhD research utilises in-depth case studies of the XP Customer Role, on a wide range of projects across Australasia, the United States and Europe.

David Hussman (david.hussman@sgfco.com) – *Customer Team Struggles*
>*"If you can find that one person who knows the whole domain, is will-ing to make quick decisions, and can put up with a room full of nerds, you are likely to be successful." – Kent Beck*

This quote from Kent Beck's "One Team" paper is as strong today as it was when the paper was released in 2001. Having been both customer and developer, I find the customer team's job often requires more courage. To make matters worse, the job often becomes more difficult as a project's agility needs grow or the project becomes successful.

Of the many customer struggles, the "proxy customer syndrome" looms large at larger organizations. Short example: the customer team cannot respond to developer requests / questions because they are not empowered to make direction decisions and their ability to gather information from the real business is too slow. For a few stories, this is not a problem, but when the number of un-answerable questions grows, it is the customer team that feels the pressure.

My hope is the agile community avoids replacing the super hero, do-all project managers of the past with customer team superstars of the future. Instead, coaches, scrum masters, and other cultural guardians must help customer teams build a collec-tion of repeatable practices that fit their company's culture while adding sanity to their lives. Equal time spent coaching the customer team is often as important as ensuring that the developers adhere to a set of practices. Coaches must help create project cultures where customer teams continue to own story prioritization (defining business value) but the entire team shares tasks which are overloading the customer team (e.g. is the customer team is struggling with story tests, allow a tester - possibly working with a developer - to define story tests and perform the story sign off process). It takes a village to raise a child (or a project).

David Hussman is co-owner of SGF Software, a U.S. based company that promotes agile practices and provides agile training / coaching. David has worked on large, mission-critical systems as well as small boutique applications across various industries for more than a decade. Motivated to help software teams succeed and smile, David has evangelized agile practices for 4+ years. Recently, he has been working with large companies starting to use agile practices on a variety of projects. David has participated and presented at various agile conferences as well as contributing to the Cutter Consortium Agile Project Advisory Service and similar publications.

Chris Matts (cjmatts@thoughtworks.com) – *Observations of a Business Coach*

The business coach role will replace the traditional business analysis role. The business coach focuses on learning about a business problem and then coaching the development team in domain knowledge and the problem. The business coach coaches the business so that they can interact with the development team in the most effective manner. The business coach adopts a "zero documentation" approach to analysis. The "deliverable" is a developer trained in the business domain and problem rather than documentation. Traditional analysis tools should be used for learning rather than documentation or communication. Projects should be set up to deliver business value. Business value is created by improving or protecting cash flow, profit or return on investment in alignment with the strategy of the organisation. A project should develop a business value model. The business value should be broken down and referenced on story cards.

Chris Matts is a Business Coach with ThoughtWorks in London where he helps clients to develop business value models. Prior to joining ThoughtWorks, Chris lead the Internal Business Analysis Consultancy at Dresdner Kleinwort Wasserstein where he introduced Pair Analysis. Chris has been a business analyst and project manager since 1995. He started out his career as a developer. Chris's has analysis experience in all aspects of investment banking and specializes in Equity Derivatives and Credit Derivatives Trading Systems, and Market and Credit Risk Systems. Chris co-presented the Customer Role session at XP Day 3 in London in December 2003.

Mary Poppendieck (mary@poppendieck.com) – *A Line in the Sand?*

The role of the customer in XP is cast so that it draws a line in the sand. On the one side of the line are the developers, who aren't expected to understand the business, and on the other side is the customer, upon whose shoulders rests the responsibility for understanding everything that must be done, the order which things should be done, and the tests to determine if things were done correctly. The developers are not expected to understand the domain or question customer decisions, thus making sure that if any wrong decisions get made, the developers won't be at fault.

I think XP draws too much of a distinction between developers and the customer role. XP expects developers to play the role of DBA, user interaction designer, even tester, but developers are not supposed to take on any work of the customer role. But the customer role is a huge burden for one person, and I think it appropriate that developers feel responsibility to assist people in the customer role. In particular, I think it inappropriate to expect customers to write tests.

In my experience, the best software results when the technical team develops a deep understanding of the domain, rather than working through an intermediary. XP calls for 'customer on site,' so that developers have access to someone playing the customer role at all times. In my experience we have generally used the practice of 'developer on site' instead; the development team works at the site of the real users of the system. They go to lunch with the people who use their software, understand what users do for a living, and felt their pain when the system is balky. The success of a system is determined by the value it brings to end-users and other stakeholders. This success should be the responsibility of the entire team, not just one individual or one role.

Mary Poppendieck a Cutter Consortium Consultant, is a seasoned leader in both operations and new product development with more than 25 years' of IT experience. She has led teams implementing lean solutions ranging from enterprise supply chain management to digital media, and built one of 3M's first Just-in-Time lean production systems. Mary is currently the President of Poppendieck LLC and located in Minnesota. Her book *Lean Software Development: An Agile Toolkit,* which brings lean production techniques to software development, won the Software Development Productivity Award in 2004.

Linda Rising (risingl@acm.org) – *Customers Are Important?*

Is there anyone who doesn't think customers are important? The problem with concentrating on one element of an agile approach – such as the role of the customer – is that everything (ideally) is hooked to everything else. John Muir, the founder of the Sierra Club said this profound statement! I tend to see the world as full of patterns, and we know that you never see a pattern in isolation. It should be connected to a collection or pattern language. Since I've written a pattern language for customer interaction – I think many of those patterns (if not all) would apply in an agile development environment, even though they were not expressly written for that setting. Here are some of those patterns (and others that are in related pattern languages):

It's a Relationship, Not a Sale: Develop a relationship with the customer. Focus on this relationship, not the current transaction. Use: Customer Understanding and Trust Account. *Customer Understanding:* Learn as much as possible about the customer. Use: Effective Listening, Timely Response and Meetings Around the Meeting. *Trust Account:* Every contact with the customer is a chance to Trust Account. Take advantage of it. Use: Effective Listening, Timely Response and Meetings Around the Meeting. *Effective Listening:* Listen to the customer with intent to understand. Use Personal Integrity, Aware of Boundaries, Customer Relief, and Good Manners. *Beautiful Termination with Satisfaction:* When a relationship built on trust has been established with a customer, you can end agreements without rancor. *Timely Response:* When you receive a request from the customer let the customer know you received it and how you plan to resolve it. *Meetings Around the Meeting:* Arrive at meetings early enough to meet other attendees and spend time socializing. After the meeting, allow a little time to talk to others with common business interests. *Personal Integrity:* Don't withhold important information from the customer but stay Aware of Boundaries. *Customer Relief:* Don't argue. Try to understand how the customer's business is impacted. Don't try to appease the customer by making promises you can't keep. Be Aware of Boundaries and use Good Manners. *Aware of Boundaries:* Treat every conversation with the customer as part of a negotiation. Don't discuss commercial considerations, e.g., price, cost, schedule, and content that aren't part of your responsibilities. Use Good Manners. *Good Manners:* Be polite. Dress appropriately to meet customer expectations. Show respect for everyone, including competitors. Be careful in interactions with others in front of the customer.

Linda Rising has a Ph.D. from Arizona State University in the area of object-based design metrics. Her background includes university teaching experience as well as work in industry in the areas of telecommunications, avionics, and strategic weapons systems. She has been working with object technologies since 1983. She is the editor of "A Patterns Handbook, A Pattern Almanac 2000," and "Design Patterns in Communications Software". She has a number of publications including: "The Scrum Software Development Process for Small Teams," IEEE Software, July-August 2001, "Agile Meetings," STQE, July/August 2002, and "The Role of Product Champion," STQE, March 2003. These and other articles are available on her web site: www.lindarising.org. She is a regular contributor to the DDC-I On-line Newsletter: ddci.com/news_latest_news_archive.shtml. She has presented a number of tutorials and workshops at JAOO, OOPSLA, and other conferences. She is currently co-authoring a book with Mary Lynns: "Fear Less: and Other Patterns for Introducing New Ideas into Organizations," scheduled for publication in 2004.

Fishbowl: XP Tools

Joshua Kerievsky[1] and Steven Fraser[2]

[1] joshua@industriallogic.com
[2] sdfraser@acm.org

Abstract. This session is an opportunity to learn more about the tools that enable teams to be extreme. Using a "fishbowl format", participants will discuss and debate the pros and cons of such tools as Eclipse, IntelliJ and Visual Studio, NUnit and CSUnit, Continuous Integration and Cruise Control, FIT and Fitnesse, and more. If you're looking for practical advice on tools for XP teams – their selection, usage and whatever improvements are desired -- you'll enjoy this session.

Joshua Kerievsky (joshua@industriallogic.com) – Fishbowl Moderator
Joshua Kerievsky has been programming professionally since 1987 and is the founder of Industrial Logic, a company specializing in Extreme Programming (XP). Since 1999, Joshua has been coaching and programming on small, large and distributed XP projects and teaching XP to people throughout the world. He is the author of numerous XP and patterns-based articles, simulations and games, including the forthcoming book, "Refactoring to Patterns."

Steven Fraser (sdfraser@acm.org) – Fishbowl Impresario
Steven Fraser has been involved in the development and deployment of software tools and processes for more than 15 years. Steven is an independent consultant in Santa Clara California. Previous to 2002 Steven held a variety of diverse software technology program management roles at Nortel Networks including: Process Architect, Senior Manager (Disruptive Technology), Process Engineering Advisor, and Software Reuse Evangelist. In 1994 he spent a year as a Visiting Scientist at the Software Engineering Institute (SEI) collaborating with the Application of Software Models project on the development of team-based domain analysis techniques. Steve is an avid operatunist and videographer.

J. Eckstein and H. Baumeister (Eds.): XP 2004, LNCS 3092, p. 347, 2004.

The XP Game

The XP Game is a playful way to understand XP Planning.

Olivier Lafontan[1], Ivan Moore[2], and Vera Peeters[3]

[1] Egg plc, Pride Park, Riverside Road,
Derby DE99 3GG, England
Olivier.Lafontan@egg.com
[2] ThoughtWorks, Peek House, 20 Eastcheap,
London EC3M 1EB, England
ivan@thoughtworks.com
[3] Tryx bvba, Colomastraat 28, B-2800 Mechelen, Belgium
vera.peeters@tryx.com

Abstract. The XP Game is a playful way to familiarize the players with some of the more difficult concepts of the XP Planning Game, like velocity, story estimation, yesterday's weather and the cycle of life. Anyone can participate. The goal is to make development and business people work together, they both play both roles. It's especially useful when a company starts adopting XP.

1 Audience and Benefits of Attending

Anyone can participate. Developers and customers benefit from experiencing both sides of the planning game. The XP Game explains velocity, in particular, showing how velocity is not the same as business value. This tutorial demonstrates how you can quickly learn to make predictable plans.

2 Content Outline

In real life Planning Game, development and business people are sitting on opposite sides of the table. Both participate, but in different roles. The XP Game makes the players switch between developer and customer roles, so that they understand each other's behaviour very well.

Some of the concepts in the Planning Game are difficult to grasp, for developers and for customers. What exactly is the meaning and background of stories, iterations, consequent estimations, velocity, yesterday's weather, planning game, feedback? The XP Game is a simulation of the XP Planning Game, which includes the following

J. Eckstein and H. Baumeister (Eds.): XP 2004, LNCS 3092, pp. 348–350, 2004.

phases: story estimation, story prioritization, planning, implementation and feedback. No knowledge of coding is required.

This XP Game is a practical way to demonstrate how the rules of the XP Planning Game make up an environment in which it becomes possible to make predictable plans. After all, the easiest way to get a feeling for the way it works is to experience it. This tutorial will differ slightly from the XP Game available from http://www.xp.be/xpgame/download/ with the inclusion of innovations from its use at Egg.

3   Presenter Resumes

Olivier Lafontan has spent the last six years working in programme/project management, specializing on Customer Relationship Management business aspects. He has alternated roles from both "Technology" and "Business" sides of the fence in companies such as BT, Lexmark, Unipart and Freesbee. Olivier currently works for Egg plc, and has been using the XP Game as a tool to aid the Agile transformation Egg has undertaken.

Ivan Moore works for ThoughtWorks in England, helping people deliver software using Agile methods. He has a PhD in "Automatic Restructuring of Object-Oriented Programs", and has (co)authored papers published at OOPSLA, TOOLS, XP, XPUniverse conferences, reviewed papers for OOPSLA and TOPLAS and co-edited a book on Prototype-Based Object-Oriented Programming. He is known for two open source projects, Jester (a mutation testing tool for JUnit tests) and MockMaker (for automatically creating Mock Objects).

Vera Peeters is an independent consultant. She runs her own company TRYX. She has more than 13 years experience in developing software systems, using different OO languages, such as C++ and Java, and this in high-technological environments. She has been exploring the eXtreme Programming practices for several years, and she currently spends most of her time coaching companies in transitioning their way of working. She focuses on the change from structural to OO development, on OO design, and on process changes (towards agility). Vera Peeters has presented workshops at XP2001, XPUniverse, OT2002 and OT2003. She developed the XP Game together with Pascal Van Cauwenberghe, and is the co-organizer of the Belgian XP User Group Meetings. She's in the organizing commitee of the Benelux XPDay and the Javapolis conferences.

4   History of Tutorial

This tutorial has been presented at XP2001 in Sardinia, XPUniverse 2001 in North Carolina and XPDay03 in London.

5   Examples of Supporting Material

The XP Game materials are available from http://www.xp.be/xpgame/download/

XP and Organizational Change: Lessons from the Field

Diana Larsen[1], David Hussman[2], Mary Lynn Manns[3], David Putman[4], and Linda Rising[5]

[1]diana@industriallogic.com
[2]david.hussman@supergofaster.com
[3]manns@bulldog.unca.edu
[4]dputman@exoftware.com
[5]rising1@acm.com

Abstract. As interest in XP continues to spread, the organizational challenges of adopting a new development method become more apparent. Some say that the implementation of XP values, principles and practices alone is enough to successfully navigate a change to XP. Others say that an understanding of change management concepts from the field of organizational development is needed. Views vary on whether to employ a change model, and if so, which change models are best. In this activity panel we use an interactive storytelling and analysis approach as we pause to consider the implications of XP and organizational change, through real-life tales from this time in the history of XP's migration into the mainstream of software development.

In preparation for the interactive session at the conference, instead of asking for opinions and positions, I asked four panel participant to send me a story in response to this request: „Thinking back over all your experiences with introducing XP and other new ideas/approaches to organizations, whether as a consultant to the change or a participant in it, what stands out to you as the peak or highlight moment? Why do you think this particular moment is significant or stands out in your memory? What conditions were present in the organization? What did other individuals do to contribute to making it a highlight? What patterns, models or techniques added value, if any? What is the most important idea or skill you have taken away from that experience? What about you, as a participant or consultant in the change, added the most value to the situation? What about the experience have you carried forward into other change efforts?"

A synthesis of their stories forms the basis of the interactive storytelling and analysis during the activity session. Excerpts from the stories follow.

David Hussman (david.hussman@supergofaster.com)

The Big Company had a history of software project that were large and costly. One day, one of the IT leaders started an initiative to see what could be accomplished with smaller teams. A visionary director decided to fund the hiring of an agile coach, who was to work with two small for a short time. As the director witnessed the success and

J. Eckstein and H. Baumeister (Eds.): XP 2004, LNCS 3092, pp. 351–355, 2004.
© Springer-Verlag Berlin Heidelberg 2004

happiness of the small teams, she requested that the coach help with a much larger and higher visibility project that had been working for one year and had not yet produced any working code. The project was split across companies, countries, cultures, and methodologies, and the political landscape was rough. If this was not enough, the project schedule was so aggressive that several industry leaders told the director that the project could not succeed.

The coach took in his bag of tricks, with the notion that iterative development would help imbue quality as well as provide measurable results in short windows. The development team quickly embraced many agile practices. A second coach was brought in, and the coaching effort was split between development and customer coaching. A group of leaders was to meet once per week to discuss progress and issues, as well as help guide each of the various project teams. Although initial iterations produced working code, happily reviewed by the sponsors, the project culture was not well. Political struggles were pulling the team in many directions and forcing many member changes. The coaches' ability to help steer was waning, frustrating the coaches, and agile practices gave way to old habits. The testing team was not fully engaged, and the customer team was struggling to overcome the politics so they could gather enough information to write meaningful and cohesive stories

The high level of project's visibility placed the project and the coaches in communication with a host of leaders from other teams, often defending attacks to the process which would crush the existing development practices at the company. Leaders outside the development space(s) needed to understand the project, but they could not speak the language of the project. As a key change agent, the coach became the translator. The unspoken question and concern was simple: „will you be done on time and with what level of quality?" Using metrics and coaching notes gathered during the iterations, the coach explained the issues to the director during a review of the project charter. The biggest concern was that the many forces acting on the team / project had so disrupted the ability to create a healthy project culture, that there was not team chemistry. The coach suggested trying to rally the team (and many of its proponents and critics) around several simple measures of project success, one of these being project health.

As the project continues, there is not yet an end to this story....

David Hussman - David is co-owner of SGF Software, a U.S. based company that promotes and practices agile development. Motivated to see IT folks succeed and smile, He has evangelized agile practices as a developer, coach, customer, and manager for 4 years. He has participated and presented at agile conferences as well as contributing to the Cutter Consortium Agile Project Advisory Service and similar publications.

Mary Lynn Manns (manns@bulldog.unca.edu)
I was hired [Dedicated Champion]** to build a patterns repository that captured best practice in the organization's software development efforts. At the same time, employees needed to be informed about patterns and how they might use them in their

projects. I began by seeking advice [Ask for Help] from friends in the larger patterns community who had some experience introducing patterns into other organizations [Shoulder to Cry On]. I also began meeting with managers in the organization. Some managers provided names of people in their groups that could help with the effort [Respected Techie, Connectors]. However, most managers simply listened politely to what I had to say. I began to realize that, although it was important to inform these managers about patterns, a top-down approach was not what would light the fire.

Therefore, I began concentrating on the developers, talking with anyone who would listen about how patterns could be useful in their work [Personal Touch]. Since I was new to the organization, this was not an easy task because I had to first learn what the developers did. I had to tell them about my work without interfering with theirs. When someone said, „Oh, you're the person who is going to **make** us use patterns," I realized I had to encourage them to appreciate patterns rather than be suspicious of them—and of me. After all, I was the „new kid on the block." I knew it was important to get them to like me [Evangelist]. I looked for opportunities to talk with people [Personal Touch]. This was usually during lunch or when I suggested a coffee and bagel break [Do Food]. In addition, I attended project meetings to hear what the teams were doing, and often brought patterns materials with me [Plant the Seeds].

After these meetings, some developers would come up to learn more about patterns [Innovators]. I asked them to help me discover what others were doing, how they could benefit from patterns, and how I could spread the word throughout the organization [Ask for Help]. The first significant pattern event for the organization happened during a monthly „tech talk" scheduled on the topic of patterns [Piggyback]. I gave an overview of patterns and cited references where they could learn more [Just Enough]. One of the developers described his use of patterns in a recent project [Hometown Story]. Approximately thirty employees attended – more than any other previous „tech talk." This made me feel that there was interest in patterns and also helped me identify those who were open to learning more [Innovators, Early Adopters]....

Dr. Manns is a member of the Department of Management and Accountancy at the University of North Carolina at Ashville where she teaches courses in management information systems and management science. Prior to joining the Department of Management and Accountancy, she was in the Computer Science Department at UNCA for 18 years. She has taught courses in various programming languages, research methods, analysis and design methodologies, microcomputer applications, management issues and object-oriented technology. Her areas of research are: introducing new ideas into organizations, patterns and „pattern mining", and project retrospectives. With Linda Rising, her co-author, Dr. Manns has written: *Introducing Patterns into Organizations,* schedule for publication, Spring 2004. ** Pattern names enclosed in [] can be found at: http://www.cs.unca.edu/~manns/intropatterns.html

David Putman (dputman@exoftware.com)

I was asked to call on the development director of a multinational telecommunications company. „I'd like to discuss our development process with you", he said. „We've never had a project that succeeded and I think it's about time we did something about it."

So it was that a few weeks later I sat in his office with a colleague explaining to him and his senior staff how agile processes, in particular XP, could help alleviate his situation. There were nods of appreciation and general agreement from around the room apart from one unhappy looking individual in the corner. „You know, you consultants have always got something new to sell" said the Head of Programme Office, „a few years back it was OO and before that it was something else. Next year it will be something else again. None of it has ever made any difference to us and I seriously doubt if anything *you* can offer will make any difference either." Aggressive words from an angry and physically intimidating person. The meeting deteriorated fairly badly after that and there was little we could do to get it back on track. We left feeling fairly despondent.

We persisted, though, and later came back to the organisation and did some seminars with their developers, giving them a basic introduction to the XP practices, before eventually being engaged to run a project for them using XP. I should say though that our friend, the Head of Programme Office, had especially selected this project for us. The project manager himself told us that, although it was one of the highest priority projects they had, it had evaluated to have a less than 3% chance of success. He had drawn the short straw of managing it because he was on secondment from a different branch of the company. It was a hot potato nobody wanted to handle.

The details of the project are fairly immaterial but, needless to say, we realised that we would easily hit the target after the first two (two-week) iterations. Five iterations later we were done but it was the events after we first realised that we would make it that were the highlight for me. The Head of Programme Office came to me and told me that he was so pleased that we were able to make the project work and congratulated me on a job well done. Before we were anywhere near finished! He then surprised me even further by asking if I could supply him with some overheads from my library, as he wanted to do some presentations on the work we were doing to some of the customers. Later, he attended a two-day XP Customer training workshop I ran and was one of the most pro-XP people you could hope to have. We used the experiences gained on that first project as a case study for the rest of the programme office who received it enthusiastically....

David Putman's role as a Senior Mentor for the Irish training and mentoring company, eXoftware, takes him to many software development organisations and he has acted as an advisor on software development to companies in three continents. His work continues to give him interesting and practical examples of all kinds of management and software development issues. He currently writes the "Models and Methodologies" column for "Application Development Advisor" magazine and has had articles published in other publications including the Cutter IT Journal. His main interests are learning organisations, the management of software development projects and how to make work satisfying to all those involved.

Linda Rising (rising1@acm.com)

I was very enthusiastic about patterns after having attended OOPSLA '94. I was talking to everyone in my company about them. I gave a couple of Brown Bags and passed out copies of articles about patterns to interested persons. Then after one meeting, a guy in my group said, „Patterns are a good idea but no one knows you. You have no credibility since you've only been with the company a few months. Why don't you talk to Randy or Jeff?" My first reaction was, „How could Randy or Jeff improve my credibility? They don't know me and they don't know anything about patterns." But, I stopped by their offices and gave them my „elevator speech." I loaned first Randy, then Jeff, my copy of the Design Patterns text and I personally invited them to the next Brown Bag. I was amazed to see how attendance increased at the next meeting. I realized that patterns (or whatever) is not about me (or the change agent). It's about the new idea. If you're going to reach others, you need help and you need help from some special people. In this case, people who can lend credibility to the idea...

Linda says: I can help your organization get going with patterns. I also do project retrospectives. My favorite implementation of this important process is to combine it with patterns writing to capture all those valuable lessons learned. I also do road shows with Mary Lynn Manns, another patterns expert and retrospectives fan. Mary Lynn and I have written: *Introducing Patterns into Organizations*. I have a Ph.D. from Arizona State University in the area of object-based design metrics. My background includes university teaching experience as well as work in industry in the areas of telecommunications, avionics, and strategic weapons systems. I have been working with object technologies since 1983. I began my interest in patterns while I was working at AG Communication Systems, where I spent five happy and productive years. I have presented a number of tutorials and workshops at OOPSLA and other conferences.

Diana Larsen (diana@industriallogic.com) – Panel Moderator

Diana Larsen is a senior organizational development and change management consultant. Identified as a „benchmark" consultant by clients and an exceptional facilitator by colleagues, Diana partners with leaders of software development and other technical groups to strengthen their ability to create and maintain company culture and performance. She facilitates processes that support and sustain change initiatives, attain effective team performance and retain organizational learning. As a certified Scrum master and specialist in the human side of software development, Diana serves as a coach, consultant and facilitator to directors, program and project managers, development teams and others. She also has special expertise in using Appreciative Inquiry approaches, Open Space Technology and other large group processes, as well as in leading teams through Project Chartering and Retrospectives. A frequent speaker at software industry conferences, Diana also authors articles on Agile /XP management, team development and organizational change.

Author Index

Lecture Notes in Computer Science

For information about Vols. 1–2976

please contact your bookseller or Springer-Verlag